SPAIN AND ITS WORLD
1500–1700

SPAIN
AND ITS WORLD
1500–1700

Selected Essays

J.H. ELLIOTT

YALE UNIVERSITY PRESS
NEW HAVEN AND LONDON · 1989

Copyright © 1989 by Yale University

Fourth printing 1997

Designed by Gillian Malpass

Set in Linotron Bembo by Best-set Typesetter Ltd, Hong Kong
Printed and bound at The Bath Press, Bath, Great Britain

Library of Congress Cataloging in Publication Data

Elliott, John Huxtable.
Spain and its world, 1500–1700.

Includes index.
1. Spain—History—House of Austria, 1516–1700.
2. Spain—Colonies—America.   3. Spain—Relations—
Europe.   4. Habsburg, House of.   I. Title.
DP171.E42   1989   946'.05   88–26139
ISBN 0–300–04217–5 (hbk.)
ISBN 0–300–04863–7 (pbk.)

CONTENTS

CONTENTS

'Now for Spain, his Majesty there, though accounted the greatest Monarch of Christendom, yet if his estate be enquired through, his root will be found a great deal too narrow for his tops.'

Francis Bacon,
'A short view to be taken of Great Britain and Spain',
The Letters and Life of Francis Bacon,
ed. James Spedding, vol. 7 (London, 1874), p. 25.

PREFACE

The essays assembled in this volume illustrate a number of themes and reflect a number of concerns arising out of my interest in the history of the European world, and especially the Hispanic world, in the sixteenth and seventeenth centuries. During the period of almost thirty years which separates the first of these essays from the most recent, our knowledge and understanding of the sixteenth and seventeenth centuries – the Early Modern period, as it has now come to be called – have undergone a profound transformation as new areas of inquiry have been opened up, and the insights acquired from disciplines other than history have been brought into play. I count myself particularly fortunate to have embarked on historical research and writing at a moment of such intellectual vitality and ferment, when it appeared, especially in the wake of Braudel's great work on the Mediterranean, that the whole of Early Modern European history was ripe for rethinking.

I was fortunate, too – more fortunate than I realized at the time – in my choice of a country and a topic. My interest in Spain had first been aroused by an extended tour of the Iberian peninsula with a party of friends from Cambridge University during the summer vacation of 1950. When the time came to choose a subject for research, I already knew that Spain, and particularly the Spain of the seventeenth century, was what I wanted to investigate. I suspect that my choice, although initially inspired by the visible reminders of the brilliance of seventeenth-century Spanish civilization, and especially the paintings of Velázquez, was also influenced at some level by my sense, as an Englishman living in the aftermath of the Second World War, that the collective predicament of the last great imperial generation of Spaniards after the triumphs of the sixteenth century was not entirely dissimilar to the collective predicament of my own generation after the triumphs of the nineteenth and early twentieth. At least this may have given me a certain sympathy across the centuries with the aspirations and dilemmas of men who, as heirs to a glorious historical legacy, were seeking for national renewal in the midst of perceived decline.

When, as an embryonic research student, I told Professor Herbert Butterfield of my hopes and plans, his heart leapt, as he characteristically put it, at the thought of a British historian taking a professional interest in the history of Spain. There was in fact a distinguished British tradition of Hispanic studies, but primarily in the field of literature, and the history of Spain was not much cultivated in British universities at the time when I began my researches. Oddly enough, however, it was a British historian, Martin Hume, working in the early years of this century, who had written what was still in effect the standard account of the period of Spanish history that had attracted my interest. His colourful but somewhat glib study of *The Court of Philip IV* (1907) was to be my introduction to the period, and his references to papers preserved in the British Museum, and written by the Count-Duke of Olivares, were to serve as my initial guide to the policies and career of a statesman who was to become the central historical figure in my subsequent research.

Even a cursory survey of Spanish publications showed that Spanish historians themselves had paid little attention to the history of their own seventeenth century. The climate of Franco Spain in the early 1950s was hardly conducive to historical research, and least of all to research into a period of national 'decadence'. Moreover, Spanish historical writing, like Spain itself, had become fossilized. While the regime insistently proclaimed the existence of eternal Spanish values transcending the historical process, its opponents were themselves all too often engaged in a kind of meta-history, which sought to explain Spain's failure to emerge as a modern society as the outcome of a national character shaped by a unique historical experience. As a result, Spanish historiography was out of step with the historiographical trends in post-war Europe, and largely innocent of the new kinds of interests and approaches that were appealing to the post-war generation of European historians.

There was, however, one outstanding exception to this 'exceptionalist' interpretation of the course of Spanish history. This was to be found in the little group of young Catalan historians clustered around the charismatic figure of Jaume Vicens Vives at Barcelona University. Vicens Vives had realized that the French had become the pace-makers in European historical writing, and, turning his back on the German influences in his own historical training, he set out to acquaint himself and his pupils with the ideas and methods of the *Annales* School, and to reinterpret the history of Spain along more modern lines. I was wonderfully fortunate in arriving to work in Barcelona in 1953 just as the Vicens historiographical revolution was getting under way. I found here a group of talented historians who seemed to be speaking the same historical language as myself –

historians who were attempting to see Spanish history in its wider, European, context, and who were prepared, under the guiding and sometimes impulsive genius of Vicens, to reject the sacred symbols of Spanish, and Catalan, historiography in the pursuit of historical truth. It was at times a heady experience, especially in the suffocating intellectual atmosphere of the Spain of the 1950s, and it did much to reinforce my own instinctive sense that Spanish history, no less than Spain itself, was in urgent need of exposure to the winds of change now blowing through Europe.

My original intention, to some extent inspired by my reading of Martin Hume, had been to focus on the 'centralizing' policies of the Count-Duke of Olivares in the Spain of the 1620s and 1630s. Although the tension between unity and diversity, between centre and periphery, is a recurrent theme in Spanish history, it is a theme by no means confined to the history of Spain. I found it attractive because it seemed to me to go to the heart of the more general, European, question of the relationship of power and society in the dawning age of 'absolutism'. Where Philip IV of Spain had his Catalonia and Portugal, Charles I had his Scotland and Ireland, and Louis XIII his Languedoc and Béarn, and these analogies made me feel that I was here confronted with a central problem in the history of the seventeenth-century state. But my initial inability to find in the national archives of Simancas, or elsewhere, the kind of policy papers I had expected to find, drove me out from the centre to the periphery, in the hope of discovering, through the explosive reactions of a peripheral province under pressure from a central government, the nature of those centralizing policies which had eluded my documentary search. It was thus that I came to concentrate my researches on what one of my Cambridge mentors was later to describe, rather unkindly, as a very 'rum' subject, the origins of the Catalan Revolution of 1640 against the government of Philip IV.

These researches forced me to immerse myself, as otherwise I would never have done, in the microhistory of a provincial society, Catalonia in the seventeenth century. But they also opened my eyes to a theme which frequently surfaces throughout this selection of essays – the intrusive role of the state. Anyone who spends any length of time in the great state archive of Simancas cannot fail to be impressed by the overwhelming mass of documentation generated by the Spanish administrative machine in the sixteenth and seventeenth centuries. Habsburg Spain was a pioneer of the modern bureaucratic state, and the presence of the state can be felt at every turn in the history of Spain and its overseas possessions, at once influencing and being influenced by the societies it seeks to control. The awareness of this made me sceptical from the start about efforts to write social history, in the manner of the *Annales*, without serious reference to the question of power. In writing my general survey of *Imperial Spain* (1963) I realized that, unless the dimension of state power and its exercise is constantly borne in mind, the history of Early Modern Spain fails to make sense. The ambitious foreign policies pursued by the Spanish Habsburgs, and the acute financial needs to which they gave rise, had a profound effect on Spanish, and especially Castilian, society, encouraging certain tendencies and stultifying others, as the state sought desperately to mobilize the resources required for its incessant wars.

The need to incorporate a strong political component into any attempt to reassess Early Modern Spanish history was all the greater because even the treatment of political events – the normal stock in trade of nineteenth-century historians – was so painfully inadequate, at least where seventeenth-century history was concerned. Historians of seventeenth-century Spain have no equivalent of S.R. Gardiner's massive *History of England from the Accession of James I to the Outbreak of the Civil War*. Nor is there any Spanish equivalent of the *Dictionary of National Biography* to smoothe the researcher's path. The major political figures of the seventeenth century are still largely unstudied, the lesser figures unknown, even by name. Economic and social histories of the period were non-existent when I began my researches, although Don Antonio Domínguez Ortiz was by then engaged on a series of studies which would add a wealth of new documentation and insight to our understanding of the century. Anyone working on the period therefore had, and still has, to start from a level of information which is pathetically slender when compared with the material available in print to historians of other west European societies of the seventeenth century. This situation is not entirely without its advantages, and certainly adds excitement to the chase, but it also dictates certain strategies, both for research and writing. As far as I was concerned, it pushed me into concentrating my attention on what seemed to me a particularly critical period for the understanding of the whole trajectory of seventeenth-century Spain – the period of the ministry of the Count-Duke of Olivares, from 1621 to 1643, when, as I saw it, major policy decisions were being taken, which had profound long-term implications for the future of Spanish society and the Spanish political structure. If I was right in identifying these years as among the most decisive in the whole of Spanish history, then it seemed to me that this justified the investment of considerable time and energy in reconstructing, both in its broad outlines and in close detail, the age of Olivares.

It also seemed to me that there was a strong case for publishing the results of my findings, when feasible, in the form of books rather than of articles. In this I was guided primarily by the state of the subject, and the feeling that it was preferable at this stage to describe for others the general lie of the territory, as I saw it, rather than embark on close mapping of small pieces of the terrain. But I was also influenced by the consideration that the history of Spain was not exactly central to the interests of an Anglo-American readership, and that the publication of articles in learned journals was not the most effective method of giving it the exposure which I thought it deserved. Essays and articles, however, like books, have their own special part to play, both in providing a succinct statement of the state of knowledge in a particular field, and in focusing attention on specific problems and suggesting new lines of inquiry. The pieces brought together in this volume, some of them written for special occasions and purposes, and others deriving from lectures, are therefore complementary to the books I have written, but have not, I hope, been rendered entirely superfluous by them. In brief introductions to each section of the volume I have attempted to explain the circumstances which prompted the writing of individual essays, and the ways in which they relate to one or other of my books.

Many of the essays, as will be seen, derive from my special interest in the Spain of Olivares, but I have included others for the additional light they may be able to throw on the position and role of Spain in the sixteenth- and seventeenth-century world. This world was European but it was also American, and a study of Spain that excludes its American dimension is, to my mind, no more satisfactory than one that excludes its European dimension. If Spain was a pioneer among the bureaucratic states of modern Europe, it was also a pioneer among the European colonial powers, and I believe that the implications of this pioneering role for both Spanish and European history have scarcely begun to be considered. Spain's answers one year were frequently to be Europe's the next, and so, too, were some of the difficulties and the dilemmas that they brought in their suite. Pioneering has its advantages, but it also has its costs, and the price of pioneering as a clue to the course of modern Spanish history is a topic that has yet to be explored.

In particular, it may help to place in a fresh perspective the question discussed in the final section of this book, the question of decline. The causes, the character and the extent of the phenomenon traditionally known to European historiography as the 'decline of Spain' are topics that present themselves insistently to any historian of the Spanish seventeenth century. This is, after all, one of the great themes of European history, and – because of its problematic character and its universal implications – is likely to remain so. My own views on the subject, as will be apparent from these essays, have shifted and evolved as I approached it at different times and from different angles. Given the complexity of the phenomenon, and its many facets, this is only to be expected. But the problem of decline, for all its fascination, should not be allowed to dictate the entire agenda. The shadow of decline has hung for too long over the history of modern Spain, casting it in the form of a prolonged history of failure. But new ages bring new perspectives, and the story of the Spain of the 1970s and 1980s suggests that the time has come to re-think the Spanish past in less apocalyptic terms. This was a past, as I hope to have shown in these essays, of monumental achievements as well as monumental failures; and, if an argument based on the price of pioneering has any explanatory value, many of the failures may be seen as the understandable, although sometimes avoidable, long-term consequences of often surprisingly successful immediate responses to challenges novel either in themselves or in their complexity and scale.

There is, then, nothing definitive about these essays, which I have left, with the exception of a few minor corrections and verbal changes, in the form in which they first appeared, precisely because I see them as part of a continuing process of rethinking and reevaluating a history that had become fossilized through an excess of introversion and the neglect of archival possibilities. I hope that their assembling under one cover will give some indication of why this rethinking seems to me worth while. At the least it may suggest something of the historical richness of Spain and its world; and if it can persuade others to follow some of the half-explored pathways and probe deeper into that world, their publication in book form will have more than served its turn.

ILLUSTRATIONS

The following have kindly supplied photographs:

The Museo del Prado, Madrid; The National Gallery of Ireland; The National Gallery, London; The National Museums and Galleries on Merseyside; The National Trust Photographic Library.

Plate 1 has been taken from John Lynch, *Spain under the Habsburgs*, I: *Empire and Absolutism. 1516–1598* (Basil Blackwell, Oxford: 1986) and is reproduced courtesy of the publisher. Plates 17 and 20 are reproduced courtesy of The National Gallery of Ireland (Beit Collection). Plates 19 and 22 are reproduced courtesy of The Trustees of The National Gallery, London.

PART I

THE AMERICAN WORLD

INTRODUCTION

The first of these essays, on 'Spain and its Empire in the Sixteenth and Seventeenth Centuries', was originally prepared in 1977 as a lecture for St. Mary's College of Maryland. It formed part of a series of lectures by different speakers on the colonization of Maryland, and my assignment was to give a general survey of the Spanish Empire and Spanish imperialism in order to provide a global context for subsequent lectures in the series. Its descriptive and introductory character make it an appropriate opening essay for this volume, where it can also help to set the subsequent pieces into context. It was clearly impossible, in the short time allotted to me, to examine the history of the Spanish colonization of America in any detail, and in any event this seemed a rather superfluous exercise in view of the many excellent surveys of the subject in print. I therefore felt that it might be more valuable to take a rather different approach, and look at the history of Spanish imperialism from the standpoint of its impact on the colonizing power, rather than on the colonized. While considerable attention has been paid to certain aspects of the economic consequences of empire for metropolitan Spain, and especially the impact on the Spanish economy of the influx of precious metals from the Indies, other aspects which I touch on in this essay have received relatively little attention. One of the reasons for this is an unfortunate compartmentalization, both inside and outside Spain, which has tended to separate the study of Spanish history from that of Spanish America. A similar compartmentalization has existed, and with similarly unfortunate consequences, in the study of British history, and the history of the English colonies in America. While transatlantic distances were vast, the connections between metropolis and colonies were close and continuous. These connections – personal and psychological, as well as economic, administrative and cultural – need to be patiently reconstructed before we can adequately assess what the possession of overseas empire meant to Spain, and how it shaped its history.

It is enough to look at the remarkable figure of Hernán Cortés, the subject of the second essay, to see how complex was the interaction of Spain and America, even in the career of a single personality. Here was a man who exercised a decisive influence on the subsequent history of the New World, but also one on whom the experience of America etched itself indelibly. Unexpectedly finding himself the master of an alien world, he somehow had to explain and interpret this miraculous event not only to others but also to himself. Happily, the evidence survives to show how he accomplished this. Cortés' famous letters from Mexico, which have all too often been taken at face value as a truthful relation of events, prove on closer inspection to be an extraordinary tissue of truth, lies, misconceptions and special pleading, which can only be disentangled by a prolonged scrutiny of the texts and their collation with other sources. These texts also provide a series of clues to the man himself, and to the way in which his upbringing and the environment of late medieval and Renaissance Spain had both prepared him, and failed to prepare him, to meet the unprecedented opportunities and challenges that awaited him in the Indies. I first became interested in Cortés in 1964, during my own first visit to the Indies. The absence in Mexico City of any public statue to the destroyer, and founder, of Mexico brought home to me, perhaps more vividly than anything else, the ambiguities and the controversy that surround the Spanish legacy to America. This essay, written after my return, was delivered as a paper to a session of the Royal Historical Society in 1966.[1]

A further stimulus to explore the relationship between Spain and America was provided by an invitation to give the Wiles Lectures at the Queen's University, Belfast, in 1969, on some broad issue relating to the general history of civilization. In these lectures, published in 1970 under the title of *The Old World and the New, 1492–1650*, I examined the impact on European history and the European consciousness of the discovery of America. Inevitably the Spaniards, as pioneers in the exploration and settlement of America, deserved particular attention, and I found myself reading extensively in the writings of sixteenth-century Spanish clerics and laymen who sought to grapple with the enormous theological, moral and cultural problems posed by the discovery of a hitherto unknown world whose millions of inhabitants lived, for some inexplicable reason, in total ignorance of the Christian gospel. Anyone who looks at this literature is likely to be impressed, as I was impressed, by the high

---

[1] A further essay on Cortés, entitled 'Cortés, Velázquez and Charles V', and devoted to his Machiavellian strategies in dealing with his immediate superior and his monarch, is published in the form of an introduction to the English translation by Anthony Pagden of Hernán Cortés, *Letters from Mexico* (New York, 1971; new ed., New Haven and London, 1986).

seriousness of the enterprise, and by the degree of intellectual sophistication brought by the more acute among Spain's missionaries
and officials to the study of the character and customs of the indigenous peoples of America. At the same time, it seemed to me that,
in their areas of blindness as well as in their areas of perception,
they revealed a good deal about the preconceptions and prejudices of
their own civilization. In the third of these essays, given in 1972 as
the Raleigh Lecture on History to the British Academy, I attempt to
pursue this double theme of the perception of others and the
revelation of self. Like many of the other essays in this volume, this
is no more than an exploratory probe. There is a vast sixteenth-
century literature on the New World awaiting systematic analysis,
and much unpublished material, in the form of reports and letters,
survives in the archives. But the conceptualization of America and
American man revealed even by these tentative soundings may help
to suggest the rich possibilities of this material for the history of
Spain, America, and Europe as the new lands and peoples were
incorporated into the Spanish Monarchy and empire, and into the
European consciousness.

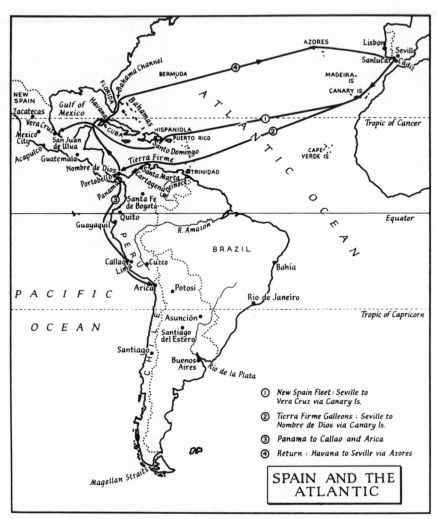

1   Spain and the Atlantic.

I

SPAIN AND ITS EMPIRE IN THE SIXTEENTH AND SEVENTEENTH CENTURIES

One of the greatest empires in world history is known to us as the 'Spanish Empire', but this is not the name by which it was known to the Spaniards themselves.[1] In the sixteenth and seventeenth centuries there was only one true empire in the western world – the Holy Roman Empire – even if other western monarchies were beginning to appropriate the title of empire for their own special purposes. With Charles I of Spain securing in 1519 the title of Holy Roman Emperor as Charles V, there was no possibility at that moment of the Spaniards formally accepting the existence of two distinctive empires, the Holy Roman and the Spanish; and even after the imperial title passed in 1556 to Charles's brother Ferdinand rather than to his son, Philip II, 'the empire' continued to denote for Spaniards the Holy Roman Empire, the German lands. Their monarch was not an emperor but a king, ruling over an agglomerate of territories known as the *monarquía española* ('the Spanish Monarchy') and consisting of Spain itself, the possessions of the king in Italy and northern Europe, and his American territories, known to Spaniards as *las Indias*.

But this does not mean to say that Spaniards lacked the capacity to think in imperial terms about the widespread dominions of their king. Already in 1520 Hernán Cortés was writing, in his second letter to Charles V from Mexico, that 'one might call oneself the emperor of this kingdom with no less glory than of Germany.'[2]

---

[1] Since this essay was intended as a general exposition rather than as a presentation of new research, only a few references will be given. Interested readers can find a more detailed discussion of many of the themes touched upon here in some of the standard works on Habsburg Spain and Spanish America. Expecially recommended are John Lynch, *Spain under the Habsburgs*, 2 vols. (2nd ed., Oxford, 1981); J.H. Parry, *The Spanish Seaborne Empire* (London, 1966); Charles Gibson, *Spain in America* (New York, 1966); see also J.H. Elliott, *Imperial Spain* (London, 1963), and *The Old World and the New, 1492–1650* (Cambridge, 1970).

[2] Hernán Cortés, *Letters from Mexico*, trans. and ed. A.R. Pagden (New Haven and London, 1986), p. 48.

Almost at the start of the discovery, conquest, and colonization of
the American mainland there existed in some quarters, then, the idea
that the King of Spain was in the process of acquiring an empire.
Philip II would later be urged to style himself 'Emperor of the
Indies', a title which was sometimes applied to him and his
successors; and 'empire of the Indies' was a phrase that acquired a
certain currency in the seventeenth century. But the Indies tended to
be set into the context of a wider and more nebulous imperialism that
was at once ideological and geographical in conception.

The humanist circle around Charles V embraced the imperial
theme with enthusiasm and represented him as being on the way to
achieving universal empire – an empire in which, in the words of
Saint John's Gospel as used by Ariosto in the *Orlando Furioso*, 'there
shall be one flock and one shepherd.'[3] Here, ready to hand, was the
theme of a providential mission, of the union of all mankind beneath
the government of a single ruler, foreshadowing the return of
universal harmony.

Along with this rather vague messianic universalism there went a
more specific sense of geographical expansion of a kind appropriate
to the great European age of discovery. The traditional limits of
Europe were the Pillars of Hercules, 'beyond which', as Dante
wrote, 'one does not go.' That 'beyond which' (*piu oltre*, rendered
into Latin as *Plus Ultra*) became the imperial device of Charles V,
twisting in scrolls around the twin pillars. *Plus Ultra*, symbolizing
first the endless expansion of the dominions and power of Charles V,
came to incorporate the more specific idea of the exploration and
conquest of the New World.[4] In mentally and physically breaking
out beyond the confines of the Pillars of Hercules into a wider world,
the Spaniards were conscious of achieving something that surpassed
even the feats of the Romans. They were on their way to a universal
empire which was genuinely universal, in the sense of being global.
This global advance can be simply plotted by a series of dates: the
1490s and early 1500s, the conquest of the Caribbean; the 1520s,
the conquest of Mexico; the 1530s, the conquest of Peru; the 1560s,
the Philippines; 1580, the annexation of Portugal and the consequent
acquisition of Portuguese Africa, the Far East, and Brazil. From this
moment the empire of the King of Spain was indeed one on which
the sun never set.

As such it surpassed in extension, and in the number of inhabitants, the greatest empire in the history of Europe, that of Rome.
This is a fact of great importance for understanding the Spanish

[3] See Frances A. Yates, *Astraea* (London, 1975), p. 26.
[4] See Earl Rosenthal, '*Plus Ultra, Non Plus Ultra*, and the Columnar Device of Emperor
Charles V', *Journal of the Warburg and Courtauld Institutes*, 34 (1971), pp. 204–28.

– or, more exactly, the Castilian – mentality of the sixteenth and seventeenth centuries. The Roman empire became a model and a point of reference for the sixteenth-century Castilians, who looked upon themselves as the heirs and successors of the Romans, conquering an even more extended empire, governing it with justice, and laying down laws which were obeyed to the farthest ends of the earth. It was a potent myth, and it had important psychological consequences for those who believed in it. The sixteenth-century Castilians saw themselves as a chosen, and therefore a superior, people, entrusted with a divine mission which looked towards universal empire as its goal. This mission was seen as a higher one than that of the Romans because it was set into the context of Catholic Christianity. The highest and most responsible duty of Castile was to uphold and extend the faith, bringing to a civilized and Christian way of life (and the two were regarded as synonymous) all those benighted peoples who, for mysterious reasons, had never until now heard the gospel message.

It seems that every empire needs its ideology, that the empire-builders have to justify to themselves in terms of a higher mission their government of dependent peoples. The Spanish crown and the Spanish ruling class found this sense of justifying mission in their obligations to their faith. Whatever services this or any other imperial mission may perform for the conquered, its impact on the conquerors does not generally seem to have been very healthy. Empire-builders, seeing themselves as entrusted with a providential mission, are all too prone to arrogance. This was one of the principal charges levelled against the Castilians, and it was essentially they who conquered and governed Spain's overseas empire. The psychological effect of their successes was betrayed in their attitude to the king's non-Castilian subjects, both in Spain itself and in other parts of Europe. For instance, a comment scribbled on a letter sent to Philip II by the governor of Milan in 1570 reads: 'These Italians, although they are not Indians, have to be treated as such, so that they will understand that we are in charge of them and not they in charge of us.'[5] This is the characteristic comment of a member of a master race, and it is not surprising to find a Catalan writing in the 1550s that the Castilians 'want to be so absolute, and put so high a value on their own achievements and so low a value on everybody else's, that they give the impression that they alone are descended from heaven, and the rest of mankind are mud.'[6] If we are to look, then, at the

[5] Quoted in H.G. Koenigsberger, *The Government of Sicily under Philip II of Spain* (London, 1951; emended ed. *The Practice of Empire*, Ithaca, N.Y., 1969), p. 48.

[6] Christòfol Despuig, quoted in J.H. Elliott, *The Revolt of the Catalans* (Cambridge, 1963; repr., 1984), p. 13.

implications of empire not so much for the peoples of that empire as for the imperialists themselves, it seems important not to ignore one of the most intangible but also one of the most far-reaching implications of empire – the psychological. It is in this context of a conscious sense of imperial mission, imperial functions, and imperial duties that I want to examine some of the consequences for sixteenth- and seventeenth-century Castile of its conquest and possession of a global empire, and more especially of an empire in America.

These Castilians, consciously following in the steps of the Romans, first had to conquer, then to colonize, and then to organize, govern, and exploit their conquests. A great deal of research has been done into the impact of their imperial activities on the subject populations of America. We have been told much about the devastating demographic impact of their presence: the decline of the indigenous population of Mexico from 25 million to 2.5 million between 1520 and 1600 as a result of war, subjugation, enforced labour services, and contact with European diseases. We know a good deal about the attempts to Christianize this population and to bring it within the confines of a European polity. We know too about some of the ecological, technical, social, and economic changes brought to the life of the inhabitants of the Indies by Spanish rule. These are fascinating and important subjects, which have received a considerable amount of attention. What has received much less attention – and this is equally true of the history of other empires, such as the British – is the way in which the possession of overseas empire affects the mother country.

What did its great overseas extension, its heroic conquering and colonizing effort, its attempt to rule over and defend its far-flung possessions, mean for the history of Habsburg Spain? The acquisition and retention of overseas empire necessarily represent a vast national investment of people, energies, and resources. Investments yield benefits, at least in theory, but they also imply costs. No serious attempt has been made to measure the costs and benefits of empire to Habsburg Spain, and indeed such an undertaking is not really feasible. There are, after all, intangible consequences, like the development among Castilians of messianic nationalism, which is obviously unquantifiable in terms of benefits or costs. It may be counted as a benefit that the morale and determination of Cortés and his colleagues were no doubt immensely fortified by their identification of their cause with that of God, Charles V, and Castile. But equally it may be counted as a cost that this confidence in their cause was rated by others as arrogance, that the Castilians earned for themselves the hatred of their fellow Europeans, and that their barbarous exploits in the New World added a whole new dimension to that vision of Spain and the Spaniards which has come to be known as the Black Legend. By the late sixteenth century, Spain stood condemned in the European dock for its atrocities against innocent peoples. The effect of this European consensus on the innate barbarism and cruelty of the Spaniard was to fortify the resolution of Spain's numerous enemies to prevent the Continent from falling beneath its bloody domination.

So there are, and must always be, strict limits to any attempt to balance the gains and losses arising to metropolitan Spain from the possession of its 'empire of the Indies.' But something can be done to suggest profitable areas of inquiry for an investigation into the ways in which investment in empire influenced the history of the imperial power itself.

If we ask ourselves what the acquisition of an American empire entailed for sixteenth-century Spain, it clearly entailed first of all the export of people. It is difficult to say with precision how many people were involved, but the most recent estimates suggest that about 240,000 men and women emigrated from Spain to the New World during the course of the sixteenth century, and perhaps some 450,000 in the seventeenth. An emigration of some 700,000 over the course of two centuries would average out at just under 4,000 passengers a year, as compared with a suggested emigration rate from the British Isles in the seventeenth century of 7,000 a year. If the total population of the Iberian peninsula was around 7 to 8 million, this implies a yearly emigration rate of 0.5 to 0.7 for every 1,000 Spaniards, which would not in itself appear a very high figure. But it is a misleading one in the sense that emigration was not evenly spread over the peninsula as a whole, and some parts of Spain produced far more emigrants than others. This is especially true of the southern areas of Andalusia and Extremadura, where the emigration rate was something like 1.4 per 1,000. But to make sense of this figure, and of the kind of demographic impact which it represents, much more information is required about the character and quality of these emigrants. In the later sixteenth century, for example, about a third of the emigrants from Spain were women. If this rate of female emigration was maintained, the loss of potential population to the Iberian peninsula must have been considerable.[7]

In the circumstances of sixteenth-century Europe, where an

[7] The figures and arguments in this paragraph are drawn from two important essays: Woodrow Borah, 'The Mixing of Populations', and Magnus Mörner, 'Spanish Migration to the New World prior to 1800', in Fredi Chiappelli, ed., *First Images of America*, 2 vols. (Berkeley and Los Angeles, 1976), 2, pp. 707–22 and 2, pp. 737–82. The fundamental work on emigration statistics has been done by Peter Boyd-Bowman, whose publications are cited in these essays.

expanding population was pressing more and more heavily on limited food resources, this loss of population or potential population may have been beneficial. America represented a safety value for the excess population of the Iberian peninsula, and contemporaries thought that this had important political and social consequences for Spain. During the period of the French religious wars, some Frenchmen believed that the lack of colonies in which to dump France's surplus inhabitants was one of the causes of their country's domestic troubles, and they contrasted their own situation with the extraordinary political stability of the Spain of Philip II. 'It is an established fact', wrote La Popelinière in 1582, 'that if the Spaniard had not sent to the Indies discovered by Columbus all the rogues in the realm...these would have stirred up the country.'[8] In other words, the export of riffraff and desperadoes was the best way to avoid a civil war.

But were they the riffraff? Emigrants emigrate because they think they can do better overseas than at home. This means that disadvantaged groups will be particularly liable to emigrate if they can. One of the major disadvantaged groups in sixteenth-century Spain consisted of the *conversos* – those who, because of their Jewish ancestry, were penalized by the statutes of purity of blood and excluded from important opportunities and positions in Castilian society. It would seem a plausible guess that the emigrants included a significant proportion of Spaniards of Jewish blood, many of whom were likely to be of above-average ability. Is it, for instance, a coincidence that the seven brothers of Saint Teresa of Avila, now known to have been of Jewish ancestry, all emigrated to the Indies? It is worth remembering, however, that the emigration of these people did not neccessarily mean a permanent loss to the mother country. One at least of Saint Teresa's brothers came home to Avila, having made his fortune in America.[9]

In general, though, even those emigrants who intended to stay in the Indies only long enough to get rich were liable to end their lives on the far side of the Atlantic. The lure of the Indies was very powerful, and those who had successfully emigrated would write home to their relatives begging them to join them. 'Don't hesitate. God will help us. This land is as good as ours, for God has given us more here than there, and we shall be better off.'[10] It seems a fair

---

[8] Henri de la Popelinière, *Les Trois Mondes* (Paris, 1582), introduction.

[9] Valentín de Pedro, *América en las letras españolas del siglo de oro* (Buenos Aires, 1954), pp. 262–8.

[10] Cited in Elliott, *Old World and the New*, p. 76. For a fascinating anthology of letters from emigrants, see James Lockhart and Enrique Otte, eds., *Letters and People of the Spanish Indies* (Cambridge, 1976).

assumption that the emigrants were drawn from the abler and more dynamic sections of the Castilian and Andalusian population, and if some of these were misfits at home, and their departure for America was therefore a source of relief to the authorities, it also deprived Spain of people who possessed certain talents, like entrepreneurial capacity, which it could ill afford to lose. One also could argue that, in the circumstances of sixteenth-century Spain, even the export of missionaries had its disadvantages. By 1559 there were 802 members of the religious orders in Mexico,[11] and one would assume that some of the ablest and most intelligent members were drawn to an overseas mission. But there was missionary work to be done at home, too, among the Moorish population of Andalusia and Valencia; and the failure of the sixteenth-century Spanish church to tackle the problem of effectively Christianizing the Moriscos may have been the price of devoting its best men and energies to the task of Christianizing the Indians of America.

To create its American empire, Spain had to export people – people to convert the Indians to Christianity, to found cities, and to settle the land. But these new territories, once conquered and settled, had also to be governed. By its nature, the acquisition of empire poses an enormous challenge for the metropolitan authorities. In studying the history of Habsburg Spain, it is too easy to ignore the unprecedented problems and the heroic effort involved in providing effective government for a global empire. No European society until this moment had been faced with an administrative task of such magnitude and such complexity. First of all, the Spaniards had to resolve a problem for which again they had few precedents to guide them, that of determining the juridical status of the large indigenous populations which had now become subjects of the crown of Castile. Were the Indians, for instance, to be treated as slaves, or were they free men? And, if free men, what tributes and services could be demanded of them as vassals of the crown? These were not easy problems to solve. For Europeans these Indians were a new kind of people, and there was great uncertainty and confusion about their origins and capacities. Were they men, in the full sense of the word, or sub-men, whose inferior capacities demanded that they be placed under some kind of tutelage? This was the type of problem with which the Spaniards found themselves confronted as soon as they arrived in the Antilles, and it became even more complex when they came face-to-face with the peoples of the settled empires of the Aztecs and the Incas. The problem led to a passionate debate during the first half of the sixteenth century in governmental circles, in the

[11] Robert Ricard, La 'conquête spirituelle' du Mexique (Paris, 1933), p. 35.

universities, and among the clergy and members of the religious
orders – a debate with which the names of Las Casas and Sepúlveda
will forever be associated. The effective outcome of this fifty-year
debate was that the Indians were not slaves and were not to be treated
as such; that, lacking Christianity and true civility, they had to be
instructed in the faith and in the ways of Christian men; that this
required close spiritual and temporal supervision, which placed the
Indians in a special but subordinate status where they must be given
the protection of the crown; and that it was right that they should
perform certain services in return for this protection.

A prime object of imperial government, then, was the protection
of the Indians, and this meant especially protecting them from
exploitation by the colonists. Consequently, one of the great problems facing the Spanish crown was how to prevent rebellions
and breakaway movements by the settler community, and it was a
problem which it successfully solved. Apart from the struggle
between the crown and the followers of Pizarro in the aftermath of
the conquest of Peru and the abortive conspiracy by Martín Cortés in
Mexico in 1566, there was no major open challenge to the crown
from the settler community in the New World in the nearly three
hundred years of Spanish rule before it was overthrown by the
independence movements of the early nineteenth century. Considering that it might take as much as two years for a message to travel
from Madrid to Lima and the reply to come home, this is an
extraordinary achievement. The Spanish crown managed to overcome the unprecedented problems of time and space to the extent of
preventing the centrifugal forces inherent in a worldwide empire
from triumphing over the forces of control emanating from
Madrid.

How did the crown succeed in achieving this degree of control?
The very challenge of empire – of having to govern such distant
territories – acted as a major stimulus to the development in
Habsburg Spain of a strong bureaucratic structure and an administrative class to staff it. In terms of well-developed and professionally
run bureaucratic organization, the Spain of Philip II was the most
advanced state in sixteenth-century Europe. In reality it could not
afford to be otherwise, since in the absence of a large and formalized
bureaucracy it could never have held its empire together. We all
know the defects of this bureaucracy, that it was cumbersome,
corrupt, and appallingly slow, and we may well recall the despairing
comment of one viceroy patiently waiting for his orders: 'If death
came from Madrid, we should all live to a very old age.' But perhaps
more significant than these glaring defects is that Spain did succeed in
building a global bureaucracy, that the bureaucracy did function

with greater or lesser efficiency, and that it did manage to hold the king's many disparate territories together.

The challenge of empire therefore produced a bureaucratic response, in the form of government by paper, on a scale previously unknown in European history. We have hardly yet begun to grasp the sheer quantity of paper used for the government of the Spanish Monarchy and empire in the sixteenth and seventeenth centuries. For example, when a viceroy or any major official left office, a formal investigation, known as a *residencia* or *visita*, was conducted into his tenure of office, with sworn statements being taken from those in a position to speak. In 1590 one such *visita* was begun on the retirement of the Count of Villar as viceroy of Peru. By 1603 the judge conducting this *visita* had used 49,555 sheets of paper and was not yet finished. The ex-viceroy himself was long since dead.[12] What a different world this was from the world of seventy or eighty years before, when the Emperor Charles V had allegedly asked for pen and ink and none was to be found in the palace![13] Although royal administration was not really as casual in the early years of Charles V as this story would suggest, the avalanche of paper in the later sixteenth century (not to mention the plethora of pens and the torrents of ink) suggests that, between the early years of Charles and the later years of Philip, there had intervened a revolution in the operations of government.

The essence of this revolution was the creation of an administrative structure designed to link the centre of the Spanish Monarchy with its periphery. The method used was to elaborate and build upon a system already in existence in the Spain of Ferdinand and Isabella, which owed much to the practice of government in the Catalan-Aragonese empire of the later Middle Ages. In accordance with this system, the king was represented in his distant territories by a viceroy, while the territories were represented in the presence of the king by councils composed of spokesmen for those territories. This was the conciliar system developed in the Spanish Monarchy during the first half of the sixteenth century: a system of councils meeting at the court, and receiving information from – and sending orders to – viceroys at the periphery. It was accompanied by a judicial system which acted as a check on the viceroys, whereby each of the territories had its tribunal of judges, known as the *audiencia*, which

---

[12] See Lewis Hanke, 'El visitador licenciado Alonso Fernández de Bonilla y el virrey del Perú, el conde del Villar', *Memoria del II congreso venezolano de historia* (Caracas, 1975), 2, pp. 13–127.

[13] The story is told by the Count of Gondomar in a letter of 28 March 1619 (*Correspondencia oficial de Don Diego Sarmiento de Acaña, Conde de Gondomar*, in *Documentos inéditos para la historia de España*, 10 vols. (Madrid, 1936–55), 2, p. 143).

was responsible for the administration of justice and could when
necessary curb and control the viceroy's administrative powers. For
example, the government of Mexico (New Spain) depended first of
all, in Spain itself, on the Council of the Indies, sitting at court and
advising the king on all major questions relating to Mexican affairs.
Its recommendations, if approved by the king, were then transmitted
to Mexico, where the viceroy might or might not put them into
effect; his activities were watched by the *audiencia* sitting in Mexico
City, which advised, warned, or defied him according to the
situation and the personalities involved.

This system, which functioned reasonably well, inevitably led to a
proliferation of paper and a proliferation of officials. The government needed secretaries to draft the regulations, scribes to write
them out, and a whole host of lesser officials to ensure their
enforcement, along with another tier of officials to ensure that the
first tier of officials had indeed ensured it. All this required a massive
bureaucracy, which had to be recruited and trained. This in turn
meant an expansion of Spain's educational system. At the beginning
of the sixteenth century there were eleven universities in Spain. A
hundred years later there were thirty-three. Much of this growth is
explained by the state's growing need for officials to man the higher
echelons of the bureaucracy, and especially officials trained in the
law. It has been estimated that under Philip II Castile supported an
annual university population of 20,000–25,000 students, representing perhaps 5.43 percent of its eighteen-year-old male population – a
figure that seems to have been very high by contemporary European
standards.[14] Those students who studied the law and survived their
course emerged as *letrados*, law graduates who formed the recruiting
pool for the bureaucracy. Since supply was outrunning demand by
the end of the century, many of these graduates would then find
themselves without jobs. But the best of them – or, perhaps more
accurately, the best-connected – might with luck secure a foothold
on the lowest rung of the bureaucratic ladder, which they would be
painfully climbing for the rest of their lives.

It was these *letrados* in government service who really held the
Spanish Monarchy and empire together. Their whole career was
spent in the service of the crown, and they would be moved around
the world in accordance with the king's orders. One such official was
Antonio de Morga, born in Seville in 1559, the son of a banker.[15] He
was sent to Salamanca University, where he graduated in canon and

---

[14] See Richard L. Kagan, *Students and Society in Early Modern Spain* (Baltimore, 1974), esp.
pp. 199–200.

[15] Morga's career is related in John Leddy Phelan, *The Kingdom of Quito in the Seventeenth
Century* (Madison, Wis., 1967).

then in civil law. In 1580 he entered government service as a lawyer. Thirteen years later, aged thirty-five, he was appointed (being a man with good connections) to a legal post in the Philippines, where in due course he became the senior judge of the *audiencia*. In 1603, at forty-five, he was transferred to the *audiencia* of Mexico. Here he was enough of a success to secure promotion ten years later to the presidency of the *audiencia* of Quito, Ecuador. This could have been the last stop before a post at the very top of the bureaucratic hierarchy, a seat in the Council of the Indies back in Spain. Morga petitioned for this in 1623, but unfortunately by this time his addiction to women and gambling had got the better of him. His conduct became a source of grave scandal, bad enough to prompt an official inquiry into his activities. He was sentenced to be relieved of his office, but before the news reached him he died in Quito, aged seventy-six, after a not very distinguished twenty-one-year presidency.

Assuming that Morga had achieved his ambition of a seat in the Council of the Indies, the council would have been reinforced by a man of enormous practical experience in the problems of overseas administration. But he would have been over sixty-five by the time he took up his appointment in Madrid, and it seems improbable that he would have been a dynamic or innovating councillor. On the whole, the government of the Spanish empire was a gerontocracy because it took such a long time for officials to pass through the various stages of their administrative careers. One therefore finds, as one would expect to find, that the councils were staffed by elderly, status-conscious officials, tenacious of tradition and legalistically inclined, who were above all determined to enjoy in comfort the prestige and rich pickings of the high office which they had worked for so long to secure. They were not a dynamic crowd, but they were nothing if not tenacious. They kept the empire in being, but they also kept it static.

Throughout their careers these men looked to the king, for both their orders and their promotion. They had a very exalted sense of the royal authority of which they were the representatives and official upholders, whether in the Philippines, Ecuador, or Mexico. This sense of the royal authority, reinforced by firsthand awareness of the vast extent of the king of Spain's dominions, created a kind of mentality which deserves to be taken into account in any history of Habsburg Spain. It was difficult to get away from the sense of the overwhelming and universal authority of the king, and while this sense helped to bind the bureaucrats of the empire together in a kind of fraternity of loyal adherents of the crown, it may also have led the government in Madrid to exaggerate the resources of power at the king's command. Madrid for these men was the centre of the universe, the bureaucratic capital of a worldwide empire. A judge who returned from Lima to serve on the Council of the Indies or a returning viceroy – a Castilian grandee like the Marquis of Montes-claros, who served as viceroy of Mexico and Peru and was then appointed a member of Philip IV's Council of State – saw the world from a peculiar angle, which was not the angle of other men. From Madrid it must have seemed that one could rule the whole world. But unfortunately this did not always happen to be true.

The acquistion of empire, then, entailed the creation of a vast bureaucratic structure whose central point was Madrid. The creation of Madrid itself was in reality a response to the problems of empire. In the early sixteenth century Spain had no capital city, and the court moved around the peninsula with the king. Madrid itself was little more than an overgrown village, with some 5,000 inhabitants. But from 1561, when Philip II settled his court there, it began to grow very fast indeed, and had reached over 100,000 inhabitants by the 1620s. This mushroom growth of Madrid as the capital of a world-wide empire was enormously significant for the future history of Spain. Here was a city at the very centre of the barren tableland of Castile: an artificial city of courtiers and bureaucrats, deriving its rather febrile prosperity from the profits of empire which flowed into it from all over the world; a distorting element in the economic life of the Castilian *meseta* in its role as a centre of conspicuous consumption for luxury goods brought from other parts of Europe and paid for with the silver of the Indies.

If we can regard the rather unhealthy growth of Madrid as a direct consequence of the bureaucratic demands created by the growth of empire, we can regard the equally remarkable growth of Seville as a direct consequence of the economic demands of empire. Just as Madrid was the bureaucratic capital of Spain's global Monarchy, so Seville was its commercial capital. Early seventeenth-century Seville was one of the largest cities of the western world – a city of some 150,000 inhabitants, against 70,000 a hundred years before. Thanks to its monopolistic position as the sole Iberian port for the Indies trade, it had become the centre of the so-called Spanish Atlantic system. Its extraordinary prosperity, and the prosperity of its hinter-land in southern Andalusia, was directly related to the sixteenth-century prosperity of that trading system. As the system began to break down, from the second decade of the seventeenth century, so Seville's prosperity began to crumble.

This system was so crucial for the European as well as the Spanish economy in the sixteenth century that its actual working is a matter of some importance. The Indies were prized, developed, and ex-ploited primarily as a source of commodities which were highly valued and in short supply in Europe itself: pearls, obtained from the waters round the coasts of Venezuela; dye-stuffs; emeralds; and, most important of all, gold and silver. Between 1500 and 1650 something like 181 tons of gold and 16,000 tons of silver reached Europe from America officially, which means that further very large quantities must have arrived by contraband. At first more gold arrived than silver, but the proportion began to change as a result of the great silver discoveries of the 1540s: the Potosí mines of Peru in 1545 and the Mexican mines of Zacatecas in 1546. But it took both time and the introduction of new refining processes by means of an amalgam of mercury to get a large-scale and regular output from these mines. Silver remittances to Spain were already substantial in the 1550s and 1560s, but it was only from the 1570s – after the discovery of mercury mines in Peru and the introduction of the new refining process there in 1571 – that the remittances became very large indeed, with Peru producing two-thirds of the silver to Mexico's one-third.

Spain and Europe needed this silver. The King of Spain needed it to meet his expenses (especially the expenses incurred in war), and Europe's mercantile community needed it to lubricate its transactions and to provide a means of paying for luxuries from India and the East. Therefore the organizaton of the silver mines and the silver trade became a major preoccupation of the Spanish crown, and the whole Spanish system – and to some extent the European international system – came to depend very heavily on the regular flow of precious metals from America to Europe. But all the silver had to be paid for, apart from the *quinto*, or one-fifth of the mines' production, which belonged to the Spanish crown of right. Payment came from the export to America of Spanish and European commodities to meet the needs of the growing settler community, which hankered for luxury objects and articles of consumption unobtainable in the newly settled lands. From the start, therefore, Seville's commerce with America was a two-way trade, designed on the one hand to satisfy the needs of a growing American market, and on the other to satisfy Europe's insatiable demand for precious metals.

The receiving point at the European end of the transatlantic network was Seville, with its port of San Lúcar enjoying a monopoly of the American trade. By the system of the treasure fleets, which was finally regularized in the 1560s, two fleets left San Lúcar each year, both in convoy with armed protection. The first of these fleets, the *flota*, left in May, destined for Vera Cruz in Mexico. The second, the *galeones*, left in August, and took a slightly more southerly course, making for Nombre de Dios (Portobello) on the isthmus of Panama; and then, after unloading its cargoes for the colonists – wine,

oil, grain, swords, books, clothes, and luxury objects – it would
retire to the more sheltered harbour of Cartagena for the winter.

The outward journey took five to six weeks, and the size of the
fleets varied a good deal, but the average was around sixty to seventy
ships. Once they had unloaded their cargoes, both the fleets would
winter in the Indies. The trickiest problem was to arrange the timing
of the return journey to Seville. The pattern was for both fleets to
rendezvous at Havana and start back with their precious silver cargoes
in the early summer, before the hurricane season arrived. To do this,
the Mexican *flota* had to leave Vera Cruz in February, laden with
silver and cochineal and other goods from Mexico, to make its three-
to four-week voyage against the trade winds to Havana. The isthmus
fleet, the *galeones*, had a much more tricky assignment, because it had
to pick up, while en route for Havana, the silver coming from the
Peruvian mines. Its voyage therefore had to be synchronized with
the transport of silver all the way from the Potosí mines to
Panama.[16] This in turn depended, in the final analysis, on the rainfall
in Bolivia. If the rains came late, there was insufficient waterpower
for the mills to prepare the ore and turn the silver into bars. From the
point of view of the return journey of the fleets, the Peruvian silver
should have been in Panama by March in order to get to Havana
before the hurricane season started. But usually the rain was so
delayed in the Bolivian altiplano that the silver only reached Panama
in May. Once the rains had fallen and the silver had been minted, a
great llama train carried it down from the mountains on the
fifteen-day journey from Potosí to Arica. At the port of Arica the
silver was transferred to ships, which took eight days to reach
Callao, the port of Lima. Here it was transferred into three or four
special treasure ships, which took twenty days to reach Panama. At
Panama it was taken out of the ships and placed on the backs of
mules, and the mule train took four days to cross the isthmus, where
the *galeones* were waiting at Nombre de Dios to load the silver. They
then sailed for Havana and joined up with the Mexican *flota*; with
luck, the combined fleets were back in Seville by the late summer or
early autumn.

This, very briefly, was the mechanism of the Seville trade – a
cumbersome and expensive, but on the whole efficient, mechanism,
which, with only two or three exceptions, got the fleets safely across
the Atlantic and back for over two centuries. This itself was a

[16] For a good account of this process, see Carmen Báncora Cañero, 'Las remesas de metales
preciosas desde el Callao a España en la primera mitad del siglo XVII', *Revista de Indias*, no. 75
(1959), pp. 35–88. The Seville trade has been exhaustively studied by Huguette and Pierre
Chaunu, *Séville et l'Atlantique, 1504–1650*, 8 vols. (Paris, 1955–59), which is the starting point
of all later work.

remarkable feat of organization, considering how dependent it was on careful synchronization all the way along the line. It demanded, in the first place, reasonably accessible deposits of silver, a regular supply of Indian labour to work them, and a regular supply of mercury to refine the metal. It demanded rains at the right time in Bolivia, llama trains and mules in abundance, and large fleets whose sailings had to be carefully arranged according to the winds and the seasons. When we talk, therefore, about the Spanish empire, we must think not just in terms of vast and widely scattered territories, nor even simply in terms of a complex bureaucratic structure, but also in terms of an intricate economic mechanism which required the most careful regulation.

What did the existence of this mechanism mean for the Spanish economy and Spanish society in the sixteenth century? Obviously the gold and silver of the Indies meant a windfall for Spain, although it could be argued that much of this windfall was unprofitably squandered. Riches were flowing into Seville in large and growing quantities, and those which did not almost immediately flow out again to pay debts to foreign bankers were transmuted into benefits for a wide variety of individuals. Aristocratic families fallen on hard times would hope to recoup their fortunes with revenues from the Indies; hence the competition among the Castilian grandees for the American viceroyalties, since a viceroy of Mexico or Peru could reasonably expect to reline his coffers during a normal tenure of office. We should therefore regard the overseas empire as a means of providing outdoor relief for at least a section of the high Castilian aristocracy. Government officials and clerics, and the relatives of settlers who had done well in the Indies and chose to remit money home to their families, would also acquire their silver nest eggs, and then use them as they would: to pay off debts, acquire property, send a favorite nephew to Salamanca University, or construct a family chapel in the local parish church. The merchants of Seville, who were the recipients of large quantities of silver, would use it for their own transactions, and especially for purchasing cargoes for the next Indies fleet. Apparently half the silver that arrived in the fleets of 1568 and 1569 was used to fit out and freight the next two fleets.[17] This meant that the system was, as it were, self-generating. Something like half the annual revenues of the Indies were needed for shipping commodities back there in order to yield more revenues in the future. But all this activity in the dockyards of Seville itself generated employment and new skills; it encouraged artisans to develop

[17] José Gentil da Silva, *En Espagne. Développement économique, subsistance, déclin* (Paris, 1965), p. 65.

products for the Indies trade and Andalusian farmers to produce more wheat or wine or oil for shipment to America. If Castile experienced a minor economic boom during the opening and middle decades of the sixteenth century, part of the explanation for this lies in the opening of the new American market, with the new demands that it created.

The influx of all this silver into the Spanish, and then the European, economy has notoriously been held responsible for the 'price revolution' of the sixteenth century. Much debate has been generated around the thesis of Earl J. Hamilton's *American Treasure and the Price Revolution in Spain* (1934), which attempted to illustrate statistically the existence of an extremely close correlation between the increase in sixteenth-century Spanish prices and the quantities of American silver arriving in Seville. There would seem, however, to be many other besides purely monetary reasons for the sixteenth-century price rise, although American silver played its part in pushing up prices and still more in keeping them at a high general level. Hamilton's thesis tends to assume that all the silver which arrived in Seville found its way into the Spanish economy, and this clearly did not happen. Large quantities were in fact shipped abroad again, for one purpose or another, immediately after registration. It is very difficult to secure exact figures, but in the later years of the sixteenth century it is probable that, in an annual consignment of 10 million ducats from America, 6 million at once left Spain.[18]

There are various explanations of this rapid exit of silver almost before entry. A certain amount went to pay for European rather than Spanish commodities, which were then shipped to the Indies. But much of it was sent abroad, largely through bankers, to keep Spain's various European armies in pay and to sustain the expensive foreign policy of the Spanish crown. For one of the greatest of all the implications of overseas empire for sixteenth-century Spain was that it helped provide the crown with the resources to launch military ventures which were quite beyond the scope of its European rivals.

Sixteenth- and seventeenth-century Europeans saw America, with some justice, as the true source of the Spanish monarch's power. Sir Benjamin Rudyard told the House of Commons in 1624: 'They are not his great territories which make him so powerful... for it is very well known that Spain itself is but weak in men, and barren of natural commodities.... No, sir, they are his mines in the West Indies, which minister fuel to feed his vast ambitious desire of universal monarchy.'[19] Rudyard was probably correct, in so far as

[18] F. Ruiz Martín, *Lettres marchandes échangées entre Florence et Medina del Campo* (Paris, 1965), p. xlix.
[19] Quoted in Elliott, *Old World and the New*, pp. 90–1.

the possession of the Indies made the thought of universal monarchy thinkable and encouraged the rulers of Spain to assume that grandiose schemes could in fact be realized. But in terms of the actual figures, America's contribution to the king's coffers was not quite as impressive as Rudyard's remarks might lead one to believe. It is true that, in the second half of the reign of Charles V, the emperor became increasingly dependent for his revenues on Spain, at the receiving end of the American silver supply, and less and less on his traditional sources of income, Italy and the Netherlands. But even as late as 1554 the American contribution amounted to only 11 percent of the crown's total income.

Things were rather different under Philip II, but even when the silver of the Indies was flowing into Seville in enormous quantities, it still hardly reached 25 percent of Philip's total revenues. But to speak simply in terms of proportional contributions is unsatisfactory. Silver was a highly desirable international commodity; it was because the King of Spain had at his disposal large and regular supplies of silver that the great international bankers of the sixteenth century, the Fuggers and the Genoese, were prepared to serve as royal bankers and perform the necessary bridging loan operations between the arrival of one fleet and the next. The imperialism of Charles V, and then of Philip II, was financed by borrowing, and neither of these monarchs would have been able to borrow for so long, or on such a massive scale, if they had not been able to attract the international financial community with the lure of New World silver.

It would be fair, then, to say that the possession of America helped to sustain Europe's first great imperial venture of the sixteenth century, that of Charles V, even if it did not originally launch it. But Charles' empire was and remained obstinately European; it was only in the second half of the century that the political organization of Europe adjusted to the new economic realities, and that Habsburg imperialism reconstituted itself around the Spanish Atlantic of the age of Philip II. Madrid, Seville, Lisbon, and Genoa – not Augsburg or Antwerp – were the effective centres of this new imperial system, and it was because the resources of those centres were accessible to him that Philip II could attempt with some success over half a century to check and throw back the forces of heresy and disorder which threatened to engulf the orderly, hierarchical world that was the only world he understood. The effort was an enormous one, as witnessed by the three million ducats a year (the equivalent of the crown's total annual revenues from the Indies) required to sustain the famous army of Flanders in its desperate struggle to crush the revolt in the Netherlands. In the end, it is hardly surprising that the strain began to break the system. Sooner or later the moment was bound to come when the costs of empire began to outweigh its presumed or real benefits. It is not easy to pinpoint this moment, and perhaps it is a mistake even to make the attempt. But between the 1590s and the 1620s there seems to have been a significant shift in the relationship of Spanish America to the metropolis – a shift which began to raise doubts in certain quarters about the value to Spain of having an empire at all.

There was, for example, the question of emigration. In the sixteenth century the Indies may have represented a useful outlet for an excess population which Castile could neither feed nor employ. But Castile was struck by a devastating plague in 1599–1600 and increasingly began to be perceived as an underpopulated country. The rapid rise in Castilian wages in the reign of Philip III suggests that Castile could no longer afford the loss of able-bodied men. Yet it was at this moment that the deepening misery of Castile led to a massive increase in illegal emigration, and the consequent drain of people to the Indies became a cause for profound concern.

About the same time, it also began to look as though Castile could no longer take for granted the benefits of empire which it had for so long regarded as a matter of course. During the sixteenth century both the Spanish crown and the Castilian economy had become dangerously dependent on the Seville trade and on the regular arrival of silver from the Indies. In moments of crisis they had looked to the New World and had not looked in vain. But now, in the early seventeenth century, circumstances had changed. The American market was beginning to dry up, at least as far as Spanish commodities were concerned. The colonists no longer wanted traditional Spanish goods in the same quantity as before; the Seville trade itself began to run into difficulties after 1610; and the silver remittances started to decline. This, for a variety of reasons, is especially true of remittances for the Spanish crown, which slumped from 2 million ducats a year at the beginning of Philip III's reign in 1598 to around 1 million in 1615 and 1616, and to a mere 800,000 in 1620, before rising again to around 1.5 million a year in the following decade.[20]

So the tangible benefits of America to Spain were dwindling, and they were dwindling at a moment when the costs of empire were climbing sharply. English attacks on Spain's American possessions in the reign of Elizabeth had already forced the crown to embark on a costly programme for building fortifications in the Indies. Under Philip III, money had to be scraped up year after year for the war in Chile against the Araucanian Indians, and the issue of naval defence

[20] Elliott, *Revolt of the Catalans*, p. 189.

in the Atlantic and the Pacific grew increasingly urgent as the threat from the Dutch increased. This problem of imperial defence began to overshadow everything else in the final years of Philip III because of the enormous burden that it was now imposing on the Castilian taxpayer and the Castilian economy. It compelled ministers to reconsider the general distribution of taxation within the Spanish Monarchy and to reassess the various ways of defending an empire consisting of widely scattered territories. The solution devised in the 1620s by the Count-Duke of Olivares was an ambitious scheme for a Union of Arms – a pooling of the Monarchy's resources for military and naval defence – which placed such an intolerable strain on the fragile constitutional structure of the Spanish Monarchy that by the 1640s it seemed on the verge of total collapse.

This growing realization of the burdens of empire was sharpened by the intense awareness of the misery of Castile. The Castile of Philip III and Philip IV went through a period of deep soul-searching, accompanied by many anxious attempts to identify and analyze the causes of distress. It seemed an extraordinary paradox that Castile, the head of a great empire, should be poverty-stricken, that it should be so rich and yet so poor. González de Cellorigo, analyzing in 1600 the troubles of Castile, traced at least some of them back to the psychological effects of the discovery of the Indies.[21] In his view, the effect of an apparently endless flow of American silver into Seville had been to create a false sense of wealth as consisting of gold and silver, whereas true wealth lay in productive investment and the development of industry, agriculture, and trade. If this was so, the discovery of America could even be considered as prejudicial to Spain, because it had diverted the country's attention from the real sources of prosperity and dazzled it with the mirage of false riches. The Castilian, as a result, had abandoned work for dreams. The Flemish scholar Justus Lipsius wrote to a Spanish friend in 1603: 'Conquered by you, the New World has conquered you in turn, and has weakened and exhausted your ancient vigour.'[22]

Once the overseas empire was beginning to be seen as a liability rather than a benefit, as a source of misfortune rather than prosperity, there was an inevitable revulsion against it. The Count-Duke of Olivares himself said at a meeting of the Council of State in 1631: 'If its great conquests have reduced this Monarchy to such a miserable condition, one can reasonably say that it would have been more powerful without that New World.'[23] This was an extraordinary

[21] *Memorial de la política necesaria y útil restauración a la república de España* (Valladolid, 1600), p. 15v.
[22] Alejandro Ramírez, *Epistolario de Justo Lipsio y los españoles* (Madrid, 1966), p. 374.
[23] Archivo General de Simancas, Estado, legajo 2332, *consulta* of 7 September 1631.

statement, coming from the principal minister of the Spanish crown. Here was the anti-imperialist thesis finding expression in the very highest governmental circles of the Spanish Monarchy – the rejection, as it were, of a hundred years of Spanish history. Although this was the despairing remark of an exhausted minister and should not be taken too seriously, it does seem to indicate a striking change of mood from the heady days of Charles V. In the early sixteenth century the Castilians had seen themselves as a people divinely favoured with the gift (or the trust) of a global empire. Now, a century later, they had lost their confidence. The gift of empire had proved a poisoned chalice, which had sapped their vigour and aggravated their ills. This change of attitude appears to correspond to a change in the objective situation. The liabilities of empire *had* increased, and its immediate benefits had diminished. The difficulty came in adjusting to this changed situation.

Sixteenth-century America had made it possible for Castile to sustain itself as the dominant world power, but at an economic, administrative, and psychological cost which only slowly became apparent. When the cost did begin to appear, and the bills came in for payment, it was hard for a ruling class accustomed to thinking in imperial terms to change its policies and its ways. The possession of empire had created expectations and assumptions which it was difficult to jettison, and by the mid-seventeenth century the commitments of Madrid had so far outstripped its capacity to meet them that the jettisoning of expectations had become essential for the Monarchy's survival. In fact, empire had become a psychological burden which made it almost impossible to think in realistic terms about the changing international situation. The sad history of the Spain of the middle and later seventeenth century is the history of a people and a ruling class which failed to rid themselves in time of imperial delusions.

The fate of Spain, and of other imperial powers which followed in its steps, prompts a final reflection as to whether the adverse psychological consequences of empire for the imperialists do not, in the long run, outweigh all the more tangible assets that empire is supposed to bring in its train. And as we look at the course of Spanish history since the days of Charles V, and consider the remarkable achievements of a uniquely gifted people, we can still hear the mocking echo of those words of Justus Lipsius: 'Conquered by you, the New World has conquered you in turn.'

II

THE MENTAL WORLD OF HERNÁN CORTÉS

So many books and articles have been devoted to the life and career of Hernán Cortés that it may well seem presumptuous to add to their number. But there is still no satisfactory biography, and it is only quite recently that his writings – his 'letters of relation' to Charles V, his general correspondence, and his military and administrative directives – have been subjected to the close critical scrutiny which they deserve. In particuler, Dr. Richard Konetzke has drawn attention to the constructive aspects of Cortés' career as the founder of a colonial society, while an Austrian historian, Dr. Viktor Frankl, has analysed with extraordinary ingenuity Cortés' idea of empire and his indebtedness to Spanish medieval traditions and ways of thought. Other important contributions have been made by Mexicans: Dr Manuel Alcalá, who has drawn an extended parallel between Caesar and Cortés, without, however, proving any direct influence of one on the other, and Srta. Eulalia Guzmán, whose annotated edition of the first two letters of relation is intended to expose the conqueror of Mexico as a consummate liar and a monster of depravity.[1] Although these four historians approach Cortés from very different stand-points, they have all shown how much can still be learnt about him from an examination of his writings, and how much remains to be discovered before we shall be able to see him in the round – not only as a military leader, but also as a colonist and an entrepreneur, and as an unusually astute politician with a remarkable gift for putting old ideas to new uses in the unprecedented situation in which he found himself in Mexico.

[1] R. Konetzke, 'Hernán Cortés como poblador de la Nueva España', *Estudios Cortesianos* (Madrid, 1948), pp. 341–81; V. Frankl, 'Hernán Cortés y la tradicón de las Siete Partidas', *Revista de Historia de América*, no. 53 (1962) pp. 9–74, and 'Imperio particular e imperio universal en las cartas de relación de Hernán Cortés', *Cuadernos Hispanoamericanos* no. 165 (1963), pp. 443–82; M. Alcalá, *César y Cortés* (Mexico, 1950); Eulalia Guzmán, *Relaciones de Hernán Cortés a Carlos V sobre la invasión de Anáhuac* (Mexico, 1958). The writings of Cortés have been collected in a single volume by Mario Hernández Sánchez-Barba, *Hernán Cortés. Cartas y Documentos* (Mexico, 1963). All quotations in this article are drawn from this volume, cited as *Cartas*.

Their work has also emphasized the need to set Cortés very firmly into the context of the society from which he sprang, the society of late medieval and early Renaissance Spain, for he at once mirrors the ideals and aspirations of that society, and shares the pattern of its development. Between 1485, the year of his birth, and 1547, the year of his death, Spain passed through a whole cycle of experiences which are strangely reflected in Cortés' personal career. He was born at a time when Ferdinand and Isabella had succeeded in imposing royal justice and royal authority on a society which had threatened to disintegrate under the pressure of conflicting individual ambitions. They had restored the community of the realm, and had helped to imbue it with that sense of confidence and purpose which would enable it to complete the reconquest of its own territory from the Moors and to embark on its career of overseas expansion in Africa, Italy, and the Antilles. The Castile of the Catholic Kings was a country which, while deeply attached to medieval traditions and values, was being stirred by Italian humanist ideals; and stirred, too, by those aspirations for spiritual renewal and regeneration which were agitating all Europe in the later Middle Ages. This was the society from which Cortés came, and he retained its imprint to the end of his days.

Cortés left Spain for the West Indies in 1504, the year of Isabella's death, and did not return to it until 1528, when her grandson, Charles V, was firmly established on the Spanish throne. In the intervening period the carefully articulated society built up by the Catholic Kings was subjected to a series of severe strains, culminating in the revolt of the *Comuneros* between 1519 and 1521, the very years in which Cortés committed his own personal act of revolt against lawfully constituted authority, and went on to conquer Mexico for his imperial master.[2] The Spain to which he returned in triumph in 1528 was Erasmian Spain – a country painfully adjusting itself to a new historic role under the leadership of men fired by ambitious ideas of universal empire, and by Erasmian ideals of general reform. But already the universal ambitions of Charles and his advisers were clouded by the threat of heresy, and when Cortés came home for the last time, in 1540, the humanist Spain of his first visit had become deeply tinged by the sombre hues of the Counter-Reformation.

The life of Cortés therefore spans an extraordinarily rich and varied period of Spanish history – a period in which a reorganized and re-articulated medieval society, increasingly exposed to external

[2] See M. Giménez Fernández, *Hernán Cortés y su revolución comunera en la Nueva España* (Seville, 1948), which attempts to draw a parallel between the revolt of Cortés and that of the Comuneros.

intellectual influences, turns outwards to acquire an overseas empire, and finds itself endowed with a unique imperial and religious mission. But Cortés, while spanning the transition from Middle Ages to Counter-Reformation, seems also to reflect it in his own mental development. His correspondence, when read in the light of the political and intellectual pre-occupations of contemporary Spain, gives the impression of having been written by a man with exceptionally sensitive mental antennae, alert to detect the most subtle shifts of opinion in a world thousands of miles away.

This very sensitivity, however, makes it extremely difficult to trace the course of Cortés' intellectual development, and the problem is further complicated by the almost total absence of external evidence about his interests and attainments. It is known only that, as the son of *hidalgo* parents in Extremadura, he was sent at the age of fourteen to Salamanca where he remained for two years. There is some dispute about the way in which he was supposed to be spending his time at Salamanca, but it seems probable that he embarked on the study of Latin grammar with the intention of proceeding to the study of law, but then tired of his studies and returned home to Medellín, to the annoyance of his parents, who had hoped to see him equipped for a profitable legal career.[3] But there is no doubt that his two years in Salamanca, followed by a long period of training and experience as a notary, first in Seville and then in Hispaniola, gave him a working knowledge of Latin and a close acquaintance with the methods and the technicalities of Castilian law.[4] There is a story that, as a child, he was an acolyte in the church of Santa María in Medellín, and that here he learnt the Psalms, but the relatively few Biblical allusions in his writings are drawn almost entirely from the New Testament, and his one direct quotation from the Gospels is produced (in Latin) with such a flourish as to induce some scepticism as to whether he was capable of producing many more: 'I even called to mind a passage from the Gospels which runs: "*Omne regnum in se ipsum divisum desolivatur*".'[5]

If his knowledge of the Bible, although very effectively exploited when the occasion demanded, tended to be sketchy, he was obviously well versed in the types of literature with which a late-fifteenth-century Castilian *hidalgo* would normally expect to be acquainted. This meant, in particular, the legal codes of Castile, and especially the famous code of Alfonso X, the *Siete Partidas*, compiled between 1256 and 1263, and first printed in Seville in 1491. Dr. Frankl has

---

[3] See Salvador de Madariaga, *Hernán Cortés* (London, 1942), pp. 22–4.
[4] See Alcalá, *César y Cortés*, pp. 134–8, for examples of Latin quotations in Cortés' writings, and for the influence of Latin constructions on his style.
[5] *Cartas*, p. 47.

convincingly shown the extent of Cortés' knowledge of the *Siete Partidas*, and his extraordinary skill in exploiting the *Partidas* to justify and legalize his own very difficult position after breaking with the governor of Cuba, Diego Velázquez, and setting out unauthorized on the conquest of Mexico.[6] Once Cortés' knowledge of the contents of the *Partidas* is accepted, whole areas of his thought are illumined, for the *Partidas*, with their references to Aristotle and antiquity, and their vivid definitions of such concepts as 'fame', 'treason', and 'tyranny', constitute at once an encyclopaedia of law and theology, and a code of military and legal conduct, capable of providing the Castilian *hidalgo* with an admirably coherent framework of ideas.

The other literary companions of a Castilian gentleman, besides the *Partidas*, were histories, chronicles, and romances of chivalry. The *conquistadores*' acquaintance with the romances is vividly attested by Bernal Díaz's account of the conquest of Mexico; and Cortés himself is quick to see the allusion when, on landing at San Juan de Ulúa, Puertocarrero quotes four lines from the ballad of Montesinos – an allusion which has recently been shown to express graphically Cortés' plan for vengeance against his mortal enemy, the governor of Cuba.[7] Equally well attested by Bernal Díaz is the tendency of the *conquistadores* to compare their exploits with those of the Romans, as in Cortés' own speech to the troops during the Tlaxcala campaign: 'As for your observation, gentlemen, that the most famous Roman captains never performed deeds equal to ours, you are quite right. If God helps us, far more will be said in future history books about our exploits than has even been said about those in the past.'[8] Here already was that sense of superiority to the achievements of antiquity which distinguishes the later phases of the Renaissance, and which was one day to be expressed in the dedication of a book to Cortés: 'you displayed so many new stratagems in matters of war that it cannot be said that in any of them Your Excellency imitated the Ancients.'[9]

Whether Cortés himself had ever actually read any classical authors is not clear. It has been suggested, on the strength of a reference to 'necessity' in his fourth letter of relation, that he had read Livy, and was therefore acquainted with that idea of necessity which

[6] 'Cortés y la tradición de las Siete Partidas', *op. cit.* The Partidas constitute vols. 2–4 of *Los Códigos Españoles concordados y anotados* (Madrid, 1848–51).

[7] Frankl, *op. cit.*, pp. 29–31.

[8] *Historia verdadera*, 1 (Mexico, 1944), p. 260. Translated J.M. Cohen (London, 1963), p. 159.

[9] *Obras que Francisco Cervantes de Salazar a hecho, glosado, y traducido* (Alcalá de Henares, 1546). 'Diálogo de la dignidad del hombre', f. 4.

was to be so important to Machiavelli.[10] But it would hardly seem essential to have read Livy to produce the particular aphorism used by Cortés – 'there is nothing like necessity for sharpening mens' wits' (*no hay cosa que más los ingenios de los hombres avive que la necesidad*). Almost the same words are in fact used by a character in the famous contemporary novel, the *Celestina*, first published in 1499, when he says that there is no better 'sharpener of wits' (*avivadora de ingenios*) than 'necessity, poverty, and hunger'.[11]

There is indeed some danger that Cortés will be endowed with too elaborate an intellectual ancestry in the search for the origins of his ideas. He reels off a striking phrase such as 'there should be nothing superfluous (*cosa supérflua*) in all the earth' – a phrase which can be, and has been, traced back to the Aristotelian formula: *Natura nihil facit frustra*.[12] He uses it very skilfully as a justification for the forcible subjection of the Chichimeca Indians to the rule of Charles V, but where did he originally find it? The general cast of his thought, as might be expected, was Aristotelian and Thomist, but this phrase again was apparently one in contemporary use, for it is uttered by no less a person than Celestina herself (*ninguna cosa ay criada al mundo supérflua*).[13]

It would seem, on the whole, that Cortés had an extraordinarily quick ear and eye for the arresting phrase, and a genius for putting it to unexpected use. This tends to create an impression both of originality and of erudition, which is not always justified. He is capable, for instance, of beginning a letter to an oriental potentate with a resoundingly Aristotelian sentiment: 'It is a universal condition of mankind to want to know.' But this, too, was probably a commonplace of the times, and appears in the *Siete Partidas* in the form of 'all men naturally want to hear and know and see new things.'[14] His use of such phrases, and in particular the constant insistence in his letters of relation on the importance of 'knowing and inquiring' or of 'finding out the secret of things' (*saber el secreto*) have frequently been taken to display a typically Renaissance attitude to knowledge. Cortés' own intense thirst for knowledge is not in doubt, but it is worth noting that both these expressions appear in the instructions given him by Diego Velázquez when he entrusted him with the command of the expedition to Mexico.[15] It is entirely

---

[10] Frankl, 'Imperio particular', pp. 32–3.
[11] *La Celestina*, ed. M. Criado de Val and G.D. Trotter (Madrid, 1958), p. 165.
[12] Frankl, 'Imperio', p. 19.
[13] *Celestina*, p. 141, and see F. Castro Guisasola, *Observaciones sobre las fuentes literarias de La Celestina* (Madrid, 1924), p. 33.
[14] *Cartas*, p. 478; *Siete Partidas*, Partida I, tit. 1, ley xix.
[15] *Cedulario Cortesiano* (Mexico, 1949), p. 14.

typical of Cortés that he should have seized on the words and tirelessly reproduced them in his letters to the emperor, in order to display his deep regard for the letter of the instructions which in other respects he was actively defying.

Perhaps only once is there anything approaching a plausible hint of first-hand acquaintance with a classical author. When a *residencia* was held against him in 1529 a witness alleged that he frequently heard him say that ' "if the laws had to be broken in order to reign, then broken they must be", and he also used to repeat "Caesar or *nihil*." ' The remark about the breaking of the laws derived originally from Euripides, and was quoted both by Cicero and by Suetonius in his life of Caesar. It would not be surprising if at some stage in his life Cortés had read Suetonius on Caesar; but the evidence remains hearsay, and the fact that the chronicler Gonzalo Fernández de Oviedo, living in Santo Domingo, himself uses the quotation when describing Cortés' defiance of Velázquez, suggests that it enjoyed some currency among sixteenth-century Spaniards.[16]

These instances suggest something of the extreme difficulty involved in defining with any degree of precision the sources of Cortés' thought. The difficulty is hardly surprising, for Cortés, although an highly intelligent man with an instinctive capacity for literary craftsmanship, cannot be described as learned or well-read; and during his active life his reading was probably largely of a professional character, consisting of the Castilian legal codes and of those notarial and official documents which he taught himself to gloss and interpret with such consummate skill. Susceptible as he was to the influence of his environment, and adept at reproducing ideas and expressions which caught his attention, it is only possible to assess in the most general terms the important formative influences in his life. In particular, regrettably little is still known of local conditions in his native Extremadura during his childhood years,[17] and many of the military and administrative ordinances at present taken as examples of his organizing genius may well prove on closer investigation to be directly inspired by models deriving

[16] 'Sumario de la Residencia tomada a Don Fernando Cortés', *Archivo Mexicano*, 1 (Mexico, 1852), p. 64; Fernández de Oviedo, *Historia general...de las Indias*, BAE (Biblioteca de Autores Españoles), vol. 118 (Madrid, 1959), p. 149. The original quotation reads: 'Si violandum est ius, regnandi gratia violandum est' (C. Suetoni Tranquilli, *Divus Iulius*, ed. H.E. Butler and M. Cary, Oxford, 1962, p. 14). That Cortés at least had a good stock of stories from classical history is shown by his apt allusion to the dispute between Marius and Sulla over the captured Jugurtha when his own captains were quarrelling over the captured Cuauhtémoc (Bernal Díaz, *Historia verdadera*, 2, p. 299).

[17] Late-fifteenth-century Extremadura, the home of so many *conquistadores*, deserves serious investigation. There is a pioneering article by Mario Góngora, 'Regimen señorial y rural en la Extremadura de la Orden de Santiago', *Jahrbuch für Geschichte von Staat...Latein-Amerikas*, 2 (1965), pp. 1–29.

from Extremaduran conditions and from the circumstances of the war in Granada. The dominant figure in late-fifteenth-century Extremadura, Don Alonso de Monroy, the Master of Alcántara, was probably Cortés's cousin, and Cortés' father had fought at his side in the fierce civil wars. Although Monroy survived in exile until 1511, he had passed into legend long before his death, and much of the legend, as recounted by a contemporary biographer, reads almost like a preview of the greater career of the conqueror of Mexico.[18] There is the same style of military leadership; the same style of harangue to the troops; and there are even the same omens. Monroy's followers told him to turn back when his horse died under him, but he paid no attention to their warnings, because, in his biographer's words, 'the hour of his ill-fortune was at hand.' Cortés, too, refused to turn back when five of his horses fell as he left the camp one night at Cempoala: 'I held on my course, considering that God is more powerful than nature.' Where Monroy went on to disaster, Cortés came to no harm. His hour of ill fortune was still far away.[19]

The Extremaduran upbringing, the relationship with a legendary figure in Extremaduran life, and the typical *hidalgo* education in the chronicles, the romances, and the code of the *Siete Partidas*, were all, therefore, important formative influences on Cortés' career. So, too, were the Salamanca episode and the period of notarial training, which gave him his knowledge of Latin, his very considerable legal learning, and his skill in the drafting and interpretation of documents. Finally, there were the fifteen years spent in Hispaniola and Cuba as notary, secretary to the governor, municipal official and *encomendero* – years which gave him administrative and political experience, and a first-hand acquaintance with American conditions and the problems of a settler society. All these experiences helped to provide the intellectual equipment of the Cortés who set out in 1519 to conquer Mexico.

In leaving Cuba for Mexico, Cortés carried with him a strong conviction of the influence of *Fortuna* on the affairs of men. In his *Crónica de la Nueva España* Cervantes de Salazar tells how Cortés, while still a public notary in the little town of Azúa, near Santo Domingo, dreamt one night that suddenly his poverty was gone, and that he was dressed in fine clothes and waited on by innumerable retainers who addressed him with high-sounding titles of honour. 'And although', continues Cervantes de Salazar,

---

[18] Alonso Maldonado, *Hechos del Maestre de Alcántara Don Alonso de Monroy*, ed. A. Rodriguez Moñino (Madrid, 1935). For Cortés family relationships, see F. Gómez de Orozco, '¿Cuál era el linaje paterno de Cortés?', *Revista de Indias*, 9 (1948), pp. 297–306.

[19] Maldonado, p. 106; *Cartas*, p. 43.

he, as a wise man and a good Christian, knew that credit should not be given to dreams, he was none the less very happy, because the dream had been in conformity with his own thoughts. . . . They say that, after the dream, he took paper and ink, and drew a wheel with buckets. He wrote one letter on the full buckets, another on those that were being emptied, another on the empty ones, and another on those that were moving upwards, while on the ones at the top he placed a nail. . . When he had done this, he said to certain of his friends with unusual cheerfulness that either he would dine to the sound of trumpets, or perish on the gallows, and that now he began to know his fortune (*ventura*) and what the stars promised him. . .[20]

The image of Fortune's wheel was well known to late fifteenth and early sixteenth-century Spaniards, and 'adverse fortune suddenly turns her wheel' several times in the course of Bernal Díaz's history of the conquest of Mexico.[21] Cortés' wheel, however, has become the *noria* – the traditional water-wheel with hanging buckets to be found in Extremadura and other parts of Spain. Whether at that time this was a common conception of Fortune's wheel is not clear, although Clestina herself, in Rojas' novel, envisaged it in this form: 'We are like pots in a water-wheel. . .one up, and another down; one full, and another empty; it is fortune's law that nothing can continue any long time in one and the selfsame state of being.'[22] But the most important feature of the wheel for Cortés was that it could be stopped – a point he further emphasized when, tilting at the ring in Coyoacán after Mexico had fallen, he chose as his device a wheel of fortune and a silver figure of a man with a hammer in one hand and a nail in the other. The motto read: 'I shall hammer in the nail when I see that there is nothing more to possess.'[23]

This belief that the wheel could be stopped in its revolution by hammering in a nail, suggests an attitude to Fortune not unlike that of Machiavelli. Fortune could, after all, be mastered by man; but this task needed divine help, for, as in Machiavelli's Florence,[24] Fortune was integrated as far as possible into a Christian world. Throughout Cortés' correspondence divine Providence is at hand to guide and

[20] Vol. 1 (Madrid, 1914), pp. 120–1.

[21] *Historia verdadera*, 2, p. 67. For the idea of Fortune, see H.R. Patch, *The Goddess Fortune in Medieval Literature* (Harvard, 1927); José Antonio Maravall, *El mundo social de la Celestina* (Madrid, 1964), c. 7; Florence Street, 'The Allegory of Fortune. . .in. . .Juan de Mena', *Hispanic Review*, 23 (1955), pp. 1–11.

[22]*Celestina*, p. 175 (translated James Mabbe, ed. H. Warner Allen, London, n.d., p. 150).

[23] 'Clavaré quando me vea do no aya más que posea'. 'Residencia', 1, p. 64.

[24] Felix Gilbert, *Machiavelli and Guicciardini* (Princeton, 1965), p. 41.

govern. Nothing, he reminds the emperor, is impossible to God.[25] Battles are won, with God's help, against hopeless odds,[26] and on many occasions God 'mysteriously' comes to the aid of Cortés and his men.[27] But there exists in Cortés' mind a special relationship between God and Charles V. 'Since Your Majesty's childhood', he writes in his second letter, 'God has always taken care to direct your affairs.'[28] This divine favour reserved for the emperor is a matter of great moment to Cortés, for, as the loyal servant of the emperor, he could expect to share in the blessings that Providence showered upon his master. 'The royal good fortune (*real ventura*) of Your Majesty' is therefore a recurring theme in Cortés' letters, and he sees his own victories won 'with the help of God and the royal *ventura*.'[29]

But if Cortés looked on the divine and royal favour as a talisman for success, he knew that the man who aspired to master Fortune must possess innate qualities of resourcefulness and guile – those qualities which for Machiavelli helped to constitute *virtù*. The idea was familiar enough to Renaissance Spaniards, and nothing could be more Machiavellian than the remark of one of the characters in the *Celestina*: 'It is knowing the times and seizing the opportunity which makes men prosperous.'[30] Cortés, like the underworld figures of the *Celestina*, longs for the wealth that will enable him to crash the barriers of the social hierarchy, and bask in the pleasures enjoyed by the titled and the rich; and his chosen weapons for achieving this ambition were the same as theirs. He too must know the times and seize the opportunity, and this required not only native wit but also the wisdom that came of experience. There is in Cortés' correspondence a constant insistence on the importance of *experiencia* – that personal and individual knowledge of men and of things which an increasing number of early sixteenth-century Spaniards were coming to regard as superior to the knowledge derived from traditional authority.[31]

There was no lack of resourcefulness in Cortés' approach to the conquest of Mexico, which was as much a political as a military operation, and one conducted simultaneously against the Aztec emperor and the governor of Cuba. The contemporary chronicler

---

[25] *Cartas*, p. 44.

[26] *Cartas*, pp. 18, 41.

[27] *Cartas*, p. 97.

[28] *Cartas*, p. 52.

[29] *Cartas*, p. 104. *Cf*. Frankl, 'Cortés y la tradición', p. 18.

[30] *Celestina*, p. 39.

[31] See J.A. Maravall, *Los factores de la idea del progreso en el Renacimiento español* (Madrid, 1963), pp. 109–31. *Cf.* the Florentine 'experientia, que rerum est magistra' (Gilbert, *Machiavelli*, p. 39).

Fernández de Oviedo refers at one point to Cortés' capacity to 'construct romances (*novelar*) and devise schemes appropriate to a resourceful, astute, and cunning captain.'[32] Recent work on Cortés, particularly by Dr. Frankl and Srta. Guzmán, has helped to confirm his extraordinary skill in the constructing of romances and the devising of schemes. The first letter of relation, as Dr. Frankl has shown,[33] is a brilliant fictional reconstruction of the course of events leading up to the defiance of the governor of Cuba and the founding of Vera Cruz – a reconstruction which draws heavily on the political and juridical ideas embedded in the *Siete Partidas*. The governor, Velázquez, is painted in the darkest colours as a man consumed by greed and personal interest, whereas Cortés himself emerges as the faithful servant of the Spanish crown and a staunch upholder of the common weal.[34]

But it is in his account of the confrontation with Montezuma that Cortés' powers of imagination and invention are revealed at their best. Although the whole episode remains deeply mysterious, it at least seems clear that Cortés' account of what passed between the two men should not be taken, as it has long been taken, at face value. In all probability, two distinctive layers of legend now surround the relationship between Cortés and Montezuma. The outer layer, which forms the basis of modern interpretations of the conquest of Mexico,[35] holds that Cortés was the unwitting beneficiary of an Aztec tradition that the priest-king Quetzalcóatl would one day return from out of the east and reclaim his own. No evidence has apparently been found, however, to prove the existence of any pre-conquest tradition of Quetzalcóatl leading his followers to the land of Anáhuac. It is possible that the stories of a return from the east, like those of the omens which paralysed Montezuma's powers of decision, sprang up only *after* the conquest; and the identification of Cortés with Quetzalcóatl (who is never mentioned in the writings of Cortés), may first have been made in the 1540s by the Franciscans Motolinía and Sahagún.[36]

But wrapped within this legend lies another, for which Cortés himself may have been largely responsible – a legend similar in theme but less specific in its details. Cortés retails two speeches by Montezuma,[37] both of them so improbable in content and tenor as to

[32] Fernández de Oviedo, *op. cit.*, BAE, 120, p. 42.

[33] 'Cortés y la tradición'.

[34] *Cartas*, pp. 26–7; P. Mariano Cuevas, *Cartas y otros documentos de Hernán Cortés* (Seville, 1915), p. 5.

[35] *E.g.* Madariaga, *Hernán Cortés*.

[36] Eulalia Guzmán, *Relaciones*, p. 223; Henry R. Wagner, *The Rise of Fernándo Cortés* (Berkeley, 1944), pp. 187–98.

[37] *Cartas*, pp. 59–60, 68–9; Guzmán, pp. 221–30, 276–81.

suggest that they were founded more on fantasy than facts. The two speeches are couched in tones quite alien to an Aztec but familiar enough to a Christian Spaniard; for they subtly combine the themes of the coming of a Messiah and the return of a natural lord to his vassals, in order to lead up to the grand climax of Montezuma's renunciation of his imperial heritage into the hands of Charles V. 'We give thanks to our gods', says Montezuma, 'that in our time that which was long expected has come to pass.' Srta. Guzmán has shrewdly pointed out how this whole passage echoes the strains of the *Nunc Dimittis*.[38] But the New Testament analogies do not end here. Montezuma ends his first speech of welcome with the dramatic gesture of lifting his clothes to show Cortés his body, saying: 'you see that I am of flesh and bones like yourself and everyone else, mortal and tangible.' Does not this contain overtones of Jesus' words to the disciples ('a spirit hath not flesh and bones as ye see me have') and of Paul and Barnabas at Lystra ('we also are men of like passions with you')?

It is hard to avoid the impression that Cortés was drawing on all his very considerable reserves of imagination in order to paint for Charles V a solemn and spectacular picture of a scene that may never have occurred. If the scene had a faintly Biblical setting, it would be all the more impressive, especially as Montezuma's forefathers were now in the process of being endowed with distant Christian origins; and, with a nice irony, Cortés introduces his account of Tenochtitlan with words that themselves have a Biblical ring: 'I know that [these things] will seem so remarkable that they cannot be believed, for what we behold with our own eyes, we cannot with our understanding comprehend.'[39] But if Cortés drew on the Bible for his general setting, and on Castilian legal codes for the ideas of suzerainty and vassallage which he put into Montezuma's mouth, there still remains a third crucial element in the story – the myth of the ruler returning from the east. It has been suggested that Cortés heard some such story from the Indians in the Antilles,[40] but it seems equally possible that he heard it on his march to Mexico, and stored it up for future use. According to Bernal Díaz, two *caciques* at Tlaxcala told Cortés of a prophecy that men would come from the region where the sun rises and would subjugate the land.[41] If so, the prophecy may have related not to Quetzalcóatl but to Huitzilopochtli, the god of war, who appears in the writings both of Cortés and Bernal Díaz, under

[38] Guzmán, p. 279.
[39] *Cartas*, p. 71. *Cf.* Matthew 13:14 ('Hearing ye shall hear, and shall not understand; and seeing ye shall see, and shall not perceive').
[40] Guzmán, pp. 223–5.
[41] *Historia verdadera*, 1, p. 288.

the guise of 'Ochilobos'. In a letter written by Don Antonio de Mendoza, the first viceroy of New Spain, to his brother, it is specifically stated that the Aztecs welcomed Cortés thinking that he was 'Orchilobos' – not Quetzalcóatl.[42] Fernández de Oviedo, commenting on the letter, disbelieves the stories both of Orchilobos coming from the north-east, and of Cortés being mistaken for him; but this does not affect the possibility that Cortés picked up some local legend, which he then proceeded to embellish and turn to account with his customary skill.

Whatever the exact origins of the myth of the returning ruler, the whole Montezuma episode, as related to Charles V, bears witness to Cortés' remarkable fertility of invention. This creative ability, the capacity to build on a grand scale, often starting from the most slender foundations, is perhaps the most striking of all the characteristics of Cortés. It carried him through the delicate problems involved in the defiance of Velázquez; it carried him through the conquest of Mexico itself; and it inspired his approach to the work of reconstruction when the Aztec empire had fallen.

His plans for the New Spain to be established on the ruins of the old Mexico were deeply influenced by his experiences in the Antilles where he had seen the Indian population destroyed.[43] A repetition of the Antilles experience must at all costs be avoided, and he wrote, like the great Renaissance builder he was, of the conservation of the Indians as being 'the foundation on which all this work has to be built'.[44] But behind his schemes for the creation of an ordered society of Spaniards and Indians lay a vision which he had borrowed from the friars. It was in August 1523 that the first three Franciscan missionaries (all Flemings) arrived in Mexico, to be followed in May 1524 by the famous 'twelve apostles' headed by Fray Martín de Valencia. In the fourth and fifth letters of relation, dated October 1524 and September 1526, there are clear signs of Franciscan influence on Cortés' thought. The Franciscans, the majority of whom seem to have been less influenced by Erasmus than by Italian apocalyptic traditions and the doctrines of Savonarola,[45] arrived with a burning desire to establish, in a Mexico still uncorrupted by European vices, a replica of the church of the apostles. Cortés, in the first of his letters, had emphasized the importance of informing the pope of his discoveries, so that measures could be taken for the conversion

[42] Fernández de Oviedo, *Historia general*, BAE, 120, pp. 245–47.
[43] *Cartas*, p. 351 (*Ordenanzas de buen gobierno*, 1524).
[44] *Cartas*, p. 397 (*Memorial de servicios*, 1528).
[45] J.A. Maravall, 'La utopia político-religiosa de los Franciscanos en Nueva España', *Estudios Americanos*, 1 (1949), pp. 199–227. For Cortés and the Franciscans, see Fidel de Lejarza, 'Franciscanismo de Cortés y Cortesianismo de los Franciscanos', *Missionalia Hispánica*, 5 (1948), pp. 43–136.

of the natives.[46] But now, in his fourth letter, he couples his pleas for assistance in the work of conversion, with an attack on the worldliness of the church and the pomp and avarice of ecclesiastical dignitaries. His diatribe, so typical of contemporary European protests against the wealth and corruption of the church, is clearly inspired by the friars, for whom he requests exclusive rights in the conversion of Mexico. It is the Franciscans, too, who inspire the prophecy in the fifth letter that there would arise in Mexico a 'new church, where God will be served and honoured more than in any other region of the earth.'[47]

The Franciscans provided Cortés with an enlarged vision, not only of the new church and the new society to be built in Mexico, but also of his own special role in the providential order. He had already, in his first letter, been careful to insist that God had arranged the discovery of Mexico in order that Queen Juana and Charles V should obtain special merit by the conversion of its pagan inhabitants.[48] It followed from this that he himself, as the conqueror of Mexico, enjoyed a special place in the divine plan. The attitude of the Franciscans was bound to encourage him in this belief, for to them he inevitably appeared as God's chosen agent at a vital moment in the ordering of world history – the moment at which the sudden possibility of converting untold millions to the Faith brought the long-awaited millenium almost within sight. It was, therefore, with the concurrence of the Franciscans that Cortés could now designate himself as the 'agency' (*medio*) by which God had been pleased to bring the Indians to an understanding of Him.[49]

Since the Franciscan vision was a world-wide vision, it is not surprising that Cortés received from the Franciscans a fresh encouragement to look beyond the confines of Mexico, once its conquest was achieved. On his ill-fated Hibueras expedition of 1524–26 he was accompanied by two Flemish Franciscans, one of whom was Juan de Tecto, a distinguished theologian and a former confessor of Charles V.[50] It was perhaps Tecto's first-hand acquaintance with the imperial ideology of the Emperor's advisers and with Erasmian currents of thought in his native country, which furnished Cortés with his new vision of a world empire subject to a Charles V who would become 'monarch of the universe' – an empire which he himself would help to found by pressing on from Mexico, across the Pacific to the East.[51] The vision was a complex one, compounded as

[46] *Cartas*, p. 25.
[47] *Cartas*, pp. 238–39, 318.
[48] *Cartas*, p. 25.
[49] *Cartas*, p. 241.
[50] Gerónimo de Mendieta, *Historia eclesiástica Indiana* (ed. Mexico, 1870), p. 606.
[51] *Cartas*, pp. 320 and 482. For the evolution of Cortés' idea of empire, see Frankl, 'Imperio'.

it was of Cortés' own dreams of the conquest of Cathay, Erasmian and Imperial dreams of a universal empire, and Franciscan dreams of the conversion of mankind as the essential prelude to the ending of the world. He pursued it for year after year, but, like some will-of-the-wisp, it persistently eluded him, for already by 1526 it seemed that his luck was gone.

There seems no reason to doubt that his harrowing experiences on the Hibueras expedition permanently changed Cortés, giving him a new awareness of the inscrutability of Providence and the impotence of man. The fifth letter of relation, which describes the expedition, is very different in spirit from those that preceded it. The phraseology is that of a man who has passed through a deep spiritual ordeal, which has left him at once with a sense of his own unworthiness and of the infinite power of God. Gone is the confidence which, seven years earlier, had enabled him to press on at Cempoala in spite of the misfortune to the horses. Now, when his ship is forced back to port three times, he sees this as a signal from heaven, and abandons his plans for return.[52] Gone, too, is the earlier confidence in the unbounded powers of man. In a language very different from that of his earlier letters, he writes: 'no wit of man could ever have found the remedy, if God, who is the true remedy and succour of those in affliction or want, had not provided it.'[53]

Fortune, after all, was not so easily to be commanded, and, from the time of the Hibueras expedition, it became clear that the wheel had begun its inexorable downward turn. Thwarted by royal officials and dogged by royal ingratitude, he wrote bitterly to his father in 1526: 'I had rather be rich in fame than in wealth.'[54] Although his fame was anyhow assured, he soon found a group of men both ready and able to cultivate it for him, for on his return to Madrid in 1528 he struck up a friendship with the Polish ambassador to the Imperial court, John Dantiscus, a friend of Copernicus and the centre of a wide humanist circle which included Erasmus and Valdés. The friendship was duly celebrated by Dantiscus in a Latin poem written after Cortés had gone back to Mexico: 'Great Cortés is far away, the man who discovered all these huge kingdoms of the New World. He rules beyond the equator as far as the star of Capricorn, and though so far away, he does not forget me.'[55]

This flattering interest of the humanists in the conqueror of

[52] *Cartas*, pp. 304, 460.
[53] *Cartas*, p. 257.
[54] *Cartas*, p. 468.
[55] *Ioannis Dantisci poetae laureati carmina*, ed. Stanislas Skimina (Cracow, 1950), carmen xlix, lines 85–90. For Dantiscus, see A. Paz y Mélia, 'El embajador polaco Juan Dantisco en la corte de Carlos V', *Boletín de la Real Academia Española*, 11 and 12 (1924–25). Dantiscus' diplomatic correspondence was published in *Acta Tomiciana* (12 vols., ed. S. Gorski, Posnan, 1855–1901), but there is no trace of the letters to or from Cortés.

Mexico was fully reciprocated by Cortés in the last years of his life when, in retirement in Madrid, his house became the centre for an 'academy' holding regular discussions on matters of humanist and religious concern.[56] The circle of intellectuals who sought the company of Cortés did much to perpetuate both his fame and his ideas. There was Sepúlveda, whose discussion of the Indian question may well owe much to conversations with him.[57] There was Gómara, his first biographer, who transformed him into a typical hero of Renaissance historiography.[58] There was, too, that minor but interesting figure in the Spanish literary world, Cervantes de Salazar, who in 1546 dedicated to Cortés a dialogue on the dignity of man.[59] The dedication, couched in suitably fulsome terms, presents Cortés to the world exactly as he must have wished. It contains the obligatory reference to his distinction both in arms and letters, and the inevitable comparison with Alexander and Caesar; and it manages incidentally to propagate a new Cortés legend – that he burnt his ships instead of beaching them after landing at Vera Cruz.[60] But it also includes a comparison even more flattering than that with the heroes of antiquity, for the role of Cortés among the pagans of Mexico is compared with that of St Paul in the primitive church.

At this point the humanists made common cause with Cortés' other band of admirers, the friars. The Franciscans, as they were well aware, owed him much, and they repaid the debt by representing him in their histories of the conquest as the man chosen of God to prepare the way for the evangelization of mankind. But the debt of Cortés to the Franciscans – a debt generously acknowledged in his last will and testament – was no less great, for, at a time when humanist Spain was only just embarking on its subtle transmutation into the more complex Spain of the Counter-Reformation, they had done much to add a new religious dimension to his world. And no world was so rich in imagination and so infinitely adaptable as the mental world of Hernán Cortés.

[56] Madariaga, *Cortés*, p. 482; Pedro de Navarra, *Diálogos de la preparación de la muerte* (Tolosa, 1565), f. 41.

[57] Angel Losada, 'Hernán Cortés en la obra del cronista Sepúlveda', *Revista de Indias*, 9 (1948), pp. 127–69.

[58] Ramón Iglesia, *Cronistas e historiadores de la conquista de México* (Mexico, 1942), pp. 100–103; H.R. Wagner, 'Francisco López de Gómara and His Works', *Proceedings of the American Antiquarian Society*, 58 (1948), pp. 263–82.

[59] See above p. 30 n. 9.

[60] For the legend of the burning of the ships, see especially F. Soler Jardón, 'Notas sobre la leyenda del incendio de las naves', *Revista de Indias*, 9 (1948), pp. 537–59. Soler Jardón suspected that the legend of the burning originated in the desire to compare Cortés with classical heroes, but failed to find any reference earlier than the 1560s. If, as seems possible, Cervantes de Salazar originated the legend, at least in its written form, he reverted to fact and described the ships as being beached in his *Crónica de la Nueva España*, which he began writing some thirteen years after the publication of the dedication to Cortés.

III

THE DISCOVERY OF AMERICA AND
THE DISCOVERY OF MAN

'Two things', wrote Michelet in a famous passage, 'belong to this age [the sixteenth century] more than to all its predecessors: the discovery of the world, the discovery of man.'[1] By 'the discovery of man' Michelet meant European man's discovery of himself as both a physical organism and a moral being, whose mysteries were now explored to their innermost depths. But the simultaneous discovery of the world also represented a discovery of man – the European discovery of non-European man, a creature whose strange, varied, and frequently repulsive habits proved to be a source of consuming curiosity.

During the course of the sixteenth century sufficient new information became available about the distant, and sometimes hitherto unknown, peoples of the world to furnish the European reader with a rich and varied picture of the races of mankind. By 1556, for instance, the Spanish translator of that standard repository of ethnographical information, Boemus's *Manners, Laws and Customs of All Nations*, was able to expand the original text with two hundred informative pages on the inhabitants of the New World of America.[2] Although some of the most valuable material never found its way into print or general circulation, the sheer quantity of ethnographical information at the disposal of the sixteenth-century European reading public remains very impressive. The printing-press and the long-distance sailing ship had between them brought the world to Europe's doorstep.

But it is one thing to arrive on the doorstep and another to pass through the door. How far was the discovery of man, in Michelet's sense of the phrase, really affected by the discovery of non-European

---

[1] Jules Michelet, *Histoire de France*, 7 (Paris 1855), pp. ii–iii.
[2] Francisco Tamara, *El Libro de las costumbres de todas las gentes del mundo y de las Indias* (Antwerp, 1556).

man? The experiences of Spanish officials and missionaries among the American Indians offered a novel source of first-hand information on man's capabilities and behaviour. But while that remarkable treatise on human psychology and aptitudes, the *Examination of Men's Wits* by the Spanish doctor Juan Huarte (1575),[3] reveals a profound acquaintance with the classical world of Hippocrates and Galen, it completely ignores the findings of his compatriots in the New World of America – findings which were by no means irrelevant to his interests. This seems to have been sadly typical. The evidence of sixteenth-century treatises on manners and morals suggests that, with the occasional distinguished exception like Montaigne, most authors felt that the Christian and classical traditions were sufficient to enable them to explore the mysteries of human behaviour without any need for recourse to the new worlds overseas. No doubt the disturbing figure of Caliban would soon be discovered on his enchanted island; but even Caliban's ancestry can be traced back beyond the Caribbean to the legendary wild man of medieval Europe.[4]

It seems that most sixteenth-century Europeans could manage well enough on their voyages of self-discovery without having to land for fresh provisions on exotic shores. But circumstance and opportunity drove a certain number of them to apply their minds to the study of strange men in alien environments; and when they did this, they found themselves confronted with fundamental questions about the nature of man himself. Their attempts to answer these questions may, at least in the sixteenth century, have had little or no resonance in their European homelands.[5] But they did something, if only in restricted circles, to widen the boundaries of perception. And if the answers were often inadequate and ill-informed, the questions, once posed, remained creatively disturbing. What were the essential characteristics of humanity? What constituted a civilized man, as distinct from a barbarian? In what respects were certain peoples of the world deficient, and how best could their deficiencies be remedied?

European travellers to Asia, Africa, and America often returned with valuable information about distant lands. But the travellers and explorers, although they saw much and heard more, were essentially birds of passage. They were in too great a hurry, and too concerned

[3] Juan Huarte de San Juan, *Examen de ingenios para las ciencias*, ed. Rodrigo Sanz, 2 vols., (Madrid, 1930).
[4] See Richard Bernheimer, *Wild Men in the Middle Ages* (Cambridge, Mass., 1952).
[5] For a discussion of this point, see J.H. Elliott, *The Old World and the New, 1492–1650* (Cambridge, 1970), chs. 1 and 2.

with the portrayal of the curious and the exotic, to formulate the crucial questions or undertake the systematic inquiries that would provide material towards an answer. It is for this reason that Spain's conquest and settlement of America play a unique part in the process of Europe's discovery of mankind. Millions of non-European peoples, whose very existence was unknown a generation earlier, were now exposed to a sustained missionary effort and to the experience of permanent European rule. As a result, observation based on casual contact could be replaced by observation based on intimate acquaintance over a prolonged period of time. The new-style colonial relationship represented by the Spanish domination of central and southern America created a new kind of opportunity for systematic ethnographical study.

The opportunity, as might have been expected, was only very partially seized. Yet enough information was collected, for one purpose or another, to create an impressive corpus of ethnographic source-material on the beliefs and customs of the peoples of the Spanish New World in the pre-conquest and immediate post-conquest periods. Enthusiastic lay amateurs like Juan de Betanzos studied native history and antiquities, while missionaries incorporated descriptions of native rites and superstitions into their narratives of the spiritual conquest of the Indies. Memoranda on Indian affairs were prepared by members of the religious orders for presentation to the Council of the Indies or consideration by ecclesiastical councils. Crown officials drew up innumerable reports – detailed accounts of local visitations, careful replies to the famous royal questionnaire of 1577, and elaborate treatises on the Indian problem, like those produced in the middle of the sixteenth century by Alonso de Zorita in New Spain and Juan de Matienzo in Peru. On top of all this, there were the massive investigations into Indian history and civilization undertaken by those two great friars, the Dominican Diego Durán and the Franciscan Bernardino de Sahagún, and three supremely ambitious 'natural and moral' histories of the Indies by Fernández de Oviedo, Bartolomé de las Casas, and José de Acosta respectively.

These sixteenth-century observers of the Indian societies of America did not, on the whole, approach their work in a spirit of scientific detachment. Instead, they began with a clear conviction of the superiority of their own Christian civilization, and their inquiries were generally guided by considerations of utility. Crown officials needed precise information on Indian land tenure and inheritance patterns if they were to dispense justice according to custom, which was the essence of good government to sixteenth-century Europeans. Missionaries needed precise information on pagan superstitions if they were to cast down the idolaters. 'To preach against those things,' wrote

Sahagún, 'and even to know if they exist, it is necessary to know how they used them in the time of their idolatry.'[6]

As against these directed inquiries, there are relatively few which were primarily inspired, as was Oviedo's *History of the Indies*, by sheer intellectual curiosity. But the intellectual calibre of some of the inquirers was so high as to enable them to produce studies of indigenous society and institutions which triumphantly transcend the limitations of scope and purpose inherent in their origins. This is especially true of Sahagún's *General History of the Things of New Spain*, which represents an attempt, unique in the sixteenth century for its range and penetration, to provide a comprehensive linguistic and ethnographic survey of Aztec society by means of carefully controlled investigations making use of native informants.[9]

While the sophistication of Sahagún's technique places him in a class of his own, his material is similar in kind to that of his contemporaries. Between them, Spanish observers touched on all the major aspects of Amerindian life. Birth, marriage, and death; domestic life and customs; inheritance systems and methods of education; clothes, hygiene, and medicine; tributary systems and economic organization; government and warfare; popular beliefs, practices, and superstitions – all of these receive some attention, and many are studied in detail. When this information is more systematically exploited, it should become possible for historians and anthropologists to explore in considerable depth the Central American and Andean civilizations of the immediate pre-conquest period and the impact upon them of European rule.[8]

This does not, however, exhaust the possibilities of sixteenth-century investigations. For if they open a window on to non-European societies with few or no records of their own, they also allow us to observe the observers – to glimpse something of their underlying assumptions and attitudes as they embarked on their discovery of non-European man. These sixteenth-century Spaniards were faced with the challenging test of confrontation with alien societies and alien systems of belief. It is not surprising if under this test they reveal something of themselves, even as the twentieth-century anthropologist may also reveal more of himself and his own

---

[6] Fr. Bernardino de Sahagún, *Historia general de las cosas de Nueva España*, ed. Angel María Garibay K., 4 vols., (Mexico, 1969), 1, p. 27.

[7] For Sahagún's method see his own account in the *Historia General* 1, pp. 105–8. Also Luis Nicolau D'Olwer, *Historiadores de América. Fray Bernardino de Sahagún, 1499–1590* (Mexico, 1952).

[8] Pioneering work along these lines is being done by Professor John V. Murra of Cornell University and his colleagues. See in particular his edition of the *Visita de la provincia de León de Huánuco en 1562* by Iñigo Ortiz Zúñiga (Huánuco, 1967).

society to future generations than he is ever liable to suspect. In setting up, however unconsciously, an objective reality against which to measure an alien society, the investigator offers his own hostages to fortune. For the sixteenth-century European, the great line of division lay between the Christian and the pagan. For his twentieth-century successor, the product of a scientific civilization, it lies between the 'irrational' and the 'rational'.[9]

The sixteenth-century Spaniard who tells us something of the Indian cannot fail in the process to tell us something of his own conception of man. But difficult questions of method at once present themselves. Spanish commentators on the Indians were sharply differentiated by background and profession. Many, but not all, of them – Oviedo and Durán are both distinguished exceptions – had received a university education. Some were religious, and some secular; some trained in the law and others in theology. Among the religious themselves, there were significant disagreements between religious and secular clergy, and between members of the different orders. Interest and partisanship, too, led to deep-seated differences. Those who spoke for the settlers' lobby were likely to depict the Indian in a very different light from those who were primarily interested in the salvation of his soul. Moreover, any conception of man with which the Spaniards arrived in the Indies was itself liable to be modified in one direction or another by the sheer fact of prolonged contact with their alien inhabitants. Is it permissible, then, to assume the existence among Spaniards of a commonly agreed and relatively unchanging conception of man?

For all their differences, however, they were the products of a society united by certain strongly defined attitudes – Christian in its values, legalistic in its outlook, corporate and hierarchical in its organization. On arrival in the Indies they were all confronted, whether consciously or not, with the same fundamental problem – that of the unity and diversity of the human race. How far were the Indians the same kind of beings as themselves? If they differed, how was their diversity to be explained; and indeed how far could it be tolerated among peoples subject to their rule? For all the varieties of response to this problem, it still remains possible to detect certain assumptions, spoken or unspoken, which point to a common vocabulary among the conquerors. And although due allowance must be

[9] J.D.Y. Peel, 'Understanding Alien Belief-Systems', *British Journal of Sociology*, 20 (1969), pp. 69–84, provides a suggestive study of some of these questions, as also does Peter Winch, 'Understanding a Primitive Society', *Religion and Understanding*, ed. D.Z. Phillips (Oxford, 1967).

made for the strongly Aristotelian cast of much sixteenth-century Spanish thought, a large part of this common vocabulary would seem to have been shared by Christendom as a whole.

From the moment when Columbus reported that he had found 'no human monstrosities' among the Caribbean islanders,[10] there existed at least a presumption in favour of the humanity of the peoples of the Indies. The presumption acquired the status of dogmatic certainty when Paul III's bull of 1537 described the Indians as 'true men... capable not only of understanding the Catholic faith, but also, according to our information, desirous of receiving it'.[11] Spiritually, then, as well as biologically, the Indians were officially accepted by Christendom as descendants of Adam, and consequently as members of the family of man.

This represented a decisive victory for the party of humanity, and it was consolidated by the scholastic arguments of Vitoria and others – arguments tacitly accepted by the Spanish crown in its dealings with the Indians – that pre-conquest Indian society was a valid society in spite of its ignorance of Christianity. By living in polities, and regulating their lives in accordance with fixed rules and regulations – however defective these may have been from a Christian standpoint – large numbers of American Indians had satisfied the Aristotelian criteria for acceptance as political and social beings.[12] Although there remained the difficult problem of those tribes so savage and nomadic that they appeared to live outside society,[13] the application of Aristotelian arguments to the peoples of America conferred proper credentials on uncounted millions. Socially, as well as biologically and spiritually, they had established their claim to be regarded as men.

In a moving passage in the prologue to his *History of the Things of New Spain*, Sahagún writes: 'it is very certain that these people are all our brethren, proceeding like us from the stock of Adam. They are our fellow creatures, whom we are obliged to love as ourselves, *quid quid sit.*' Had they not, he argued, shown their aptitude for the mechanical and liberal arts? Had they not displayed in warfare their

[10] Letter on first voyage in *The Journal of Christopher Columbus*, trans. Cecil Jane, revised L.A. Vigneras (London, 1960), p. 200.

[11] See Lewis Hanke, 'Pope Paul III and the American Indians', *Harvard Theological Review*, 30 (1937), pp. 65–102.

[12] Francisco de Vitoria, *Relectio de Indis*, eds. L. Pereña and J.M. Pérez Prendes (Madrid, 1967), pp. 29–30. For the development of scholastic arguments see especially Joseph Höffner, *Christentum und Menschenwürde. Das Anliegen der Spanischen Kolonialethik im Goldenen Zeitalter* (Trier, 1947).

[13] Bartolomé de Las Casas attempts to deal with this problem in book 3, ch. 47 of his *Apologética historia sumaria*.

capacity to support hunger and thirst, cold and lack of sleep? 'Then they are no less capable of learning our Christianity.'[14]

But the very fact that such arguments were still felt to be necessary in the 1570s suggests the depth of disagreement over the nature of the Indians. Although the words 'beast' and 'bestial' figured prominently in the debate, the critical point at issue was not the humanity of the Indians *per se*, but the exact degree of humanity with which they could be credited.[15] Could the Indians really be regarded as men, in the full sense of the word as understood by sixteenth-century Europeans, or were they in some, or indeed in all, respects defective human beings – sub-men perhaps, requiring special treatment appropriate to their status?

Various criteria could be used to determine this point. It is significant that physical characteristics, which were to assume such prominence in nineteenth-century discussions on the non-European races of the world, were not among the criteria most commonly applied. It was not until Europeans became obsessed with the idea of a graded, and then of an evolutionary, scale of being, that physical traits moved to the forefront of the argument.[16] Colour in particular was treated, at least in so far as the Indians were concerned, in largely neutral terms. This was partly because the colour of the Indians, which was described by the cosmographer of the Indies, Juan López de Velasco, as resembling cooked quince,[17] lacked the historical and emotional overtones which were beginning to be associated with the more familiar black. It was difficult, too, to attach guilt to the non-white as long as colour was primarily attributed to long exposure to the sun.[18]

Yet for Europeans nurtured in the Aristotelian and Hippocratic traditions, colour took its place alongside other physical characteristics as one among many clues to the natural condition of a man.

[14] *Historia general*, 1, p. 31.

[15] For critical discussions of the Indian 'bestiality' thesis, see Edmundo O'Gorman, 'Sobre la naturaleza bestial del indio americano', *Filosofía y Letras*, 1 (1941), pp. 141–56 and 305–15, and Lino Gómez Canedo, '¿Hombres o bestias?', *Estudios de Historia Novohispana*, 1 (1966), pp. 29–51.

[16] For the change in European attitudes in the late seventeenth and early eighteenth century see Margaret T. Hodgen, *Early Anthropology in the Sixteenth and Seventeenth Centuries* (Philadelphia, 1964), ch. 10, and especially pp. 417–18.

[17] *Geografía y descripción universal de las Indias* (1571–4; ed. Madrid, 1894), p. 27.

[18] Francisco López de Gómara, however, was already arguing in 1552 that the colour of the Indians was the result of *naturaleza* and not exposure (*Primera parte de la historia general de las Indias*, BAE (Biblioteca de Autores Españoles), vol. 22, Madrid, 1825, p. 289). The Jesuit Alonso de Sandoval, writing in 1627, considers blackness an 'intrinsic quality' (*De Instauranda Aethiopum Salute*, ed. Bogotá, 1956, p. 26). The explanation of colour in Iberian literature of the sixteenth and seventeenth centuries deserves closer and more documented study than it has so far received.

Physical appearance testified to the disposition of the soul; but the testimony could, it seemed, be variously interpreted. For Las Casas, as might have been expected, the Indians had fine complexions and well-proportioned bodies – fitting receptacles for noble souls.[19] But those who regarded the Indians as naturally inferior beings had no difficulty in turning the same evidence to provide support for their views. The Spanish jurist Juan de Matienzo, in his *Government of Peru* of 1567, pronounced all Indians to be 'pusillanimous and timid', and ascribed these defects to their special brand of melancholic humour. 'Men of this type or complexion are, according to Aristotle, very fearful, weak and stupid.... It is clear that this is their complexion from the colour of their faces, which is the same in all of them....' Both the appearance and the behaviour of the Indians led Matienzo to an irresistible conclusion: that they were 'naturally born and brought up to serve. And it can be known that they were born for this because, as Aristotle says, such types were created by nature with strong bodies and were given less intelligence, while free men have less physical strength and more intelligence. So it can be seen that the Indians are physically very strong – much stronger than the Spaniards – and can bear more than them, for they carry burdens on their backs of twenty-five to fifty pounds and walk along beneath them without difficulty.' 'The stronger they are', he concluded, 'the less intelligence they have.'[20]

Matienzo was no arm-chair theorist like Sepúlveda, condemning Indians to natural servitude from a well-stocked library thousands of miles away. On the contrary, he was a highly intelligent royal official (unfortunately we have no information as to his physique), with six years of experience in the viceroyalty of Peru. His remarks suggest how profoundly an Aristotelian training – acquired in this instance in the University of Valladolid – could colour Spanish attitudes towards the indigenous population of the Indies. Just as Aristotle described some of the races of distant barbarians as irrational by nature and living only by their senses like the beasts,[21] so too for Matienzo the Indians were 'animals who do not even feel reason, but are ruled by their passions'.

Matienzo's prime evidence for this sweeping assertion was that the Indians ate and drank without thought for the morrow.[22] It is clear that we are faced here with a failure both of sympathy and

---

[19] *Apologética historia sumaria*, ed. Edmundo O'Gorman (Mexico, 1967), 1, p. 207.
[20] *Gobierno del Perú*, ed. Guillermo Lohmann Villena (Paris–Lima, 1967), pp. 16–17.
[21] *Nicomachean Ethics* 7, 1149ª9 ff. See Arthur O. Lovejoy, *A Documentary History of Primitivism and Related Ideas*, 1 (Baltimore, 1935), p. 179.
[22] *Gobierno del Perú*, pp. 17–18.

understanding – sympathy for the plight of a people numbed by the shock of European conquest, and understanding of the system of social organization and food provisioning to which the Andean Indians were accustomed. At the same time, it must be remembered that Matienzo was writing to a brief. In the difficult political climate of the 1560s, Crown officials felt it incumbent upon them to justify the substitution of Spanish rule for that of the Incas.[23] Aristotle's theory of natural servitude, based on the idea of innate inferiority and incapacity, provided this justification. Working from a *parti pris*, it was not hard to find the evidence to fit.

In the context of Spanish attitudes to man, however, the exact motivation is less important than the underlying assumptions, which are often, as with Matienzo, almost casually betrayed. Matienzo's assumptions about Indian waywardness were based, as was only natural, on expectations which were derived from European patterns of behaviour. As Las Casas clearly saw, these false expectations could only be dispelled by the acquisition of a proper understanding of Indian life and Indian psychology. This in turn demanded a greater willingness to learn Indian languages than his compatriots had so far displayed. 'From this failure has sprung an error that is by no means insignificant, and whose pernicious character will be realized on the day of the Last Judgment – the tendency to regard them as beasts.'[24]

It would have been equally possible to argue that lack of knowledge had led to the depiction of Indians as paragons of prelapsarian innocence; but such assumptions – unlike those of bestiality – did not long survive a closer intimacy with the peoples of America. Increasing acquaintance with the Indian character, and bitter experience of spiritual backsliding among their native converts, produced a growing disillusionment even among those friars who were their most fervent partisans. This disillusionment, although explicable in terms of American conditions, may also reflect changing attitudes to man in Europe itself. As the optimistic view of human nature current in Renaissance and Erasmian Europe gave ground before a renewed emphasis on the innate sinfulness and depravity of man, so the character of the American Indians came to be more unfavourably assessed.

The change can be traced in the deliberations of the clergy of New Spain, as one generation of missionaries gave way to the next. In these deliberations one can follow that fateful progression – from enchantment to total disenchantment and thence to paternalism –

---

[23] For the background to Matienzo's treatise, see the valuable introduction by Lohmann Villena (separately printed in his *Juan de Matienzo*, Seville, 1966).
[24] *Apologética historia*, 1, p. 545.

which was to repeat itself so often in the history of European colonial enterprise. While a meeting of the clergy in Mexico in 1532 insisted on the spiritual and intellectual capacity of the Indians, they emerge twenty years later from the first Mexican Provincial Council of 1555 as intellectually feeble and inconstant creatures, distinguished by a natural inclination to vice.[25] This increasingly pessimistic consensus about the nature of the Indians had obvious implications for the way in which they should be treated. These were spelt out by Fray Pedro de Feria, bishop of Chiapa, in a memorandum submitted to the third Mexican Provincial Council of 1585. 'We must love and help the Indians as much as we can. But their base and imperfect character requires that they should be ruled, governed and guided to their appointed end by fear more than by love. . . . These people do not know how to judge the gravity of their sins other than by the rigour of the penalties with which they are punished.'[26]

In the bishop's words we hear the echoes of the sixteenth-century schoolroom; and it was indeed as archetypal children that many of the Spanish religious, irrespective of their order, came to look upon the Indians.[27] But what did this imply? Huarte, in his *Examination of Men's Wits*, describes the child as 'no more than a brute animal', moved exclusively by anger and desire. Childhood, which lasted till the age of fourteen – to be followed by 'adolescence' from fourteen to twenty-five – was the period in which the rational spirit was submerged in a hot and humid temperament, which inhibited the child from making use of his understanding and free will. Yet if the child was close to the beast, he was also not too far removed from the angels. 'The virtues of childhood are many', wrote Huarte, 'and its vices few.' Children were amenable to discipline and easy to persuade. They were bland and tender, generous and simple.[28]

From a theological standpoint, the analogy with children was not perhaps entirely satisfactory. As one of its critics, the Augustinian Alonso de la Vera Cruz, pointed out in a course of lectures delivered in the University of Mexico in 1553, 'if they were incapable like children and simple-minded, it would follow that they could not sin; and so all their vices. . . would not any more be imputed to them than to brute animals. But they are held responsible, and rightly so. Therefore they have sufficient discernment to commit sin. . . .'[29] But

[25] See José A. Llaguno, *La personalidad jurídica del Indio y el III Concilio Mexicano* (Mexico, 1963), pp. 13 and 35.

[26] *Ibid.*, p. 195.

[27] Antonio de Egaña, 'La visión humanística del indio americano en los primeros Jesuitas peruanos, 1568–1576', *Analecta Gregoriana*, 70 (1954), pp. 291–306.

[28] *Examen de ingenios*, pp. 76 and 90–1.

[29] *The Writings of Alonso de La Vera Cruz*, trans. and ed. Ernest J. Burrus S.J., 2 (St. Louis, 1968), § 718.

the analogy served its turn in suggesting that the Indians were something less than full men, while at the same time implying some hope
for the future, in that the Indian mind, like a child's mind, was a
tabula rasa on which any suitable doctrine could gradually be impressed.[30]

But what doctrines needed to be impressed on these tender minds?
Those of Christianity, clearly enough. But were the Indians not also
deficient on other counts? Bishop Landa ends his description of
Yucatán, written around 1560, by providing a conventional list of
the benefits brought to the Indians by Spain – horses, domestic
animals, iron, the mechanical arts, the use of money. 'Although', he
concludes, 'the Indians managed to do without them, they live now
that they have them incomparably more like men.'[31] The Indians, in
fact, lacked some of the prerequisites of a civilized way of life as
understood by the Spaniards, and in so far as they lacked these things
they were something less than men.

The obvious answer for the partisans of the Indians when faced
with the argument that the barbarian was defective as a human being
by virtue of his barbarism, was to widen the definition of barbarism as a concept, while limiting its applicability to the peoples of
America. This was the approach adopted by Las Casas, who distinguished four different contemporary uses of the word 'barbarian'. Of these only one – a man so lacking in reason as to behave
like a beast – was accounted for by essence rather than by accident,
and it was not applicable to the Amerindian.[32] But most of those
who had dealings with the Indians remained unconvinced by such
arguments. No observer could fail to be impressed by the glaring
cultural disparities to be found among the numerous different
peoples of the American continent; and most Spaniards believed that
even the Indians with the highest standards of civility were in some
respects inadequate. They might indeed have shown their capacity
for a civil life in conformity with the most rigorous Aristotelian
criteria; but even if this proved, as it did to Alonso de la Vera Cruz,
that they were neither simple-minded nor children, he found himself
unable to deny that 'even the most outstanding among them if

---

[30] Matienzo, *Gobierno del Perú*, p. 18, talks of 'printing' or 'impressing' (*imprimir*) doctrines
upon them. Las Casas (*Apologética historia*, 2, p. 262) uses the words *tablas rasas*. Vasco de
Quiroga and Gerónimo de Mendieta both used the image of soft wax (see John Leddy Phelan,
The Millennial Kingdom of the Franciscans in the New World, 2nd edn., Berkeley and Los Angeles,
1970, p. 150).

[31] Fray Diego de Landa, *Relación de las cosas de Yucatán*, ed. Angel María Garibay K. (8th
edn., Mexico, 1959), p. 138.

[32] *Apologética historia*, 2, pp. 637–54. 'Barbarian' could also be used of non-Christians; of
men who lived without laws or ordered polities; and of those who spoke strange languages and
lacked the art of writing.

compared to our Spaniards are found to be deficient in many respects'.[33]

In what, then, did these deficiencies lie? When Bishop Landa argued that the Indians lived, as a consequence of Spanish rule, 'incomparably more like men', it is clear that he equated 'man' with 'European man', and regarded any deviation from this norm as a diminution of manhood. Similarly, when even so sympathetic an observer as Sahagún concerned himself with the aptitude of the Indians for the study of the mechanical and liberal arts and theology,[34] it is clear that much of the argument turned on whether they possessed sufficient intellectual and rational capacity to lead of their own volition a style of life which approximated to the Christian and European model.

To live like a man meant, ideally, to live like a Spaniard. America was not the first place in which Spaniards had attempted to promote this ideal among their subject peoples. Within a few years of the conquest of Granada, Hernando de Talavera, the first archbishop of Granada, was telling the newly baptized Moors of the Albaicín that it was necessary for them to conform in all things to the practices of the Christians, 'in your dress and your shoes and your adornment, in eating and at your tables and in cooking meat as they cook it; in your manner of walking, in giving and receiving, and, more than anything, in your speech, forgetting in so far as you can the Arabic tongue'.[35]

The archbishop's words suggest how difficult it was, even had the desire existed, to separate the doctrinal requirements of a newly baptized Christian from the patterns of his social behaviour. Doctrine and behaviour were so closely associated in the minds of most Europeans that the friar who wrote of 'reducing those who lived like barbarians and brute animals to a Christian and human polity'[36] would probably have been hard put to it to distinguish between the two. Marriage and funeral customs, education and dress – especially when it was a question of dress or undress – all came within the ambit of a Christian way of life.

There was, however, a difference of views on the question of language. To some Spaniards, the languages spoken by the Indians were a clear indication of their barbarism. In a memorandum drawn

---

[33] *The Writings of Alonso de la Vera Cruz*, 2, § 742.

[34] See above, pp. 47–8.

[35] Antonio Gallego y Burín and Alfonso Gámir Sandoval, *Los moriscos del Reino de Granada* (Granada, 1968), Appendix 4, p. 163.

[36] Padre Araya, *Segunda parte de la historia de San Esteban*, quoted by Luis G. Alonso Getino, *El Maestro Fr. Francisco de Vitoria* (Madrid, 1930), p. 184.

[37] Llaguno, *La personalidad jurídica*, p. 200.

up for the ecclesiastical council of 1585 Dr. Ortiz de Hinojosa of the University of Mexico described some of the languages of New Spain as being 'so inaccessible and difficult that they appear to have been introduced not by men but by nature, as the illiterate noise of birds or brute animals, which cannot be written down with any kind of character, and can scarcely be pronounced for being so guttural that they stick in the throat.'[37] On the other hand, Europe, and Spain itself, was used to a diversity of tongues; and although knowledge of Castilian would enable the Indians of New Spain to acquire, in the words of a royal decree of 1550, 'our civilized way of life (*nuestra policía*) and good customs',[38] the principal deficiency of Indian languages seems to have been considered not so much their obscurity as the fact that they lacked a written alphabet.

Themselves the children of a civilization increasingly dependent on the written word, sixteenth-century Europeans naturally regarded the absence of it among the American Indians as a sign of barbarism. Did not the Venerable Bede, argued Las Casas, introduce letters into England so that his fellow-countrymen should no longer be regarded as barbarians?[39] For Acosta, even the Chinese, who formed the highest of his three categories of barbarians, did not possess 'true writing and reading, since their words are not made up of letters but of little figures of innumerable things'. But he was deeply impressed by the pictographs of the Mexicans and the *quipus* of the Peruvians – two peoples which he placed in a second, intermediate, category of barbarian. 'If this is not ingenuity', he wrote, 'and if these men are beasts, judge who will....'[40]

The correlation between civilization and possession of the alphabet was clearly taken for granted by sixteenth-century Europeans; and even the most zealous friends of the Indians, like Las Casas, were unable to conceal the existence of some deficiency on this score. But the lack of a written language was no more than one among the many points which made the Indians vulnerable in the eyes of those who doubted their capacity to conduct their lives in a suitable manner without the benefit of firm Spanish control.

Even the most prejudiced witnesses were prepared to concede that the Indians differed widely among themselves. In particular, some lived settled lives in towns and villages, while others were hunting and food-gathering nomads. Civilized man, for the sixteenth-century Spaniard, was essentially urban man; and it was for this

---

[38] Richard Konetzke, *Colección de documentos para la historia de la formación social de Hispano-América*, 1 (Madrid, 1953), p. 272.

[39] *Apologética historia*, 2, p. 638.

[40] Joseph de Acosta, *Historia natural y moral de las Indias*, ed. Edmundo O'Gorman (2nd edn., Mexico, 1962), pp. 288 and 292.

reason that Las Casas, following in the steps of Aristotle, had found it necessary to devote so much space in his *Apologética Historia* to towns and urban life in pre-conquest America.[41] But even where the Indians met Aristotelian requirements by living in settlements, their way of life still left much to be desired in the eyes of those who doubted their rational capacity.

Writing in 1599, Captain Vargas Machuca was ready to admit that those Indians who lived in more temperate climes were superior to those in the tropical lands. 'They are people who wear clothes, and have more civility (*policía*).' 'But all of them', he continued, 'are barbarous peoples, as is shown by their houses, dress, food and curious clothing, of which anyhow they wear very little except in the temperate regions. And even here they did not know what stockings and shoes were until, as a result of contact with us Spaniards, they were reduced to civility and put on clothes, and covered their bare bodies with shirt, doublet and hose, stockings and shoes, hats and cloaks.'[42] Matienzo, in Peru, had shown a similar preoccupation with dressing at least upper class Indians in European clothes. Among other advantages, this would allow them to become 'more like men'.[43] But he was unexpectedly tolerant of the Indian practice of wearing the hair long. 'Some people consider this bad. But I can find nothing worng with it, except perhaps on the score of cleanliness.'[44] His limited understanding of Andean civilization was sufficient to make him realize that ordering an Indian to have his hair cut was equivalent to sentencing him to death.

The member of a civilized polity, then, as conceived by the sixteenth-century Spaniard, was a town-dweller who was dressed in doublet and hose, and wore his hair short. His house was not overrun with fleas and ticks. He ate his meals at a table and not on the ground. He did not indulge in unnatural vice, and if he committed adultery he was punished for it. His wife – who was his only wife and not one among several – did not carry her children on her back like a monkey, and he expected his son and not his nephew to succeed to his inheritance. He did not spend his time getting drunk; and he had a proper respect for property – his own and other people's.[45]

The fact that so many of these desiderata were more honoured in the breach than the observance in Europe itself was irrelevant to the

---

[41] *Apologética historia*, book 3.

[42] Bernardo de Vargas Machuca, *Milicia y descripción de las Indias* (Madrid, 1599), f. 131ᵛ.

[43] *Gobierno del Perú*, p. 69 ('...porque comiencen a tener algún ser de hombres').

[44] *Ibid.*, p. 80. For a similar preoccupation in the British reaction to the North American Indian, see *The Complete Writings of Roger Williams*, 1 (New York, 1963), p. 136, and n. 97.

[45] For all these and other adverse criticisms of Indian customs and behaviour see Vargas Machuca, *Milicia*, fs. 132ᵛ–137ᵛ.

attempt to realize them in the New World of America. They fixed a
standard by which Europeans could assess non-European man.
Admittedly the standard was not adopted without a challenge. The
strain of primitivism and the hankering for innocence in Renaissance
thought created a continuing ambiguity in the European response to
the customs of the unspoilt peoples of America.[46] But the ambiguity
affected most deeply those who were farthest removed from the
Indians. The officials faced with the task of incorporating their
charges into the new-style Spanish polity had fewer doubts. They
found their Indians intolerably idle, for reasons which to them were
perfectly plain. Aristotle had taught them that it was attachment to
private possessions which made a man work. 'So it is not surprising',
argued Matienzo, 'that these poor Indians should be idle and take no
trouble to work, because up to now they have had no private property, but everything in common.' His solution was to offer them
their own plots of land, and wages for their labour, so that they
would begin to purchase Spanish goods. This, he believed, would
gradually transform them into civilized men.[47] The same view was
held by another Spanish official in Peru, Hernando de Santillán, for
whom the Indians, although 'of little understanding and civility',
were not as brutish as the Spaniards made them out to be. Wages
would create in them the acquisitive instinct, and a consequent pro-
pensity to work.[48]

   The determination of these officials to bring the Indians into a
wage economy, which they saw as an essential constituent of a
civilized polity, suggests how far European civilization, even in its
Hispanic version, had travelled by the later sixteenth century
towards the modern western view of economic man. This view
remained obnoxious to those who, like Las Casas, clung to the ideal
of apostolic poverty. It was only, he argued, because Europeans in
their greed were obsessed with the acquisition of riches, that they
described the Indians as idle, whereas in fact their land was so
abundant as to allow a minimum of labour, and they could devote
the remainder of their time to hunting and crafts and *fiestas*.[49] But
with a few exceptions[50] the ceremonial and ritualistic character of
labour in Amerindian society was too alien to be understood by

[46] For an illuminating example of this ambiguity, as it affected one particular individual, see
Elizabeth Armstrong, *Ronsard and the Age of Gold* (Cambridge, 1968).

[47] *Gobierno del Perú*, p. 20 ('. . .entrar en ellos la pulicía').

[48] 'Relación del origen. . .y gobierno de los Incas', in *Crónicas peruanas de interés indígena*, ed.
Francisco Esteve Barba (BAE, 209, Madrid, 1968), p. 140.

[49] *Historia de las Indias*, ed. Agustín Millares Carlo, 2 (Mexico, 1951), pp. 463–4.

[50] Notably Alonso de Zorita, *The Lords of New Spain*, trans. Benjamin Keen (London,
1965), pp. 202–4.

Spaniards who themselves, however inadequately, had by now entered the world of wages and the clock.

While certain qualities elicited respect, and even admiration – the bravery and independence of the Araucanian Indians of Chile,[51] for instance, or the remarkable aptitude of many of the Mexican and some of the Peruvian Indians for European arts and crafts – the Indian, measured by the yardstick of sixteenth-century European man, was clearly a failure. This was partly because the yardstick itself derived from the European situation and was totally inadequate for assessing the non-European races of the world; and partly, too, because the Indian, demoralized and psychologically crippled by the experience of conquest and colonization, conformed all too well to the low expectations of a post-Renaissance generation deeply persuaded of the depravity of man. If the Indian was all too often as he was depicted – 'vicious, lazy, idle, melancholic, cowardly, base, evil-intentioned, mendacious, ungrateful, with little memory and no constancy, idolatrous, and given to wicked and abominable sins', to quote the description of the unfortunate inhabitants of Hispaniola by the Spanish translator of Boemus, Francisco Tamara,[53] – this may largely have been because the Europeans had made him so.

Faced with this unsatisfactory human being, the instinctive reaction of the Spaniard was to thank God, as Tamara thanked Him, for 'making us Christians and not heathen; civilized and not barbarians; Spaniards and not Moors or Turks, dirty idolaters'.[54] The only way to break this crust of complacency was to introduce a historical dimension – to look at the Indian not simply as he was now, but also as he had been in the past.

This was the great achievement of men like Durán, Las Casas, Sahagún, and Acosta. By a patient process of historical reconstruction, worthy of men who had read the historians of classical antiquity, they were able to recapture the lineaments of indigenous civilizations which had already vanished beyond recall. Although they found in this process of reconstruction much that was repellent to them as Europeans and Christians, they also discovered much that they could genuinely admire. They were impressed in particular by the achievements of the higher civilizations of pre-conquest America in government, education, and public works. There were, as Sahagún wrote, 'many notable things in the government of these

[51] E.g. Acosta, *Historia natural y moral*, p. 131.
[52] Cf. Matienzo, *Gobierno del Perú*, p. 18, and Bernardo Vargas Machuca, *Refutación de Las Casas* (ed. Paris, 1913), p. 229.
[53] *El Libro de las costumbres*, p. 253.
[54] *Ibid.*, p. 5.

pagans'[55] – things which a sixteenth-century European could appreciate and to some extent understand.

Certain contradictions are to be found in Spanish reactions to the governmental systems of the Incas and Aztecs which reflect the contradictions in sixteenth-century Europe itself. They were admired for their power and efficiency, as also for their provision for the well-being of their subjects, and for their capacity to mobilize them for great public works.[56] Yet their power was at the same time equated with tyranny, which, as Acosta argued, represented an inherent characteristic of barbarism. 'The nearer men are to reason, the more humane and less arrogant is their government....But among barbarians everything is the reverse, because their government is tyrannical and they treat their subjects like beasts....'[57] The logic of this argument would seem to be that the highest admiration is reserved for those tribes which refused to tolerate kings and absolute rulers, and lived in what he described as *behetrías* – the old Castilian areas of jurisdiction by freely elected lords – electing their captains and chiefs for temporary emergencies. But in practice Acosta is soon affirming that the best government in the New World was the monarchical government of Montezuma and the Incas, 'although these were in considerable part tyrannical'.[58]

Acosta's mental acrobatics vividly illustrate the conflict in sixteenth-century European society between the competing claims of liberty and order; and it is not surprising to find that it is for order that a late sixteenth-century European finally opts. Yet the very existence of this conflict in European thought had a bearing on assessments of pre-Columbian state organization, which tended to fall short of unqualified enthusiasm. As soon as discussion moved, however, from the state to the family the qualifications could be safely dropped. Las Casas, Sahagún, and Acosta all discussed in great detail, and with undisguised admiration, the strict Aztec system for the training of children, and the deferential nature of the child's relationship to his parents. 'Nothing has impressed me more', wrote Acosta, 'or seemed to me more worthy of praise and remembrance, than the care and order shown by the Mexicans in the upbringing of their children. For realizing that the future hopes of a republic lie in the training and education of children and young people (a subject discussed at length by Plato in his *Laws*), they set out to turn away their children from

[55] *Historia general*, 2, p. 282.

[56] Las Casas, as might be expected, makes the most of these achievements of the pre-Columbian civilizations, and is especially enthusiastic about the solicitude of the Incas for widows, orphans, and the poor (see the *Apologética historia*, 2, pp. 598 and 626–7).

[57] *Historia natural y moral*, p. 293.

[58] *Ibid.*, pp. 304–5.

indulgence and liberty, which are the two plagues of childhood, and to occupy them in useful and honest exercises.'[59] Is it possible that Acosta and his fellow-observers glimpsed in the Aztec educational system a disciplined relationship which they felt to be breaking down in European homes?[60]

The introduction by men like Sahagún and Acosta of a historical approach into their study of non-European man, did much to reinforce in their own minds the case for attributing to the Andean and Central Mexican Indians a high degree of rationality. But there was always liable to come a moment when history faltered. It could be used, as Las Casas used it, to draw elaborate parallels between the American Indians and the peoples of Europe before the arrival of Christianity; but certain practices only became explicable to these sixteenth-century inquirers when the debate was transferred from the realm of history to that of theology. Even in the great work of Sahagún, which is perhaps as 'objective' as any sixteenth-century work of ethnographical inquiry could hope to be, there stands in the background a sinister shadow – that of Satan himself.

The devil stalked the America of the sixteenth century as surely as he stalked the continent of Europe, and the results of his machinations were everywhere to be seen. It was well known that, as Vargas Machuca said, 'the malice of the devil customarily attempts to deprive men of their reason, and turn them into beasts'.[61] From drunkenness to cannibalism the story was the same. Drunkenness, for Las Casas, was 'a defect of all the heathen thanks to the industry of the devil'.[62] The 'bestial and diabolical practice' of infant sacrifice among the Aztecs was blamed by Sahagún not on the parents, but on the 'most cruel hatred of our ancient enemy Satan, who with the most malign cunning persuaded them to engage in such infernal acts'.[63] In confronting the more puzzling features of alien societies, a sixteenth-century Europe obsessed with the cosmic conflict between God and the devil found the answers to its puzzlement in the *diabolus ex machina*.

[59] *Ibid.*, p. 315.
[60] Las Casas at least is not slow to point a moral for European parents. *Apologética historia*, 2, p. 421.
[61] *Refutación de Las Casas*, pp. 170–1.
[62] *Apologética historia*, 1, p. 183. Drunkenness among the Indians was one of the problems which most preoccupied the missionaries and officials, and it constituted, in the eyes of their detractors, one of the clearest indications of their natural inferiority. The question was, however, sympathetically and intelligently discussed by Alonso de Zorita (*The Lords of New Spain*, pp. 132–3), who saw that it might well be a post-conquest phenomenon, brought about by the new circumstances of Spanish rule. For brief modern discussions see, for Mexico, Charles Gibson, *The Aztecs Under Spanish Rule* (Stanford, 1964), p. 150, and, for Peru, Fernando de Armas Medina, *Cristianización del Perú* (Seville, 1953), pp. 577–81.
[63] *Historia general*, 1, p. 142.

In some respects this European obsession with the powers of darkness provided a further incentive to inquiry. Without it, Sahagún and his colleagues would never have probed so deeply into the complexities of the Aztec calendar. 'This artifice of counting', wrote Sahagún in the prologue to his fourth book, devoted to Aztec feast-days and prophecies, 'is either an art of sorcery or a compact and fabrication of the devil, and it must with all diligence be up-rooted.'[64] Yet at the same time Europe's preoccupation with the devil represented an obstacle to the deeper understanding of indigenous societies. It was hardly necessary to probe much further into Indian belief-systems or social behaviour for explanations of cannibalism and human sacrifice when such horrible rites were known to be inherent in the condition of paganism itself. The heathen, as Acosta pointed out, were by virtue of their paganism slaves to the prince of darkness, and prone, in consequence, to every form of evil.[65]

Paradoxically, however, the diabolical explanation of repugnant rituals helped to ease the task of those who saw the Indians as rational human beings. If the responsibility for bestial acts could be attributed to the devil, the Indian could be presented as a man who was deluded rather than deficient. Inevitably, then, as the light of Christianity dispelled the darkness, the delusions would vanish and these benighted heathen would recover true soundness of mind.

Behind this argument lay a critical assumption: that cultural diversity – the deviation from the norm which the inhabitants of Christendom had furnished for themselves – could be explained by the process of degeneration which afflicted the descendants of Adam in their wanderings through the earth.[66] If this was so, the coming of the Spaniards with the Christian gospel could help to redress the baneful consequences of time and disobedience. Spain's consequent duty towards these unfortunate peoples was nowhere better described than by Acosta towards the end of the sixteenth century: 'All those who are scarcely men, or only half men, must be taught how to become men, and be instructed as if they were children.'[67]

A policy of civilization along Hispanic lines had always had its critics among those whose prime concern was the preaching of the

[64] Ibid., 1, p. 315.
[65] Historia natural y moral, p. 216. The devil in America hardly receives his due in Rafael Heliodoro Valle, 'El diablo en Mesoamérica', Cuadernos Americanos año 12, no. 2 (1953), pp. 194–208.
[66] For sixteenth- and seventeenth-century explanations of cultural diversity, see Hodgen, Early Anthropology, especially chs. 6 and 7.
[67] De Procuranda Indorum Salute, ed. Francisco Mateos (Madrid, 1952), p. 48.
[68] Phelan, The Millennial Kingdom of the Franciscans, p. 87.

gospel. The friars, jealous of their own influence over their Indian charges, were naturally anxious to keep them uncontaminated by European vices. The ideal, for them, remained the superimposition of Christianity on the old pagan social structure.[68] The condition of the Indians after a few decades of Spanish rule only confirmed the fears they had always entertained. They saw them turned into a broken and demoralized people; and the Franciscan Mendieta wrote in 1596 of the 'shame which we Christians should feel that pagans, of less talent than ourselves, should have been better ruled and ordered in matters of morality and behaviour during the time of their heathendom' than they now were as Christians under the government of the Spaniards.[69]

What had gone wrong? – if indeed it had. For many Spaniards remained less impressed by the disasters than by the miraculous transformation wrought among the Indians by the introduction of European civility.[70] Sahagún, for one, had an explanation. After describing the organization and way of life of the Mexicans in the pre-conquest period, he noted that all this had come to an end with the arrival of the Spaniards, who overthrew their customs and governmental system, 'and wanted to reduce them to the Spanish way of life'. This, he believed, was a disaster for environmentalist reasons. Good government was government attuned to the special needs of a people, and these were determined both by temperament and climate. The nature of Mexico, and the constellations under which it lay, made it a land whose inhabitants were naturally inclined to idleness and vice. The Aztecs, instinctively recognizing this fundamental fact, had devised a form of government that was characterized by sobriety and restraint, and had consequently succeeded in holding vice in check. The Spaniards, on the other hand, had ignored the special properties of the regions they had conquered, and had introduced a system ill-adjusted to the temper of the land.[71]

This was an argument with far-reaching implications for Europe's 'civilizing' mission in the overseas world. It was all very well for Acosta to argue that 'all those who are scarcely men, or only half men, must be taught how to become men'; but what in practice happened when this was attempted? The answer was supplied by a young doctor, Juan de Cárdenas, a native of Mexico City, who in 1591 published a book called *Problems and Marvellous Secrets of the Indies*.[72] He devoted a number of pages to the Chichimeca Indians of

---

[69] Fray Gerónimo de Mendieta, *Historia eclesiástica Indiana* (ed. Mexico, 1870), p. 75.
[70] E.g. Vargas Machuca, *Refutación*, pp. 229–30.
[71] *Historia general*, 3, pp. 158–60.
[72] *Problemas y secretos maravillosos de las Indias* (Facsimile edn., Madrid, 1945).

northern Mexico, whom he described as 'a savage and barbarous people, never subjected or tamed by any other nation'. They lived among the rocks and crags; they wore no clothes, and stank to heaven; they had no God, no rites, nor customs; they committed in public every bestial act, and their whole life was given over to the killing of animals and men. But he admitted that in their own country they were brave, strong, and healthy in spite of their repulsive diet.

Capture a Chichimec, however, and try to civilize him, and what happened? He languished and declined. Cárdenas found the explanation for this sad change in environment and custom. Spanish food was unnatural to a man who had lived all his life on a diet of roots and berries. The decline and death of Chichimecs in the hands of the Spaniards was to be ascribed, then, to 'the change of air, diet, customs and way of life, so that one can with justice say of them that change of custom is equivalent to death.'[73]

Cárdenas' treatise betrays an orthodox mind, brought up on the standard authorities studied in sixteenth-century Europe – Aristotle, Galen, Hippocrates. His arguments, along with those of Sahagún on the unfortunate results of the attempt to reduce the Mexican Indians to a Spanish way of life, indicate how Europe's classical inheritance had once again come to its rescue in its confrontation with alien peoples and customs. The only cure for ethnocentric complacency was a sense of perspective – the perspective of time and the perspective of space. The perspective of time was provided by men who, nurtured on Herodotus and Pliny, were ready to embark on historical research into the social organization and customs of the peoples with whom they now found themselves in contact. Similarly the perspective of space was provided by men whose classical training had made them alive to the significance of geography and climate. The environmentalism which is all too often exclusively associated with the towering figure of Bodin, but which in fact was deeply rooted in sixteenth-century thought,[74] was itself an important incentive to tolerance. For if different climatic and topographical conditions created different humours and temperaments, this in turn suggested the logic of accepting that different regions of the earth should enjoy the style of life and social organization appropriate to their needs.

These environmentalist assumptions may in some respects have inhibited the development of anthropology in sixteenth-century

---

[73] Folios 200^v–203^v.

[74] M.J. Tooley, 'Bodin and the Medieval Theory of Climate', *Speculum*, 28 (1953), pp. 64–83. Also Clarence J. Glacken, *Traces on the Rhodian Shore* (Berkeley, 1967), ch. 9.

Europe, for if the explanation of diversity lay in places rather than in people, there was little to be done except accumulate information about the varieties of human behaviour and note the repetition of certain patterns in the light of roughly similar topographical conditions.[75] Yet at the same time these assumptions made at least a handful of Europeans uneasily aware that the imposition of European standards on non-European peoples subjected to their rule, might not, after all, be an unmixed good. They had, in fact, made the disturbing discovery that man and European man were not necessarily identical. And, even more disturbing, that they did not have to be so.

It was, admittedly, one thing to accept the fact of diversity for alien peoples living outside the sphere of European jurisdiction, and quite another to accept it for those who were the subjects of European kings. The Spanish crown was unlikely to be deflected from the attempt to introduce 'civility' in its American dominions by the expression of a few doubts about the social and psychological consequences of the process for its Indian vassals. Yet the very expression of doubt and hesitation had an importance of its own in the slow and painful process of Europe's discovery of man. No Christian could accept a wholly determinist explanation of human diversity as an unalterable fact of existence. Religion and education must, by degrees, transform even those who lived in the most unfavourable natural conditions. But the awareness of diversity, and of the need to temper policy according to the demands of environment and social characteristics, was itself an acknowledgement of the complexity of man.

Applied to Europe itself, this awareness was nothing new. Indeed it was a truism that laws and governments should be appropriately framed in the light of local circumstances.[76] Diversity was, after all, an established fact of European life. But applied to non-European conditions in regions where Europeans enjoyed the mastery, the truism raised a number of awkward questions which were bound to reflect on the criteria and values of the European world. The Spaniards in America were among the first Europeans to be faced with these questions. The discovery and settlement of this strange new world compelled them to confront the problem of the nature of man, not only as a creature capable or incapable of salvation, but also as a physical and social being who should, or should not, conform to some pre-determined image. Their questions were sometimes badly

[75] See John H. Rowe, 'Ethnography and Ethnology in the Sixteenth Century', *The Kroeber Anthropological Society Papers*, no. 30 (1964), pp. 1–19.
[76] Cf. Tooley, 'Bodin', pp. 78–80.

posed, and their answers sometimes wrong. But America drove some of them at least to widen and deepen their concept of man, and to draw upon Europe's inherited historical and geographical traditions in order to understand better the peoples entrusted to their charge. In the process of inquiry, they found themselves led irresistibly towards an acknowledgement of the simultaneous unity and diversity of the human race. In the circumstances, therefore, it was entirely appropriate that, in portraying the Indians, they should also unconsciously have been portraying themselves.

PART II

THE EUROPEAN WORLD

INTRODUCTION

The Kings of Spain, as rulers of 'the empire of the Indies', were faced with problems of government at long distance on a scale unprecedented in European history. But they were also faced with some extremely difficult problems of government a good deal nearer home. Ironically, it was in some ways easier to govern the Mexican viceroyalty of New Spain, with a travelling time of three months or more from Madrid, than the peninsular viceroyalty of Catalonia, with a travelling time of three days. As I worked on the history of seventeenth-century Catalonia for my study of *The Revolt of the Catalans* (1963), I was impressed by the force of the famous argument of the Count of Olivares to Philip IV in 1624 that although he might be King of Portugal, Aragon and Valencia, and Count of Barcelona, he was not yet King of Spain. From the standpoint of Madrid, the principality of Catalonia, with its own distinctive language, laws, history and institutions was an almost ungovernable province. In Catalonia it was not so much distance as diversity that represented the principal challenge to statecraft.

In 1640 Madrid failed the challenge, and Catalonia revolted. But, after twelve years of rebellion, it returned to allegiance to Philip IV. Both the rebellion, and the return to allegiance, seemed to me to raise important questions about the character and the durability of the Spanish Monarchy. While the institutional structure of the Monarchy offered some significant clues, I had learnt from my time in Barcelona with Jaume Vicens Vives to look behind the institutions to the interest groups and the balance of social forces for an explanation of the workings of political power. The essay here reprinted on the Catalan ruling class was originally published in 1965 in a two-volume homage to his memory. As the essay itself makes clear, although it is focused on Catalonia, its implications extend well beyond the borders of the principality. Extreme diversity was a fact of life in the Iberian peninsula and in the Spanish Monarchy as a whole, but the form of government of this congeries of kingdoms and provinces was dictated by certain constants, and in particular by

the need for Madrid to establish and maintain a *modus vivendi* with
the local elites. The Catalan example suggests at once the problems
and the opportunities in this process for the Spanish crown.

My study of the progressive alienation of the Catalan elite from
Madrid, culminating in the 1640 rebellion, was undertaken at a moment when the simultaneity of revolts and revolutions in the Europe
of the mid-seventeenth century was a subject of vigorous historical
debate. The Catalan revolt, one of the *Six Contemporaneous Revolutions* discussed by Roger B. Merriman in 1938, inevitably figured in
this great debate of the 1960s. Influenced as I was by the debate in the
presentation of my own findings, I felt that they did not invariably
support the more audaciously speculative of the interpretations of
'the general crisis of the seventeenth century' that were currently
being propounded. When I came, therefore, to give an Inaugural
Lecture in 1968 at King's College, University of London, I decided
to survey both the debate, and the general problem of 'Revolution
and Continuity in Early Modern Europe', and naturally drew for this
purpose on the experience of Spain and Catalonia. As readers of this
essay will appreciate, my researches in Catalonia had made me very
conscious of the sense of collective identity of the local community
under pressure from outside forces – a sense that found expression in
the idea of the *patria*. The defence of the *patria*, of an idealized vision
of the community, seemed to me to play a critical part in Early
Modern European revolts and revolutions, and I felt that this aspect
was being neglected in the current controversy.

The nature of the perceived threat to the community raised, for its
part, the whole question of the aspirations and intentions of central
governments, and of the character of the pressures to which they in
turn were subject. Of all these pressures, the most insistent was war.
In recent years the role of warfare in the development of the Early
Modern state, and not least in that of Spain,[1] has been the subject of
renewed historical attention. But less attention has been paid to the
decision-making processes which involved states in war. This neglect of foreign policy in its widest sense – of the choices that were
made in foreign affairs, and of the assumptions that underlay them –
has been, in my view, one of the great weaknesses in contemporary
writing on Early Modern Europe. Historians of seventeenth-century
Spain are here particularly fortunate, thanks to the extraordinarily
full accounts in the documentation of the Council of State of discussions on matters of war and peace. These make it possible to identify
and follow individual points of view, while also, with the help of

---

[1] See I.A.A. Thompson, *War and Government in Habsburg Spain, 1560–1620* (London, 1976).

other material, reconstructing the mentality of the ruling group at the centre of power.

This process of reconstruction has yet to be undertaken on any systematic basis over the span of the century, but close studies have been made at a number of points, and in particular for the years of Spain's involvement in the Thirty Years' War. In 1984 an International Colloquium was held at Munich on the Thirty Years' War, and Professor Roland Mousnier and I were asked to present papers on 'Foreign policy and domestic crisis' in France and Spain respectively. This invitation seemed to me to provide an opportunity to examine some of the underlying policy preconceptions and concerns of successive regimes in Madrid, and also to show the connection (or, more accurately, the frequent lack of connection) between the financial and economic situation and major foreign policy choices. In working on my political biography of the Count-Duke of Olivares I had been very struck by the repeated references to the theme of 'reputation', not only by the Count-Duke but also by his colleagues. The same theme surfaces in the papers of Cardinal Richelieu, which I studied in preparation for a short comparative study of the two statesmen, *Richelieu and Olivares* (1984). The parallel here seemed to me significant, and a salutary reminder that Spain formed part of a political culture common to western Europe, however strong some of its own local variations. An excessively 'internalist' approach to the history of Early Modern Spain has too often tended to obscure this fact, and to conceal the many resemblances between developments in Spain and other European monarchies in these centuries of intense Spanish involvement in European life.

IV

A PROVINCIAL ARISTOCRACY: THE CATALAN RULING CLASS IN THE SIXTEENTH AND SEVENTEENTH CENTURIES

The administrative history of the Spanish Empire is generally treated as the history of a limited number of governmental institutions. These were the institutions by which the government in Madrid sought to maintain its control over the numerous, and often remote, possessions of the King of Spain. In Madrid itself a set of councils, operating under the king, jealously supervised the administration of those territories for which they were responsible.[1] Government in the various territories was exercised by viceroys, closely dependent on Madrid for their instructions, while the administration of justice was entrusted to *audiencias*. Councils, viceroyalties and *audiencias* were therefore the essential institutions of an elaborately organized governmental system whose nerve-centre was Madrid. Together they constituted the working mechanism of the 'centralized' Spanish Monarchy.

In spite of the importance of these institutions, curiously little attention has been paid to the men who composed them. Of all the councils, only the Council of the Indies has so far been systematically investigated.[2] A thorough study of the Spanish bureaucracy in the sixteenth and seventeenth centuries – of the background and education of the officials who staffed the councils and governed the Monarchy – would add an extra dimension to our understanding of the institutions, and hence of the workings of government. But, invaluable as such a study would be, it would still provide no more

---

[1] For a brief survey of the conciliar system, see the foreword, by Dr. Batista I Roca, to H.G. Koenigsberger, *The Government of Sicily under Philip II of Spain* (London, 1951).

[2] Ernesto Schäfer, *El Consejo Real y Supremo de las Indias*, 2 vols. (Seville, 1935). [See now also the important prosopographical study by Janine Fayard, *Les Membres du Conseil de Castille à l'époque moderne, 1621–1746* (Geneva, 1979). For the education of royal officials there is now the pioneering work of Richard L. Kagan, *Students and Society in Early Modern Spain* (Baltimore and London, 1974).]

than a partial picture of the Spanish governmental system. The bureaucracy did not work in a vacuum; nor was its power exclusive and unlimited. It was not even a monolithic structure. Recent studies have made it increasingly clear that the Spanish system of government, in the Old World as much as in the New, was essentially a system of checks and balances, and that government depended upon the delicate interplay of a number of bodies, constantly re-adjusting their relationship to maintain a precarious equilibrium.[3] Much of this interplay occurred within the bureaucracy itself: in the New World, in particular, viceroy was held in check by *audiencia, audiencia* by viceroy, and each in turn was checked by the council in Madrid. But restraints came from without as well as from within. The powers of officials were limited, in the dominions of the King of Spain as everywhere else, by considerations of time and space, by local autonomies and jurisdictions, by privileges and exemptions, and by all the pressures, legal and covert, which powerful local interests could bring to hear upon the agents of the crown.

Little is known about these pressures because little is known about the groups that were in a position to exert them. Yet these groups were as essential a part of 'government' as was the official bureaucracy. Far from being a graceful minuet danced solely by the central and local officials of the crown, the Spanish system of government more closely resembled a highly intricate quadrille, with the 'ruling classes' of the various provinces[4] as indispensable partners. A viceregal administration could only function effectively if it enjoyed the cooperation of the natural ruling class in the province it governed – the upper clergy, the nobles, the gentry, and the municipal oligarchies, who in practice ran the province under the general direction of the viceroy and, ultimately, of Madrid. A knowledge of the character of the provincial aristocracies in the Spanish Monarchy would therefore seem an essential prerequisite for the understanding of the Habsburg system of government. Yet, with the partial exception of the Netherlands aristocracy in the sixteenth century, the provincial aristocracies have been largely neglected; and, in particular, the aristocracies of the various kingdoms of the Spanish peninsula remain an unknown quantity.

[3] See especially Koenigsberger, *The Government of Sicily*, and K. Garrad, *The Causes of the Second Rebellion of the Alpujarras* (unpublished Ph.D dissertation of 1955 deposited in the Cambridge University Library).

[4] Technically, the Spanish Monarchy was a complex of kingdoms, duchies, principalities and counties, and the word 'province' suggests nowadays a degree of subordination to the central government which often existed neither in practice nor in theory. For convenience sake it is, however, simpler to speak of 'provinces'; and it is noticeable that during this period the Catalans, at least, often referred to the principality as 'this province', without apparently intending to imply by this any sense of subordination or inferiority.

What was the composition and character of a provincial aristocracy? Through what agencies did it exercise power and influence? How far was it successful in asserting and maintaining its control against constant pressure from Madrid? The answers to some of these questions are suggested by a study of the ruling class in the principality of Catalonia.

The union of the Crowns of Castile and Aragon as a result of the marriage of Ferdinand and Isabella had left Catalonia with its system of government formally unchanged. The contractual nature of Catalan kingship was preserved; the king's government operated within the limits laid down by the traditional 'constitutions'; laws could only be made or altered, and taxes voted, at a session of the Catalan *Corts,* which the king must attend in person; justice continued to be administered by the *Audiència* established in Barcelona; and the permanent committee of six, known as the *Diputació,* continued to watch over the rights and liberties of the principality, and to represent its interests in disputes with royal officials. The only real change, although a crucial one for the future development of Catalan social and political life, was brought about by the permanent departure from the principality of the king and his court. Catalonia, no stranger to absentee kingship during the fifteenth century, was to find itself ruled during the sixteenth and seventeenth centuries by monarchs whom it scarcely ever saw. Inevitably the absenteeism of its rulers made certain administrative modifications essential. The traditional royal council of the kings of Aragon, transformed into the Council of Aragon, followed the king out of the principality and eventually settled with him in Madrid; and the king's place in Barcelona was taken by a viceroy who, alone of the royal officials in the principality, was permitted by the constitutions to be a foreigner.[5]

The administration over which the viceroy of Catalonia presided was very small. The police arm consisted of the Governor of Catalonia and his colleague, the Governor of the counties (Rosselló and Cerdanya), assisted by four *agutzils* and a number of minor officials, operating in conjunction with rather under two hundred local officials of the crown (known as *veguers, batlles* and their subordinates).[6] There were three financial departments in Barcelona, run by a small staff; there was a chancery; and, for the administration

---

[5] For a more detailed account of the viceregal administration see chapter 4 of my *The Revolt of the Catalans. A study in the decline of Spain, 1598–1640* (Cambridge, 1963).

[6] A(rchivo de la) C(orona de) A(ragón), C(onsejo de) A(ragón) leg(ajo) 373, *Memorial of salaries of royal officials in Catalonia* (1624). This memorial lists 152 local offices in the principality itself and a further 35 in the counties.

of justice, there was an *Audiència* which consisted at the end of the sixteenth century of seventeen judges, who had come to assume the additional task of acting as advisers to the viceroy. This viceregal administration was responsible for governing, under instructions from the Council of Aragon in Madrid, a province with large tracts of rocky and mountainous country, a land of isolated valleys, of small coastal settlements and remote inland villages, with a population approaching 400,000.

The administration's hands were tied by a permanent shortage of money; by immunities and exemptions which severely restricted its scope (some 70% of all the jurisdictions in the principality seem to have belonged to barons and to the church);[7] and by a constitutional inability to enlarge itself at will, for no new offices could be created without the consent of the *Corts*.[8] Shortage of cash and wide aristocratic immunities were common enough in the dominions of the King of Spain, but Catalonia appears to have differed from provinces like Sicily and Naples in the fierceness of the constitutional restraints which it imposed on royal officials, and in the severity of the legal restrictions which it placed in the way of even the most minor administrative reforms. The king's government in the principality was therefore dependent, perhaps to a degree unusual even in the Spanish Monarchy, on the cooperation, active as well as tacit, of the province's own ruling class.

In spite of the formal division of Catalan society into three *estaments* or estates – *eclesiàstic, militar* (aristocratic) and *reial* (popular) – each with its own chamber in the *Corts,* it is none the less possible to speak of a homogeneous ruling class composed of members of all three estates. As a ruling class, it probably possessed more social cohesion than that of seventeenth-century France, with its sharp divisions between *noblesse d'épée* and *noblesse de robe*. In some respects, indeed, it displayed a greater degree of social and economic uniformity than its equivalent in Jacobean England, for there were certain features, both within the ranks of the aristocracy and in the relationship between aristocracy and upper bourgeoisie, which were peculiarly favourable to the formation of a closely knit social group.

Within the aristocracy itself, cohesion was enhanced by the almost complete absence of titled nobles. During the sixteenth century such of the great Catalan families as had survived tended to leave the

---

[7] Calculated from the list of jurisdictions provided in part 3 of Don Luis De Peguera, *Pràctica, forma y estil de celebrar Corts Generals en Cathalunya* (Barcelona, 1701). First published in 1632.

[8] *Constitutions y altres drets de Cathalunya* (Barcelona, 1704), lib. I tit. LXXI.

principality and become assimilated into the aristocracy of Castile. 'Loyset is continuing his studies and speaks Castilian very prettily', wrote Doña Estefanía de Requesens in 1534 of her six-year-old son, the future governor of the Netherlands, who was being educated at court;[9] and so yet another of the old Catalan houses loosened its ties with its native land. When the Catalan *Corts* were assembled in 1626, they were attended by only nine native holders of titles: one duke (Cardona), seven counts and a viscount – and all the counts held titles created by Philip III in 1599.[10]

Beneath this very small group of titled nobles came the mass of the aristocracy, divided into two classes. The higher class consisted of the nobles proper, recognizable by the prefix *Don,* which was inherited by all their sons, and which in Catalonia, unlike Castile, was reserved exclusively for those with a privilege of nobility. The lower class were the gentry, or *cavallers,* who again transmitted their rank to their children, but possessed no distinguishing title.

The distinction between nobles and gentry was more nominal than real. Together they made up the *estament militar,* and together they constituted the aristocratic chamber – the *braç militar* – at meetings of the *Corts.* There seems to have been no sharp economic division between the two groups, and indeed by European standards most of the Catalan aristocracy would probably be classed as gentry. A noble in Catalonia nominally required an annual income of some 2,000 *lliures* in the early seventeenth century to live as befitted his station,[11] but it is doubtful whether more than a small section of the nobility possessed as much. Many nobles were younger sons, and the inheritance system in the principality was carefully designed to ensure that the bulk of the family estate was preserved intact in the hands of a single heir. As a result, the claims of younger sons on the estate were customarily bought off with cash payments, which were often much too small to provide them with a living. The sons of Don Josep de Pons, for example, were to be maintained by the heir until the age of twenty when they would inherit 1,000 *lliures* apiece[12] – a sum so small that a secular or ecclesiastical appointment, or a good marriage, was likely to be essential. Younger sons of nobles in such circumstances as these were indistinguishable from gentry, for whom an annual income of about 600 *lliures* seems to have been regarded as a proper figure,[13] although again it was by no means universally attained.

[9] José M.ª March, *Niñez y juventud de Felipe II* (Madrid, 1942), 2, p. 194.
[10] ACA Cancillería R(egistro), 5515 f. 217. List of those summoned to 1626 *Corts.*
[11] Cf. the petition of Joan Francesc Brossa (1626), ACA, CA leg. 500.
[12] A(rchivo de) P(rotocolos) B(arcelona), A.J. Fita, lib(ro) 7 de testaments fs. 95–98v. Will of Don Josep de Pons, 24 Jan. 1639.
[13] Cf. the petition of Antoni Magarola (1613?), ACA, CA, leg. 488.

Outside Barcelona, where, until 1621, nobles as distinct from *cavallers* were excluded from municipal office, there was little to distinguish a noble except his prefix; and the general trend during the course of the sixteenth century had been towards an upgrading of *cavallers* into the ranks of the nobility. This can be seen from a comparison of the lists of those summoned to attend the *Corts* of 1518 and 1626 respectively:[14]

Date	Nobles	Cavallers	Total
1518	37	451	488
1626	254	526	780

While there had been a seven-fold increase in the number of nobles, the total numbers of the *estament militar* had not even doubled. The prime reason for this is almost certainly to be found in deliberate royal policy. There were obvious disadvantages in swelling indefinitely the ranks of an aristocracy any one of whose members was in a position to bring the *Corts* to a standstill by the use of a *dissentiment* or veto. It was preferable to promote existing *cavallers* into the ranks of the nobility, although Philip III, always prodigal of honours, created sixty new *cavallers* in 1599.[15]

In spite of a certain caution on the part of the crown in adding to the numbers of the aristocracy, this socially homogeneous *estament militar* was by no means a closed caste. Its 488 members in 1518 were drawn from about 290 families; its 780 members in 1626 came from some 410 families, of which only about 120 were represented in 1518.[16] This points to the extinction during little more than a century of well over half the male lines of the Catalan aristocracy, and the reinforcement of the aristocracy by the ennobling of new families. Ferdinand the Catholic had ennobled several wealthy peasants for their services to the royal cause during the civil wars of the fifteenth century,[17] but since his reign the new creations had been drawn from the ranks of the landowners, of the upper bourgeoisie and of the officials who staffed the viceregal administration. Property and office were therefore the essential passports to aristocracy, and aspirants to social distinction would either attempt to gain entry into the royal administration – usually by way of the law – or would buy their way into the ranks of the propertied upper bourgeoisie, like Cánoves and Morgades, two notoriously rich merchants, 'natives of Vic liv-

---

[14] ACA, CA, Cancilleria R. 3896 fs. 25–33 (*Corts* of 1518) and R. 5515 f. 217 (*Corts* of 1626). Neither of these lists can be accepted as completely accurate.

[15] ACA, CA, leg. 358 *Certificación...de los caballeros y nobles...*1599.

[16] These figures must be regarded as a very rough approximation, based on a comparison of surnames.

[17] P. Negre Pastell, *La Cofradía de San Jorge y la noblesa gerundense* (Girona, 1952), p. 56.

ing in Barcelona, who the day before yesterday were peasants, yesterday merchants, and today *cavallers* engaged in commerce – and all in the space of thirty years.'[18]

The links between the aristocracy and the leading citizens in the larger towns were, by the seventeenth century, very close, and this closeness again helped to increase the homogeneity of the Catalan ruling class. The easy interchange between the two groups can partly be ascribed to the success of prominent citizens in turning themselves into exclusive urban aristocracies. In spite of Ferdinand the Catholic's attempts to break the hold of the municipal oligarchies over urban life by the introduction of a lottery system for office, the oligarchies had skilfully managed to re-constitute themselves and to retain their control of the important municipal offices. While the lottery system continued to operate, the list of names from which the draw was made was carefully restricted, and the system was so weighted that the most influential citizens – lawyers, merchants, doctors – dominated urban government.[19]

During the sixteenth century some of these powerful municipal oligarchies, having successfully wrested the control of municipal affairs from the hands of the humbler citizens, found themselves confronted by a new challenge. After the civil wars of the fifteenth century, many nobles and gentry abandoned their remote, and often ruined, castles for the greater comforts of a town house.[20] Here they chose to pass the greater part of the year, though perhaps retreating to their country estates during the hot summer months. Once they had taken up residence in the towns, most of them appear to have lost interest in the running of their estates, which they were content to administer through a *procurador*, or to lease for a fixed annual rental.[21] Their interests were becoming those of townsmen, and increasingly they associated themselves with the lives of the towns. In 1639 174 members of the *estament militar* (between a quarter and fifth of the entire aristocracy) were listed as resident in Barcelona,[22] while several others rented houses in the city and presumably lived in them for at least part of the year;[23] and several of the more important

---

[18] A(cademia de) B(uenas) L(etras, Barcelona). *Dietari* de Pujades (1621–5), f. 164v.

[19] See for example the lists of eligible names for the four posts of *consellers* in Manresa (Archivo Histórico de Manresa, *Llibre de ànimes*).

[20] Joaquín Pla Cargol, 'Proceso del desarrollo urbano de Gerona a través de los tiempos', *Anales del Instituto de Estudios Gerundenses*, 2 (1947), p. 218.

[21] The most striking exception to this is a Lleida noble, Don Francesc de Gilabert, who was overcome by remorse at the neglect of his estates and took to farming them himself. In 1626 he published a book, *Agricultura prática*, in the hope of persuading others to follow suit.

[22] ACA, G(eneralitat), Caja 26 List of aristocracy resident in Barcelona, 3 Dec. 1639.

[23] E.g. Don Pau de Ager rented a house in Barcelona belonging to Dona Lluisa d'Ardena (APB, A.J. Fita, lib. 7 de testaments fs. 106–115v. Will of Dona Luisa d'Ardena, 16 July 1639).

towns, like Girona, Lleida, Perpinyà and Vic, had their resident
nobles, whose presence is still commemorated by a 'street of the
cavallers', lined with spacious, well-appointed houses.

These resident nobles and gentry were naturally anxious to part-
icipate in municipal government and to hold municipal office. Town
charters, however, often expressly forbade this, and the existing
urban oligarchies were not keen to open their ranks and to widen the
circle of power. But gradually they gave way. By the end of the
sixteenth century most towns were in debt, and nobles and *cavallers*
stubbornly refused to pay rates as long as they were excluded from a
share in municipal government. Under threat of bankruptcy Girona
opened the doors of its town hall to nobles and gentry in 1601;[24]
Perpinyà followed suit in 1602;[25] and by the 1620s nobles and gentry
played a part in the government of most of the larger towns.

The eventual union of the aristocracy and the dominant municipal
families in the government of the towns was no doubt facilitated by a
constant process of intermarriage. Bourgeois wealth could enable the
younger sons of nobles to live as befitted their status, and they in
turn could confer the distinction of their name upon a 'new' family.
Maria, daughter of Nofre Boixadors, a wealthy Barcelona citizen,
brought her aristocratic husband, Don Felip Vilana, the very large
dowry of 13,000 *lliures*;[26] conversely, Joan Francesc Brossa, a rich
citizen of Vic of humble origins, felt justified in petitioning the king
for a title of nobility, partly on the strength of his wealth, but also
on the grounds that he had twice been married to daughters of
cavallers.[27] If at times the social gulf seemed forbiddingly wide, it was
frequently bridged by an institution peculiar to Barcelona and one or
two of the other principal towns, known as honoured citizenship. At
the summit of the Barcelona hierarchy were some fifty citizens called
ciutadans honrats. The title of *ciutadà honrat* (a hereditary title) was conferred either by the king or, more frequently, by vote of the existing
ciutadans honrats at an annual meeting held on 1 May.[28] Once elected,
the recipients were entitled to all the privileges of the *estament militar*
except that of participating in the *braç militar* in sessions of the *Corts*.
To all intents and purposes, therefore, *ciutadans honrats* were indistinguishable from the traditional aristocracy, whose interests and
pursuits they shared, and to which they were related by numerous
ties of kinship.

[24] ACA, CA, leg. 347, Memorandum on Girona government, c. 1605.
[25] ACA, CA, leg. 347, Duke of Feria to King, 15 March 1602.
[26] APB, A.J. Fita, lib. 6 de capítols matrimonials. Marriage contract, 5 Feb. 1622.
[27] ACA, CA, leg. 500, Petition of Brossa, 1626.
[28] Joan Pere Fontanella, *De Pactis Nuptialibus* (Barcelona, 1612), clàusula III, glosa II, c. 77.
[For this institution and the patriciate it produced, see now James S. Amelang, *Honored Citizens
of Barcelona: Patrician Culture and Class Relations, 1490–1714* (Princeton, 1986).]

As a result of these ties between the 'military' aristocracy and the urban aristocracy, the social and family cohesion within the upper échelons of Catalan society was very considerable. In practice, some five hundred families, closely interrelated and enjoying a broadly similar social status, dominated the life of the principality. The same names constantly recur: Alemany and Alentorn, Boixadors and Calders, d'Oms and Llupiá, Magarola and Peguera, Rocabertí, Sentmenat and Sorribes. Families such as these were well represented in the municipal hierarchies; they occupied many of the best available ecclesiastical posts, although, to their deep distress, the principality's nine dioceses were not exclusively reserved for Catalans; they provided recruits for the *Audiència* and for the small viceregal administration; and they owned the many baronies and jurisdictions that pockmarked the face of the country. Together they constituted the Catalan 'ruling class'.

In Catalonia, as in other parts of sixteenth- and seventeenth-century Europe, the ruling class tended to assume a double role. On the one hand, it helped the crown to maintain the established order against possible upheaval from below; on the other, it sought to preserve, and, if possible, to extend, its rights and privileges against real or alleged encroachments by the crown – a process which it tended to identify with the preservation of the country at large from arbitrary royal government.

The assistance which a governing class could render the crown in the task of preserving public order could be either tacit or open. In Jacobean England it was open: the gentry, in their role as justices of the peace, acted as the filters through which the commands of the central government were transmitted to the localities, and ensured that these commands – in so far as they did not run too strongly counter to their own interests – were generally obeyed. In Philip III's Catalonia, on the other hand, the assistance was largely tacit. Where the English gentry were willing, and even anxious, to serve as unpaid justices, their Catalan equivalents had, by the seventeenth century, contracted out of local office – on the grounds that salaries were too low.[29] As for unpaid service, 'nobody wishes to work without payment' nowadays.'[30] An investigation of the motives that lay behind the opposing attitudes to local government of the Catalan and English gentry might provide a valuable insight into the comparative development of European societies in the Early Modern

[29] ACA, CA, leg. 344, Duke of Feria to Marquis of Denia, 28 Dec. 1598.
[30] Francisco de Gilabert, *Discursos sobre la calidad del principado de Cataluña* (Lérida, 1616), Discurso I, f. 9.

period. One or two possible explanations of the negative attitude of the Catalan governing class towards local office under the crown do, however, spring to mind. The permanent absenteeism of a monarch able to reward the deserving from first-hand knowledge, and to give them places in his court and about his person, had deprived the Catalan aristocracy of a prime incentive for public service in any form; infrequent sessions of the Catalan *Corts* in relation to the English parliament, together with the fact that all gentry, as well as nobles, attended by right, meant that there was little of that competition for positions of local influence which in England was an essential preliminary to the acquisition of a place at Westminster; and, perhaps most important of all, the extent and scope of private baronial jurisdictions in the principality placed large areas of the country right outside the scope of royal authority, and thus did much to diminish the attraction of holding local office under the crown.

But although Catalan nobles and gentry refused to serve as royal officials in the localities, they none the less ruled the country through their own baronial courts. Don Rafael de Biure forbade his vassals to indulge in blasphemy or to play card games, to cut wood or go hunting; he ordered them to repair the roads in the month of June, and he attended his court to mete out justice when one family quarrelled with another over a marriage settlement or a disputed boundary line.[31] Baronial authority was still, in the seventeenth century, the most powerful authority in the lives of a large part of the rural population, especially in those baronies where the lord possessed *mer i mixt imperi* – full civil and criminal jurisdiction, including the right to sentence to death, grimly symbolized by the gallows erected on his land.[32]

Through baronial courts, therefore, potential agrarian unrest was held in check, except when barons chose to exploit it for their own ends. Similarly, the municipal oligarchies succeeded in maintaining order in the towns, except when corn ran short and famine threatened. At two moments in the first half of the seventeenth century, however, the principality fell prey to incipient social upheaval: in 1615, when the bandit movement in the countryside reached its climax, and in 1640, when political revolution against the Spanish

---

[31] Cf. the *Registre de la Cort del... batlle del lloch de Praeixens per lo Ill. y Noble Señor Don Raphael de Biure* (Archivo Histórico de Barcelona, Archivo Patrimonial, leg. III-15).

[32] Although it was legally possible to appeal from a baronial court to the *Audiència*, many vassals can hardly have been in a position to take advantage of this right. Professor Koenigsberger shows, in his *Government of Sicily*, pp. 137–9, how the Spanish Crown tried and failed to prevent the extension of *mero e misto imperio* among the Sicilian nobility. I am not sure how far a conscious effort was made to check it in sixteenth-century Catalonia. In both provinces the crown signally failed to substitute royal for baronial jurisdiction.

crown was accompanied by widespread popular risings in both the country and the towns. On both occasions there were grave dissensions and uncertainties within the ruling class, which prevented it from effectively exercising its function of preserving public order. But, with these two exceptions, its tacit assistance enabled the crown to maintain, however precariously, what was euphemistically known as 'royal authority' throughout the principality.

While fulfilling this task, which naturally coincided with its own sectional interests, the ruling class was quick to react to any signs that the crown was extending its powers at its own expense. Whereas in Sicily during the sixteenth century the crown at least managed to construct a solid basis for its power,[33] its progress in Catalonia during the same period was minimal, and may perhaps have been limited to the establishment of an additional chamber in the *Audiència* to hear appeals from baronial courts.[34] Whenever the crown attempted to sharpen its authority and extend its control over the principality, the ruling class was almost invariably able to check it in mid-course. The new-style Inquisition, for instance, which Ferdinand the Catholic had imposed on the principality in the face of strong opposition, was quietly undermined during the course of the sixteenth century, and deprived of much of its influence.

These successes were achieved by the skilful exploitation of the principality's traditional laws and institutions. Most of the Catalan constitutions were, in any event, so specific as to allow the crown few loopholes, and the chances of the crown securing alterations in the constitutions with the consent of the *Corts* were slight. From the beginning of Philip II's reign sessions of the *Corts* became increasingly infrequent, and the king was usually so anxious for a subsidy that he rarely put up a strong fight for what his viceroys considered to be essential constitutional changes. Instead, the *Corts* became a useful vehicle for the ruling class to extract valuable administrative and legal concessions from the crown as a reward for the granting of a subsidy.

When the *Corts* were not in session, the ruling class possessed another admirable instrument for bringing pressure to bear on the crown, in the form of the *Diputació*. The Diputació or *Generalitat* is customarily treated in Catalan historiography as a well-nigh perfect institution – a unique expression of the general will of the Catalan nation in its struggle against arbitrary government. Nominally this

---

[33] Koenigsberger, p. 105.
[34] Increasing use seems to have been made of proclamations by the viceroys, but restrictions were placed on these in the *Corts* of 1599. Cf. *Constitutions fetes per la SCR Magestat del Rey . . . 1599* (Barcelona, 1603) const. ix.

was its *raison d'être,* and on certain occasions in the sixteenth and seventeenth centuries it no doubt acted, at least momentarily, in line with the interests of the community at large. But admiration for its achievements in the Middle Ages has tended to obscure its real character in a later period, and to confer upon it a representative role which, in the eyes of contemporaries, it no longer invariably possessed.

'The house of the *Generalitat* in Barcelona is nothing but a house of damnation', declared the town council of Cervera (although it subsequently erased the remark).[35] One of the explanations for this unpopularity of the *Diputació,* which was by no means confined to the citizens of Cervera, is to be found in an anonymous statement of 1626 that 'the people of Catalonia ordinarily have little love for the *Generalitat* because they do not all enjoy offices in it.'[36] To understand the force of this remark it is necessary to see how the *Diputació* worked.

The fact that the three *Diputats* and the three *Oidors* were chosen, like town councillors, by a lottery system, has fostered the impression of an admirably equitable institution – its officers selected by the sternly impartial hand of chance in the shape of a small boy selecting names at random from an ornate silver basin on 22 July of every third year. But while the way in which the names were drawn from the basin is well enough known, less attention has been paid to the manner in which they had originally found their way there. In practice, the draw was only the final stage of a long and intricate process whereby a total of 524 names, out of a population of 350,000, were selected as being eligible for participation in the triennial lottery. These 524 names, from which two were chosen for each estate, were apportioned as follows:

> *Ecclesiastics* :   66
> *Braç militar* : 250
> *Braç reial*   : 208 (of whom 85 were citizens of Barcelona)

The ecclesiastics consisted solely of bishops, abbots and canons, so that no parish priest would ever hold office; and the members of the *braç reial* were the nominees of the municipal oligarchies of a mere twelve towns, whose inclusion was determined not by their present standing but by their past importance.[37]

By its very composition therefore, the *Diputació* was exclusively

[35] Archivo Histórico de Cervera. Varia. Instructions for syndics to *Corts* of 1626.
[36] Biblioteca de Catalunya, Barcelona. Ms. 979, fs. 66–70, *Diversos Discursos.*
[37] ACA, G, 78/4, *Llibre de habilitacions.*

the preserve of those who belonged to the principality's ruling class. Moreover, its decisions tended to be dictated by a particular segment of that class. When royal officials were alleged to have committed some grave illegality, the *Diputats* would summon a meeting of the *braços* or estates. These nominally consisted of all those qualified to attend the *Corts,* except that the *braç reial* was represented on these occasions solely by the city of Barcelona, and that the *braç militar* included Barcelona's *ciutadans honrats.* Since meetings were inevitably held at short notice, they were attended only by those who happened to be in or near Barcelona at the time, and, as a result, the Barcelona oligarchy enjoyed a preponderant voice in any decisions taken. These decisions might involve formal protests to the viceroy, the sending of a special embassy to Madrid, and, as a last resort, the taking of sanctions against the royal officials involved. The conduct of the principality's relations with Madrid therefore resided in the hands of a very small group; and there was enough evidence to suggest, both to the ministers in Madrid and to the principality at large, that this group was not overscrupulous in its administration of the great financial resources of the *Diputació*, nor in preserving the distinction between its own interests and those of the Catalan nation.

In the *Diputació*, then, the ruling class possessed a powerful institution for checking the advance of royal power. But, quite apart from *Diputació, Corts* and all the other various legal and institutional devices conveniently ready for use, it could also employ less obvious methods for ensuring that its interests were not flouted and over-ruled. There were, for instance, grandees and influential ministers at court who had close ties with the Catalans and were willing to put in a word on their behalf. There were two Catalan regents in the Council of Aragon – a body which, by its very composition, was likely to pay considerable attention to the interests of those it governed. In addition, the viceregal administration itself was far too closely associated with the principality's ruling class to act as a blind instrument of royal authority. Many judges in the *Audiència* were themselves drawn from prominent Catalan families; and viceroys despaired of obtaining either secrecy or complete impartiality from a tribunal whose members were so closely connected by kinship or friendship with the provincial aristocracy.[38]

As a result, the king needed the greatest political skill if he were to extend his authority over the principality by any means other than naked force. At every turn he found himself baulked by laws and institutions which drastically curbed the exercise of royal power. His officials were few and unreliable, and were obstructed by a provinc-

[38] ACA, CA, leg. 273, núm. 14, Bishop of Urgell to King, 31 Oct. 1626.

ial aristocracy possessing many privileges and great influence. The Count of Oñate's comment during the *Corts* of 1632 that its members were trying to transform the principality 'virtually into a free republic under Your Majesty's protection'[39] was not far short of the truth. To all appearances, the Catalan ruling class held all the trumps.

Yet appearances were, in some respects, deceptive. While the ruling class had ample opportunties for doing very much what it wanted, its capacity to make the most of these opportunties depended on its attaining a wide measure of agreement as to what exactly it really wished to do. This presupposed a sense of direction and of common purpose which proved, in practice, to be sadly lacking.

The ruling class was at least united in its determination to keep the royal power at arm's length. In this respect it fulfilled a function of extreme importance in preserving Catalonia's national identity and its contractual relationship with its ruler at a time when these were seriously threatened by an authoritarian government in Madrid. However much the ruling class may be accused of acting solely to further its own selfish ends, those ends were frequently so closely identified with the preservation of Catalonia's historic constitutional character as a state with real traditions of political liberty, that the aristocracy should receive at least some credit for its success in keeping constitutionalism alive at a time when this was threatened all over Europe by the advance of royal power. Moreover, as a Dutch historian has pointed out in a protest against the tendency to label sixteenth-century revolts against absolutism as inevitably conservative and mediaeval, 'particularism was the only weapon that the municipal and provincial regents had at their disposal in order to guarantee local interests against royal centralism.'[40] This was as true of Catalonia as it was of the Netherlands.

But if the preservation of constitutionalism can be duly marked in the credit column of the provincial aristocracy, there is also a list of debits to be placed on the other side. There are many indications in later sixteenth- and seventeenth-century Catalonia of deep popular resentment against the aristocracy. A 'constitutionalism' which gave landowners enormous powers and privileges naturally seemed the very antithesis of liberty to those whom they oppressed. The anxiety of villages to exchange baronial for royal jurisdiction is itself a suggestive sign: government by royal official was much to be pre-

[39] ACA, CA, leg. 278, núm 23, Oñate to King, 2 June 1632.
[40] J.W. Smit, 'The present position of studies regarding the revolt of the Netherlands', *Britain and the Netherlands*, ed. J.S. Bromley and E.H. Kossmann (London, 1960), p. 27.

ferred to government by 'little lords and barons who usually tyrannize over them and gnaw them down to the bone with unjust taxes.'[41] But hopes of escaping from baronial jurisdiction were generally disappointed. Lawsuits were expensive and endlessly protracted, and Catalan barons, like those of Naples,[42] seem on the whole to have been extending their jurisdiction – sometimes by purchase from a needy crown and sometimes by usurpation.[43]

As long ago as 1883 a Catalan historian made the illuminating suggestion that the late sixteenth and early seventeenth centuries saw a recrudescence of the social struggles of the fifteenth century.[44] Indeed it may well be legitimate to speak of a 'new feudalism', both fiscal and judicial, in seventeenth-century Catalonia. The widespread agrarian unrest of the time may partially have been a response to an extension of baronial power and to a new harshness shown by barons and landlords in their dealings with vassals and tenants – although so little is known of Catalan rural life that this can be no more than a hypothesis. But the great explosion of anger against aristocracy and municipal oligarchies during the revolutionary year 1640, is itself the clearest possible indication of widespread hatred of a ruling class which had exploited the principality's laws and institutions in order to buttress its own privileged position in the body politic.

The latent hostility to the ruling class, symbolized by the bonfires lit by the vassals of Don Joan Terés, Archbishop of Tarragona, when they heard the news of his death,[45] provides an interesting comparison with the unrest in the French countryside in the 1630s and 1640s. Professor Mousnier has convincingly shown that the unrest cannot summarily be dismissed as a simple struggle of oppressed vassals against their 'feudal' lords.[46] On the contrary, the lords were the best defenders of the peasants against fiscal oppression by agents of the crown, and the bonds between peasantry and aristocracy were strong. But in Catalonia, unlike France, there was no direct taxation by royal officials. Taxation, which was indirect, was managed by officers of the *Diputació*; and, at least in the first half of the

---

[41] Archives du Ministère des Affaires Etrangères, Paris. Corresp. Espagne Supplément no. 3, f. 265, *Advertissement donné ou Roy*...(1643).

[42] Alfred von Reumont, *Die Carafa von Maddaloni* (Berlin, 1851), 1, pp. 142–53. Of the 1973 communes in the kingdom of Naples in 1586, 1900 were listed as being under feudal jurisdiction, and only 69 under the jurisdiction of the crown, so that the position was even more serious than it was in Catalonia. I owe this reference to the kindness of Professor H.R. Trevor-Roper.

[43] E.g. Cervera was complaining of usurpations by local barons in 1609 (ACA, CA, leg. 484 Petition from the town of Cervera).

[44] José Pella y Forgas, *Historia del Ampurdán* (Barcelona, 1883), p. 722.

[45] ABL, *Dietari* de Pujades (1601–5), f. 178.

[46] 'Recherches sur les soulèvements populaires en France avant la Fronde', *Revue d'Histoire Moderne et Contemporaine* (1958), pp. 81–113.

seventeenth century, the taxes paid by Catalans to the crown were very light. Consequently, the Catalan aristocracy did not appear in the countryside as the protector of the peasantry against royal oppression, and this must have done much to reduce that sense of a real community of interest which to some extent in France softened the harsh lines of social division.

It was indeed the lack of a sense of responsibility towards the community at large which most characterized the Catalan ruling class in this period. There was very little in the political structure of the Spanish Monarchy to give provincial aristocracies a sense of corporate purpose that extended beyond the protection of their own sectional interests, and the Catalan aristocracy provides a striking example of the results of this vacuum. Things might have been very different if Charles V and Philip II had deliberately fostered among their various territories some sense of unity and of service to a common ideal, or even if they had engaged in a frontal assault on their liberties. But, as it was, the creation of a Spanish Monarchy meant no more to the Catalans than the departure of their native prince from their soil. It did not, for over a century, present them with an obvious threat to their national survival; nor, on the other hand, did it offer them glorious new opportunities. With a few exceptions Catalan nobles and gentry were not drawn into the service of the kings of Spain. A few of them served in the Spanish army in Flanders and Milan, and one or two may have studied in a Castilian university,[47] but it seems that the majority had never travelled beyond the borders of their native province. Such education as they received at home, at the aristocratic college of Cordelles in Barcelona or at the very inadequate university of Lleida, apparently did little to widen their horizons. Castilian plays and literature had become fashionable in Barcelona, and a section of the ruling class was gradually assimilating Castilian culture and learning to express itself in Castilian turns of phrase. But there is very little sign of real cultural interests, or even of any awareness of the intellectual trends of the times. 'Really', remarked an exasperated Olivares, 'the Catalans ought to see more of the world than Catalonia'[48] – although he failed to add that his predecessors in Madrid had given them little inducement to do so.

The narrow parochialism of the ruling class, its lack of outlets and opportunities for service, inevitably drove it in upon itself, with sad

[47] The numbers seem very small. For the year 1599–1600 I can find in the list of the law-students at Salamanca no more than a dozen Catalans, of whom only one was a noble (Archivo de la Universidad de Salamanca, *Matrícula*, 1599–1600).

[48] *Segrédos públicos* (Lisbon, 1641) Appendix. Olivares to Count of Santa Coloma, 29 Feb. 1640.

consequences for the principality as a whole. The solidarity and cohesion that came from the intermingling of aristocracy and upper bourgeoisie and from the absence of any sharp distinction of rank, rapidly dissolved in the enervating political atmosphere of the sixteenth century. Lacking anything better to do, the provincial aristocracy of Catalonia, like that of Sicily,[49] consumed itself in internal feuds. Since the later Middle Ages, two rival factions had existed in the principality: the *nyerros* and the *cadells*. The feud between them seems to have flared up with renewed ferocity in the late sixteenth and early seventeenth centuries. There were long and bloody vendettas between rival families, and the more lawless nobles like Joan Cadell, *senyor* of Arsèguel, and Don Alexandre d'Alentorn, *senyor* of Seró, moved round the country with armed bands of retainers, and gave shelter in their castles to the outlaws and bandits who kept the principality in a state of turmoil during the first half of the reign of Philip III. 'They say that the *caballeros* here are free', wrote the Castilian Marquis of Almazán, viceroy of Catalonia in the years when banditry was mounting to a climax. 'But in my opinion they are more oppressed than those of Castile, because they cannot go out of a town without a large number of men, whereas I could travel from Madrid to Almazán alone, or with a single servant, without being afraid of anyone. That is what I call freedom, and not what passes for freedom in Catalonia.'[50]

While the ruling class was split by family feuds into warring factions, it also seems to have been divided by an increasing differentiation between the urban and the rural aristocracy. The poorer gentry, finding that 'they could not command in the cities with reputation and authority' had 'retired to the mountains abashed.'[51] Here they remained immune from the civilizing influence of the towns, and looked with mingled jealousy and contempt upon the more fortunate of their number who possessed town houses, had married into bourgeois wealth, and acquired bourgeois ways. Uneasily aware that they were condemned to live out their lives in their own 'little corner of land',[52] they attempted to compensate for the decline in their prestige and status by vigorous and often brutal assertion of their authority over the peasantry and villagers in the countryside.

It was these rural gentry who played a prominent part in the bandit movement which swept the principality in the first fifteen years of

[49] Koenigsberger, *Government of Sicily*, p. 99.
[50] Jaime Villanueva, *Viage literario a las iglesias de España* (Valencia, 1821), 7, pp. 130–134. Almazán to Provincial Council of Tarragona, 1613.
[51] *Súplica de... Tortosa* (Tortosa, 1640), f. 30.
[52] Gilabert, *Discursos*. Discurso, 1, f. 11.

the seventeenth century.[53] This movement brought them into direct conflict with the interests of the towns, which found their livelihood threatened by the lack of security on the roads. Although the urban oligarchies had their own links with the bandit gangs, the clash between town and country was sufficiently sharp to divide the ruling class; and the Duke of Alburquerque, viceroy from 1616–19, was quick to exploit the division. His achievement in restoring order to the principality is primarily to be explained by his skilful creation of an alliance between the urban oligarchies and the viceregal administration.

Alburquerque's success showed how fragile was the solidarity of the Catalan ruling class, and how easily its innate divisions could be exploited by skilful ministers of the crown. At moments of crisis, as in the conflict of 1622–3 over the appointment of a viceroy,[54] appeals to self-interest and a careful distribution of bribes were capable of winning over the most inveterate opponents of royal authority, and of breaking what at first sight appeared to be the solid opposition of a united ruling class. So long as the viceroys of Catalonia were able to divide, they could also expect to rule. But, in the twenty years between the departure of Alburquerque and the outbreak of revolution in 1640, the opportunities to exploit division were thrown away. The tactlessness and intransigence of Alburquerque's successor as viceroy, the Duke of Alcalá, destroyed in three short years the hopeful alliance of the administration and the towns; and eighteen years of government by Olivares, with his constant threats to the financial resources of Barcelona and his notorious hostility to provincial rights and liberties, completed the alienation of the Catalan ruling class from the Spanish crown. But, in spite of the policies of Madrid, the break, when it came, was reluctant, and was effected, for the most part, with a notable lack of enthusiasm. During the 1630s, the municipal oligarchy of Barcelona, while vigorous in the defence of its privileges, showed as great a determination to avoid a break with Philip IV as did the city of London, under similar provocation, to avoid a break with Charles I.[55] This is all the more striking in that Barcelona, unlike London, was not the home of the court, and the financial and commercial interests of the oligarchy were not closely

[53] It will be seen from this that Catalan banditry conformed to the general pattern of Mediterranean banditry, enjoying aristocratic support, as described by Professor Braudel (*La Méditerranée et le Monde Méditerranéen à l'époque de Philippe II*, Paris, 1949, pp. 655 ff.). For Italian parallels, see Giuseppe Coniglio, *Il Viceregno di Napoli nel Sec. XVII* (Rome, 1955), pp. 17–19 and Jean Delumeau, *Vie Economique et Sociale de Rome dans la seconde moitié du XVIᵉ siècle*, 2 (Paris, 1959), p. 543.
[54] For this controversy, see chapter 6 of my *The Revolt of the Catalans*.
[55] See Valerie Pearl, *London and the Outbreak of the Puritan Revolution* (Oxford, 1961).

involved with those of the king. The rupture with Madrid came only when the popular revolt against the *tercios* was getting out of hand; when the *Diputats* and a small group of determined men had taken the fateful step of opening negotiations with France; and when the majority of the ruling class, faced on the one hand with popular revolution and on the other with the intransigence of Madrid, saw itself left with no alternative but to follow where a few of its more resolute members led.

For a few moments, then, in 1640, the ruling class found itself united, if only in a common movement of revulsion against the principal ministers of the King of Spain. This itself was a marked contrast to the hopeless divisions of 1615, when the political ambitions of a discontented noble like Don Alexandre d'Alentorn had consumed themselves in sterile banditry. The leaders of the generation of 1640 – Claris and his friends – displayed a greater degree of political sophistication than their predecessors in the generation of 1615.[56] They were skilful enough to turn an admittedly favourable international situation to their own advantage, and to carry the ruling class into an alliance with France. They showed a greater awareness of their obligations to the community than had been shown twenty-five years before. At a crucial moment in the history of Catalonia, they made effective use of the principality's laws and institutions to preserve its national identity intact.

But this achievement of 1640 proved to be short-lived. The concept of a 'Catalan republic' turned out to be but a shadowy ideal, and any fleeting sense of corporate unity and purpose was soon destroyed by a resurgence of the faction struggles which had bedevilled the country in the past. After the fall of Olivares, the government in Madrid was able to exploit these divisions, and to win back the allegiance of a class which had been terrified by the spectre of popular revolution, and which found to its cost that the King of France was no more to be trusted than his brother of Spain. With the return of the principality to Spanish control by the end of 1652, and with the renewed promise of Philip IV to observe its constitutions, the *status quo* of the pre-revolutionary era was unobtrusively restored. The ruling class had discovered, by bitter experience, that its interests were best served by continued membership of a Spanish Monarchy in which it had never felt itself really at home.

The Catalan ruling class, while it possessed marked characteristics of its own, was not unique. It had its counterparts in Aragon and

[56] I am grateful to Professor Vicens Vives for making this point to me.

Valencia, Sicily and Portugal,[57] and therefore a study of its character and of its relations with the government in Madrid can help to throw light on the way in which a large empire was governed and preserved.

At first sight, its grievances were many. It was the constant lament of provincial aristocracies that not enough favours flowed their way. Aragonese, Catalans, Portuguese, all complained that they were deprived of the presence of their prince, and that offices, pensions and favours were the exclusive preserve of the privileged aristocracy of Castile. Yet, for all the sense of bitterness and neglect, an actual rupture with Madrid was surprisingly rare. The ruling class of the northern Netherlands, under the skilful leadership of William of Orange, eventually brought itself to renounce its allegiance to the King of Spain; and the Portuguese ruling class, after a brief union of sixty years, followed suit in 1640. Otherwise, the Monarchy held fast. It even managed to survive the revolutionary movements of the 1640s, which for a moment seemed to portend its total disintegration. In the event, however, neither Naples nor Sicily nor Catalonia was permanently lost: the erring sheep returned to the fold.

The history of the Catalan ruling class hints at the reasons for the Monarchy's survival. Disgruntled and neglected as it was, it none the less found continuing association with the Spanish crown preferable to any of the possible alternatives. Partly the maintenance of royal authority was desirable because it helped to preserve a social order essentially favourable to aristocratic privilege, as it also helped to preserve territorial integrity in a world of warring powers. But there was perhaps a deeper reason. Paradoxically, the greatest strength of the Monarchy lay in its very weakness. It was precisely because the 'centralized' Spanish Monarchy was *not* effectively centralized that provincial aristocracies could look upon continuing government by the King of Spain as a tolerable prospect. However many orders might issue from Madrid, viceregal administrations were incapable of carrying them out without the assistance of the local governing class. Even if Madrid should employ all the resources of patronage at its disposal to divide and break the opposition, a provincial aristocracy – as the Catalans showed – possessed innumerable devices for evading or sabotaging the measures it disliked. Government in the Spanish Monarchy therefore remained a compromise: a compromise

---

[57] The position in Spain's American possessions was in some respects different, since the crown, no doubt with its European experiences in mind, was at least partially successful in preventing the establishment of an aristocracy enjoying the same powers and privileges as the aristocracies of the Old World. See Richard Konetzke, 'La formación de la nobleza en Indias', *Estudios Americanos*, 3 (1951), pp. 329–59.

which was generally less favourable to the government than to the governed. And, as they basked in a freedom which was not, alas, graced by frequent manifestations of royal favour, most provincial aristocracies sooner or later became dimly aware that there was after all at least something to be said for an absentee king.

V

REVOLUTION AND CONTINUITY
IN EARLY MODERN EUROPE

Of all the debates which have agitated historians during the past few years, none has been more lively, or less conclusive, than the great debate surrounding what has come to be known as 'the general crisis of the seventeenth century.' While dissenting voices have been raised here and there,[1] the current fashion is to emphasize the more turbulent characteristics of the age. It was in 1954, which seems in retrospect to have been an unusually crisis-conscious year, that Professor Roland Mousnier published a general history of sixteenth-and seventeenth-century Europe, in which the seventeenth century was depicted as a century of crisis, and especially of intellectual crisis.[2] In the same year, Dr. Hobsbawm, in an article which now stands as the classic formulation of the 'general crisis' theory, argued that the seventeenth century was characterized by a crisis of the European economy, which marked a decisive shift from feudal towards capitalist organization.[3] Since then, Professor Trevor-Roper, with one eye on the political revolutions of the 1640s, and the other on Dr. Hobsbawm, has produced a uniquely personal interpretation of the seventeenth century as an age of crisis for the 'Renaissance State'.[4]

It is, I think, striking that three such distinguished historians, of very different views and persuasions, should have united in depicting the seventeenth century in such dramatic terms. They all represent some aspect of the age – whether economic, intellectual or politi-

---

[1] Many of the contributions to the debate are to be found reprinted in *Crisis in Europe, 1560–1660*, ed. Trevor Aston (London, 1965). For expressions of dissent, see E.H. Kossmann, 'Trevor-Roper's "General crisis" ', *Past and Present*, no. 18 (Nov., 1960), pp. 8–11; A.D. Lublinskaya, *French Absolutism: The Crucial Phase, 1620–1629* (Cambridge, 1968); and I. Schöffer, 'Did Holland's Golden Age coincide with a period of crisis?', *Acta Historiae Neerlandica*, 1 (1966), pp. 82–107. Dr. Schöffer's admirable article, of which I was unaware when I originally drafted this essay, makes a number of points which coincide closely with my own.

[2] *Les XVIe et XVIIe Siècles* (Paris, 1954).

[3] Aston, *Crisis in Europe*, pp. 5–58.

[4] *Ibid.*, pp. 59–95.

cal – in terms of discontinuity, in the sense either of a change of direction or a change of pace. The change, too, is a violent one, as the use of the words 'crisis' and 'revolution' suggests. But the crisis of one historian is a chimera to another, and the consensus collapses as soon as attempts at definition begin.

It is not my intention now to embark on the daunting task of reconciling the irreconcilable. Nor do I intend to examine the evidence for and against an interpretation of the seventeenth century as an age of economic and intellectual crisis. Instead, I have chosen to concentrate on the narrower, but still, I think, important question of the 'political' revolutions of the middle years of the century – those revolutions which (in Professor Trevor-Roper's words) 'if we look at them together...have so many common features that they appear almost as a general revolution.'[5]

The revolts and upheavals which may be held to constitute this 'general revolution' have frequently been listed: the Puritan Revolution in England, flanked by the revolts of Scotland and Ireland; the insurrections in the Spanish Monarchy – Catalonia and Portugal in 1640, Naples and Palermo in 1647; the Fronde in France between 1648 and 1653; the bloodless revolution of 1650 which displaced the *stadtholderate* in the Netherlands; the revolt of the Ukraine from 1648–54; and a string of peasant risings across the continent. Nor should we disregard the plea of Professor Michael Roberts that 'if we are really determined to bring the Cossacks and the Ironsides within the scope of a single explanation,' we should not 'leave Sweden out of the reckoning.'[6] For did not the year 1650 see a dangerous social and constitutional crisis in the troubled realm of Queen Christina?

This clustering of revolts was a subject of fascinated concern to contemporaries, who saw them as part of a great cosmic upheaval; and it has frequently been commented upon by historians. It is thirty years now since Professor R.B. Merriman published his *Six Contemporaneous Revolutions*. But for Merriman the six revolutions afforded 'an admirable example of the infinite variety of history.'[7] Since the 1950s, however, the tendency has been to emphasize their similarities rather than their differences; and the concept of a 'general revolution' of the 1640s has effectively come to influence the history of seventeenth-century Europe only in our own generation.

Not the least of the attractions of a 'crisis' interpretation of the seventeenth century to our own age, is that it offers the possibility of a unified conceptual approach to a complex period. It has, too, the

[5] *Ibid.*, p. 59.
[6] *Ibid.*, p. 221.
[7] Published Oxford, 1938, p. 89.

additional advantage of plausibility, with that dramatic decade of the 1640s to bear witness to the turbulence of the times. Opinions may vary about the long-term consequences of the revolutions. Not everyone, for instance, would agree with Professor Trevor-Roper[8] that the seventeenth century 'is broken in the middle, irreparably broken, and at the end of it, after the revolutions, men can hardly recognize the beginning.' But there would probably be a fairly general measure of agreement with his view that 'the universality' of revolution in the seventeenth century pointed to 'serious structural weaknesses' in the European monarchies – weaknesses which gave rise to revolutionary situations.

Whether these weaknesses were more or less serious at this moment than in preceding generations, need not at present concern us. All I wish to do for the time being is to draw attention to the way in which the argument is couched. It is the 'universality' of seventeenth-century revolution which points to structural weakness. This argument from universality underlies most of the theories about the 'general crisis' of the seventeenth century. Six contemporaneous revolutions (at a minimum count) – does not the very number and pervasiveness of revolutionary movements suggest a moment of unique gravity, and a crisis of unique proportions, in the history of Early Modern Europe?

But supposing this unprecedented epidemic of revolutions was not, after all, unprecedented.... Let us look back for a moment to the sixteenth century, and in particular to the decade of the 1560s. 1559-60, revolt in Scotland, culminating in the abdication of Mary Queen of Scots in 1567; 1560, revolt of the Vaudois against Emmanuel Philibert, duke of Savoy; 1562, outbreak of the French civil wars; 1564, revolt of the Corsicans against Genoa; 1566, the beginning of the revolt of the Netherlands; 1568, revolt of the Moriscos of Granada; 1569, the Northern Rebellion in England. Seven 'contemporaneous revolutions'; and perhaps I may be allowed to anticipate Professor Roberts and plead that the rising of the Swedish dukes against Eric XIV in 1568, and his subsequent deposition, should not be overlooked.

This sudden rash of revolts would hardly have come as a surprise to that doughty professional rebel John Knox, who was able to announce reassuringly to Mary Queen of Scots in 1561: 'Madam, your realm is in no other case at this day, than all other realms of Christendom are.'[9] But while contemporaries seem to have felt that they

[8] Aston, op. cit., pp. 62 and 63.
[9] John Knox's History of the Reformation in Scotland, ed. W.C. Dickinson, 1 (London, 1949), p. 367.

were witnessing the beginnings of a general conflagration, or what Calvin called 'Europae concussio',[10] I am not aware that any historian has grouped them together under the title of 'the general revolution of the 1560s', or has used them as evidence for a 'general crisis of the sixteenth century.'[11]

Perhaps it is not unreasonable to speculate for a moment on the possible reasons for this apparent discrimination in the treatment accorded the seventeenth century. Merriman seems to have been led to his six contemporaneous revolutions partly by his study of seventeenth-century political histories, and partly by the preoccupation of the 1930s with the possibility of a coming 'world revolution'. He was also influenced by the example of 1848, which gave him the opportunity to draw parallels and comparisons. His principal concern was to consider the relationship of the various revolutions to each other, and his principal conclusion from a study of the 1640s and the 1840s, was that 'national rivalries proved stronger than the virus of revolution' – an encouraging conclusion, no doubt, in the circumstances of the 1930s.[12]

Merriman's approach to the seventeenth-century revolutions by way of diplomatic history was of little interest to historians of the post-war generation. But he had bequeathed them a magnificent subject, ready for exploitation. In the context of the post-war historiography of Early Modern Europe, exploitation proved easy enough. The French economist Simiand had taught Early Modern historians to see the sixteenth century as an age of economic expansion, and the seventeenth as a century in which expansion was first halted, and then, around 1650, succeeded by a slump. Given the existence of a major reversal of economic trends in the middle years of the century, Merriman's contemporaneous revolutions seemed both relevant and suggestive. Here, surely, were the social and political manifestations of a crisis affecting the entire European economy. Had his revolutions been those of the 1560s rather than those of the 1640s – the products of an age of expansion rather than of an age of contraction – they might have attracted less attention. Yet even assuming that we can legitimately speak of a general crisis of the European economy in the

[10] R. Nürnberger, *Die Politisierung des Französichen Protestantismus* (Tübingen, 1948), p. 91 n. 57.

[11] The links between the Huguenot and the Dutch revolts have, of course, received considerable attention, especially from nineteenth-century historians. Cf. in particular Kervyn de Lettenhove, *Les Huguenots et Les Gueux*, 6 vols. (Bruges, 1883–5). See also H.G. Koenigsberger, 'The Organization of Revolutionary Parties in France and the Netherlands', *Journal of Modern History*, 27 (1955), pp. 335–51, which draws interesting parallels between the organization of the revolts in France, the Netherlands and Scotland.

[12] Merriman, *op. cit.*, pp. 209 and 213.

mid-seventeenth century – and the evidence, though impressive, is not conclusive – it seems odd that the assumed relationship between economic crisis and political revolution has gone unquestioned. Why should we ignore for the seventeenth century De Tocqueville's perception that revolution tends to come with an improvement rather than with a deterioration of economic conditions?

But the decisive element in the concentration of interest on the revolutions of the 1640s is clearly the supreme importance attributed to the Puritan Revolution in England, as the event which precipitates the collapse of Europe's feudal structure and the emergence of a capitalist society. If the Puritan Revolution is seen as the essential prelude to the Industrial Revolution, it is obvious that a constellation of revolutions benefiting from its reflected glory, is likely to outshine any other in the revolutionary firmament. This, at least, seems to be the attitude of the Soviet historian, Boris Porshnev. His Fronde is a bourgeois revolution *manquée*. 'It was', he writes, 'a French variant of the English bourgeois revolution which was breaking out on the other side of the Channel, and a distant prologue of the French Revolution of the eighteenth century.' He presents the sixteenth-century civil wars, on the other hand, as a combination of feudal quarrels and popular insurrections.[13] Yet, given the upsurge of revolt in the towns of the Ligue in 1588, it is not easy to see any intrinsic reason why the French civil wars should not also be categorized as a bourgeois revolution *manquée*. But perhaps the Ligueurs lacked a progressive ideology.

A contest in the revolution stakes between the 1560s and the 1640s does not seem in itself a particularly profitable enterprise. But it does give rise to a larger and more important question – the question of our general conception of revolution, and its applicability to the study of Early Modern Europe. Here the distinction between Marxist and non-Marxist historian dwindles in importance. The language of our age is pervasive – so pervasive that Professor Mousnier, after cogently criticizing Professor Porshnev for his interpretation of the Fronde in terms of class conflict, can refer to the English civil war, in his most recent book, as 'perhaps the first great bourgeois revolution of modern times.'[14]

Coming from the pen of a historian whose approach to the history of his own country is as staunchly anti-Marxist as that of Professor Mousnier, these words hint at the existence of what seems to be a

---

[13] Boris Porchnev [Porshnev], *Les Soulèvements Populaires en France de 1623 à 1648* (Paris, 1963), pp. 537, 17, 47.

[14] *Fureurs Paysannes* (Paris, 1967), p. 7.

central problem in the history of Early Modern European insurrections. We are all of us the children of our age, but in this particular
field of historical writing, the tricks of time have proved to be more
than usually deceptive. Between us and Early Modern Europe lies
the late eighteenth century, dominated for us by two events which
seem to have done more than anything else to shape our own civilization – the French Revolution and the Industrial Revolution in
England. During the nineteenth century, each of these became a
paradigm – an exemplar, in one instance, for political and social
development, and in the other for economic development. The
twentieth century has appropriated these paradigms from its predecessor, and continues to make use of them as best it can.

How far the current paradigm of the French Revolution actually
corresponds to what occurred in the course of that Revolution
has been a matter for fierce debate. But the paradigm has not been
confined to the French Revolution and the insurrections that have
succeeded it. Consciously or unconsciously, nineteenth-and twentieth-century historians have looked at revolts in Early Modern
Europe in the light of the late eighteenth-century revolutions, and of
their assessment of them. This has frequently provided them with
valuable insights into the origins of great events; but the very fact
that they applied to many of these Early Modern revolts the word
'revolution' suggests the possibility of unconscious distortions,
which may itself give us some cause for unease.

It is true that 'revolution' was by no means an unknown word in
sixteenth- and seventeenth-century Europe, as applied to upheavals
in states. A Spaniard looking back in 1525 on the revolt of the
Comuneros expressed his fear of a 'revolution of the people';[15] and
in 1647 and 1648 two Italians, Giraffi and Assarino, published accounts of recent insurrections, which they entitled 'The Revolutions'
of Naples and Catalonia.[16] But a close study of the concept of
'revolution' by Professor Karl Griewank has shown how slowly, and
with what uncertainty, the idea of revolution was brought down
from the heavens of Copernicus and applied with any precision to
the mutations of states.[17] Sedition, rebellion, *Aufstand*, mutation,
revolt, revoltment (John Knox)[18] – these are the words most commonly employed in sixteenth-century Europe. Gardiner's Puritan

---

[15] J.A. Maravall, *Las Comunidades de Castilla* (Madrid, 1963), pp. 243–4.
[16] A. Giraffi, *Le Rivolutioni di Napoli* (Venice, 1647); Luca Assarino, *Le Rivolutioni di Catalogna* (Bologna, 1648). See also Vernon F. Snow, 'The concept of revolution in seventeenth-century England', *The Historical Journal*, 5 (1962), pp. 167–74.
[17] *Der Neuzeitliche Revolutionsbegriff* (Weimar, 1955).
[18] Knox, *op. cit.*, 1, p. 193.

Revolution was Clarendon's Great Rebellion. Only towards the end of the eighteenth century, under the impact of events in America and France, did 'revolution' effectively establish itself in the European political vocabulary, and acquire those connotations by which we recognize it today.

These include the idea of a violent, irresistible and permanent change of the political and constitutional structure; a powerful social content, through the participation of distinctive social groups and broad masses of the people; and the urge to break sharply with the past and construct a new order in accordance with an ideological programme.[19] Modern historians, accustomed to expect these ingredients of a revolution, have instinctively sought to detect them in Early Modern revolts. Presuming the existence of social protest and class conflict, they have duly found them in the uprisings of the populace. Conditioned to look for minority parties scheming to subvert the state by violence, they have anatomized with great skill the techniques of revolutionary organization. Expecting of a revolution that it should have an innovating ideology, they have effectively isolated and explored the aspirations of those who sought to establish a new order on earth. The work which has been done along these lines has proved immensely fruitful. It has made us aware of motives and forces behind the movements of unrest which were largely veiled from the participants. It has told us things which we could never have known, or glimpsed only obscurely, about the patterns of political and social cohesion and the underlying causes of failure or success.

But it would be foolish to ignore the possibility that, in using a concept of revolution which is relatively recent in origin, we may unconsciously be introducing anachronisms, or focusing on certain problems which accord with our own preoccupations, at the expense of others which have been played down or overlooked. Some recognition of this is implied in recent discussions and debates, particularly on the question of the applicability of the idea of class conflict to Early Modern European society.[20] Although Professor Mousnier has insisted against Professor Porshnev that the popular uprisings in Richelieu's France were fomented by the upper classes and testified to the closeness of the relationship between the peasants and their lords, it would be unwise to disregard the evidence for the existence of fierce social antagonisms in Early Modern Europe. These found

[19] Griewank, op. cit., p. 7.
[20] See Mousnier, Fureurs Paysannes, p. 29, and also p. 322 n. 1 for reference to his debate with Porshnev. Further discussion of the question of class in Early Modern society may be found in R. Mandrou, Introduction à la France Moderne (Paris, 1961), pp. 138–64, and F. Mauro, Le XVIe Siècle Européen. Aspects Economiques (Paris, 1966), pp. 337–44.

expression at moments of unbearable tension – whether in the fury of the Neapolitan mobs in 1585,[21] or in the assault of the Catalan peasants and populace on the nobles and the rich in the summer of 1640.[22]

But it is one thing to establish the existence of social antagonisms, and another to assume that they are the principal cause of conflict. The Catalan rebels first attack royal officials and royal troops; and it is only after disposing of them that they turn on their own ruling class. A revolt may frequently have started, as in Catalonia, against the agents of the state, and then been transformed into a war on the rich. But the parallels between this and a modern class conflict cannot be automatically taken for granted, if only because the ordering of society in Early Modern Europe tended to militate against class solidarity. A society grouped into corporations, divided into orders, and linked vertically by powerful ties of kinship and clientage, cannot be expected to behave in the same way as a society divided into classes. Intense rivalries between guildsmen and non-guildsmen, and between the guilds themselves, helped to disrupt community action in urban revolts;[23] and it hardly seems a coincidence that one of the rare examples of a fair degree of urban solidarity is provided by the Comuneros of Castile, where guild organization was weak.

The applicability of the modern notion of ideology to Early Modern revolts seems equally open to question. If by ideology we mean 'a specific set of ideas designed to vindicate or disguise class interest',[24] the uncertainties about 'class' in Early Modern Europe must also be extended to 'ideology'. If we employ it more loosely to mean simply the programme of a particular movement (and this is presumably the way in which it is employed by most western historians), there still remain large unanswered questions about the extent to which it faithfully represents the character of the movement as a whole. To talk, for instance, of Calvinism as the ideology of the Dutch rebels, is to ascribe to the rebellion as a whole, a series of ideals and aspirations which we know to be those of only a small minority – and a minority whose importance may well have been inflated, simply because they are the group whose ideals correspond most closely to our notions of what an ideology should be.

Perhaps our principal expectation of a revolutionary ideology is that it should break with the past and aspire to establish a new social

---

[21] R. Villari, *La Rivolta Antispagnola a Napoli* (Bari, 1967), p. 44.

[22] J.H. Elliott, *The Revolt of the Catalans* (Cambridge, 1963), pp. 462–5.

[23] For a classic example, see Gene A. Brucker, *Florentine Politics and Society, 1347–1378* (Princeton, 1962), p. 55.

[24] A. Gerschenkron, *Continuity in History and Other Essays* (Cambridge, Mass., 1968), p. 65.

order. In a society dominated, as Early Modern European society was dominated, by the idea, not of progress, but of a return to a golden age in the past, the best hope of finding an ideology of innovation lies in certain aspects of the Christian tradition. In particular, the chiliastic doctrines of later medieval Europe look forward to the coming of a new age on earth – the age of the Holy Ghost, characterized by a new social and spiritual order. Up to a point, therefore, it is possible to see the Bohemian Taborites of the fifteenth century as belonging to the tradition of revolutionary innovation by means of violent action. It is certainly arguable that the Taborites did in practice establish for themselves a society in which new forms of social and political organization predominated over the old.[25] But, on the other hand, the Taborites did not reject the traditional three-fold ordering of society; and although they were attempting to establish a new spiritual order on earth, the character of this order was determined by reference to the past – in this instance to the primitive church.

The same kind of difficulties are likely to bedevil attempts to bring religiously-inspired movements of the sixteenth century into the category of ideological innovation. The peasant movements in early sixteenth-century Germany, for all their millenarian and egalitarian aspirations, were still dominated by the desire to return to a past order, which was held to be eternally valid.[26] The same would also seem to be true of the Calvinist ideal of the advancement of the kingdom of God – an advancement which was anyhow to be achieved by the winning of the state authorities to the cause, rather than by the action of the revolutionary masses.[27]

Even if we dignify – or debase – these religious aspirations with the name of 'ideology', it would be misleading to see them as providing a programme of action appealing to the majority of the participants in Early Modern revolts. The Taborites, the Anabaptists and the Calvinists all singularly failed to win anything like universal acceptance of their ideas; and it is not clear why we should regard them as speaking with the true voice of the movements to which they belong, unless it is because they happen to be the most articulate. With our ears straining to catch one particular theme, there is always a danger that, amidst the general uproar, other notes and other voices will go unheard. This danger is not always recognized with such clarity, or expressed with such candour, as it has been by Michael Walzer, in his reference to the English sectaries:

[25] H. Kaminsky, *A History of the Hussite Revolution* (Berkeley, 1967), pp. 481 ff.
[26] Griewank, *op. cit.*, p. 102.
[27] Nürnberger, *Die Politisierung*, pp. 19–21.

'However important they are to latter-day genealogists, the sects (even, the Levellers) are of very minor importance in seventeenth-century history.'[28]

Doubts of this kind might profitably be extended. A fuller recognition of the degree to which our own thinking about revolutions is affected by preconceptions derived from the nineteenth century, might at least enable us to isolate more effectively those points at which distortions are most liable to occur. If we accept this possibility, a number of uncomfortable questions about our method and our approach may suggest themselves. I have already hinted at one such question: how far can historians accustomed to look for *innovation* among revolutionaries, enter into the minds of men who themselves were obsessed by *renovation* – by the desire to return to old customs and privileges, and to an old order of society? How far, too, has our preoccupation with violence as an essential ingredient of revolution concentrated attention on the agitators and the organizers, at the expense of the more passive and the less committed? For all the brilliance of Calvinist organization in the Netherlands, it is arguable that the fate of the revolt was determined elsewhere – by the great mass of people whose religious affiliation was lukewarm or indeterminate,[29] and by those stolid burghers of Holland and Zealand, who edged their way with such extreme caution along the precipitous path that divided loyalty from rebellion.

Most of all, it is open to question whether our persistent search for 'underlying social causes' has not let us down blind alleys, and has concealed from us more profitable ways of approach. I speak here, as in so much else, as one of the errant wanderers. Not that I would claim to have received some sudden illumination on the road to Damascus. It is simply that the constant reading of modern accounts of sixteenth- and seventeenth-century insurrections is likely in due course to induce a weariness of the spirit, and to provoke a certain critical questioning. While it is clear that all the major upheavals in Early Modern Europe represent a combination of different revolts, animated by different ideals and reflecting the aspirations of different groups, it is less clear why 'social' revolts should be regarded as in some way more 'fundamental'. Nor is it clear why we should be expected to assume that the outbreak of revolt in itself postulates structural weaknesses in society. Political disagreement may, after all, be no more and no less than political disagreement – a dispute about the control and the exercise of power.

---

[28] *The Revolution of the Saints* (London, 1966), p. x.
[29] See J.W. Smit, 'The present position of studies regarding the revolt of the Netherlands', *Britain and the Netherlands*, ed. J.S. Bromley and E.H. Kossmann (London, 1960), pp. 23–5.

An age as acutely attuned as ours to the distress signals of the poor and the starving, may be correspondingly less sensitive to the cries of the more fortunate for freedom from arbitrary power. The innumerable peasant revolts – the *soulèvements populaires* – which are now being analysed in such painstaking detail, provide a terrifying revelation of the misery in which most of Europe's population lived. But we should not, I believe, be afraid to ask the apparently brutal question: did they make any difference? Or, indeed, *could* they make any difference, in a world in which technological backwardness had at least as much to do with the condition of the populace as exploitation by an oppressive ruling class? And if we conclude that they could and did make a difference, we should then go on to determine the precise areas in which that difference was made.

If we can recognize that contemporary preconceptions about the nature of revolution may have helped to shape our treatment of Early Modern revolts, we are at least in some position to attempt remedial action. Our priorities, for instance, can be set against those of contemporaries, in an attempt to discover which of theirs have receded into the background, or have come to be overlooked. It is a salutary experience to watch the development of the French civil wars through the sharp eyes of Estienne Pasquier, whose evaluation of events is that of an intelligent and well-read sixteenth-century layman. 'There are three things', he wrote, 'of which one should be infinitely afraid in every principality – huge debts, a royal minority, and a disturbance in religion. For there is not one of these three which is not sufficient of itself to bring mutation to a state.'[30]

No doubt Pasquier's analysis is inadequate, even by contemporary standards. His historical analogies were essentially political, and he set the unfolding drama of conflict in France into the context of famous faction feuds. 'Two miserable words of faction, Huguenot and Papist, have insinuated themselves amongst us', he wrote in 1560; 'and I fear that in the long run they will lead us to the same calamities and miseries as the Guelfs and Ghibellines in Italy, and the White and the Red Rose in England.'[31] But this was not an unreasonable assessment of events from the standpoint of 1560; and if he omitted the social and economic considerations – the discontents of the gentry, the social consequences of rising prices – which loom so large in modern accounts of the French wars, this does not necessarily mean that he was unaware of their influence on events. Pasquier and his contemporaries were capable enough of seeing the existence of a relationship between political and social grievance. It

[30] *Lettres Historiques (1556–1594)*, ed. D. Thickett (Geneva, 1966), p. 100.
[31] *Ibid.*, p. 47.

was in the degree of significance to be accorded to this relationship that a sixteenth-century approach diverges most sharply from our own. An age which has devoted itself to meticulous research into the fortunes of nobles and gentry is likely to find something almost comically casual about the words which Joachim Hopperus slips into his account of the origins of the Dutch revolt: 'Several of the principal leaders were at this time very heavily burdened with debts. This is sometimes considered a source of unrest and attempted innovation, since such people hope to take advantage of disturbances in the state to re-establish their fortunes.'[32]

But it may be that we have been equally casual in our approach to what contemporaries themselves regarded as important: Pasquier's 'royal minorities', for instance, and indeed the whole question of kingship. It is now almost impossible for us to grasp the degree to which changes in the character of kingship affected the dispositions of power in the state. In societies where all the threads of patronage ultimately come to rest in the hands of the king, any of the accidents and hazards to which hereditary kingship is prone, are likely to have profoundly disturbing consequences. The apparent turbulence of politics in the 1560s may therefore not be entirely unrelated to a remarkably high mortality rate among monarchs in the preceding decade, and the accession of new and inexperienced rulers, some of whom were women or children. Similarly, if a comparison is to be made between the histories of France and Castile, it does not seem entirely irrelevant to consider how far Castile's immunity from rebellion after 1521 is to be ascribed to a high degree of social stability, and how far to the accident that it escaped royal minorities and the baneful presence (except for a short period in the reign of Philip IV) of adult cadet princes.[33]

There is, however, another area in which most modern historiography seems to have been even less at home, and with far more considerable consequences. The search for the causes of discontent is nowadays more likely to lead to religious or social grievance, than to a sense of national loyalty. Yet the apparent uncertainty of modern historians when faced with the question of nationalism in Early Modern Europe stands in marked contrast to the increasingly confident use in the sixteenth century of the words *patria* and *patrie*. When the Corsican leader, Sampiero Corso, turned to Catherine de

---

[32] J. Hopperus, 'Recueil et Mémorial des Troubles des Pays Bas', *Mémoires de Viglius et d'Hopperus sur le commencement des Troubles des Pays Bas*, ed. A. Wauters (Brussels, 1868), p. 237.

[33] It is significant that Olivares was greatly exercised by the problem of how to educate and employ the Infantes Don Carlos and Don Fernando, and complained of the lack of precedents to guide him: British Library, Egerton MS. 2081 f. 268, *Papel del Conde Duque sobre los Infantes*.

Médicis for help in the early 1560s to free his native island from Genoese domination, she presented him with a number of banners bearing the heroic inscription: *pugna pro patria*.[34] The rebels of Ghent in 1578 not only spoke of defending their *patrie,* but also referred to themselves as *patriotes*.[35] The lawyers and judges in the reign of Charles I gained a reputation with parliament of being 'good patriots';[36] and Masaniello, the hero of the Neapolitan revolt of 1647, was hailed as *liberator patriae*.[37]

It is possible that, in approaching these apparent manifestations of patriotic sentiment, we have again been both influenced and inhibited by our nineteenth-century inheritance. 'The Commonwealth', wrote Lord Acton, 'is the second stage on the road of revolution, which started from the Netherlands, and went on to America and France. . . .'[38] For all the qualifications introduced by Acton himself, there was a strong temptation to look at Early Modern revolts through the lens of the French Revolution, interpreted this time in accordance with the liberal-national tradition. The modern reaction against the historiographical excesses of this tradition is natural enough. But the manifestations of some kind of community consciousness in Early Modern revolts are too numerous and too forceful to allow the question of nationalism to be left in a kind of historical limbo.

There are obvious difficulties about attempting to equate these various manifestations with a nationalism of the nineteenth-century variety. All too often a supposed allegiance to a national community turns out, on inspection, to be nothing of the kind. The *patria* itself is at least as likely to be a home town or province as the whole nation,[39] and a revolt, like that of the Dutch, which is represented in nineteenth-century historiography as a nationalist uprising, may just as convincingly be depicted as a manifestation of particularist, rather than nationalist, sentiments.[40]

Yet even though *patria* might apply in the first instance to a native city, it could at times be extended, as in the Castile of the Comuneros,[41] to embrace the entire community of the realm. But whether the community was local or national, expressions of allegi-

[34] A. De Rublé, *Le Traité de Cateau-Cambrésis* (Paris, 1889), p. 77.

[35] G. Malengreau, *L'Esprit particulariste et la Révolution des Pays-Bas au XVIe Siècle* (Louvain, 1936), p. 82 n. 4.

[36] T. Hobbes, *Behemoth,* ed. F. Tönnies (London, 1889), p. 119.

[37] A. Giraffi, *An Exact Historie of the late Revolutions in Naples* (London, 1650), p. 160.

[38] *Lectures on Modern History* (London, 1907), p. 205.

[39] Cf. the description of Barcelona as his *pàtria* by Pujades (Elliott, *Catalans,* p. 42).

[40] As it is by G. Malengreau, *L'Esprit Particulariste*. . . .

[41] Maravall, *Las Comunidades,* p. 55. See also G. Dupont-Ferrier, 'Le sens des mots "patria" et "patrie" en France au Moyen Age et jusqu'au début du xviie siècle', *Revue Historique,* 188 (1940), pp. 89–104.

ance to it assumed the same form: a deep and instinctive antipathy to outsiders. Throughout the Early Modern period, this antipathy was a powerful driving-force behind popular revolt. It moved the Corsican peasants in the 1560s to take up arms against the Genoese, and the Catalan peasants in 1640 to take up arms against the Castilians. *Visca la terra* – long live the land! – is the perennial cry of the Catalan populace as it turns out, to the summons of the church bells, to attack the bands of Castilian soldiers making their way to their embarkation-point at Barcelona.[42]

This popular nationalism figures prominently in the accounts of revolts written by nineteenth-century historians, who were themselves so often the products of a Romantic culture nurtured on the legends and the songs with which the deeds of the rebels were kept alive in folk memory. But in idealizing it, they helped to discredit it, and oversimplified a complex phenomenon. What was often, at its least attractive, no more than an instinctive hatred of outsiders, was transmuted into a self-conscious identification with a national community, embodying certain specific ideals. But the Romantic historians were not totally mistaken in assuming the existence in Early Modern Europe of some such sense of identification, although they may have expected too often to find it expressed even at the very lowest social levels. For alongside the more obvious manifestations of popular sentiment, there was also to be found another phenomenon, which has yet to receive the attention and the analysis it deserves. This might perhaps best be described as a corporate or national constitutionalism; and while it may have reached down, in some form, to the lower levels of society, it was essentially the preserve of the dominant social and vocational groups in the state – nobles and gentry, urban patriciates, the lawyers, the clergy, the educated.

Perhaps it may be defined as an idealized conception of the various communities to which allegiance was owed; and it embraced, in ever-widening circles, the family and vocational community to which they belonged, the urban or provincial community in which they lived, and ultimately, and sometimes very hazily, the community of the realm. This idealized conception of the community was compounded of various elements. There was first, and most naturally, the sense of kinship and unity with others sharing the same allegiance. But there was also a sense of the corporation or community as a legal and historical entity, which had acquired certain distinctive characteristics with the passage to time, together with certain specific obligations, rights and privileges.

---

[42] Elliott, *Catalans*, p. 253.

The community was founded on history, law and achievement, on the sharing of certain common experiences and certain common patterns of life and behaviour. As such, it was an ideal – indeed an idealized – entity, already perfect in itself. It was, though, for ever subject to attacks from enemies, and to erosion at the hands of time. The highest obligation incumbent upon its members was therefore to ensure that in due course it should be transmitted intact to their successors. The plea for the faithful fulfilment of this obligation echoes right through the history of Early Modern Europe, from the Florentine who urged his fellow-citizens in 1368 to 'leave to posterity that which was left to us by our ancestors',[43] to the Catalan canon who begged his brother canons in 1639 not to 'let us lose in our own time what our forbears have so bravely won.'[44]

The sixteenth century seems to have contributed a new sophistication and a new awareness to the sacred task of defending a community whose rights and liberties were embodied in written constitutions and charters, and kept alive in the corporate memory. In particular, it engaged with enthusiasm in legal and historical research. The great revival of interest in the customary law – a revival symbolized in France by the names of Bodin and Hotman – [45] not only provided new defences against arbitrary power decked out with the trappings of Roman Law, but also helped to establish the idea that each nation had a distinct historical and constitutional identity.[46] By endowing the community with a genuine or fictitious constitution, set firmly into a unique historical context, the sixteenth-century antiquarian movement gave new meaning to the struggle for the preservation of liberties. The corporation, the community, the *patria* all acquired a firmer identity as the historical embodiment of distinctive rights.

The idea of the *patria* was also fostered by the new humanist education. A governing class which had imbibed the history of Greece and Rome from an early age would have no great difficulty in making an identification between its own idealized community and the polities of classical antiquity.[47]

[43] Brucker, *Florentine Politics*, p. 396.

[44] Elliott, *Catalans*, p. 344.

[45] Julian H. Franklin, *Jean Bodin and the Sixteenth-Century Revolution in the Methodology of Law and History* (New York, 1963), esp. ch. 3.

[46] Ralph E. Giesey, *If Not, Not* (Princeton, 1968), p. 245. On the general question of constitutionalism, see in particular J.G.A. Pocock, *The Ancient Constitution and the Feudal Law* (Cambridge, 1957) and Michael Roberts, 'On Aristocratic Constitutionalism in Swedish History', *Essays in Swedish History* (London, 1967). I have also greatly benefited from discussions on this subject with Mr. Quentin Skinner of Christ's College, Cambridge, who kindly read an early draft of this essay and made valuable comments on it.

[47] For the influence of classical polities on seventeenth-century English thought, see Zera S. Fink, *The Classical Republicans* (Evanston, 1945).

There were [says Hobbes in the *Behemoth*] an exceeding great number of men of the better sort, that had been so educated, as that in their youth having read the books written by famous men of the ancient Grecian and Roman commonwealths concerning their polity and great actions; in which books the popular government was extolled by the glorious name of liberty, and monarchy disgraced by the name of tyranny; they became thereby in love with their forms of government. And out of these men were chosen the greatest part of the House of Commons.

The core of rebellion, as you have seen by this, and read of other rebellions, are the Universities...

The *Universities* have been to this nation, as the wooden horse was to the Trojans.[48]

Until a great deal more research has been done on education in Early Modern Europe, it is impossible to determine what degree of importance should be attached to Hobbes' angry denunciations. But the intellectual influences which went to shape the conception of their own community among the governing classes of Europe, are obviously a matter of the greatest interest, since it was the idealized community or the *patria* which gave them the frame of reference by which they determined their own actions and assessed those of others. In *The Community of Kent and the Great Rebellion*, Professor Everitt has shown how the political behaviour of the dominant groups in Kentish society between 1640 and 1660 can only be understood in the light of their intense devotion to an idealized local community. While the gentry of Kent included convinced royalists and parliamentarians among their number, the principal aim of the majority was to 'stand for the defence of the liberties of their unconquered nation' against assaults from either camp.[49]

This devotion to an idealized community can be paralleled all over Europe, on a local, a regional, and a national scale. Everywhere, the instinct of the ruling classes was to preserve a heritage. While in some instances this heritage might become indissolubly bound up with religious loyalties, the preservation of a heritage seems to have outweighed every other cause, including that of religion, in its appeal to the majority of the ruling nation. 'If religion be not persuaded unto you', wrote the Lords of the Congregation to the nobility, burghs and community of Scotland in 1559, 'yet cast ye not away the care ye ought to have over your commonwealth, which ye see manifestly and violently ruined before your eyes. If this will not

---

[48] *Op. cit.*, pp. 3, 58, 40.
[49] Published Leicester, 1966, p. 269.

move you, remember your dear wives, children and posterity, your ancient heritages and houses....'[50]

Eloquent appeals for action in defence of laws and liberties were obviously likely to carry additional conviction when the arbitrary power that threatened them was also an alien power. In Scotland, Corsica and the Netherlands in the 1560s, in Catalonia and Portugal in the 1640s, the rebels found it easier to rally support, because the oppression came from foreign rulers, foreign officials and foreign troops on native soil. In these circumstances, a revolt originally sparked by religious protest, or sectional discontents, was capable of gathering support and momentum by combining in a common patriotism the constitutionalism of the privileged classes and the general antipathy to the outsider felt by the population at large.

This combination almost always proved fragile and transitory, because the idea of a national community to which all sections of society owed their prime allegiance, was still so weakly developed. The national community was shot through with rival allegiances, and riven by sectional and social hatreds. Moreover, the constitutionalism of the privileged was all too often no more than a convenient device for defending the interests of an exclusive caste on the basis of bogus history and bogus law. Yet, in recognizing this, one must also recognize that the defence of liberties could, in certain circumstances, broaden into the defence of liberty; and that the pursuit of sectional advantage was not necessarily incompatible with the furtherance of a genuinely constitutional cause. For all its obvious deficiencies, constitutionalism provided the political nation with an ideal standard against which to measure current realities. Once this ideal standard existed, it was always capable of extension by a leader of political genius. The *patrie*, as glimpsed by William of Orange, was something more than a society in which the rights and liberties of the privileged were safe from the exercise of arbitrary power. It was also a society which included freedom of conscience among its liberties; an essentially open society, in which men were free to come and go and educate themselves without restrictions from above.[51]

Given the existence of an idealized vision of the community, however restricted that vision, movements of protest are likely to occur within the political nation when the discrepancy between the image and the reality comes to seem intolerably wide. In Early Modern Europe it is these movements of protest from above, and not the popular uprisings, which are capable of leading to a 'mutation in the state'. The problem, though, is to relate them to other

[50] Knox, *op. cit.*, 1, p. 225.
[51] *Apologie ou defense de...Prince Guillaume* (Leyden, 1581), esp. p. 91.

manifestations of discontent, simultaneous or complementary, which have their origin in religious, fiscal or social grievances among the general population. 'Then is the danger', as Bacon appreciated, 'when the greater sort do but wait for the troubling of the waters among the meaner, that then they may declare themselves.'[52] But it is impossible to establish here any common pattern of revolt. In the Netherlands of the 1560s an aristocratic movement benefited from simultaneous movements of religious and patriotic protest. But the aristocratic movement was halted in its tracks by the popular uprising – the iconoclastic fury – of August 1566. In Catalonia in 1640 the popular uprising, provoked by the behaviour of foreign troops, encouraged the leaders of the political nation to seize the initiative, and to transform a long-standing movement of protest into a decisive break with the crown. In the England of the 1640s, it was only *after* the political nation had seized the initiative, and then itself split down the middle, that the people began to move. In Naples in 1647 the popular movement failed to evoke an effective response among the dominant social classes, and doomed itself to destruction.

In states displaying such varieties of political and social organization great variations in the pattern of revolt are only to be expected. There will always be men bold enough, angry enough, or frightened enough to seize the opportunity afforded by an upsurge of popular fury or by a sudden weakening of the state. The crucial question then becomes the attitude adopted by the mass of the uncommitted among the ruling class. Will they rally behind the crown and the agents of royal authority in an emergency, or will they allow the leaders of the insurrection to have their way? The answer is likely to depend on a delicate balance between the ruling class's persistent fear of social upheaval, and its feeling of alienation from the crown. In the Netherlands in 1566, for example, the political nation rallied to the government of Margaret of Parma when social upheaval threatened it. But in 1572, after five years of repressive government by the Duke of Alba, it had become so alienated from a régime which had launched an assault on its liberties, that it adopted a position of neutrality when the emergency came. The same is true of the Catalan political nation in the summer of 1640: the extent to which it had been alienated from Madrid by the policies of Olivares over the past twenty years was sufficient to prevent it making any serious move to check the course of the revolt. In Naples, on the other hand, the nobles and gentry, for all their discontents, had remained closely associated with the viceregal administration, which had bribed them

---

[52] 'Of Seditions and Troubles', *The Works of Francis Bacon*, ed. J. Spedding, 6 (London, 1858), p. 411.

with favours and privileges because it needed their help in mobilizing the resources of Naples for war. This association made them the immediate objects of popular hatred in 1647; and they had nothing to gain from breaking with a régime which had shown itself more responsive to their interests than any that was likely to replace it.[53]

If the 1560s and the 1640s prove to be decades of more than usual unrest in Europe, it does not seem a coincidence that they were both periods in which the traditional loyalty of ruling classes to their princes had been subjected to very considerable strain. In both decades, several states were still engaged in, or were only just emerging from, a long period of warfare which had imposed heavy demands on national resources. In both decades, too, there was deep discontent among the ruling classes over the prevailing style of government. In the 1560s resentment was focused in particular on the rule of secretaries and professional civil servants: Cecil in England, Persson in Sweden,[54] Granvelle in the Netherlands. In the 1640s, it was focused on the rule of favourites – Strafford, Richelieu, Olivares – all of whom had shown a degree of political ruthlessness which was all the more objectionable because, as nobles, they had been traitors to their kind.

At a time when there was already something of a coolness between the crown and the political nation, the situation was aggravated in both periods by signs of unusually energetic activity on the part of the state. In the late 1550s or early 1560s, the state's preoccupation with religious dissidence as a threat to its own authority had made it exceptionally vigorous in its employment of counter-measures. These brought the central power into conflict with sectional interests and those of local communities, and aroused widespread disquiet about the infringement of rights and liberties. In the 1630s and 1640s the main thrust of state power was fiscal rather than religious, but the consequences were not dissimilar. The financial demands of the state brought it into direct conflict with important sections of the political nation, which expressed its discontent through its representative institutions, where these still existed, and through the tacit withdrawal of allegiance.

In these circumstances, a group of determined rebels is well placed to make the running. The crown, and those sections of the governing class immediately dependent upon it, finds itself temporarily isolated. The privileged and propertied classes hold aloof, or lend their sympathy and support to the rebels. But in practice the rebels

---

[53] The extent of the crown's concessions to the Neapolitan nobility, and the political consequences of this policy, emerge very clearly from R. Villari, *La Rivolta Antispagnola*. . . .

[54] Michael Roberts *The Early Vasas* (Cambridge, 1968), p. 224.

have very little time at their disposal. Not only do their actions give rise to new feuds and vendettas, but a society which thinks essentially in terms of restoration is likely to baulk at measures which smack of innovation. 'From the beginning of the rebellion', wrote Hobbes, 'the method of ambition was constantly this: first to destroy, and then to consider what they should set up.'[55] Rebels who contrived to give this impression were bound to alienate the body of uncommitted but conservative opinion in a political nation which was anyhow terrified that its own internal disputes would place power in the hands of the populace.

Rebels, therefore, could not count on continuing support from within the ruling class. Their movement, too, was likely to have only a narrow social base in a vertically articulated society. In the circumstances, they were bound to be driven back on alternative sources of help – and these could only come from outside. Merriman, with world revolution at the back of his mind, was impressed by the lack of cooperation between rebel régimes in different states. But much more impressive is the extent to which rebels sought, and secured, foreign assistance at vital stages in their revolts. Foreign aid, in fact, seems to have been an indispensable requirement for any revolt, if it were to have a chance of perpetuating itself. It was English military assistance which enabled the Scottish rebels to triumph in 1560. It was the French, the Germans and the English who saved William of Orange and the Dutch. It was the support of foreign Protestant or Roman Catholic powers which gave an additional lease of life to the rebel factions in France. In the 1640s, the story was the same. The Scots came to the help of the English, the French to the help of the Catalans, the French and English to the help of the Portuguese.

The dependence of Early Modern revolts on external assistance suggests something of their character and their limitations. Sometimes they were furthered, sometimes impeded, by popular uprisings; but these were ephemeral movements, which could achieve little or nothing without assistance from groups within the ruling class. The prime aim of this class was to conserve and restore; and this aim at once determined the scope of the rebels' action, and the extent of their support. A ruling class alienated from the crown by encroachment upon its liberties was prepared to let royal authority be challenged, and this allowed the rebels such successes as they in fact achieved. But once the heritage had been saved, the political nation reverted to its traditional allegiance, and those rebels who chose to persist in rebellion were compelled to look abroad for help.

[55] *Behemoth*, p. 192.

The sixteenth and seventeenth centuries did indeed see significant changes in the texture of European life, but these changes occurred inside the resilient framework of the aristocratic-monarchical state. Violent attempts were made at times to disrupt this framework from below, but without any lasting degree of success. The only effective challenge to state power and to the manner of its exercise, could come from within the political nation – from within a governing class whose vision scarcely reached beyond the idea of a traditional community possessed of traditional liberties. But this proved to be less constricting than it might at first sight appear. Renovation in theory, does not of itself preclude innovation in practice; and the deliberate attempt to return to old ways may lead men, in spite of themselves, into startlingly new departures. There remained, too, sufficient room for the ruling class to be able to challenge the state at the two points where its activities were most likely to influence the character of national life. By resisting the state in the matter of taxation, it might destroy, or prevent the establishment of, a major obstacle to economic development; and by resisting its claims to enforce religious uniformity, it might remove a major obstacle to intellectual advance. If significant change came to certain European societies in the sixteenth and seventeenth centuries, it came because this challenge was effectively carried through.

By the eighteenth century, the growing awareness of man's capacity to control and improve his environment would make it more fashionable than it had been in the seventeenth century to think in terms of innovation. At this point the character of revolt would also begin to change; and rebellion might come to assume the characteristics of revolution. Until then, revolts continued to be played out within the context of the ambitions of the state on the one hand, and the determination of the dominant social groups to preserve their heritage, on the other. If this determination came to be expressed in an increasingly sophisticated language, this was because the political nation itself was becoming more sophisticated. National constitutionalism learnt the language of law, of history and antiquity. Perhaps, then, it is to the rise of a literate and educated lay establishment, not to the rise of new social classes, that we should look if we are to understand the eventually decisive achievement of Early Modern revolts – the transformation of liberties into liberty. That one man, at least, guessed as much, we can see from the dialogue of the *Behemoth*:[56]

[56] *Ibid.*, p. 71.

B. For aught I see, all the states of Christendom will be subject to these fits of rebellion, as long as the world lasteth.

A. Like enough; and yet the fault (as I have said) may be easily mended, by mending the Universities.

VI

FOREIGN POLICY AND DOMESTIC CRISIS: SPAIN, 1598-1659

In his *Ragion di Stato*, first published in 1589, nine years before the death of Philip II, Giovanni Botero asks 'whether it is a greater task to extend or preserve a state'. His answer is unhesitating: 'Clearly it is a greater task to preserve a state, because human affairs wax and wane as if by a law of nature, like the moon to which they are subject. Thus to keep them stable when they have become great and to maintain them so that they do not decline and fall is an almost superhuman undertaking. Circumstances, the weakness of the enemy and the deeds of others all play a considerable part in conquest, but only most excellent qualities can hold what has been conquered. Might conquers, but wisdom preserves.'[1]

Botero's maxim became the conventional wisdom for those who succeeded to the inheritance of a king commonly regarded as a by-word for political prudence. The Spanish Monarchy – the *monarquía española* – as inherited by Philip III in 1598 was, in terms of its extension and military might, the greatest power in the world, and therefore the supreme test of statesmanship for those in charge of its policies became its conservation. 'It is an established fact in politics that good government is still more strikingly revealed in knowing how to conserve than in acquiring more', the Portuguese merchant, Duarte Gomes, reminded the Duke of Lerma in 1612. For this, 'much prudence is required.'[2]

The reminder was hardly necessary. The men responsible for the management of Spain's foreign policy in the first half of the seventeenth century were acutely aware of their responsibility to preserve intact a cherished inheritance temporarily entrusted to their safe keeping. They were imbued with a deep pride in that inheritance,

---

[1] Giovanni Botero, *The Reason of State*, Eng. trans. P.J. and D.P. Waley (London, 1956), pp. 5–6 (Book 1, 5).

[2] Duarte Gomes, 'Carta para el Duque de Lerma escrita en Lisboa a 12 de Deziembre 1612', *Discursos sobre los comercios de las dos Indias* (1622), ed. Moses Bensabat Amzalak (Lisbon, 1943), p. 239.

and placed themselves in a historical tradition which saw the Spanish Monarchy as surpassing in power and grandeur its glorious predecessor, the empire of ancient Rome. This gave them, at least in the eyes of their foreign contemporaries, an intolerable arrogance. But behind the confident facade there lurked a certain insecurity. As successors to the Roman empire they could hardly forget its fate. They knew that states, like every living organism, were subject to the process of rise and decline; and, while many of them shared the providentialist vision of Fray Juan de Salazar, who declared in his *Política española* of 1619 that 'the Spanish people is like the Hebrew, in that it is the chosen people of God',[3] they could never quite escape the uneasy feeling that through their own shortcomings they might forfeit their privileged status, and so condemn themselves to that same organic process of decline which only divine decree could set aside. As a result, they approached the world with a wary defensiveness, conscious that the ambitions of others and their own failings might at any time destroy their precious inheritance.

A defensive mentality, however, does not necessarily imply a defensive posture. Attack may, after all, be the best form of defence. We should not therefore necessarily expect to see a foreign policy establishment in the Spanish Monarchy consistently committed to the purely passive policy of holding the line. On the contrary, periods of caution – dictated either by 'prudence' or circumstance, or a combination of the two – might well alternate with periods of dynamic activism, in which Spanish foreign policy was perceived by non-Spaniards as an attempt to secure 'universal monarchy' by open aggression rather than by the subtle and underhand methods in which Spain's diplomats were believed to be uniquely skilled. These external perceptions of Madrid and its intentions often bore very little relation to the perceptions that Spain's imperial ruling class held of its own situation and that of the Monarchy. In periods of restraint and activism alike, it tended to be animated by a siege mentality which took it for granted that all the world was Spain's enemy, and that only supreme political skill could avert a fatal erosion of its global primacy.

On the death of Philip II in 1598 such a reading of the international scene did not seem entirely misplaced. If Philip's policy in the Mediterranean had successfully consolidated Spain's hold over Italy and kept the Turks at bay, there was much less room for optimism as the new government of Philip III surveyed northern Europe. It was true that heresy had not triumphed in France, but a former heretic

---

[3] Fray Juan de Salazar, *Política española* (1619), ed. Miguel Herrero García (Madrid, 1945), p. 88.

was now on the French throne, and the peace of Vervins of 1598 was a tacit recognition of the failure of Philip II's interventionist policies. In the Netherlands, a massive expenditure of men and money had failed to crush heresy and rebellion, while the England of Elizabeth remained a continuous threat to the shipping lanes which linked Spain to northern Europe and to the silver of the Indies. The first priority of the Duke of Lerma's regime was therefore to complete the unfinished business of the late king, and to ensure the defeat of Spain's northern enemies before they could subvert Catholic Europe and Spain's transatlantic system.

In spite of a major commitment of resources to the northern struggle in the opening years of the reign, the effort simply proved too great for an exhausted Castile and a royal treasury close to bankruptcy. The peace with England in 1604 and the Twelve Years' Truce with the United Provinces of the Netherlands in 1609 were a direct consequence of financial, economic and psychological exhaustion. Little is known about the motivation of Lerma's foreign policy; but while it is possible that his own inclinations were for peace, it was an acccumulation of pressures, culminating in the royal bankruptcy of 1607, that forced upon him a temporary peace which many outside the magic circle of power regarded as profoundly humiliating for a King of Spain.

With its widely scattered global interests, the Spanish crown was always faced with conflicting choices, and it is possible that Lerma's alleged 'pacifism' reflects at least in part a desire to reorder Spain's priorities. It was difficult, if not impossible, to sustain dynamic 'northern' and 'Mediterranean' policies simultaneously for any length of time, and Lerma may well have been planning to pay more attention to the Mediterranean theatre, where the activities of Algiers pirates were becoming an increasingly serious menace.[4] His concern at the revival of French power under Henry IV may also have encouraged him to seek a respite from the unsuccessful and costly war against the Dutch. France, after all, was the traditional enemy, and a truce with the United Provinces was a prudent insurance policy at a time when a new confrontation of the two crowns was beginning to look unpleasantly close.

The assassination of Henry IV in 1610 not only averted this confrontation, but also created new opportunities for Spain to reassert its European preeminence without resort to war. The sudden lifting of the French threat and the reluctance of the regency government of Marie de Médicis to pursue a bellicose foreign policy gave the gov-

[4] R.A. Stradling, *Europe and the Decline of Spain. A Study of the Spanish System (1580–1720)* (London, 1981), pp. 41–2.

ernment of Philip III a welcome breathing-space. The ensuing years were preeminently to be the years of the *pax hispanica,* when it seemed that Spainsh diplomats, assisted by Spanish money, and by pro-Spanish cliques operating in the principal European courts, were subtly ensnaring one state after another in their gigantic spider's web with its centre at Madrid.[5]

If Lerma, however, succeeded in trapping France – the choicest prize of all – in his spider's web with his policy of royal marriages, he did so at the expense of the tradition which gave the relationship between Madrid and Vienna priority over all other alliances. By identifying himself with a pro-French, rather than pro-Austrian, foreign policy, he made himself more vulnerable to the attacks of his enemies at court, where Austrian influence remained strong in spite of the death of Queen Margarita in 1611.[6] These enemies could point to a rapidly lengthening list of failures on the part of his regime: corruption, maladministration, and the crying neglect of pressing economic and financial problems at home; and weakness and humiliation abroad, symbolized by the Dutch truce of 1609, the discreditable Italian settlement at Asti in 1615, and the growing perception of looming crisis in central Europe, where Spain's ambassadors were urging Madrid to lend support to the Austrian Habsburgs before it was too late.

In its final years before his fall from power in 1618, the Duke of Lerma's torpid regime was being engulfed by a rising tide of activism. The leading activists were Spain's representatives in foreign parts – military men, viceroys, ambassadors – who chafed at the restraints imposed on them by a slow-moving and hesitant administration in Madrid, and looked back with growing nostalgia to the age of Philip II in which they had spent their youth and early manhood. Such men as Don Pedro de Toledo in Milan, the Duke of Osuna in Naples, Don Baltasar de Zúñiga in Prague, were acutely conscious of the decline that had overtaken the 'reputation' of Spain and Spanish power since the days of Philip II. They believed, with some justification, that 'reputation' was itself an important weapon in the conduct of diplomacy, and that a successful assertion of power in one theatre of operations would have beneficial results in all the others, and prove to the world that Spain had not lost the martial qualities which had given it its global preeminence. They also believed that such an assertion of power was long overdue, and that

[5] For a survey of Spanish foreign policy under Philip III, see H. R. Trevor-Roper, 'Spain and Europe, 1598–1621', *The New Cambridge Modern History,* 4 (Cambridge, 1970), pp. 260–82.

[6] For the feud between Lerma and the Austrian Habsburgs, see María Jesús Pérez Martín, *Margarita de Austria, reina de España* (Madrid, 1961), and E. Rott, 'Philippe III et le Duc de Lerme', in *Revue d'Histoire Diplomatique,* 1 (1887), pp. 201–16, 363–84.

unless Madrid took prompt action, the enemies of Spain, the House of Austria and the Catholic cause would before long triumph throughout Europe. They therefore brought growing pressure to bear on Madrid to act decisively where Spanish interests were thought to be at stake, and were not above taking independent action of their own when the crown failed to issue the orders which they had urgently requested.

If any one event can be said to mark the transition from the quiescent Lerma epoch to the new activism that would distinguish Madrid's policies in the 1620s and 1630s, it was the return from Prague of Don Baltasar de Zúñiga to take up his seat on the Council of State in Madrid in July 1617.[7] Zúñiga, with his long first-hand acqaintance with the affairs of northern and central Europe, became the natural spokesman on the council for the 'Austrian' party, and, with them, for the activists. Profoundly convinced of the need to save the Emperor from the rising tide of heresy and subversion in the hereditary Habsburg lands, it was he who inspired and guided the hesitant process of Spanish intervention in Bohemia and central Europe between 1617 and 1621.[8] It has not yet been established what part, if any, foreign policy considerations played in the overthrow of Lerma in October 1618, but the repudiation of the favourite was preceded by the repudiation of the 'pacific' policies which had characterized his career in the eyes of his opponents.

It has been argued that the 'last great manifestation of Spanish imperialism', in the form of intervention in central Europe in the final years of the reign of Philip III, can be related to the upsurge of the Spanish Atlantic trade between 1616 and 1619, and the consequent influx of new wealth from the Indies.[9] But it is very hard to see how this argument can be sustained. At this moment of alleged prosperity the Council of Finance was constantly complaining about the acute shortage of money in the royal treasury, and it was in these last years of the reign that American silver remittances to the crown – the indicator that most mattered – slumped disastrously, falling to a low point of only 800,000 ducats in 1620, as against two million ducats a year at the beginning of the reign.[10]

[7] Peter J. Brightwell, 'The Spanish Origins of the Thirty Years' War', *European Studies Review*, 9 (1979), pp. 409–31. See p. 411.

[8] This process is examined by Peter Brightwell in his Cambridge University doctoral dissertation, 'Spain and the Origins of the Thirty Years War', and in the posthumously published articles taken from it.

[9] Pierre Chaunu, 'Séville et la "Belgique", 1555–1648', *Revue du Nord*, 42 (1960), pp. 259–92

[10] J.H. Elliott, 'América y el problema de la decadencia española', in *Anuario de Estudios Americanos*, 28 (1971), pp. 1–23, and *The Revolt of the Catalans. A Study in the Decline of Spain, 1598–1640* (Cambridge, 1963; repr. 1984), p. 189.

The Spanish decision to intervene in support of the Emperor cannot therefore be 'explained' in terms of any sudden new-found affluence. On the contrary, Philip III ordered the intervention in spite of the shortage of money: 'The provisions are so vital that the Council of Finance must find them. Germany cannot possibly be abandoned.'[11] We must therefore look elsewhere for the motivation behind Madrid's decision, and we are likely to find it primarily in the capture of the decision-making process by Zúñiga and by those who felt, like him, that the international situation was now so grave that only vigorous military action by Spain could save the Catholic cause and the House of Austria from disaster. But why should Zúñiga's view have prevailed at this particular juncture? It is in the attempt to answer this question that the nature of the relationship between foreign and domestic affairs between 1618 and 1621 is most likely to emerge.

Zúñiga's triumph can be attributed primarily to the coincidence between the development of a power vacuum in Madrid, and the growing perception of a gathering storm over Europe as the Bohemians took up arms against their Habsburg masters, and Spain's Twelve Years' Truce with the United Provinces approached its destined end in 1621. Lerma's hold over power was already slipping when Zúñiga returned to Madrid in 1617, and his replacement in the following year by his ineffectual son, the Duke of Uceda, only served to underline the continuing crisis of authority at the very centre of government. Zúñiga was the natural beneficiary of this crisis of authority, and worked in close collaboration with his nephew, the Count of Olivares, a gentleman in the household of Prince Philip, to turn it to his own advantage.

Zúñiga and Olivares, however, were also the beneficiaries of a changing national mood. The growing awareness of 'decline' – *declinación* – in the Castile of Philip III[12] had given rise to an increasingly vociferous movement for national reform and renewal. The demands expressed in the writings of the *arbitristas* for the application of specific remedies to cure a national sickness that threatened to be terminal, were being taken up by government officials, merchants, members of the urban patriciate, and the Cortes of Castile, all of them now clamouring for a general reformation – the reformation of morals and manners, of administration and the royal finances, of economic policies and attitudes, and of the inequitable and iniquitous structure of taxation in Castile and in the Spanish Monarchy at large.

---

[11] Elliott, *Catalans*, pp. 189–90.
[12] Below, ch. 11.

This domestic demand for reformation, which had become over-whelming by the time of Philip III's sudden death in March 1621, coincided with the demand of the foreign policy activists for a revival of Spanish military and naval power in an effort to restore Spain's authority in the world. Both demands were in reality the reflections of a single movement – a movement for the regeneration and restoration of a Spanish Monarchy which was perceived as being, both domestically and internationally, in a state of decline. The clamour for 'reformation' at home and 'reputation' abroad derived from the widely held assumption that the salvation of the Monarchy would come only through the restoration of values and virtues which has been eroded by the crimes and follies of the Lerma regime and the passage of time. Zúñiga and Olivares, on securing power on the accession of Philip IV in 1621, were able to capitalize on this assumption, and place themselves at the head of the movement for the restoration of Spain. A few days after being entrusted with the state papers by the new king, Zúñiga told the Genoese ambassador that the aim of the new administration was to 'restore everything to the state it was in during the reign of Philip II and to abolish the large number of abuses introduced under the recent government.'[13]

This yearning for the restoration of Spain's greatness and glory did much to determine the climate in which the major foreign policy deci-sions of 1618–1621 – the intervention in Germany and the decision to renew the war with the Dutch in the spring of 1621 – were taken by the Council of State. That climate is reflected in some of the rhetoric at council meetings, as when the Count of Benavente, in arguing for the resumption of active hostilities against the Dutch, insisted on the therapeutic effects of war, which would ensure that Spaniards did not lose their martial virtues and grow effeminate. 'Either we have a good war or we lose everything.'[14] But such rhetoric, although it may have helped to set a mood, constituted the trappings rather than the substance of the decision-making process. The policies of 1618–1621 were not the product of a sudden war psychosis, or the automatic reflexes of a group of councillors who saw their only escape from insoluble domestic problems in military adventurism abroad. On the contrary, Zúñiga and his colleagues seem to have weighed the arguments carefully before reaching their decisions.

To judge from the *consultas* of the Council of State, these decisions were based on a wide range of political, religious, economic and geo-strategic considerations, in a context of general pessimism about the international scene. The commitment to send military assistance to

[13] Cited J.H. Elliott, *The Count-Duke of Olivares* (New Haven and London, 1986), p. 82.
[14] *Ibid.*, p. 74.

the Emperor was reached by slow and hesitant stages, but grew out of the conviction that a successful revolt by Bohemia would be followed by the spread of heresy and subversion throughout the Empire and the Habsburg hereditary lands. The occupation in 1620 of the Valtelline and the Rhenish Palatinate reflected the Council's realization of the vital necessity of retaining control over the military corridors between Milan and Flanders, at a moment when the resumption of hostilities with the Dutch already appeared imminent.

The most critical of all the decisions – and one which, in all the essentials, was reached in the last months of the life of Philip III, before the advent of the Zúñiga-Olivares regime – was for the renewal of the war in the Netherlands. It was a decision reached only after agonized debate and wide consultation.[15] Zúñiga was too wise and experienced to imagine that at this late date there was any chance of ending the revolt of the Netherlands. 'To promise ourselves that we can conquer the Dutch is to seek the impossible, to delude ourselves', he told the secretary, Juan de Ciriza, in 1619.[16] The humiliating terms of the truce of 1609 were seen as a serious blow to Spain's reputation, and this certainly played its part in the decision. But it could also be shown that the truce had had disastrous consequences for Castile and the Spanish Monarchy as a whole, without bringing comparable advantages in the form of reductions in military and naval expenditure. The Dutch had taken advantage of the truce to penetrate the Portuguese colonial empire, with potentially grave repercussions for the delicate relationship between Castile and Portugal. The activities of Dutch merchants were subverting Castile's economy and its Atlantic trade. Dutch intrigue and Dutch money were aiding and abetting the enemies of the Roman Church and the House of Austria throughout the continent.

A strong case could therefore be made, and indeed was made, that the price of renewed war against the Dutch could hardly be higher than the high price of peace. No doubt 'sentimental' considerations also entered into the final decision. The emotional ties between Spain and the loyal provinces of the southern Netherlands were strong, based as they were on a shared loyalty to the same crown and the same faith, and fortified by a complex web of personal relationships and interests. Zúñiga's own wife, for instance, came from a Flemish noble family. Historians have yet to take account of this long-standing Spanish-Flemish connection, the ramifications of which still escape us, but it would be surprising if they played no part in

[15] Peter J. Brightwell, 'The Spanish System and the Twelve Years' Truce', *English Historical Review*, 89 (1974), pp. 270–92; Jonathan Israel, *The Dutch Republic and the Hispanic World, 1606–1661* (Oxford, 1982), ch. 2.

[16] Cited Brightwell, 'The Spanish System', p. 289.

reinforcing the commitment of successive Spanish regimes to the
continuation of the struggle in the Netherlands.[17] But it is hard to
imagine that Zúñiga, essentially a realist and something of a fatalist,
should have allowed himself to be swayed by considerations of this
kind. Essentially he seems to have calculated that, unless the Dutch
were promptly taught a lesson, the whole ordering of Europe on the
basis of a *pax austriaca* would be subverted, and the *monarquía española*
itself would be threatened with collapse.

The timing of his decision was determined largely by the ex-
piration date for the truce. But the continuing ineffectiveness of
French foreign policy, the defeat of the Bohemian rebels and Spain's
recent successes in the Valtelline and the Palatinate appeared to make
the moment unusually propitious. This was the time to restore Spain's
tarnished 'reputation', and make its king respected once again in the
world; for, as he is alleged to have said in the debate on the termina-
tion of the truce with the Dutch, 'in my view, a monarchy that has
lost its *reputación,* even if it has lost no territory, is a sky without
light, a sun without rays, a body without a soul.'[18] The insistence on
'reputation', however, was more than a mere flight of rhetorical
fancy. Zúñiga's policy objectives seem to have been carefully
calculated. His long-term aim was to bring the Dutch back to the
negotiating table and secure their approval for a peace settlement
shorn of the conditions that had made the truce of 1609 so humiliating to Spain – the virtual recognition of Dutch sovereignty, the
closure of the Scheldt, the resigned acceptance of their maritime and
commercial activities in the overseas empires of Spain and Portugal.
To achieve this goal he planned a judicious combination of psychological pressure – a healthy respect for the refurbished reputation of
Spanish arms – and military, naval and economic warfare, designed
to throttle Dutch trade, which he rightly saw as the foundation of the
Republic's successes. He also hoped to bring additional pressure to
bear on the Dutch by securing the military involvement of the
Empire in the Netherlands, once stability had been restored in
Germany. If the King of Spain had come to the Emperor's help
against his rebels in Bohemia, it was only right that the Emperor in
return should come to the King of Spain's help against *his* rebels in
the Netherlands.

The policy guidelines laid down by Zúñiga – an honourable peace
with the Dutch, and a settlement in Germany which would restore
the position of the Austrian Habsburgs without driving the Protes-

[17] J.H. Elliott, 'A Question of Reputation? Spanish Foreign Policy in the Seventeenth
Century', *Journal of Modern History*, 55, (1983), pp. 482–3.
[18] Juan Yañez, *Memorias para la historia de don Felipe III* (Madrid, 1723), p. 117.

tant principalities to seek a revenge born of despair – were to be appropriated by Olivares on his uncle's death in October 1622, and were to be tenaciously followed during his two decades of power. His foreign policy, like that of Zúñiga, remained resolutely 'Austrian', and its central axiom was that 'not for anything must these two houses [the Austrian and Spanish branches of the Habsburgs] let themselves be divided.'[19] Like Zúñiga he was deeply committed to the maintenance of *reputación*. 'I have always yearned', he told Philip IV in 1625, 'to see Your Majesty enjoying in the world an esteem and reputation comparable to your greatness and qualities – a glory that Your Majesty should esteem and strive for much more than to be the conqueror of new provinces and lordships. For, by God's mercy, Your Majesty already possesses many more than are needed to be the first prince in the world.'[20] The essence of the Count-Duke's foreign policy was therefore to conserve with reputation a world-wide Monarchy that was already large enough. In this sense it was, like the policies of his predecessors, essentially defensive in outlook; but the insistence on *reputacíon* meant that – whether in the Netherlands or elsewhere – peace and security could not be bought at the price of national honour.

During the 1620s the Count-Duke sought to combine his policy of *reputación* abroad with that other policy with which he and his uncle had identified themselves: *reformación* at home. The early 1620s were to be a period of intensive reforming activity, as the Count-Duke struggled to remove long-standing abuses and bring regeneration and renewal to Castile.[21] His reform programme, however strongly predicated on the determination to return to the virtues and values of the Castile of Philip II and the Catholic Kings, was in reality characterized by the realization that, if Castile and the Spanish Monarchy were to retain their primacy, they must adjust to the realities of international life in the highly competitive world of the seventeenth century. This was the lesson that the Count of Gondomar had learnt during his embassy in London: 'Warfare today is not a question of brute strength, as if men were bulls, nor even a question of battles, but rather of winning or losing friends and trade, and this is the question to which all good governments should address themselves.'[22] Power and prosperity, as the Dutch had shown, were intimately related.

The attempt to promote prosperity and translate it into power

[19] A(rchivo) G(eneral de) S(imancas) Est. legajo 2331, Olivares in Council of State, 10 Nov. 1630.
[20] AGS Est. legajo 2039, consulta, 29 June 1625.
[21] For Olivares' reform programme, see Elliott, *The Count-Duke*, ch. 5.
[22] *Ibid.*, p. 78.

would require far-reaching economic, military and institutional reform. It would be necessary to found trading companies on the model of the Dutch East India Company, and 'to direct all our efforts', in Olivares' words, 'to turning Spaniards into merchants.'[23] It would mean radical fiscal changes, a build-up of Spanish naval power, and a reorganization of the Monarchy's system of military defence. The demands of war and foreign policy, therefore – the need to compete with foreign rivals on an equal footing – served as a major incentive to reform in the Spain of the 1620s, and as a major stimulus to innovating change. For example, the Union of Arms, the scheme whereby all the kingdoms of the Monarchy should provide a fixed quota of paid men for the Monarchy's defence, was an ingenious attempt to rationalize its archaic military arrangements and mobilize its resources more effectively for war.

But if the desire for *reputación* was itself an important driving-force for *reformación,* it was an open question whether these two principal objectives of the Olivares' regime would prove in the long run to be compatible. A policy of *reputación* was bound to be expensive, and in consequence raise awkward questions of priority. Could Spain afford to continue more or less indefinitely to give assistance to the Emperor and fight the interminable war in the Netherlands? The answer was provided by some revealing words from the Marquis of Montesclaros, who – ironically – was president of the Council of Finance. 'The lack of money', he told his colleagues, 'is serious, but it is more important to preserve reputation.'[24] His words are a fair reflection of attitudes among royal ministers when questions of cost were involved. Those who were against some line of action would advance the argument that funds were too scarce to allow it. Those who supported it, on the other hand, would brush the financial arguments aside. A systematic study of the major foreign policy decisions in Habsburg Spain would almost certainy show that, while some calculation of resources was made, political and not financial considerations were the prime determinant of policy except on those rare occasions when the crown's bankers were simply unwilling, or unable, to make further funds available.

In the mid-1620s the Count-Duke seems to have hoped and believed that he could run *reformación* and *reputación* in double harness, making use of each to promote the other. The danger of a combined assault by Spain's enemies, for instance, was used as an argument in 1626 to urge the Cortes of the three states of the Crown of Aragon to

---

[23] John H. Elliott and José F. de La Peña, *Memoriales y cartas del Conde Duque de Olivares* (2 vols., Madrid, 1978–80), 1, p. 98.
[24] Cited J. H. Elliott, *Richelieu and Olivares* (Cambridge, 1984), p. 77.

join in the Union of Arms – a project which Olivares saw as the first stage in his cherished scheme for the creation of a genuinely unified Spanish Monarchy.[25] Reform at home and victory abroad would, in this way, be mutually reinforcing. The triumphs of that *annus mirabilis* of Spanish arms, 1625 – the surrender of Breda, the expulsion of the Dutch from Brazil, the rout of the English at Cadiz – suggested that such hopes were not entirely misplaced. But everything depended on the Count-Duke's capacity to translate victory into peace within a reasonable space of time; and 'universal peace with honour' – which he told the Council at the end of 1626 was his objective for 1627[26] – continued to elude him.

In retrospect, the years 1627–1629 seem to be the turning-point in the history not only of the Olivares administration but also of the attempts of Habsburg Spain to retain its European primacy.[27] They are also years in which the interplay of domestic and foreign policy proves more than usually complex. 1627 began with a major financial convulsion, the first royal 'bankruptcy' of the reign of Philip IV. The suspension of payments to the crown's Genoese bankers was in reality a carefully designed manoeuvre to reduce the crown's dependency on the Genoese and lower the high rates of interest on the *asientos* by bringing into play a group of Portuguese businessmen to provide competition.[28] In conjunction with the belated suspension in 1626 of the minting of the debased *vellón* coinage, it represented a major attempt by the administration to place the crown's finances and the Castilian currency on a sounder footing.

These measures for the restoration of fiscal health came not a moment too soon. *Vellón* prices were rising dramatically in 1626 and 1627, and the combination of high prices and high taxation was adding daily to the unpopularity of a regime which had come to power on a wave of popular approval in 1621. The full extent of the Count-Duke's unpopularity was spectacularly revealed when the king fell dangerously ill in the late summer of 1627, and was thought for a moment to be in imminent danger of death. The pasquinades, the court intrigues, the startling emptiness of the churches in Madrid when prayers were offered for the king's recovery, made it clear that Philip's death would cause no great sorrow if it led to the downfall of his minister.[29]

[25] See Elliott and La Peña, *Memoriales y cartas*, 1, Docs, IX and X.
[26] AGS Est. legajo 2040, 'Parecer de SE el Conde-Duque...' 12 Dec. 1626.
[27] See Elliott, *Richelieu and Olivares*, ch. 4.
[28] Antonio Domínguez Ortiz, *Política y hacienda de Felipe IV* (Madrid, 1960), p. 31; Felipe Ruiz Martín, 'La banca en España hasta 1782', *El Banco de España; una historia económica* (Madrid, 1970), pp. 119–20.
[29] For the king's illness and the domestic crisis of 1627, see Elliott, *Richelieu and Olivares*, pp. 90–95, and Elliott and La Peña, *Memoriales y cartas*, 1, Docs. XII and XIII.

The revelation of the hatred in which he was held seems to have come as a shock to Olivares, who found himself in trouble wherever he turned. His foreign policy may have brought victories, but it had not brought peace; his plans for the restoration of the crown's finances and for economic revival were being crippled by the costs of war finance and by currency disorders; and his reform projects were being systematically blocked by the privileged groups in Castilian society and elements of the bureaucracy, determined to resist changes which seemed to threaten deeply entrenched interests. In such a situation he desperately needed to vindicate his record by achieving some spectacular success, and spectacular successes are often more easily secured in foreign policy than in the more mundane area of domestic affairs.

It was at this moment of great domestic difficulty, at the end of 1627, that Duke Vincenzo II of Mantua died, in the midst of doubt and dispute over his succession. Some strong arguments could be advanced, simply in terms of the Italian and international situation, against allowing the Duke of Nevers, the candidate with the strongest claims, to take over the inheritance unopposed. The fact that the strategically placed duchy of Mantua would now be in the hands of a French-born duke presented obvious risks to Milan and to Spain's general position in northern Italy. It could also be argued that, by precipitately claiming his inheritance without reference to his overlord, the Emperor, Nevers had struck a damaging blow at Imperial authority. Yet these and other questions could probably have been resolved by diplomacy if Madrid had so wished. It is hard to believe that Olivares' decision in favour of military intervention was unrelated to his current domestic difficulties. A spectacular success, and notably the permanent occupation by Spain of the fortress of Casale, would go far towards silencing his domestic critics. With Louis XIII so deeply engaged in the siege of La Rochelle, the chances of French intervention in Italy seemed remote, and the prospects for a brilliant Spanish success correspondingly good.

By temperament the Count-Duke was cautious in his approach to foreign affairs – too cautious for some of his colleagues, who profoundly disagreed with his overtures for a Franco-Spanish rapprochement in 1627,[30] and believed that France under Richelieu represented a sufficient long-term danger to Spain to justify a preemptive

---

[30] Eberhard Straub, *Pax et Imperium. Spaniens Kampf um seine Friedensordnung in Europa zwischen 1617 und 1635 (Rechts-und Staatswissenschaftliche Veröffentlichungen der Görres-Gesellschaft,* Neue Folge, Heft 31, Paderborn, 1980), pp. 277–8. For the Franco-Spanish alliance project, see Georg Lutz, *Kardinal Giovanni Francesco Guidi di Bagno. Politik und Religion im Zeitalter Richelieus und Urbans VIII* (Bibliothek des Deutschen Historischen Instituts in Rom 25, Tübingen, 1971), pp. 254–313.

strike before it grew any stronger. It seems to have been the combin-ation of domestic necessity with foreign opportunity which lured him into the uncharacteristic gamble of intervention in Mantua – a gamble which might have succeeded if the diplomatic and military groundwork had been better laid, and if Gonzalo Fernández de Córdoba had been a more resolute commander. As it was, what might have been a spectacular *coup* turned into a slow-motion disaster as Don Gonzalo's forces settled down to the interminable siege of Casale. The Count-Duke had always been well aware that a long campaign would run the risk of provoking a French intervention, but had calculated on victory at Casale before Louis XIII and Richelieu secured their own victory at La Rochelle. His calculation was wrong. The surrender of La Rochelle in October 1628 gave Richelieu a new freedom of action, and the news of Piet Heyn's capture of the treasure-fleet encouraged him to move rapidly in support of the Duke of Nevers. Once the French army was across the Alps, at the end of February 1629, a new and potentially extremely dangerous situation had developed. Olivares had prophetically war-ned the papal nuncio in January that, if French troops moved into Italy, this would mark the beginning of a conflict between France and Spain that would last for thirty years.[31] His prediction was uncannily accurate.

The three-year struggle for the control of Mantua placed an enor-mous additional strain on Spanish resources at a time when the loss of the treasure-fleet had played havoc with the royal finances, and when the Castilian economy, affected by poor harvests and rising food prices, was entering a new phase of recession.[32] These strains did much to sharpen the debate over foreign and domestic policy in Madrid. The failures in Italy encouraged Olivares' enemies to return to the attack, and make a new attempt to persuade Philip IV to dis-pense with the services of his minister.[33] Philip himself, jealous of the successes of Louis XIII, began to assert himself in the field of foreign affairs, and spoke of leading his armies in Italy in person.[34] The most serious repercussions of Mantua, however, were felt in the war in the Netherlands.

Spain's traditional dilemma of Italy or Flanders posed itself in an acute form in 1629. The Count-Duke's whole northern policy had been directed towards bringing such pressure to bear on the Dutch

[31] Archivio Segreto Vaticano, Spagna, 69, fo. 61, despatch of Cesare Monti, 5 Jan. 1629.

[32] Vicente Pérez Moreda, *Las crisis de mortalidad en la España interior, siglos XVI-XIX* (Madrid, 1980), pp. 299–300.

[33] Elliott, *Richelieu and Olivares*, pp. 101–2.

[34] See Elliott and La Peña, *Memoriales y cartas*, 2, Docs. I-IX for the uneasy relationship of king and favourite during the spring and summer of 1629.

that they would be forced back to the negotiating table. This policy
had been showing some signs of success, but it was essential that the
pressure should not be relaxed. The war in Italy meant a diversion of
valuable resources away from the Netherlands at a critical moment.
It also meant the abandonment, at least for a time, of a major element
in Olivares' strategy – the attempt to secure Imperial participation in
the Netherlands war, and an invasion of the Dutch Republic by
Wallenstein's army. The Mantuan War not only set up new strains
between Madrid and Vienna, but turned Imperial attention away
from northern Europe just when Olivares had been attempting to
harness it to his own designs. This in turn strengthened the hand of
those members of the Council of State, headed by Ambrosio Spínola,
who believed that the time had come to reach a settlement with the
Dutch, even if the terms were no better than those of 1609. In the
Flanders/Italy debate in the spring and summer of 1629, the majority
favoured war in Italy and peace in the Netherlands, and Olivares'
entire northern policy seemed on the brink of collapse.

Thanks to a long rear-guard battle by Olivares against an unsatisfactory peace with the Dutch, and the gradual restoration of the military situation in Italy with the help of the Imperial forces, the major
crisis of Spanish foreign policy represented by the Mantuan affair
was eventually overcome. But the costs of that affair were enormous,
both domestically and in terms of Spain's international position. For
three years Spain had been forced to fight simultaneously in Italy and
the Netherlands, where a total collapse of Spanish power was only
narrowly averted. This war on two fronts was only achieved by
making heavy new demands on the tax-payers of Castile, where the
fiscal requirements of war now took priority over everything. Foreign affairs – *affari di fuora* – were now paramount, as the secretary
of the Tuscan embassy in Madrid noted in 1632.[35] This primacy of
foreign affairs meant to all intents and purposes the abandonment of
the Count-Duke's domestic reform programme. *Reformación* had
been sacrificed to *reputación*.

Internationally, Spain's intervention in Mantua had reawakened all
the traditional distrust of Madrid's intentions, and driven the lesser
European states to look to France for protection. It helped, too, to
fortify Richelieu's domestic position by confirming his analysis that
the power of the Habsburgs must be checked before it was too late.
Unless there was a dramatic change in the structure of power in
France or Spain – and this was unlikely, since both Richelieu and
Olivares emerged from the crisis of 1629–31 with their authority

---

[35] Archivio di Stato, Florence, Mediceo, filza 4959, despatch of Bernardo Monanni, 6 Nov.
1632.

enhanced – the two countries were now set on a collision course. The Count-Duke's aim was now to prepare for the war that he knew was coming, by building up a system of alliances, including alliance with the Emperor, and doing all he could to bring the war in the Netherlands to a successful conclusion before the break came with France.

In the 1630s, in Spain as in France, the mobilization of resources for war became the paramount consideration. Intense fiscal pressures were brought to bear on every group in Castilian society – privileged and unprivileged alike – with the result that some of the traditional social distinctions between the tax-payer and the tax-exempt began to be eroded. War, in effect, was beginning to act as a major instrument of social change by introducing a levelling effect, to the advantage of the state.[36] But the erosion of old privileges was to some extent offset by the introduction of new ones. Like all the war-time societies of the 1630s and 1640s, Castile fell prey to the profiteers – the tax-collectors, the government officials, the military men, the bankers. Nowhere was this new war-time affluence more visible than in Madrid itself, where the Portuguese businessmen summoned by Olivares to serve as royal bankers flaunted their wealth, and caused grave scandal with their alleged Judaizing practices.[37]

Yet it was these same Portuguese financiers who kept Spain financially afloat during the 1630s, bearing a substantial proportion of the crown *asientos* which the Genoese bankers could no longer carry unaided.[38] The growing weakness of the Spanish Atlantic economy in the 1630s was at least partially offset by the Count-Duke's ability to tap the resources of the international Marrano community to finance the Spanish war effort. But this dependence on Portuguese money had its disadvantages. In particular, it reinforced Madrid's obligation to recover Brazil from the hands of the Dutch, and made it correspondingly more difficult to reach a peace settlement with the Dutch Republic, which was not prepared to abandon its Brazilian conquests.

Although the financial assistance of the Portuguese bankers did something to ease the crown's difficulties, the Count-Duke was acutely aware of Castile's extreme economic weakness, and the hazards of committing the country to additional military expen-

---

[36] For a useful summary of seventeenth-century Spanish fiscalism and its consequences, see Antonio Domínguez Ortiz, *Polítca fiscal y cambio social en la España del siglo XVII* (Madrid, 1984).

[37] See Julio Caro Baroja, 'La sociedad criptojudía en la corte de Felipe IV', in his *Inquisición, Brujería y Criptojudaísmo* (2nd. ed. Madrid, 1972), and James C. Boyajian, *Portuguese Bankers at the Court of Spain, 1626–1650* (New Brunswick, 1983).

[38] Boyajian, *Portuguese Bankers*, chs. 3 and 4.

ditures. It was for this reason that he deferred for as long as possible
the break with France, which he knew would impose almost unbearable strains on the Castilian economy and Castilian society. But at
the same time – like Richelieu – he was carefully preparing for the
inevitable confrontation. In 1634, with the prospect of imminent war
with France, ministers were asked whether any territories should be
abandoned as being too expensive to defend. The Council of State's
view was that everything should be defended to the last breath,
although the estimated expenditures for the first year of war were
alarming:[39]

	escudos
Flanders (for 1635)	3,700,000
Subsidies for princes and electors in Westphalia and Rhineland	500,000
Assistance for Germany (to be doubled if the proposed League came into being)	600,000
Assistance for Gaston d'Orléans (conditional on his launching a diversionary attack on France)	1,200,000
Invasion of France from Spain	500,000
Defence of Milan	600,000
Expedition for recovery of Brazil	1,000,000
Aid to Marie de Médicis, Gaston, and Prince Thomas of Savoy	333,000
	8,433,000

When the war finally came in the spring of 1635, the Count-Duke
was well aware that the only way to win was to win quickly. Spain
was in no condition to withstand a war of attrition. It was for this
reason that, within a few weeks of the outbreak of hostilities with
France, he drew up a plan of campaign for a massive three-pronged
assault on France from Flanders, the Empire, and across the Pyrenees, in the hope of bringing the war to a speedy conclusion. Either,
he wrote, everything would be lost, or else the ship would be saved.
Either Castile would have to bow its head to the heretics, 'which is
what I consider the French to be', or else it would become 'head of
the world, as it is already head of Your Majesty's Monarchy.'[40]

With the failure of the Corbie campaign of 1636, the conflict
settled down into the kind of war of attrition which Olivares had
been so anxious to avoid. The indecisive struggle of the later 1630s
imposed growing strains, not only on the fabric of Castilian society,

---

[39] AGS Est. legajo 2152, draft response (starting 'Este lugar') to royal order of 28 Aug. 1634.
[40] Elliott, *Catalans*, pp. 309–10.

but also on the fabric of the Spanish Monarchy itself, as Olivares sought to draw the various kingdoms and provinces into his Union of Arms. It was this growing pressure of the central power of the state on the peripheral provinces of the Iberian peninsula which provoked in 1640 those two great upheavals that were to have such profound consequences for Spain's international position: the revolts of Catalonia and Portugal.

The 1640 revolts suggested that the Spanish Monarchy was on the verge of dissolution, and gave corresponding encouragement to Spain's enemies. 'The greatness of this Monarchy is near to an end', as the British ambassador in Madrid observed.[41] In practice, reports of its demise proved premature. Olivares himself managed to hang on to power for a further two years, in spite of the calamities of 1640, and did something to contain, if not repair, the damage. He even succeeded by six weeks in outlasting Richelieu, whose death in December 1642 – especially when followed by that of Louis XIII six months later – offered new hope to Madrid just when it seemed that all hope was lost. But the two revolts of 1640 inevitably had a major impact on Spain's military effectiveness in Europe, and forced the ministers in Madrid to reassess the international situation. Olivares himself, in what may have been his last state paper before his dismissal, seized on the news of Richelieu's death as providing the occasion for a new peace initiative. The news, he wrote, 'compels His Majesty's ministers to consider the acute situation in which we find ourselves, so as to miss no opportunity afforded by this event to secure by any possible means a treaty of peace, which is all that can possibly restore our fortunes at this present juncture.'[42]

The events of the succeeding years, however, were to show how elusive peace remained. In some respects the revolts made it more, and not less, difficult to negotiate a peace settlement, since the temptation of a great power when subjected to losses and humiliations is naturally to hold on, in the hope of better times to come. The Catalan revolt, too, added further complications to the problem of peace with France, since the French could not jettison their Catalan allies, while Philip IV could not accept a treaty which did not include the return of the Catalans to their former allegiance. On the other hand, the revolt of Portugal, although equally distressing to Philip's *amour propre,* opened up new possibilities of peace with the Dutch, since the fate of Brazil was no longer of overwhelming interest to Madrid.[43] The realization of this dictated the strategy of

[41] Cited Elliott, *Catalans,* p. 523.
[42] Cited Elliott, *Richelieu and Olivares,* p. 153.
[43] Fritz Dickmann, *Der Westfälische Frieden* (4th ed., Münster, 1977), p. 261.

Olivares' successor, Don Luis de Haro, who saw that the separation of the Dutch from the French held out the best hope for a revival of Spanish power. Peñaranda's patient diplomacy at Münster in pursuit of this strategy reaped its reward in 1648.

The successful conclusion of a peace treaty with the Dutch served as a further encouragement to the ministers in Madrid to gamble on a change of fortune in the war with France – a not unreasonable gamble in view of the outbreak of the Fronde. Once again, as so often in the past, foreign policy decisions were dictated primarily by foreign policy, rather than by domestic, considerations. From the standpoint of 'rational' argument, Spain would have been well advised to cut its losses and make peace as best it could. It was suffering from an acute shortage of manpower, which made the recruitment of troops increasingly difficult. Seville's Atlantic economy was in a state of deep crisis after 1640, with a drastic decline in the Indies trade and a slump in remittances of American silver.[44] The currency manipulations of 1641–3 had played havoc with Castilian prices,[45] and the accumulation of royal debts provoked the second crown 'bankruptcy' of the reign of Philip IV in 1647, twenty years after the first.[46] Yet if these economic and financial setbacks had a serious impact on Spain's ability to sustain its armies, they failed to shake Madrid's resolution to continue the struggle with France in the hope of redressing the military balance. So, too, did the uprisings of 1647–8 in Naples and Sicily. The Italian revolts were suppressed, and the Monarchy proved sufficiently resilient in the face of adversity to chalk up some impressive successes, culminating in 1652 in the recovery of Dunkirk, the capture of Casale, and the ending of the Catalan rebellion.[47]

Yet those successes, while sufficient to encourage Philip and his ministers to continue the struggle, were insufficient to allow them to press home the war to a satisfactory conclusion. They testified as much to the weakness of France as to any new-found strength in Spain, and pointed to a stalemate which, after another seven years of hostilities, found formal expression in the Peace of the Pyrenees – a settlement which at least safeguarded Philip's *reputación,* to the extent of temporarily masking the decisive shift in the European balance of power which had occurred between 1640 and 1660. Appearances at least had been preserved, and except for the loss of Portugal the

[44] Huguette and Pierre Chaunu, *Séville et l'Atlantique* (8 vols., Paris, 1955–9), 8(2), pp. 1793–1851. For silver imports, Earl J. Hamilton, *American Treasure and the Price Revolution in Spain, 1501–1650* (Harvard Economic Studies 43, Cambridge, Mass., 1934), table 1.

[45] Hamilton, *American Treasure,* pp. 85–7.

[46] Domínguez Ortiz, *Política y hacienda,* p. 68.

[47] Stradling, *Europe and the Decline of Spain,* p. 122.

Monarchy had surmounted the crisis of the 1640's with its territorial integrity virtually intact.

The fact that it survived as well as it did is a tribute at once to the weakness of France during the minority of Louis XIV and to the resilience of the Monarchy's structure. With the failure of the Olivares experiment at a tighter integration of the structure, the very looseness of Madrid's control over the the different kingdoms and provinces became a positive advantage, suggesting as it did to the ruling elites in those provinces that there were worse fates than subjection to the King of Spain. Olivares' successors, by emphasizing their commitment to the preservation of provincial rights and liberties, were able to hold the centrifugal structure together. But none of this would have been of any help to them if Castile, the head and heart of the Monarchy, had gone up in revolt. The absence of revolution in Castile is one of the most significant phenomena in the history of seventeenth-century Europe. The essential precondition of revolt was there, in the form of intensive governmental fiscalism. But, for reasons which have still to be satisfactorily explained, the Castile of the 1640s and 1650s remained quiescent. This quiescence enabled Philip IV and his ministers to sustain with extraordinary tenacity and a surprising measure of success the traditional Habsburg foreign policy of upholding their European commitments.

Perhaps the most striking feature of Spanish foreign policy between 1598 and 1659 is this continuity of tradition. From the early seventeenth century there was a widespread perception that Spain's power was in decline, but there is no evidence that this perception ever provoked an agonizing reappraisal of its policy and objectives. It is possible that there was covert opposition, especially to the prolongation of the war in the Netherlands, but there were relatively few demands in high places that Spain should cut its coat according to its cloth. In the 1620s some of the Flanders veterans on the Council of State, like Don Fernando Girón, were notably pessimistic about the prospects for continuing war in Flanders; and in 1635 the Count of Humanes, a friend and confidant of Olivares, went so far as to advocate the abandonment by Spain of both Flanders and Milan.[48] But suggestions of this kind are startling by their very rarity. There seems to have been a striking unanimity among the men who controlled Spain's destinies under Philip III and IV that there was no alternative to the traditional policies, and a general consensus that, in the words of Baltasar de Zúñiga, 'a monarchy that has lost its *reputación*. . .is a sky without light, a sun without rays, a body without a soul.' It is only towards the very end of the reign of Philip IV, and

[48] Elliott, *The Count-Duke*, p. 491.

ironically with Olivares' own son-in-law, the Duke of Medina de las Torres, that an influential voice is raised on behalf of a more 'realistic' foreign policy. 'Your divine duty', he told Philip in 1659, 'is not to continue attempting to defend what is defenceless...The raising of new revenues, and the continuation of taxes already imposed, cannot be justified if they are to be consumed by an unnecessary and wilful war.'[49]

If we review Spanish foreign policy, therefore, over the first sixty years of the seventeenth century, it would seem that its formulation bore little relation to changing domestic circumstances. The decline of silver remittances from the Indies, the deterioriation of the Castilian economy, the inadequacy of the Castilian tax base, and the failure to distribute the fiscal burden more equitably between Castile and the other kingdoms and provinces of the Spanish Monarchy, all contributed over the course of the years to a slow erosion of Spain's European primacy. But while there was no lack of awareness of the gravity of the situation, this awareness does not seem to have translated itself into any determination to reassess the guidelines which had traditionally governed the conduct of foreign policy in Madrid. Throughout these years, the principal objectives of Spain's policy remained unchanged: the maintenance of the Catholic cause, the defence of the dynastic interests of the two branches of the House of Austria, the retention of the loyal provinces of the southern Netherlands, and the exclusion of foreigners from Spain's empire of the Indies.

Since the guidelines remained unchanged, the major foreign policy decisions during the period of the Thirty Years' War – the intervention in Germany, the resumption of the war with the Dutch, the intervention in Mantua, the confrontation with France – were taken by the Council of State on the basis of perceived interests and considerations of international power politics within a preexisting conceptual framework. They bore little or no relation to the availability of resources or to Castile's ability to sustain a further period of intensive warfare. Indeed, the decision-making process in seventeenth-century Madrid provides a classic instance of the primacy of foreign policy over domestic affairs. Foreign and domestic policy were interdependent largely in the sense that foreign policy had a profound impact on domestic policy, rather than the other way round. The fiscal demands of ceaseless warfare over the course of the years distorted the Castilian economy, played havoc with the crown's finances, stimulated major social changes, and, in the Olivares years,

---

[49] R. A. Stradling, 'A Spanish Statesman of Appeasement: Medina de las Torres and Spanish Policy, 1639–1670', *Historical Journal*, 19 (1976), pp. 18–19.

inspired an attempt to reorganize the constitutional structure of the Spanish Monarchy, which had nearly fatal consequences.

If there was any serious correlation between foreign and domestic considerations, it is probably to be found primarily at a psychological level. A creeping fatalism seems to have overcome the Spanish political establishment during the opening decades of the seventeenth century. One effect of this pessimistic approach to the changing times was to reaffirm society's traditional objectives, in the hope of returning to the virtues of a more heroic age. *Reputación,* although by no means an exclusively Spanish phenomenon in the conduct of seventeenth-century foreign policy, had a marked tendency in Spain to become an end in itself, and Medina de las Torres issued a long-overdue reminder when he argued in 1666 that 'the true reputation of states does not consist of mere appearances, but in the constant security and conservation of their territories, in the protection of their subjects and the well-being thereof, in the respect which other princes have for their authority and military strength.'[50]

An excessive commitment to upholding 'reputation' precludes a flexible response to changing situations, and casts its exponents, at least in their own eyes, as men in a heroic mould, battling gallantly against the oncoming tide. This was certainly the self-image cherished by Zúñiga and Olivares, who has constant recourse to nautical metaphors in his speeches and correspondence. In an exchange of letters in 1625 with the Count of Gondomar, who had complained that 'the ship was going down', he replied that he was well aware of the gravity of the situation, but 'as the minister with paramount obligations it is for me to die unprotesting, chained to my oar, until not a fragment is left in my hands.'[51]

It was this do-or-die mentality which kept Spain at war for decade after decade, even as the odds turned against it. It is a state of mind which needs explaining. The key to the relationship between foreign policy and domestic affairs in seventeenth-century Spain will ultimately be found to lie in the mentality of the imperial ruling class, and in its perception of the world around it. We need to know much more than we know at present about the education, the practical experience of the world, the literary tastes and the historical attitudes of Zúñiga, Olivares and their colleagues if we are to understand the mental processes which underlay their foreign policy decisions and persuaded them that death was preferable to retreat. Like gamblers with a dwindling pile of coins, they kept on hoping that one final throw would lead to a spectacular reversal of their fortunes. In this

[50] *Ibid.*, p. 19.
[51] Elliott and La Peña, *Memoriales y cartas*, 1, p. 112.

perhaps they were not totally misguided. The years of success – 1625, 1634, 1636 – suggested that shipwreck might yet be averted. And if God willed otherwise, then, in the Count-Duke's words, the most honourable response was to 'die doing something.'[52] It was a not inappropriate ambition for a great power whose days of greatness were numbered.

[52] AGS Est. K. 1416, fo. 56, consulta of Council of State, 17 Sept. 1633.

PART III

THE WORLD OF
THE COURT

INTRODUCTION

In recent years there has been a marked revival of interest in the royal court, both as a social organism and as the centre of power in monarchical states. This revival, stimulated in part by the work of Norbert Elias,[1] and exemplified by the publication in 1977 of a volume of essays on *The Courts of Europe*,[2] was long overdue. The court, for all its apparent remoteness, touched the life of Early Modern societies at so many points that its neglect in much modern scholarly writing has left a particularly unfortunate void. The character of kingship itself, the workings of the patronage system, and the attempts of regimes to develop a set of symbols for securing and maintaining allegiance – all these require some understanding of the court, of its personal and spatial relationships, and its daily routines. The documentation is often abundant, but the apparently trivial and repetitive character of much of it has tended to deter investigation into a subject which anyhow was for long uncongenial to a generation that prided itself on its anti-elitist views.

Although my researches had made me keenly aware of the importance of the more personal characteristics of kingship, I had paid little attention to the environment of the court until asked to contribute an essay on the court of Philip IV to the volume on *The Courts of Europe*. When I came to write it, I found that the inadequacy of the existing literature made it difficult to produce anything more than a rather summary descriptive survey.[3] Shortly after this, however, I embarked with a specialist in the history of seventeenth-century Spanish painting, Professor Jonathan Brown, on a collaborative project for a study of the palace of the Buen Retiro, the pleasure palace built for Philip IV on the outskirts of Madrid. Our original idea had been to

[1] Notably, *Über den Prozess der Zivilization* (Basel, 1939), which understandably evoked little interest at the time of its publication, and had to wait nearly forty years for an English translation as *The Civilizing Process* (New York, 1978).

[2] Ed. A.G. Dickens (London, 1977).

[3] For this reason, and because much of what I said there overlaps with, or is superseded by, other pieces reprinted here, I have not included it in this book.

combine our knowledge of the history and art of the reign of Philip IV to study Velázquez's *Surrender of Breda* in its historical context. But since this painting was commissioned as one of a series for the Hall of Realms in the new palace, our interest naturally extended to the Hall of Realms, and from there, by a logical progression, to the entire palace complex. Eventually, in *A Palace for a King* (1980), we found ourselves attempting to reconstruct not only the palace itself – largely destroyed during the Peninsular War – but also the history of the court and court festivities, and the ways in which the Olivares regime made use of art, literature and the theatre for purposes of image-building.

The three essays in this section all developed out of this work. The first of them, published in 1987 in a volume of essays in honour of Professor H.G. Koenigsberger, who has himself made a valuable contribution to our understanding of court culture in Early Modern Europe, surveys the history of the Spanish court over two centuries, in an attempt to discover the extent to which it did, or did not, differ from other contemporary courts. It was also intended to counter the dangers of an excessively mechanistic interpretation of court history, by showing how court ceremonies and etiquette, apparently so uniform and unchanging, could be used to very different effect in different reigns, in accordance with the personality of the monarch, or the lack of it. The next essay provides an illustration of this, by studying the interplay of 'power and propaganda' in the regime of Olivares. This essay was originally prepared as a seminar paper in 1980 as part of a programme on politics and ideology sponsored by the Shelby Cullom Davis Center at Princeton University. In it, I drew on our findings in *A Palace for a King*, to suggest the possibilities, and the dangers, inherent in the mobilization of artists and men of letters by a determined regime in order to project its aspirations and assumptions.

The final essay in this section is concerned with a particular case history, that of the great seventeenth-century Spanish writer and satirist, Francisco de Quevedo. The year 1980 was the fourth centenary of Quevedo's birth, and this piece was my contribution to a commemorative symposium held at Boston University. Any historian working on Spanish politics and society in the first half of the seventeenth century is confronted sooner or later by the need to come to terms with his brilliant and allusive writings, but my initial curiosity about this complicated genius was prompted by my chance discovery in the Archivo Histórico Nacional in Madrid of an unknown letter of 1642 from Olivares to Philip IV relating to Quevedo's arrest and imprisonment three years previously. Quevedo's incarceration in the convent of San Marcos in León has always been one of the more mysterious episodes in an often

mysterious career, and the discovery of this letter made it possible
for the first time to learn how the principal protagonist justified the
arrest. Quevedo, wrote Olivares, had shown himself to be 'treacherous, an enemy and critic of the government, and, finally, an
intimate friend of France and in correspondence with the French.'
That he should be branded as a critic of the regime was no surprise,
but the charge that he was in collusion with the French, although it
surfaced in contemporary rumours about the causes of his arrest,
was more startling, in view of Quevedo's almost fanatical Castilian
patriotism.

While not necessarily accepting the truth of Olivares' charge, I felt
that the allegation was sufficiently surprising to justify a critical
scrutiny of Quevedo's relationship with the Olivares regime, on the
basis of his writings and of my own knowledge of the Count-Duke
and his circle. This reconsideration of Quevedo's career during the
reign of Philip IV led me to a startling piece of evidence about his
family background, which still awaits evaluation by Quevedo
specialists, and also enabled me to date one or two of his writings
with greater security than has so far been possible. Quevedo's works
lend themselves particularly well to close historical scrutiny because
of their numerous topical allusions, but I have no doubt that, as
our acquaintance with the court of Philip IV is deepened, collaboration between historians and literary specialists will produce fresh insights into Spanish Golden Age literature and a greater contextual
precision. My prime purpose, however, was to make some sense of
the twists and turns in Quevedo's tortuous relationship with the
regime, and, while I do not claim to have elucidated all the mysteries,
I hope at least to have produced a plausible interpretation which may
serve as a basis for future discussion. As will be seen, it is an interpretation that, although local in context, relates to a universal issue –
that of the writer in the service of the state.

VII

THE COURT OF THE SPANISH
HABSBURGS: A PECULIAR
INSTITUTION?

According to Lord Herbert of Cherbury – but can his story really be true? – Philip II of Spain once saw fit to rebuke one of his ambassadors for neglecting some piece of business in Italy because of a disagreement with the French ambassador over a point of honour. How, he asked his ambassador, had he 'left a business of importance for a ceremony?' The ambassador boldly replied to his master *como por una ceremonia? Vuessa Majesta misma no es sino una ceremonia.* 'How, for a ceremony? Your Majesty's self is but a ceremony.'[1]

The elaborately ceremonious character of Spanish court life was notorious among Europeans of the late sixteenth and seventeenth centuries. But if they laughed, they also imitated. Charles I of England, deeply impressed by his experiences on his visit to Madrid as Prince of Wales in 1623, introduced a decorum into the ceremonial of the English court which bid fair to outdo that of the Spaniards.[2] Yet in spite of the pervasive influence of Spanish manners and ceremonial in Early Modern Europe, all too little is known about the character and organization of the court of the Spanish Habsburgs, and the ways in which it developed.[3] From the Duke of Saint-Simon to

---

[1] *The Autobiography of Edward, Lord Herbert of Cherbury*, ed. Sidney L. Lee (London, 1886), pp. 205–6. I have left Lord Herbert's unorthodox rendering of Spanish uncorrected.

[2] Peter W. Thomas, 'Charles I of England', in *The Courts of Europe* ed. A.G. Dickens, (London, 1977), p. 193.

[3] There is much material of interest in Dalmiro de la Valgoma y Díaz-Varela, *Norma y ceremonia de las reinas de la Casa de Austria* (Madrid, 1958), and Antonio Rodríguez Villa, *Etiquetas de la Casa de Austria* (Madrid, 1913) provides a useful description of various court functions and offices, but no general survey is available covering the history of the Spanish court during the two centuries of Habsburg rule. Ludwig Pfandl, 'Philipp II und die Einführung des burgundischen Hofzeremoniells in Spanien', *Historisches Jahrbuch*, 58 (1938), pp. 1–33, ranges wider than its title, and makes some suggestive points. The most extensive literature on the Spanish court during this period belongs to the reign of Philip IV, for which see J.H. Elliott, 'Philip IV of Spain', in Dickens, *The Courts of Europe*, ch. 8, and the bibliography there given, together with Jonathan Brown and J.H. Elliott, *A Palace for a King. The Buen Retiro and the Court of Philip IV* (New Haven and London, 1980). In the piece which follows I have sought to give a picture of the character and development of the court over a

Norbert Elias[4] it is the court of Louis XIV of France that has been taken as the archetype of courtly society in the age of absolutism. This is partly because Versailles became the model for so many of the courts of eighteenth-century Europe, and partly because the Spanish court by comparison is poorly documented and has elicited relatively little study.

Yet, as interest in the history of European courts revives, it is their variety that impresses, at least as much as their uniformity.[5] Courts differed markedly in character, not only from country to country, but also from one reign to the next, undergoing changes over time far more drastic than could ever be anticipated from the glacial and apparently immobile surface imposed by ceremonial and etiquette. This should hardly be a matter for surprise. Institutions can adapt to new needs while preserving the carapace of old forms, and their reaction (or the lack of it) to new challenges and requirements is likely at any given moment to be dictated by the play of personality on organization, in response to political, social and economic forces, and to the movement of ideas. The princely court, for all its regulated protocol and archaic ceremonial, can hardly be an exception to this rule of institutional history.

Certain general characteristics of the Early Modern European court can be identified from the model constructed by Norbert Elias on the basis of Versailles. Everything possible, for instance, was done by means both of ceremonial and household organization to preserve the sacred character of kingship through the maintenance of distance.[6] The monarch, as God's representative on earth, was placed at the centre of a universe carefully designed to duplicate the harmonious ordering of the heavens.

The Spanish court in this respect had little to learn and much to teach. The king was presented as a figure at once remote and yet the centre of universal attention – a presentation that became especially artful in the seventeenth century as mastery was achieved over the illusionistic devices of the theatre. When plays were performed in the palace of the Alcázar in Madrid, the king was seated some ten

longer period, offering an interpretative synthesis on the basis of contemporary descriptions and such work as has been published on the Spanish and other European courts in recent years. Some of the points here presented were first made at a conference held at Duke University in April 1981 on 'Arts, letters and ceremonial at the court of the Spanish Habsburgs'.

[4] Norbert Elias, *Die höfische Gesellschaft* (Neuwied and Berlin, 1969). I cite here from the English translation by Edmund Jephcott, *The Court Society* (New York, 1984).

[5] Dickens, *The Courts of Europe*, gives a good idea of this variety, and is likely to be the starting point for the study of European courts for many years to come.

[6] For the importance of distance, see Elias, *The Court Society*, p. 118.

or twelve feet from the back wall, at the exact point at which the perspective design of the stage set could be appreciated to the full. On either side of the room were standing ranks of courtiers, with their eyes fixed on the king and queen as much as on the play. For in a sense the king and queen *were* the play. Theatrical contrivance could be brilliantly used to underline the point, as when the curtain was raised on one occasion to reveal on centre stage a throne beneath the canopy of which were two portraits – of the king and queen. The monarchs in effect looked on themselves, as in a mirror, while the audience gazed in admiration at this double image of majesty, the original and the likeness.[7]

Setting, ceremonial, household organization, all served to emphasize the unique and remote splendour of a godlike king. 'It cannot be denied', wrote Alonso Núñez de Castro in the seventeenth century, 'that palaces which are sumptuous in the beauty of their buildings and the richness of their furnishings, are an adornment that makes majesty plausible, as also is the accompaniment of guards, servants and confidants who perform those respectful ceremonies with which princes, as human deities, ought to be venerated.'[8] We still know far too little about the composition and functioning of the Spanish court,[9] but it was well endowed with the guards and servants deemed necessary to minister to the needs of a deified monarch. As in other European courts, there were three principal functionaries responsible for attending to the king's material wants: the *mayordomo mayor*, or Lord High Steward, in charge of his feeding and housing; the Grand Chamberlain (*camarero mayor*), or, as the office fell into abeyance, the *sumiller de corps*, or Groom of the Stole, to organize his personal service; and the Master of the Horse (*caballerizo mayor*), to attend to his stables and transportation. Each of these palace officials had his own extensive staff.

An idea of the scale of the enterprise can be gained from a list of the household servants of the king and queen, drawn up in 1623 in the early years of Philip IV.[10] Excluding the three hundred members of the royal guards, and the 167 officials and servants employed for the king's sporting and hunting activities, there were around 350 principal servants in the household of the king. These included 12 *mayor-*

---

[7] See J.E. Varey, 'The Audience and the Play at Court Spectacles: the role of the King', *Bulletin of Hispanic Studies*, 61 (1984), pp. 399–406.

[8] Alonso Núñez de Castro, *Libro histórico político, sólo Madrid es corte*, 3rd edn. (Madrid, 1675), p. 192.

[9] Mr. R.G. Trewinnard is preparing a Ph.D. thesis for the University of Wales on 'The Household of the Spanish Habsburgs, 1606–65: Structure, Cost and Personnel', which should provide us with much new information.

[10] B(ritish) L(ibrary), Add(itional) Ms. 36,466, fs. 247–259v., *Relación de todos los criados que ay en la casa real del rey de España este año de 1623 años.*

domos, 18 gentlemen of the household on active duty, another 25 who had formerly served or enjoyed the right of entry, 47 gentlemen to wait on the royal table, and 10 valets or *ayudas de cámara*. In addition there was an ecclesiastical establishment under the direction of the Archbishop of Santiago as *capellán mayor*. In it were to be found the royal confessor, 10 royal preachers, some lesser clerics and a chapel master in charge of the choristers and of 63 musicians (instrumentalists and vocalists). The queen's household, for its part, included 8 *mayordomos*, 10 dames of honour, 18 ladies in waiting, 12 *meninas* – all daughters of noblemen – and 20 principal ladies as *ayudas de cámara*, 'not to mention the ladies' servants and the menial servants, of whom there are large numbers.' The total number of household officials and service staff on the court books in 1623 was around 1700.[11]

That the figure at the centre of these ministrations was of more than human character was indicated by some of the ancient rituals that were still attached to his personal service. An observer noted as late as 1655 the survival of the Castilian custom by which no one could ride a horse once it had been ridden by the king. When the Duke of Medina de las Torres sent Philip IV a splendid horse as a present, the king returned it with the words *sería lástima* – it would be a pity if he were to mount it and so prevent such a noble steed from ever being ridden again.[12]

But if the court was the residence of a quasi-divine monarch, it was also the centre of political and administrative power – a point emphasized by the layout of the royal palace of the Alcázar in Madrid, with its royal apartments on the first floor, and the council chambers and secretarial offices on the floor below. The uneasy combination of personal and bureaucratic kingship so characteristic of Early Modern European societies was reflected in Madrid in the decision of the two greatest seventeenth-century ministers, the Duke of Lerma and the Count-Duke of Olivares, to combine their governmental duties with the household offices of Groom of the Stole and Master of the Horse, which guaranteed them close proximity to the king both inside and outside the palace. The Groom of the Stole – *sumiller de corps* – was assured of access on all occasions by virtue of his duties. He had general supervision of the king's chamber and of his dining arrangements, and combined this with specific personal services. As practised in the seventeenth century, these duties involved passing him his

---

[11] Gil González de Avila, *Teatro de las grandezas de la villa de Madrid* (Madrid, 1623), p. 333. Sixty-six years earlier, in 1557, the Venetian ambassador, Federico Badoero, reported that Philip II had 1500 officials in his household service (*Relazioni di ambasciatori veneti al senato*, 8, *Spagna* [1497–1598], Turin, 1981, p. 150).
[12] 'Voyage d'Antoine Brunel en Espagne (1655)', *Revue Hispanique*, 30 (1914), p. 213.

shirt, towel and clothes when he rose each morning, handing him his goblet at lunch and dinner when he ate alone, and being in attendance at all royal audiences. He supervised the making of the king's bed, and lighted the way to the royal bedchamber at night. He was also expected to sleep in a portable bed in the royal apartment, unless – as presumably happened with Lerma and Olivares – the king dispensed him from this obligation and appointed a substitute. [13]

It was, however, not only political and administrative power that radiated outwards from the apartments of the king. The Early Modern court served also as an 'exemplary centre', [14] at once national and international in its range. The rivalry of European princes was inevitably reflected in the competitive display of their courts. But it hardly seems an accident that it was the lesser rulers who needed to be the innovators in matters of display – the fifteenth-century Dukes of Burgundy in ceremonial display, the sixteenth-century Medici in the art of court spectacle. It was only by a compensatory effort of this kind that they could hope to hold their own in a world of great powers. But the great powers in turn would follow at their own pace and convenience, conferring their own prestige on practices first developed in the lesser courts. This happened with Burgundian ceremonial, introduced by Ferdinand at the court of Vienna with his court orders of 1527 and 1537, [15] and subsequently imposed by his brother, the Emperor Charles V, on the household of the heir to the throne of Castile in 1548. The resulting Habsburg – Burgundian style, once established in Vienna and Madrid, enjoyed a European preeminence sustained by Habsburg political hegemony. It was this style which would inspire Charles I's reforms at the English court, where the ceremonial introduced by Edward IV 'after the manner of Burgundy' [16] had become tarnished with the passage of time, and dismally failed to conform to the exacting standards of Madrid.

At the national level, the court as exemplary centre had a vital part to play in the 'civilizing process'. Court etiquette, with its fine hierarchical gradations and its exact delimitation of functions, proved – whether in London, Paris or Madrid – to be an important

[13] Royal Library, Copenhagen. Ny.kgl. S.no. 190, *Etiquetas de la real cámara de SMC el señor Rey Don Felipe Quarto* (11 August 1646), f. 7v. See also Yves Bottineau, 'Aspects de la cour d'Espagne au XVIIe siècle: l'étiquette de la chambre du roi', *Bulletin Hispanique*, 74 (1972) pp. 138–57, for these duties. Edward Hyde, Lord Clarendon, who was in Madrid in 1649, uses Groom of the Stole as the English equivalent of *sumiller de corps* (*The History of the Rebellion and Civil Wars in England*, ed. W.D. Macray, 5 vols. (Oxford, 1888), 5, p. 93).

[14] The expression is borrowed from Clifford Geertz, *Negara. The Theatre State in Nineteenth-Century Bali* (Princeton, 1980), p. 13.

[15] Hubert Ch. Ehalt, *Ausdrucksformen absolutischer Herrschaft. Der Wiener Hof im 17 und 18 Jahrhundert* (Munich, 1980), p. 35.

[16] Cited by Neville Williams, 'The Tudors', in Dickens, *The Courts of Europe*, p. 148.

device for inculcating social discipline. When the Admiral of Castile in a fit of pique took from his neck the chain from which hung his golden key of office and handed it back to Philip IV during the royal visit to Barcelona in 1626, the king spoke witheringly of 'this poor, badly educated, *caballero*', and had him placed under arrest and banished to his estates.[17] Education in politeness, education in taste, education to service – the court as exemplary centre was potentially equipped to provide all three.

Like any other European court of the period, therefore, the Spanish court performed at least three major functions. It protected and sustained the sacred character of kingship. It served as a centre of political and administrative power. And it constituted an exemplary centre for foreigners and nationals alike. But inevitably it had its own distinctive way of performing these functions; and how and why it developed its own distinctive approaches still needs to be systematically explored.

If we take our stand in the middle years of the seventeenth century, two features of Spanish court life immediately seize the attention. The first is the highly religious character of Spanish kingship in its public manifestations. The bulk of the monarch's public appearances were motivated by religious occasions – the celebration of mass at one or other of Madrid's many churches and convents, and attendance at *autos de fe*. While this reflects the extreme piety of individual monarchs, it also testifies to a particular conception of kingship, in which the relationship of the king to his God is regarded as more than usually close. As the offically styled *rey católico*, and the recipient of a divine favour which had made him the greatest monarch in the world, the King of Spain had a special obligation to uphold with particular fervour the ceremonies of the church and the purity of the faith.

Commentators, however, seem to have felt a continuing need to emphasize the piety – *piedad* – of the monarch. This was partly for domestic reasons, in a society which saw itself under constant threat from the forces of Protestantism, Judaism and Islam. But their concern also had an international dimension, particularly in the light of the King of Spain's perennial rivalry with the Most Christian King of France. In this context, it is significant that the King of Spain, unlike the King of France, was not endowed with healing powers.[18]

---

[17] Instituto de Valencia de Don Juan, Madrid. Envío 109 (91). Statement by Philip IV on the behaviour of the Admiral of Castile.
[18] Marc Bloch, *Les rois thaumaturges* (Paris, 1961), p. 155.

Nor did he benefit, like the French monarch, from the public sanction of a coronation ceremony – a deficiency which gave Cornelius Jansen a certain amount of trouble when he wrote his *Mars Gallicus* in defence of Spanish policy on the outbreak of war between France and Spain in 1635.[19] This made it all the more necessary to underline the King of Spain's uniquely Catholic credentials.

> How many times [wrote Claudio Clemente of Philip IV] have we seen Your Majesty in solemn processions, on foot and bare-headed beneath a burning sun, surrounded by an innumerable multitude of every order and estate and moving through a cloud of dust to accompany the holy sacrament long distances...We have seen Your Majesty in the most ordinary dress go on foot in Holy Week to visit many temples through streets covered with mud and with rain pouring from the skies, and returning home soaked to the skin...We have seen Your Majesty enter the house of a sick person and not continue his journey until the sacrament has been returned to its temple...[20]

These highly public displays of devotion, however, were performed by a monarch who otherwise was rarely seen. For the outstanding feature of Spanish court life, at least in the eyes of seventeenth-century foreign observers, was the invisibility, and indeed the sheer inaccessibility, of the king. The Venetian ambassador describes Philip III as spending a large part of his year 'in solitude, with very little court'.[21] The Maréchal de Gramont, visiting the court of Philip IV in 1659, observes that even the grandees saw the king only when they accompanied him to mass, and again in the evening when plays were performed; 'and the only time they speak to him is in audience, when business compels them to request one'.[22] Gramont's description makes clear how different were the spatial relationships between king and court in France and Spain. In Spain, the king was approached through a succession of rooms, each one more exclusive of access than the one before. Even in the eighteenth century after the advent of the Bourbons, Saint-Simon noticed how bare these rooms in the Alcázar looked – primarily because they contained no chairs. In the suite of rooms leading to the king's private apartments there were

---

[19] French trans., *Le Mars François* (1637), Bk. 1, ch. 9. For the abandonment of the coronation ceremony in medieval Castile, see Teófilo F. Ruiz, 'Une royauté sans sacre: la monarchie castillance du bas moyen âge', *Annales*, 39 (1984), pp. 429–53.

[20] Claudio Clemente, *El machiavelismo degollado por la christiana sabdiuría de España y de Austria* (Alcalá, 1637), pp. 120–1.

[21] Simeone Contarini (1604) in *Relazioni di ambasciatori veneti*, 9, *Spagna* [1602–1631] (Turin, 1978), p. 288.

[22] *Mémoires de Maréchal de Gramont*, in A. Petitot and L.J.N. Monmerqué, *Collection des mémoires relatifs à l'histoire de France*, 77 vols. (Paris, 1820–9), 57, p. 78.

only two, both of them folding chairs, one for the use of the *mayor-domo mayor* and the other for that of the *sumiller de corps*.[23]

Lesser dignitaries were received in one or other of the outer rooms, and the right of entry to the holy of holies, the king's study or *aposento*, was restricted to the papal nuncio, the President of the Council of Castile, cardinals, viceroys, and those fortunate individuals who had been accorded special royal permission.[24] Tucked away beyond the *aposento* was the royal bedchamber. The only members of the court allowed access to it were gentlemen of the chamber on active duty. According to Gramont, these posts of gentlemen of the chamber were the only court offices coveted by the grandees 'because, serving the king at table, and dressing and undressing him, they enjoy during their week of service the privilege of seeing his Majesty, a privilege from which all the others are excluded.'[25]

This highly private bedchamber ritual contrasts strikingly with the publicity attending the *lever* and *coucher* of the King of France – events of such importance at the French court that, when Versailles came to be built, the royal bedroom occupied the central position on the first floor, and was the focal point of the palace.[26] A similar contrast was to be found in the dining arrangements. Apart from a few special occasions, by the seventeenth century the King of Spain dined alone, except for the twenty or so officials who waited upon him, carrying and removing plates with the ritual precision required of a corps de ballet. The meal was taken in complete silence, and on the rare occasions when the queen dined with the king, she had her own separate service and no words were exchanged.[27] The King of France, on the other hand, dined in public. So, too, did Charles I of England and Henrietta Maria.[28] At the Imperial court in Vienna the practice was closer to that of Madrid, although the meals seem a little less bleak. The Emperor Ferdinand II 'did ordinarily dine in his Antechamber, but most commonly sup with the Empresse...When his Imperial Majesty sits at table with the Empresse...then there is most exquisite musicke; otherwise there is no musicke at dinner, unless it be on festivals and holydaies.'[29]

The punctiliousness of the etiquette surrounding the largely invisible King of Spain, and the extreme formality of Spanish court

[23] *Mémoires de Saint-Simon*, ed. A. de Boislisle (Paris, 1879–1930), 39, p. 409.

[24] Pfandl, 'Philipp II und die Einführung des burgundischen Hofzeremoniells', p. 14.

[25] *Mémoires*, p. 81.

[26] Elias, *The Court Society*, p. 82.

[27] Pfandl, 'Philipp II', pp. 21–2.

[28] Thomas, 'Charles I', in Dickens, *The Courts of Europe*, p. 194.

[29] *The Particular State of the Government of the Emperor Ferdinand the Second, as it was at his decease in the year 1636* (London, 1637), fs. 67–67v.

ceremonial, never ceased to surprise and impress seventeenth-century visitors to Madrid. Marshal Gramont on his embassy of 1659 tells us 'there was an air of grandeur and majesty which I have seen nowhere else.'[30] But reservations are also expressed. Antoine de Brunel, visiting the Spanish court in 1655, keeps his admiration within bounds:

> no prince lives like the King of Spain; all his actions and all his occupations are always the same, and move with such regularity that, day by day, he knows exactly what he will do for the whole of his life. One could say that there is some law which obliges him never to miss what he is accustomed to. So the weeks, the months, the years and the divisions of the day bring no change in his pattern of life, and never allow him to see anything new.[31]

Coming from the subject of a king of whom Saint-Simon would later write that 'with an almanac and a watch one could tell, three hundred leagues away, what he was doing',[32] the words possess a certain piquancy. Is it possible that punctuality reached Paris by way of Madrid?

Not surprisingly, the frozen ritual of Spanish court etiquette was also reflected in the deportment of the king. Foreign observers were struck by his impassivity. Philip IV was described by François Bertaut in 1659 as a 'statue'.[33] The pattern of a royal audience was always the same. Those admitted to the king's presence would invariably find him *arrimado a un bufete* – standing at a console table – as they entered the audience chamber. He would raise his hat as they came in, and then stand motionless throughout the audience. The studiously non-comittal remark that closed the audience at least indicated that the statue talked.

We have here, then, a monarch who seems to be little more than a marionette, concealed for much of the time from public view, but occasionally brought on stage to be put through a series of carefully modulated ritual movements before a hushed and reverential audience. Does this indicate, as has been suggested, the triumph of oligarchy over personal kingship? In the France of Louis XIV, where the king lived out his life beneath the public gaze, the nobles were grouped round a highly visible monarch to enhance his prestige. In the Spain of Philip III and IV and Carlos II, court ceremonial was used to isolate the sovereign and confine him to the company of a

[30] *Mémoires*, p. 51.
[31] 'Voyage d'Antoine Brunel', p. 144.
[32] Cited Elias, *The Court Society*, p. 131.
[33] François Bertaut, 'Journal du Voyage d'Espagne (1659)', *Revue Hispanique*, 47 (1919), p. 35.

few privileged aristocrats.[34] But is it the French style of public kingship or the Spanish style of private kingship that stands in need of explanation?

Any attempt to explain the developments of distinctive court styles in terms of the relationship of king to aristocracy (important as this may have been in determining the final configuration) can easily overlook an element common to all institutional history, and nicely described by Norbert Elias in relation to royal courts as 'a ghostly *perpetuum mobile* that continued to operate regardless of any direct use-values, being impelled, as by an inexhaustible motor, by the competition for status and power of the people enmeshed in it...and by their need for a clearly graded scale of prestige.'[35] The classic instance of the operation of this 'ghostly *perpetuum mobile*' at the Spanish court is the celebrated story told by Bassompierre of Philip III contracting his fatal fever from the heat of a brazier which had been placed too close to him, and which the Duke of Alba, as gentleman of the chamber, was unwilling to move without orders from the *sumiller de corps*, the Duke of Uceda, who happened to be out of the palace at the time.[36]

Although the story does not seem to figure in any Spanish source, Bassompierre claims to have heard it from another gentleman of the chamber, the Marquis of Povar, and it does not look inherently implausible. It became popular in the seventeenth century as an example of the absurdity of Spanish court etiquette, but a parallel is to be found in an incident at the French court in the following century, when Marie Antoinette's chemise was passed ceremoniously from hand to hand, while the queen herself stood naked and shivering as the proprieties of rank were observed among her ladies in waiting.[37] Both instances, whether apocryphal or not, exemplify the tendency of court ceremonial to develop a machine-like momentum, crushing in its course those sacrosanct royal figures it has been specifically designed to protect.

In the absence of a personality strong enough to mould an institution to his will, the institution itself takes command. But in the history of the Spanish court, three personalities – Charles V, Philip II, and the Count-Duke of Olivares – proved strong enough either to arrest the 'ghostly *perpetuum mobile*' or to master it to suit their own designs. Above all, it is to that virtuoso of political stagecraft, Charles V, that we must turn for the decisions which set the pattern

---

[34] Bottineau, 'Aspects de la cour d'Espagne', pp. 152–3.

[35] Elias, *The Court Society*, pp. 86–7.

[36] *Journal de ma vie. Mémoires du Maréchal de Bassompierre*, ed. Marquis de Chantérac, 2 (Paris, 1873), pp. 240–1.

[37] Elias, *The Court Society*, p. 86.

of life for his successors on the Spanish throne. Heir to the
Burgundian traditions which had surrounded him during the first
years of his life, no man was more acutely aware of the way in which
symbols could be deployed and manipulated for political effect.
When Philip II asked the aged Duke of Alba in 1579 for a written
account of the royal household and its ceremonial, the duke confirmed that this was something he had frequently discussed with the
Emperor, 'the man who was best informed about such matters'.[38]

The Emperor's hand was everywhere to be found in the ceremonial arrangements used in Spain to ensure the royal preeminence. In
the matter, for instance, of the exclusive right of grandees to go
covered in the royal presence, Alba recalled, in response to Philip's
request, that the question did not arise under the Catholic Kings
'because all kinds of people went covered. Going bare-headed in
Castile was introduced only after His Imperial Majesty came here.'
By regulating the wearing of hats in the royal presence, the Emperor
at once distanced himself from his subjects, introduced a hierarchical
gradation at court, and created a coveted privilege which would
increase the dependence of the high nobility on the monarch.

There is no direct evidence as to why Charles entrusted a reluctant Duke of Alba in January 1548 with the task of imposing the
Burgundian style on the household of Prince Philip.[39] The political
cirumstances of the moment, however, provide a clue to the
Emperor's intentions. In the aftermath of his victory at Mühlberg,
he could begin to make the necessary dispositions for the future of
his dominions. Central to his strategy was the retention of the link
between Spain and the Burgundian inheritance of the Netherlands.
With this in mind he planned a visit by his son, as the rightful heir
to the inheritance, to his northern realms, and it was obviously
important that Philip should come to the Netherlands surrounded by
the correct Burgundian trappings. There may have been rumblings
of dissent in Castile over 'thus discrediting the Castilian style, which
on grounds of antiquity alone ought to have been preserved',[40] but
Brussels was worth a *sumiller de corps*.

If, as Charles hoped, Philip might yet succeed to the Empire itself,

[38] BL Add. Ms. 28,361, fs. 11–12, Duke of Alba to Mateo Vázquez, 15 Nov. 1579. I am
indebted to Dr David Lagomarsino for this reference, and for his general advice on points of
etiquette. I am also grateful to him for making available to me a copy of Jean Sigonney's report
on ceremonial in the Emperor's household, discussed below.
[39] Alba's reluctance is reported by his seventeenth-century biographer, Ossorio, who had
access to papers now lost. See P. Antonio Ossorio SJ, *Vida y hazañas de Don Fernando Alvarez
de Toledo, Duque de Alba*, ed. José López de Toro (Madrid, 1945), pp. 163–5. See also William
S. Maltby, *Alba. A Biography of Fernando Alvarez de Toledo, Third Duke of Alba, 1507–1582*
(Berkeley, Los Angeles, London, 1983), pp. 66–7.
[40] Prudencio de Sandoval, *Historia de la vida y hechos del Emperador Carlos V* (Barcelona,
1625), 2, p. 588.

the fact that the Burgundian style was already in use in his own household and at his brother's court in Vienna further strengthened the case for its adoption at the court of Castile. To judge from a report later drawn up for Philip by Jean Sigonney, the Comptroller of Charles' household,[41] the new-old style which he imposed on his son's household in 1548 was the one that his own household had followed for many years. It is open to question, however, how far this style was authentically Burgundian. Sigonney himself clearly had his doubts. The preface to his account of the Emperor's household arrangements suggests that Burgundian household organization first lost something of its pristine grandeur when the Habsburg Maximilian married Mary of Burgundy in 1477 and brought to the marriage his own German household. Still more was lost when Maximilian's son, Philip the Fair, married Joanna of Spain. When Maximilian gave his grandson Charles a household of his own at the age of ten, it was – so Sigonney had heard – very different in style from the household of the old Dukes of Burgundy, and not much of this now survived, except for the dining arrangements, which themselves were falling into desuetude.

Sigonney remembered that the Emperor was once questioned about the oblivion into which so many of the Burgundian practices had fallen. His answer was highly characteristic. Just as the Dukes of Burgundy 'had taken the liberty to live in their own way, he wanted a similar freedom in not having to imitate them in things he did not like.'[42] If Charles now denied his son this same freedom, it was presumably because he thought that the new style of ceremonial and household organization would enhance the prestige of his son in his dealings both with his own subjects and with his fellow-princes.

Philip, as the dutiful son of his father, seems to have accommodated himself to the Emperor's wishes, although the household organization that prevailed in his reign gives every sign of maintaining a highly syncretic character. No doubt the old forms and practices had a way of reasserting themselves. Ceremonial in the royal chapel of the Alcázar, for example, had been brought into line with the 'usage of Burgundy' in 1546. But in 1586 it was subjected to a new and definitive reform, in accordance with 'the usage of Castile and Burgundy.' This proved in practice to be a blending of Aragonese, Castilian, Burgundian and Flemish styles with those of the papal court.[43]

---

[41] Biblioteca Nacional, Madrid. Ms. 1080, *Relación de la forma de servir que se tenia en la casa del Emperador don Carlos nuestro señor. . .el año de 1545 y se avia tenido algunos años antes.*
[42] F. 4.
[43] Véronique Gérard, 'Los sitios de devoción en el Alcázar de Madrid: capilla y oratorios', *Archivo Español de Arte*, 57 (1983), pp. 275–84.

The ceremonial designed for the court of Spain by Charles V was well calculated to make kingship at once impressive and remote. The effect of Philip II's adoption and adaptation of that ceremonial was to make it impressive but withdrawn. Charles, with his peripatetic court, combined grandeur with a high degree of visibility. Philip, in settling his court and government in Madrid in 1561,[44] reduced the degree of visibility by withdrawing himself geographically to a central location in Castile. But the process of withdrawal was more than merely geographical. Philip also engaged in what might be described as a psychological withdrawal, as he moulded Spanish kingship to the forms of his own temperament and style of life. The muted style of the court under Philip II, underlined by the gravity of the king's deportment and the sobriety of his dress, found an appropriate embodiment in that mausoleum of monarchy, the Escorial.

The effect of Philip's decision to pursue an essentially reclusive form of life, more appropriate to a monk than a monarch, was to deprive him of some of the political advantages conventionally attributed to the sixteenth-century court – the prestige, for example, associated with public display, and the opportunities for occupying the high nobility in harmless court employment. It is not surprising that the nobility of Castile found little temptation to linger in so lugubrious a court. But there were compensating political advantages to be gained from sheer royal remoteness. The awe, amounting to terror, of those who found themselves in his presence makes it clear that private kingship, no less than public, could be used to powerful political effect in the hands of a master.

But Philip II's style of kingship was a highly personal one, not easily transmitted to his heirs, even though – in its religiosity and its dedication to paper work – it was consistently held up as the model that they were expected to follow. Where Philip II moulded the form of the court to suit the character of his kingship, Philip III, lacking all character to his kingship, allowed himself to be enveloped by the forms. During the first two decades of the seventeenth century, the court may be said to have imposed itself on the king.

The manner of Philip III's life, indeed, suggests a rather pathetic attempt to escape from its clutches. Whenever possible, Philip was on the move, but – in contrast to his grandfather – this was peripatetism without purpose. He was for ever travelling from one country residence to another – the Pardo, the Escorial, Aranjuez – or

---

[44] For a useful reappraisal of Philip's decision, see Juan Ignacio Gutiérrez Nieto, 'En torno al problema del establecimiento de la capitalidad de la monarquía hispánica en Madrid', *Revista de Occidente*, 27–8, extraordinario 8 (1983), pp. 52–65.

escaping into the countryside to indulge his passion for hunting, which afforded him some relief from the constraints of ceremonial and the tedious obligations of government.[45] It was only in his exemplary display of public devotion that he sustained and reinforced a central tradition of Spanish kingship.

Yet it was in the reign of this unpromising monarch that Spain acquired a genuine court life, even if Philip's own active contribution was confined to little more than court festivities. Sir Charles Cornwallis, reporting from the court at Valladolid in 1605, describes him as taking part in the equestrian sport of the *juego de cañas* – 'a thing not formerly seen in this kingdom, and done on purpose (as to us it was delivered) to honour our Nation.'[46] The new vigour of court life reflected the appearance of a new and young king, and one with a growing family of infantes and infantas – itself a striking novelty in Habsburg Spain. It also reflected the capture of the crown by a faction of the aristocracy, as the Duke of Lerma assumed power as the king's favourite and principal minister, and appointed his relatives and dependents to court and government office.

It was natural that a heavily indebted aristocracy should descend on the court, now that power and patronage were in the hands of one of its own. The process accelerated after the court's return to Madrid in 1606 from its unhappy five-year sojourn in Valladolid. Henceforth the definitive capital of a world-wide empire, Madrid became the magnet of the nobility, whose acquisition or construction of town houses brought it into daily contact with those who had some formal attachment to the court, either as palace functionaries, or as. ministers, royal secretaries and officials.

Professor Koenigsberger has pointed to the conjunction of court and great metropolis as a major formative influence on seventeenth-century European cultural developments – in the visual arts, drama and music – because it gave birth to a 'dual patronage and audience, courtly and urban'.[47] The existence of a wealthy and leisured elite in the Madrid of Philip III augured well for this conjunction. By the time of Philip's death in 1621, Madrid, with its 150,000 inhabitants, possessed most of the ingredients of what we have come to regard as standard court life in Early Modern Europe, with, however, one significant exception. The Spanish court remained in large degree a court without a king. With Philip absent at Aranjuez or away at one

[45] Pietro Gritti (1619): 'He spends a large part of the year in his country retreats, constantly engaged in hunting.' *Relazioni di ambasciatori veneti*, 9, p. 527.
[46] Ralph Winwood, *Memorials of Affairs of State in the Reigns of Queen Elizabeth and King James I* (1725), 2, p. 73 (Sir Charles Cornwallis to the Lords of the Council, 31 May 1605).
[47] 'Republics and Courts in Italian and European Culture in the Sixteenth and Seventeenth Centuries', *Past and Present*, no. 83 (1979), pp. 33–56. See p. 45.

of his hunting lodges, the court lacked a real master of ceremonies. The houses of leading aristocrats like the Dukes of Sessa or Osuna served as centres of patronage, but social and literary life lacked a single focal point. It was the accession of Philip IV in 1621, and the rise of a new favourite, the Court of Olivares, that supplied the missing centre.

The twenty-two years of the Olivares regime, from 1621 to 1643, are the climacteric years of the court of the Spanish Habsburgs, and they also mark a critical moment in the history of the court as a European institution. Olivares, bringing with him from Seville the expansive notions of patronage of the Andalusian aristocracy, perceived the possibilities of the court as an instrument of policy in a way that they had not previously been perceived in Habsburg Spain. He was helped in this by the tendency of his generation to view public life in terms of the theatre. Kings and ministers, courtiers and generals, were all seen as playing a part in the great theatre of the world. But, as Richelieu was to find with Louis XIII, a sense of theatre was not in itself sufficient if the leading actor was not prepared to enter fully into his part. In the young Philip IV, Olivares was fortunate in having first-class material to hand. Philip was intelligent enough to learn his lines, but also docile enough to take direction; he had bodily grace and an innate sense of dignity; he combined a mastery of horsemanship and open air sports with a taste for cultural and theatrical activities, and a highly discerning eye for works of art; and he possessed the punctiliousness that was essential for anyone who had to live his life according to strict laws of protocol.

Olivares' grooming of Philip IV for his star role – or, more accurately, his planetary part as the original Sun King, the *rey planeta*[48] – was a conscious act of policy, designed to restore the authority of kingship in a society in which, as he saw it, the political balance had in recent years tilted dangerously in favour of the grandee houses of Castile. The court appointments made by the Duke of Lerma had in effect made Philip III the prisoner of a grandee faction. It was one of the ironies of the Olivares regime that the only way to break the monopoly of this faction was to fill court posts with members of another – his own. The dominance of the Sandovals was therefore duly replaced in the 1620s and 1630s by that of the rival families of the Guzmáns, the Haros and the Zúñigas. But the intent, at least in Olivares' view of the world, was not to capture but to rescue kingship. In his celebrated secret memorandum of 1624,

[48] For this grooming process, see Brown and Elliott, *A Palace for a King*, pp. 40–9.

destined only for the eyes of the king, he refers admiringly to Philip II's policy of keeping the grandees dependent on the crown by sending them on embassies and employing them on ceremonial duties which would force them to dig deeply into their pockets.[49]

Although the details still escape us, there can be no doubting the intention of Olivares, patiently seconded and pursued by Philip IV, to make the court at once the focus and the regulator of aristocratic life in Spain. Alonso Carrillo in 1657 describes the court of Philip IV as 'a school of silence, punctiliousness and reverence.'[50] Philip showed himself over the years to be an exacting schoolmaster. He revised the details of court etiquette and the household arrangements in 1624 and again in the late 1640s, set the most punctilious standards for himself, and – as his scathing reference to the Admiral of Castile as 'this poor, badly educated *caballero*' indicates – was not willing to tolerate breaches of propriety.

Yet for all the efforts of king and minister to raise the standards of politeness and courtly etiquette, the court never quite became the school of virtue which Olivares had envisaged. With growing frustration he contemplated the insubordination, riotous behaviour and general aimlessness of the younger generation of nobles who frittered away their days on the fringes of the court. 'I see the Monarchy being lost because the young are not being properly brought up.'[51]

A programme of rigorous training was needed, that would produce a generation of nobles dedicated to the service of the crown in peace and war alike. The king himself, with his mastery of the equestrian arts and his intensive programme of self-education, offered an admirable example for the younger nobles to copy,[52] but they proved singularly reluctant to follow their sovereign's lead. The jousts and tourneys so lavishly staged at the new palace of the Buen Retiro notably failed to produce a more martial generation; nor were the young nobles willing to attend the new court college for the nobility, the Colegio Imperial.[53]

In the mid-1630s, as an alternative solution, Olivares proposed the creation in different parts of Spain of a number of academies, two of them at court.[54] But lack of money, and perhaps also of enthusiasm,

[49] John H. Elliott and José F. de La Peña, *Memoriales y cartas del Conde Duque de Olivares*, 2 vols. (Madrid, 1978–80), 1, Doc. IV, pp. 54–5.

[50] Alonso Carrillo, *Origen de la dignidad de grande de Castilla* (Madrid, 1657), f. 12.

[51] Elliott and La Peña, *Memoriales y cartas*, 2 Doc. XI, p. 76.

[52] *Ibid.*, Doc. XIIa, p. 81 (Olivares to President of Council of Castile, 18 Sept. 1632).

[53] See José Simón-Díaz, *Historia del Colegio Imperial*, 2 vols. (Madrid, 1952–9), 1, and Richard L. Kagan, *Students and Society in Early Modern Spain* (Baltimore and London, 1974), pp. 38–9.

[54] See Elliott and La Peña, *Memoriales y cartas*, 2, Doc. XIIc.

made his scheme a dead letter. Later, in 1639, he drew up new instructions for the education of the court pages, who came under his
charge as Master of the Horse.[55] These provide a vivid insight into
his ideal of the courtier and the way he should be trained. The pages
were to 'profess such good and exemplary customs as to make it
impossible to differentiate them from members of the most strict
religious orders.' They were to be given no home leave ('the source
of all the evils of youth'), and every hour of the day was to be
scrupulously filled. They must learn to read 'perfectly' books written
in Spanish, Portuguese, 'Lemosina' (Catalan) and French, and to
'write very well our language, Italian, and French if possible'. They
were to know Latin 'preeminently well', and read historians and
poets 'and at least understand them'. Instruction was to be given in
cosmography, geography and navigation, and pupils were to acquire
sufficient mathematics to master the art of fortification. Open air
training would be provided in military pursuits, and the young men
were to become masters of horsemanship, dancing and fencing.

According to the Jesuit Jean-Charles della Faille, who instructed
the twenty-one pages in the art of fortification, the young men
enjoyed their classes;[56] but in general there is an archaizing, medieval
character to this vision of an exemplary school for pages designed, in
Olivares' words, to be a 'mirror for the nobility of Castile'. Perhaps
the days of palace schools were passed. The lack of appeal of his
educational schemes to the nobility for whom they were intended
suggests the limitations of court culture by the seventeenth century
as an instrument for moral improvement and ethical reform.

But other, less didactic, aspects of the Count-Duke's policy for the
court enjoyed more success. In particular, he succeeded in making it
a centre of cultural patronage and a showcase for the arts, acting on
the principle that it was letters as well as arms that made a monarch
great.[57] In a town which already boasted munificent patrons, Philip
IV was to become the greatest patron of them all, giving a new impetus to patronage and picture collecting at court and among the
high nobility. A roll-call of the great collectors of the middle decades
of the century – the Marquis of Leganés, the Count of Monterrey,
Don Luis de Haro, the Admiral of Castile – suggests something of
the impact of the royal example.[58]

[55] Real Academia de la Historia, Madrid. Salazar K-8, fs. 361–7. *Instrucción para la casa de los pajes*, 30 April 1639.

[56] Omer Van de Vyver S.I., 'Lettres de J.-Ch. della Faille S.I., cosmographe du roi à Madrid, a M.-F. Van Langren, cosmographe du roi a Bruxelles, 1634–1645', *Archivum Historicum Societatis Iesu*, 47 (1977), pp. 145, 148, 149 (letters of 10 April, 18 May and 8 July 1639).

[57] For Philip IV's insistence on the importance of letters as well as arms, see Brown and Elliott, *A Palace for a King*, p. 42.

[58] *Ibid.*, p. 115; and see below, ch. 12.

No one was more aware than Olivares of the important political dividends to be derived from the patronage of artists and men of letters – a patronage that Philip IV exercised on an impressive scale. According to a recent estimate, 223 writers held positions in the personal service of the king and his family during the reign of Philip IV. This compares with sixty-six in the reign of Philip II and seventy-six in that of Philip III.[59] In their books and plays these men would sing the praises of the Planet King, and project to the world the brilliant image of Spanish kingship which the regime of Olivares was seeking to promote. The same theme was developed in the visual arts, especially in the celebrated Hall of Realms in the palace of the Buen Retiro, for which Velázquez and his fellow artists executed a series of paintings designed to glorify the dynasty and comme-morate the victories of a triumphant Philip IV.[60]

But, as at the contemporaneous court of Charles I of England,[61] the degree of system in the politics of court culture under Philip IV can be overstated. Although Olivares possessed a general pro-gramme for the king and the court, there is a marked element of improvisation in its execution. The haphazard planning of the royal pleasure palace of the Buen Retiro in the 1630s[62] was characteristic of the way in which the programme was managed. Part of the ex-planation is to be found in the exigencies of the crown's finances, which made systematic planning difficult; part, also, in what the eighteenth-century Scottish historian, Robert Watson, nicely de-scribed as the 'sublime but irregular genius' of the Count-Duke himself.[63] But modern historiography, in its search for hidden symbols and meanings, is all too prone to forget that the prime purpose of court culture was to divert and entertain. The Spanish court, like the other courts of seventeenth-century Europe, was more often speaking to itself than speaking to the world.

Yet even the ways in which it spoke to itself could not fail to project a certain image, and Olivares, with his superb sense of theatre, always had a sharp eye for the possibilities. He even turned bad weather to account, as in the inaugural ceremonies of 1633 for the Buen Retiro, when glass panels adorned with red velvet and damask were placed over the balcony to protect Philip from the rain, making him look, at least to one observer, like a holy relic in a

---

[59] José Simón Díaz, 'Los escritores-criados en la época de los Austrias', *Revista Universidad Complutense* (1981), pp. 169–78. It should be noted that 95 of these were court chaplains or preachers. These number 124 in the reign of Carlos II, out of a grand total of 190.

[60] See Brown and Elliott, *A Palace for a King*, ch. 6.

[61] See Malcolm Smuts, 'The Political Failure of Stuart Cultural Patronage', in *Patronage in the Renaissance*, ed. Guy Fitch Lytle and Stephen Orgel (Princeton, 1981), ch. 6.

[62] See Brown and Elliott, *A Palace for a King*, ch. 3.

[63] *The History of the Reign of Philip the Third, King of Spain* (London, 1783), p. 422.

reliquary.[64] Here was the king as God on earth, to be reverenced and adored. We have only to move forward fifty years, to Philip's nephew and son-in-law, Louis XIV, to see the themes that made their appearance in the Spain of Olivares marshalled into a more coherent programme for the glorification of another, and greater, Sun King. By then the court of Madrid was eclipsed by the courts both of Versailles and Vienna. Carlos II, the prisoner of oligarchy, and sheltered behind the barrier of court protocol which his father had elaborated with such meticulous attention to detail, was incapable of sustaining the role expected of a King of Spain in the theatre of the world. Quevedo once wrote that for an idle king 'palaces are the sepulchres of a living death'.[65] The palace in Madrid never resembled a sepulchre more closely than in those last tragic decades of the seventeenth century.

Anyone surveying the century and a half of Spanish court history since the imposition of Burgundian ceremonial on the household of Prince Philip in 1548 is likely to be impressed on the one hand by the continuity of forms, traditions and themes, and on the other by the way in which strong personalities could impose themselves on these traditional forms and turn them to advantage. Two different and not entirely compatible strains were to be found in the style of life which Charles V selected for the court of his son. One of these was the isolation of the king as a remote figure, visible for most of the time to only a privileged few. Royal privacy, used to great political effect by Philip II, degenerated into royal obscurity in the reigns of his son, Philip III, and his great-grandson, Carlos II. The other strand in the legacy of Charles V was the use of political imagery and court ceremonial and festivities around the person of the monarch to project the glories of the dynasty. Olivares grasped the possibilities inherent in this aspect of the Emperor's legacy, and developed them with skill to create a public image of Philip IV as Felipe el Grande, the Planet King whose brilliance illuminated the earth.

Yet splendour at court was a double-edged weapon, as the regime of Olivares discovered to its cost. The court of the Spanish Habsburgs may have been unique among the courts of Early Modern Europe in the degree of tension that prevailed between the claims of reclusive and public kingship. It was possible to combine them to powerful effect, but the balance was not easily achieved. 'One can sin through excess', wrote Núñez de Castro, 'as well as through

[64] Brown and Elliott, A Palace for a King, p. 68.

[65] 'Política de Dios y gobierno de Cristo', in Francisco de Quevedo, Obras completas, ed. Felicidad Buendía, 6th end., 2 vols. (Madrid, 1966–7), 1, p. 627 (ch. 13).

deficiency. Pomp and circumstance are fitting, but they must be controlled by reason, moderated according to the season, and regulated by prudence...Expenditure should produce decorum, not ostentation; veneration and not vainglory.'[66] The elaborate court ceremonial of the Spanish Habsburgs could be used at once to protect and project the person of the king. But if the balance was wrong, if the king was either too ostentatiously presented or became too remote, not much remained to shield him from the devastating perception that 'Your Majesty's self is but a ceremony.'

[66] *Libro histórico polítíco, sólo Madrid es corte*, pp. 192–3.

VIII

POWER AND PROPAGANDA
IN THE SPAIN OF PHILIP IV

Although power and ideology march together through the centuries, there are ambiguities in their relationship that still need to be explored. Where Early Modern Europe is concerned, the possibilities for exploration are considerable, and the prospects look promising for some redirection of a historical debate that is at present in disarray. Nineteenth- and early twentieth-century historiography tended to emphasize, and often indeed to exaggerate, the effectiveness of state building in the Early Modern period. More recent historical writing, by contrast, has moved sharply in the opposite direction. It has been less impressed by the effectiveness of monarchical power in Early Modern Europe than by its limitations. It has paid more attention to participation than coercion, more attention to resistance than to the exercise of power, more attention to survival than to innovation. In so doing, it has tended to cast doubt on what was previously taken for granted: the *transforming* power of the state.[1]

More recent fashions in research, however, have introduced a new and not yet fully integrated element into this post – Second World War picture of the Early Modern state as a leviathan *manqué*. Contemporary fascination with the problems and possibilities of image making and ideological control has done much to inspire these fashions, and has helped to stimulate historical inquiry into attempts by those in authority to manipulate public opinion by means of ritual, ceremonial, and propaganda, whether in written, pictorial, or spoken form.

Contemporary interest in the deployment of images and symbols by those in power has undoubtedly added an important new dimension to our knowledge and understanding of Early Modern Europe.

---

[1] These points are admirably made by Gerhard Oestreich in his important article, 'Strukturprobleme des europäischen Absolutismus', reprinted in his *Geist und Gestalt des frühmodernen Staats* (Berlin, 1969), pp. 179–97. An English version of this and other selected writings by Oestreich may be found in his *Neostoicism and the Early Modern State* (Cambridge, 1982).

This dimension can be especially valuable for the seventeenth century, a time when new instruments and techniques of visual representation made it possible for authority to resort extensively to those illusion-istic tricks that are essential to the process of image building. It was a century, too, that possessed an unusually acute awareness of the complex relationship of image and reality. The word *reputation* figured prominently in the vocabulary of seventeenth-century states-men, and the Spanish political theorist Saavedra Fajardo was only expressing a commonplace of the times when he wrote in his *Idea of a Political-Christian Prince* (1640): 'if the crown is not firmly planted on this central column of reputation, it will fall to the ground'[2]. Reputation was the other person's perception of oneself, and if it had to be grounded on at least a minimal basis of reality, it could still be enhanced by ingenious sleights of hand.

As an age captivated by the art of the theatre, the seventeenth century displayed an almost obsessive concern with appearance. If the world is perceived in terms of the theatre, the enhancement or transformation of appearance becomes an essential component of the statesman's art. The application of the arts of the theatre to political life, and especially to the projection of kingship, is one of the principal characteristics of seventeenth-century monarchies; and it would be valuable to have more systematic research into the ways in which the symbols of monarchy were manipulated to enhance the power and majesty of seventeenth-century kings. But at least two *caveats* should be borne in mind when this research is undertaken.

If the leviathan of the seventeenth-century state proves on closer inspection to be a beast skilled in the arts of illusion, these skills would make it less of a leviathan *manqué* than has recently been assumed. While this may indeed prove to be the conclusion, it is not a conclusion that should be embraced without some awareness of the problems inherent in the study of propaganda and image making. There is some danger of our being more impressed by the workings of a propaganda machine than were those at whom it was directed, simply because of the quantity of evidence left behind for later generations. The example of the Spain of Olivares suggests that the new propaganda resources of the seventeenth-century state were perfectly capable of being counterproductive, and of damaging the very cause they were intended to promote.

Even if we reach the plausible conclusion that ritual, ceremonial, and propaganda were capable, if deftly used, of enhancing mon-archical authority, there remains another danger: that an excessive

---

[2] Diego Saavedra Fajardo, *Empresas políticas: Idea de un príncipe político-cristiano*, ed. Quintín Aldea Vaquero (Madrid, 1976), 1, p. 310 (*empresa* 31).

concentration on them is liable to distract attention from other and possibly more potent weapons in the armoury of seventeenth-century monarchs and statesmen. The exercise of power is, after all, something more than the manipulation of images. While capitalizing, then, on our sharpened awareness of the significance of symbolism and the creation of images, it would be unwise to assume that this is enough. The effectiveness of those images in any given historical situation still needs to be tested, and then set alongside that of other and perhaps more formidable devices by which rulers elicited the obedience and assent of the ruled.

The complex nature of the relationship between power and ideology can be illustrated from the history of the Spain of Philip IV during the twenty-two years of government of his favourite and principal minister, the Count-Duke of Olivares. Many features of the Spanish situation were, as always, unique; but the way in which the Olivares regime attempted to extend the range of its power by resorting to ceremonial, propaganda, and image making is characteristic enough of seventeenth-century monarchies to suggest something of the nature of contemporary governments and the difficulties that they faced.

On coming to power in 1621 Olivares made it his principal objective to restore Spain, and especially Castile, to the greatness that it had enjoyed under Charles V and Philip II. In his view the achievements of Spain's sixteenth-century monarchs had been undermined by the ineptitude and corruption of the regime preceding his own, that of the Duke of Lerma, the favourite and first minister of Philip III. He planned also to give Spain and its empire an effective system of military and naval defence against its numerous actual or potential enemies, and especially the Dutch, who had shown in their short period of independence how intelligent economic organization could enhance the military capabilities of a second- or third-rate European power.

He aimed, therefore, both to restore and to modernize, and in so doing committed himself to a programme that may from the start have been flawed by internal contradictions.[3] A particular set of values and assumptions had made Castile what it was, and Olivares shared the common belief that the departure from these values and assumptions had set in motion the process of decline. Yet even while he sought to revive Castile's ancient virtues, he was also well aware that a society with a traditional value system needed to adapt in order

[3] Below, ch. 11.

to meet the challenge of hard economic times. Traditionally, for instance, Castilians despised the values of the marketplace, but it was Olivares' intention to 'turn Spaniards into merchants.'[4]

What were the values and assumptions on which Spain's historical greatness had been predicated – the ideological underpinnings, as it were, of the Spanish Monarchy and empire? The first of them was the sense of global mission, conceived both in religious and dynastic terms. Traditionally, it was the Holy Roman Empire, now governed by the junior branch of the House of Austria, which had universalist claims. But in practice it was the *monarquía española,* the Spanish Monarchy, which was at once truly global and imperial in character, and which could claim with good reason to be the dominant world power.

It was clear to the men who governed sixteenth-century Spain that only God's special favour could have endowed their king with so many dominions, and given him an empire of unprecedented size, on which the sun never set. Therefore the justification of Habsburg rule and Spanish domination must be the furtherance of God's cause. In consequence, Habsburg Spain had a mission: to preserve, defend, and extend the faith, acting – in close concert with the Austrian branch of the family – as the right arm of the Church. If this mission were effectively sustained, a properly ordered world would enjoy the innumerable blessings of a *pax hispanica.*

This sense of Christian providentialism – of the defence of the Catholic cause against the forces of infidels and heretics – gave Habsburg Spain its raison d'être. It found expression in a large body of apologetic literature in the sixteenth and seventeenth centuries, of which Fray Juan de Salazar's *Política Española* of 1619 provided a particularly strident example. 'The principal foundation of this high edifice', he wrote, 'the hinges and axles on which this great machine turns, lie not in the rules of the impious Machiavelli, which atheists call "reason of state"... but in religion and the service and honour of God.'[5]

This sense of global mission was complemented by a close identification of throne and altar: the ruler of Spain was the standard-bearer of God's cause. Nowhere was the historic mission of the dynasty more effectively expressed than in Titian's great portrait of Charles V at Mühlberg (1548) (Pl. 2).[6] Here Charles is represented as the *miles christianus,* an image that his descendants would seek to make their own. They took for granted the existence of a special

---

[4] John H. Elliott and José F. de La Peña, *Memoriales y cartas del Conde Duque de Olivares,* 2 vols. (Madrid, 1978–80), 1, p. 98 (*Gran Memorial,* 1624).

[5] Ed. Miguel Herrero García (Madrid, 1945), pp. 53–4 ('proposición tercera').

[6] See Erwin Panofsky, *Problems in Titian, Mostly Iconographic* (New York, 1969), pp. 84–7.

2 Titian, *Charles V at Mühlberg*.

relationship between God and themselves. God conferred victories upon a king who served Him well; and conversely, as Philip IV became agonizingly aware, defeat was provoked by royal sinfulness.

While the sacred character of Spanish kingship was taken as axiomatic, it did not assume many of the forms associated with divine kingship in other parts of Europe. The King of Spain, for example, possessed no healing powers, and Spaniards in need of healing would travel to Paris, not Madrid, for a cure.[7] Moreover, there had been no coronation ceremony in Castile since 1379: the heir to the throne would receive homage as a prince, and the only ceremonies on his accession were the raising of banners and the official proclamation of his style and titles. This seems to suggest a confidence about the divinely ordained nature of Spanish kingship, operating through a legitimate line of descent, which precluded the need felt elsewhere to reinforce the image of kingship with the visible symbols of royalty. Indeed, at the end of the sixteenth century the kings of Spain apparently had no official throne, no sceptre, no crown.[8]

It is perhaps not surprising, then, that Spanish royal portraiture of the sixteenth and seventeenth centuries fails to develop an elaborate symbolic language, in sharp contrast to the practice followed at the courts of lesser European rulers. Vasari's apotheosis of Grand Duke Cosimo I of Tuscany (Pl. 3) would have seemed out of place in the more restrained world of the Spanish court. It is as if a form of 'Avis principle' operates in the world of political imagery and propaganda: those who are only second try harder. Where, as in Habsburg Spain, the supremacy of the king is taken for granted, political imagery can be studiously understated, and there is no need to deck out the ruler with elaborate allegorical trappings (Pls. 4, 5). This form of understatement may well represent the ultimate in political sophistication.

By papal concession, however, the kings of Spain proudly bore the title of Catholic Kings, and they made a point of emphasizing their supremely Catholic character, more Catholic in their own eyes than that of their rival, *le roi très Chrétien*. Public appearances were largely connected with religious occasions, such as attendance at mass or at *autos de fe,* and participation in religious processions.[9] The special relationship between God and the king was also emphasized in the official style of court architecture inspired by the Escorial, part

---

[7] Marc Bloch, *Les rois thaumaturges* (Paris, 1961), p. 155.

[8] For the discontinuation of the coronation ceremony, and the disappearance of the regalia, see Percy Ernst Schramm, *Herrschaftszeichen und Staatssymbolik,* 3 (Stuttgart, 1956), pp. 1025–31. Schramm does not, however, explore the possible reasons for the developments in the Spanish kingdoms, for which see the article by T.F. Ruiz, cited above, p. 148 n. 19.

[9] Above, p. 147.

3 Giorgio Vasari, *The Apotheosis of Duke Cosimo*.

4 Alonso Sánchez Coello, *Philip II*.

5 Diego de Velázquez, *Philip IV*.

6   The Escorial.

palace, part church, part monastery (Pl. 6). Even Philip IV's
pleasure palace of the Buen Retiro, built on the outskirts of Madrid
in the 1630s, adjoined the royal church and convent of San Jerónimo,
and its spacious gardens were dotted with hermitage chapels. The
very name of Retiro was a play on the idea of retreat, which included
that of religious retreat. Calderón's allegorical drama, *El nuevo
palacio del Buen Retiro,* presented at court in 1634, took place
simultaneously on two planes, the celestial and the earthly. God was
equated with the king; the church with the queen; and New Jerusalem
with the new palace of the Buen Retiro. Judaism, forbidden entry
into the palace, was forced to watch the enactment of the Eucharist,
which was followed by the emergence of the king bearing the cross
aloft, after his temporary *retiro* into the bread.[10]

This constant allusion to the sacred ties that bound God and king
would seem to have had a dual purpose. To the world at large it
helped to define the position of the King of Spain as the most
Catholic of kings; but within Spain itself it also provided an
important element of political and social cohesion. Church and king
were the two common elements in the disparate and fragmented
Spanish Monarchy; and religious uniformity, enforced by king,
church, and inquisition, was the guarantee of continuing political
order and stability. It also guaranteed the continuation of a

[10] Jonathan Brown and J.H. Elliott, *A Palace for a King* (New Haven and London, 1980),
p. 230.

hierarchical social order which mirrored that of the universe. The sermon, therefore, had an important part to play in maintaining the political and social status quo,[11] and the same role was also fulfilled by the theatre. Theatre was supposed to be exemplary, or, in the words of Tirso de Molina, himself a friar, 'to teach by giving pleasure' (enseñar deleitando).[12] It is not surprising, therefore, to find that a central theme of seventeenth-century drama is that of the moral, social, or political order undermined by sin or ignorance, with a dénouement that results in the restoration of the status quo. More unqualified expressions of the divine right of kings are to be found in the work of seventeenth-century Spanish dramatists than in that of contemporaneous political theorists. 'What the king orders is never unjust', proclaims Ruiz de Alarcón.[13]

Along with the universalism of a global mission, and the recurring identification of king and altar, the Spanish Monarchy traditionally rested on a third central principle: the combination of constitutional pluralism with unitary kingship. The Monarchy was in effect a supranational community, made up of a complex of kingdoms and provinces, which differed in their laws, customs, and languages, and were united only in their adherence to a common faith and their allegiance to a common king. Jealously guarding their semiautonomous status, the different constituent parts acknowledged only the overlordship of an almost permanently absentee monarch. The king of all was also, in a seventeenth-century phrase, the king of each;[14] and the fact that he was king of each was more important to the individual kingdoms and provinces than that he was also king of all.

The Spanish Monarchy, with its capital established in Madrid in 1561, was in consequence a centrifugal structure, which the king sought to hold together by a carefully organized institutional system of viceroys and councils. In such a structure the role of the king, and the image he presents to his various peoples, must be of prime importance, since in his own person he embodies unity. To retain their allegiance and reinforce their loyalty there were various guises in which he could present himself to the subjects of his different realms. Both Charles V and Philip II were presented as the champions of militant orthodoxy, although Charles V was the more con-

---

[11] José Antonio Maravall, La cultura del barroco (2nd ed., Barcelona, 1980), pp. 299–300. Eng. trans., Culture of the Baroque (Minneapolis, 1986), pp. 142–3. The sermon in Spain deserves far more attention than it has so far received, but see Hilary Dansey Smith, Preaching in the Spanish Golden Age (Oxford, 1978).

[12] Charles Vincent Aubrun, La comédie espagnole, 1600–1680 (Paris, 1966), p. 131.

[13] See José Antonio Maravall, Teatro y literatura en la sociedad barroca (Madrid, 1972), pp. 124–7, for this and other examples.

[14] See J.H. Elliott, The Revolt of the Catalans (Cambridge, 1963), p. 8.

vincing of the two in the role of warrior king. Philip II, on the other hand, developed with great skill the image of the concerned ruler in an age of bureaucratic government, creating a new model of the king as bureaucrat toiling over his papers. He also projected himself as the supreme upholder of law and the defender of justice, a royal Solomon, whose palace of the Escorial was itself conceived as the Temple of Jerusalem.[15] It is no accident, then, that the king repeatedly appears at the climactic moment of seventeenth-century Spanish plays as the *deus ex machina* who, with Solomonic equity, redresses grievances, gives to each his deserts, and restores the political and social order jeopardized by oppressive landlords or evil councillors.

The image of a supremely just king, remote but – when necessary – available, provides the indispensable safety valve in societies subject to social and financial exploitation and administrative abuse. When rebels shouted 'long live the king and down with bad government!' as they did in Catalonia and Spanish Italy in the 1640s, the safety mechanism was working as it was supposed to work. Philip II was well aware of the political advantages to be gained from fulfilling his God-given duty to sustain justice and uphold the law. But the consequence of acting as the custodian of law in a constitutionally diversified monarchy was to condemn it to a high degree of political immobility. The laws of each kingdom were sacrosanct; the king had sworn to maintain them. It was therefore difficult, if not impossible, to change the political structure, even where this worked against the crown's best interests, because the laws could not be changed. The sixteenth-century Spanish crown had found an ingenious formula for the conservation of empire, but the price of conservation was abstention from tampering with the status quo.

These three governing principles of the Spanish Monarchy helped to determine both the shape of the programme on which Olivares embarked after the accession of Philip IV in 1621, and the constraints under which he had to operate. The Monarchy had arrived at a critical juncture in 1621, not least because of the growing incompatibility of two of these three principles: an activist foreign policy conceived in terms of a global mission to defend the faith, and a passive domestic policy dominated by the desire to avoid

[15] See René Taylor, 'Architecture and Magic. Considerations of the *Idea* of the Escorial', in *Essays in the History of Architecture presented to Rudolf Wittkower*, ed. D. Fraser, H. Hibbard, and M.J. Levine (London, 1967), pp. 81–109. For the impact of this idea on Charles I of England, by way of the Spanish Jesuit Villalpando, see Roy Strong, *Britannia Triumphans: Inigo Jones, Rubens and Whitehall Palace* (London, 1980), pp. 59–63.

disturbing the status quo in the various territories owing allegiance to the king.

The activist foreign policy, pursued over many decades, although with some recent slackening, had proved enormously expensive in terms of manpower and money; and such was the constitutional structure of the Monarchy that the burden of sustaining this foreign policy had fallen with particular intensity on the heartland of the Monarchy, Castile, which was deficient in legal and institutional defences against financial exactions by the crown. Royal fiscalism had done irreparable damage to the Castilian economy, and the damage had been compounded by twenty years of mismanagement under the rule of Philip III's favourite, the Duke of Lerma, whose corrupt administration had devalued the authority of the crown and played into the hands of sectional interests in Castilian society.

Olivares came to power in 1621 committed to an activist foreign policy, which seemed to him all the more necessary because of the simultaneous resumption of war with the Dutch and the threat posed by the outbreak of war in Germany to what were perceived as the vital interests of the House of Austria. But he came to the conclusion that the condition of Castile and of the Spanish Monarchy as a whole made it impossible to sustain this activist foreign policy without radical reform at home – a reform both of institutions and of mental attitudes. In the 1620s and 1630s, therefore, a new and unprecedented political activism overtook Madrid's domestic policy as the Count-Duke attempted to restore Spain's international standing – its 're-putation' – along with the political and economic base needed to sustain it.

His activist programme dictated the character of the Olivares regime and gave a new, if temporary, dynamism to the power of the state in seventeenth-century Spain. This more aggressive deployment of state power coincided with a similar movement in the France of Richelieu and, to a lesser degree, in the England of Charles I. Insofar as it was a general European movement, it seems to have been both a response to the renewal of warfare in the difficult economic climate of the 1620s and 1630s, and a reflection of new assumptions about the character and purpose of the state.

The critical problem confronting Olivares, as also Richelieu, was how to maximize power. Greater international power could only come from the more effective mobilization of economic and social resources to meet the demands of war; but war – or at least victorious war – was in turn one of the most effective devices for enhancing the domestic power of the state.

In setting about his task of maximizing power, Olivares lacked two important elements on which at least some of his contemporaries were able to build. One was the idea of nationality. The supranational character of the Spanish Monarchy meant that national loyalties could not be used to animate the structure as a whole. Different regions had their own sense of identity, and Castile in particular had developed its own brand of messianic nationalism, although this was faltering by the early seventeenth century and clearly had no validity beyond Castile itself. Any reactivation of Castilian nationalism was likely, indeed, to be counterproductive, setting up shock waves of local nationalism in other parts of the Monarchy. But what alternative, if any, existed? How was it possible to generate a sense of loyalty to a supranational bureaucratic organism?

Richelieu was able to make much of the state, both as a concept and a word. But where and what was the state in a worldwide monarchy of disparate provinces? Not surprisingly, although Olivares speaks of 'reason of state' or 'matters of state', he does not appear to have possessed Richelieu's high conception of the state as an abstract entity. He refers instead to the 'crown', the 'monarchy', or to the 'royal authority', operating within the framework of an organic relationship between king and people. Where Richelieu, then, sought to elevate the power of the state, Olivares sought to enhance the power and authority of the king, although the difference may have been more semantic than real. In Olivares' opinion the balance of power, both at home and abroad, had been tilting against the King of Spain, and this had to be redressed before it was too late. The king was therefore at the centre of his plans for the revival of Spain. His mission was to elevate his royal master to new heights of authority.

His first task was to enhance Philip's majesty, transforming a rather petulant and self-willed adolescent into *Felipe el Grande* – Philip the Great – a king supreme in the skills of government, and in the arts of peace and war. With an eye both to international and domestic opinion, Olivares set out to groom Philip for his stellar role. Where government was concerned, the model was to be that untiring civil servant, the king's grandfather, Philip II. The image of a working king was needed to efface the image of a *roi fainéant* governed by a favourite – an image that had survived the nominal reign of Philip III and the actual reign of the Duke of Lerma, and looked set for a repeat appearance with Philip IV and the Count-Duke of Olivares. The Count-Duke eschewed the name of favourite – *privado* or *valido* – preferring to be known as the king's 'faithful minister'. But if the old image were to be banished, he must persuade the king to work. In the opening years of the reign this proved an uphill task, since Philip preferred the pleasures of the chase to the tedium of the study. But in a mood of remorse following a serious illness in 1627 he at last began to settle down to his state papers, and was soon putting in long hours at his desk, to the delight of Olivares. If he never quite became another Philip II, he turned himself under Olivares' prompting into a conscientious monarch, and the two men seem to have established a genuine working partnership.

Where the arts of peace were concerned, Philip proved an admirable pupil. Again with Olivares' encouragement, he set out to repair the deficiencies of an inadequate education, and embarked on an impressive reading programme in the best ancient and modern authors.[16] He showed an early taste for music and the theatre, and became, like so many of his family, a great connoisseur and picture collector, adding some two thousand paintings to the royal collections over the course of his reign. He therefore moved instinctively to fill the part envisaged for him by Olivares as a prince of patrons. He was to be the *rey planeta* – the Planet King, after the sun, the fourth of the planets – and although it was left to his future nephew and son-in-law, Louis XIV of France, to develop systematically the conceit of the sun, Philip shone as the central luminary in a brilliant court.

The old palace of the Alcázar, however, was not an ideal setting for the court of the Planet King, but this deficiency was remedied in the 1630s with the construction of the Buen Retiro. Closely following the traditional style of Spanish royal architecture, the exterior of the new palace lacked grandeur by seventeenth-century standards (Pl. 23). But the principal rooms were lavishly furnished and hung with paintings, some of which constituted thematic series, although no general attempt was made to achieve a tightly woven symbolism, except in the principal hall of the palace, the famous Hall of Realms. The palace courtyards were used for tournaments and jousts. The extensive gardens were carefully laid out with different forms of royal recreation in mind; and the island set in the great artificial lake was used for the mounting of elaborate plays by Calderón and other court dramatists, staged by the brilliant Italian scenographer Cosimo Lotti. With the completion in 1640 of a special court theatre, the Coliseo, it was possible to stage complex *comedias de tramoyas* – machine plays – capable of producing the most spectacular scenic effects.

The court of Philip IV therefore became, as Olivares had planned, a great centre of patronage and a showcase for the arts. The cultural patronage of Philip's court was perhaps unsystematic by later standards, but if it did not add up to a formal programme or convey a coherent set of values, it nurtured some men of genius, among

---

[16] Brown and Elliott, *A Palace*, pp. 41–2.

them Lope de Vega, Calderón, and Velázquez, and helped project the image of a country inferior to none in the arts of peace as well as war.

The arts of war were not, as Philip IV had wistfully hoped, to be embodied in his person. His ambition to lead his armies into battle was consistently thwarted by Olivares, and he was forced to find his compensation on the hunting field. But no effort was spared to present to the world the image of a victorious king, and it was in the Hall of Realms of the Buen Retiro that the military greatness of Philip IV and the power of Spain were given visible expression. The decoration of the hall was planned and executed between 1633 and 1635, and was clearly intended to dispel the impression, created by the palace as a whole, that the king was concerned only with frivolity and pleasure in times of war and hardship. In an iconographical programme in which the desires of the king and Olivares were clearly paramount, some of the major themes of the reign were splendidly rehearsed.[17]

The ceiling of the hall, with its twenty-four coats of arms of the different realms, emphasized the multiplicity and the close mutual relationship of the many kingdoms owing allegiance to Philip IV. The two end walls were devoted to the immediate past, present, and future of the dynasty, with equestrian portraits by Velázquez of Philip III and Philip IV and their queens, and the young Baltasar Carlos, the heir to the throne (Pls. 7, 8). Along the two side walls ran ten scenes by Zurbarán of the life of Hercules, the conqueror of discord, the model of princely virtues, and the founding father of the dynasty. Placed between the windows of these same walls was the most striking feature of the room – a series of twelve great battle paintings by different Spanish artists. Five of these paintings, including Velázquez's masterpiece, *The Surrender of Breda* (Pl. 9), depicted victories won by Spain in 1625, which had passed into official mythology as the *annus mirabilis* of the reign of Philip IV. Another four commemorated the victories of 1633, the very year the paintings were commissioned, with the obvious intention of representing it as a second *annus mirabilis*. The common format of these paintings, with a victorious general prominently placed against a scene of victory or surrender, remained squarely within the Spanish iconographical tradition of narrative and literal representation, almost ostentatiously eschewing the allegorical approach that characterized, for example, Rubens' splendid cycle of the life of Marie de' Médicis.

---

[17] For an iconographical examination of the Hall of Realms, see Brown and Elliott, *A Palace*, ch. 6.

7   Diego de Velázquez, *Philip IV on Horseback.*

8. Diego de Velázquez, *Baltasar Carlos on Horseback*.

9   Diego de Velázquez, *The Surrender of Breda*.

The central message of this programme was plain for all to read. It presented Philip IV, baton in hand, as the worthy upholder of his dynasty's mission, holding in check the forces of heresy, discord, and rebellion. He was a king who had been – and still was – victorious in his wars, but at the same time (as Velázquez's *Surrender of Breda* brilliantly testified) magnanimous in the moment of triumph. Here indeed was *Felipe el Grande,* the greatest monarch in the world.

If one objective of the Count-Duke was to emphasize the majesty of Philip as supreme among the princes of the world both in peace and war, another was to make sure that he became the true master of his own dominions. He had inherited a diversified and fragmented Monarchy, and Olivares' intention was to give it unity. 'The most important piece of business in your Monarchy', he told Philip in a famous state paper of 1624, 'is to make yourself King of Spain: by which I mean that Your Majesty should not be content with being King of Portugal, of Aragon, of Valencia, and Count of Barcelona, but should secretly work and plan to reduce these kingdoms of which Spain is composed to the style and laws of Castile.'[18] If this were achieved – if the laws were made uniform, the internal customs barriers removed, the king able to deploy his ministers wherever he wanted – then Philip would indeed be in reality what he already was in name, the most powerful monarch in Christendom.

This insistence on unity conceived as uniformity, which runs right through Olivares' twenty-two years of power, directly contravened that fundamental principle of the Spanish Monarchy, its respect for constitutional diversity. It was, then, a radical and dangerous enterprise on which Olivares was embarked, and one that was bound to bring him into conflict with provincial rights and liberties. While aware of the difficulties he was also a man in a hurry, desperately anxious to mobilize all the resources of the Monarchy in order to ward off the assaults of its enemies. To preach the need for unity to peoples who prided themselves on the retention of their distinctiveness was to fly in the face of prudent tradition, but in his early years of government Olivares believed that the advantages of his proposals would speak for themselves. As the first step toward the achievement of unity he proposed a scheme for military cooperation between the different kingdoms, a Union of Arms, which was laid before the Cortes of Aragon, Valencia, and Catalonia in 1626, introduced by carefully drafted broadsheets outlining the benefits to be expected from closer union.[19]

The notable lack of enthusiasm in the Crown of Aragon for this novel idea compelled the Olivares regime, increasingly short of men and money for its wars, to resort to cruder forms of pressure to achieve its ends. As in early Stuart England, the doctrine of necessity and *salus populi* became the principal theoretical justification of the regime: the needs of self-defence were held to override all lesser laws. In a Spanish version of that great drama which was being played out all over western Europe, the resort of the crown to its prerogative power was countered by the contractualist arguments of peoples determined to retain their ancient laws and liberties. The ensuing revolts of Catalonia and Portugal in 1640 not only led to the downfall of Olivares himself, but discredited with the taint of failure his programme for a closer unification of the Spanish Monarchy.

[18] Elliott and La Peña, *Memoriales y cartas*, 1, p. 96.
[19] *Ibid.*, Docs. IX and X.

The steady opposition of the peripheral provinces of the Iberian peninsula to the Union of Arms underlines the more general problem of obedience which faced Olivares at every turn as he tried to mobilize the Monarchy for war. Recalcitrant generals, undisciplined aristocrats, and self-interested ministers all stood in the way of that smooth execution of orders which he regarded as essential for any well-governed monarchy. It was no good proclaiming the greatness of Philip if the king was not obeyed.

The enforcement of obedience therefore became as high a priority as the enhancement of majesty and the imposition of unity, and indeed constituted an integral component of the Olivares programme. The regime developed its coercive machinery, including a special *Junta de Obediencia* to deal with cases of resistance to the execution of royal orders. But repression by itself was at best a partial response to a problem that confronted the ruler of every Early Modern state. In the face of apparently endemic disobedience, princes and statesmen strove to inculcate social discipline, no doubt raising their expectations of conformity in the same degree as they raised the level of their demands on their peoples. In the early seventeenth century a convenient doctrine of social discipline lay to hand in the neo-Stoic writings of Justus Lipsius.[20] Neo-Stoicism, with its insistence on the Roman virtues of *auctoritas, temperantia, constantia,* and *disciplina,* was an eminently appropriate ideology for the aspiring absolutist state; and it is no accident that it should have been embraced by Olivares, for the influence of Lipsius was strong in Spain, and not least in the learned circles of early seventeenth-century Seville, where he spent his most formative years.[21]

Philip and Olivares were quick to see the possibilities of the royal court, with its formal procedures and rules of etiquette, as an instrument for instilling the discipline that they found so defective in the Spanish aristocracy. Philip himself revised and emended the elaborate *etiquetas* which governed palace ceremonial, and developed to perfection that impassive *gravitas* which served at once to distance himself from his subjects and to instruct them in the proper rules of comportment. Unruly nobles were banished from court, and the palace became, in the words of a contemporary, 'a school of silence, punctiliousness, and reverence.'[22]

Yet human nature remained obstinately intractable, and as Olivares despaired of disciplining the nobles of his own generation, his thoughts turned increasingly toward the education of their children.

---

[20] See Oestreich, *Neostoicism and the Early Modern State* for this theme of social discipline.
[21] Elliott and La Peña, *Memoriales y cartas,* 1, pp. xlvi–lii.
[22] Alonso Carrillo, *Origen de la dignidad de grande* (Madrid, 1657), p. 12.

His aim was to create a genuine service nobility, which would place itself unhesitatingly at the disposal of the king, serving him with absolute loyalty in government, diplomacy, and war. His first attempt in this direction was the foundation of *Estudios Reales* at court under royal patronage, and in 1629 the Jesuit-run Colegio Imperial opened its doors to aspiring nobles with much pomp and fanfare. Its curriculum included classical languages, history, natural philosophy, the military arts, 'politics and economics, including those of Aristotle, adjusting reason of state to conscience, religion, and the Catholic Faith.'[23] But the new foundation, which came under immediate attack from the universities and the religious orders, was a failure, and from the early 1630s Olivares was casting around for some alternative. His next scheme was for the establishment in the peninsula of noble academies, but enthusiasm was muted, there was no money to found them, and the proposal never left the drawing board.[24]

The extreme difficulty experienced by Olivares in securing compliance with his wishes – in itself hardly unusual in early seventeenth-century states – provides some indication of the degree of opposition, whether covert or open, to his government. The scale and character of this opposition have yet to be determined, but some of the principal centres can at least be identified. Within the court there was fierce hostility to Olivares and his men – his *hechuras* or 'creatures' in seventeenth-century parlance – among the grandees and titled nobility. The Count-Duke, too, came up against the stolid resistance of the bureaucracy, which resented his slighting of the councils and his resort to ad hoc committees, or juntas, of his own hand-picked men. He was also faced with a constitutionalist opposition, not only in the Crown of Aragon, but also in Castile, where the Cortes in the last years of Philip III and the first of Philip IV were showing surprising signs of life.[25] If this opposition spoke primarily on behalf of the urban elites, it also reflected, however imperfectly, the growing popular hostility to the regime as its fiscal demands became more insistent and extreme.

While the various elements of opposition were strikingly unsuccessful in making common cause, they did succeed in their

[23] José Simón-Díaz, *Historia del Colegio Imperial de Madrid* (Madrid, 1952), 1, pp. 67–8.

[24] See Elliott and La Peña, *Memoriales y cartas*, 2, Doc. XII.

[25] See especially Jean Vilar, 'Formes et tendances de l'opposition sous Olivares', *Mélanges de la Casa de Velázquez*, 7 (1971), pp. 263–94; and Charles Jago, 'Habsburg Absolutism and the Cortes of Castile', *American Historical Review*, 86 (1981), pp. 307–26.

various ways in harassing the regime and driving it increasingly on to the defensive. Much of the aristocratic opposition inevitably took the form of palace intrigue, especially in the 1620s, when the residence in the palace of the king's two younger brothers created alternative centres of loyalty. To judge from the plays commissioned from Tirso de Molina by members of the Pimentel family, there may have been a theatre of opposition,[26] but more serious for the regime was the posting of pasquinades and the circulation of clandestine pamphlets. This covert opposition literature, circulating either in manuscript or in clandestine imprints, repeated certain standard themes: the disastrous consequences for Spain of the Count-Duke's economic and foreign policies; the arbitrary character of his government, and his usurpation of the powers of the king.

Opposition came to a head in 1629 at a time of widespread discontent over the consequences of the Count-Duke's involvement of Spain in the War of the Mantuan Succession, and in the summer of that year serious attempts were made to detach Philip from his favourite. An anonymous manifesto on behalf of the nobility bluntly told Philip that 'Your Majesty is not a king, you are a person whom the count seeks to conserve in order to make use of the office of king – a mere ceremonial ruler.'[27]

Faced with the evidence of its unpopularity, the administration made increasing use of its machinery of repression. Already in 1627 it had introduced a new and more stringent censorship law, prohibiting the printing without formal license by the Council of Castile of 'letters and relations, apologies and panegyrics, gazettes and news-sheets, sermons, discourses, and papers on affairs of state and government';[28] but this did not prevent the clandestine printing in Castile of seditious literature, and it did not apply to publications in the Crown of Aragon, which was outside the Council of Castile's jurisdiction. The spoken as well as the written word was subjected to surveillance. Preachers critical of the regime were banished from court, and attempts made to control the contents of sermons.[29] Olivares, like any seventeenth-century statesman, had his network of spies and informers feeding him with information and misinformation alike. Evidence is scarce, but it is unlikely that the arrest of Andrés de Mendoza in 1626 for 'writing discourses'[30] was a mere isolated incident.

[26] See Ruth Lee Kennedy, *Studies in Tirso, 1: The Dramatist and His Competitors, 1620–1626* (Chapel Hill, 1974), pp. 211.–14.

[27] Brown and Elliott, *A Palace*, pp. 51–2.

[28] Elliott and La Peña, *Memoriales y cartas*, 2, p. 184.

[29] Marvall, *La cultura del barroco*, p. 158. [*Culture of the Baroque*, p. 70.]

[30] *Ibid.*, p. 160, n. 70. [*Culture of the Baroque*, p. 71.]

But the government did not restrict itself to repressive measures. It also sought, where possible, to seize the offensive, mobilizing court preachers, playwrights, and artists on its behalf. There was no equivalent in Spain to the *Gazette* founded in France in 1631 by Théophraste Renaudot with Richelieu's blessing,[31] but there was an unending stream of *avisos* and *relaciones* conveying officially inspired or authorized information. The theatre, too, was brought into service. Francisco de Quevedo's *Cómo ha de ser el privado* (1629) is an attempt to show Olivares, under the transparent anagrammatic disguise of the Marquis of Valisero, as the selfless minister, a new Spanish Seneca, totally devoted to his master's service.[32] This was how Olivares was seen by himself and his friends, and this was how he wanted to be seen by the rest of the world.

Quevedo, who wielded the sharpest pen in Spain, was also drafted to respond to the anonymous manifesto of 1629 and other contemporaneous attacks on the regime, along with two other writers in the Olivares circle, the Count of La Roca and Antonio Hurtado de Mendoza.[33] All three in their counter-manifestoes presented fundamentally similar defences of the regime, admitting to occasional and inevitable setbacks, but dwelling on its successes, and particularly the victories of 1625, as evidence of the wise management of affairs by the Count-Duke himself. But these were essentially *pièces d'occasion,* and Olivares often expatiated on the need for a proper history of the reign. He eventually found his historian in the wraithlike person of the Bolognese Marquis Virgilio Malvezzi, a man after his own heart, who settled in Madrid in 1636 and became the house historian of the regime.

Court writers, then, in singing the praises of the king, were also expected to sing the praises of his minister. It was, after all, in Olivares' interest to associate himself and his policies as closely as possible with those of his master. It was for this reason that the decoration of the Hall of Realms was not confined to the glorification of the king. It also glorified the minister as his right-hand man. Although this was implicit in all the battle paintings – especially the cluster of victories of 1625 that had been singled out by Quevedo and his colleagues as proof of Olivares' wise counsel and prudent stewardship of the king's affairs – it was explicitly spelled out in the most unusual of the twelve paintings, Juan Bautista Maino's *Recapture of Bahía* (Pl. 10).[34]

---

[31] See Howard M. Solomon, *Public Welfare, Science, and Propaganda in Seventeenth-Century France* (Princeton, 1972).

[32] For this play, and Quevedo's relationship to Olivares, see below, ch. 9.

[33] Brown and Elliott, *A Palace,* pp. 162 and 164.

[34] For a detailed analysis of this painting, see Brown and Elliott, *A Palace,* pp. 184–90.

10   Juan Bautista Maino, *The Recapture of Bahía.*

Just as Velázquez's *Surrender of Breda* drew its inspiration from a play especially commissioned for court performance when news of the surrender first reached Madrid (Calderón's *El sitio de Bredá*), so Maino's *Recapture of Bahía* borrowed some of its ideas from a play by Lope de Vega, *El Brasil restituido*. But Maino skillfully turned to account the raw material provided by Lope de Vega to make certain statements about the Count-Duke and his policies. Since Bahía was recaptured from the Dutch by a joint Spanish-Portuguese naval expedition, it was traditionally selected by the regime's defenders as a classic example of the Union of Arms in action. By showing the returning Portuguese inhabitants of Bahía tending a wounded Castilian soldier, Maino provided further evidence of that close co-operation between the peoples of the Monarchy which in the past had all too often been impeded by what Olivares called 'the separation of hearts.'

But if Maino's painting may be taken as a visual expression of the universal benefits of Olivares' policy for a Union of Arms, it also made a statement – possibly without parallel in seventeenth-century works of art – about the special relationship of king and minister. In Lope de Vega's play, the commander of the expeditionary force, Don Fadrique de Toledo, at one point repairs to his tent and addresses a portrait of the king, asking if he should offer clemency to the Dutch (a proposal to which Philip graciously nods his assent). The play culminates in the crowning of Don Fadrique with laurels by the figure of Brazil. Maino appropriates these two subjects – the king's portrait and the crowning with laurels – but strikingly reworks them (Pl. 11). In his version of the surrender of the garrison, the defeated Dutch are forced to kneel as Don Fadrique de Toledo points to a tapestry in which it is not he but the king who is crowned with a wreath of laurels, while the figures of Heresy, Discord, and Treachery lie crushed beneath his feet. Two figures place the laurels on Philip's brow. One is Minerva, the goddess of war. The other is the Count-Duke of Olivares.

At this point, then, the king's favourite and first minister makes his own dramatic personal entry into the Hall of Realms. There was no doubting the significance of his presence, as the architect of Philip's victories and his right-hand man. Here was a striking affirmation both of the king's continuing confidence in Olivares, and of the closeness of their relationship as they worked together for the salvation of Spain. If the Hall of Realms set out to magnify the king, it was also intended to vindicate resoundingly the record of his minister.

But how many were willing and able to read the message? As far as the Hall of Realms was concerned, this was essentially designed for court purposes, and the audience for its message was inevitably restricted. There is no indication of any attempt to reproduce the battle paintings for a wider public, partly perhaps because Spain lacked a native school of engravers. On the other hand, the government was able to reach the provincial public in other ways, notably through newsletters and broad-sheets; and victories were celebrated with Te Deums in the cathedrals of Spain.

In Madrid itself, and more specifically at court, there was a hard core of opposition that was unlikely under any circumstances to be swayed by the propaganda of the regime. On the other hand, there is also likely to have been a large body of the uncommitted, generally unenthusiastic about the Olivares regime but susceptible to appeals to their patriotism, especially in the spring of 1635, which saw not only the unveiling of the battle paintings in the Hall of Realms but also the outbreak of war with France. But again, although the decoration of the hall clearly had a didactic purpose, how many people were actually given the opportunity to fall under its spell?

SED
DXTERA
TVA.

11   Juan Bautista Maino, detail of *The Recapture of Bahía*.

At this point, the inadequacies of an approach to the seventeenth century couched exclusively in terms of *propaganda* begin to appear. Although the Hall of Realms, like Malvezzi's history, was designed to influence contemporary opinion, its creators obviously had in mind a much larger audience than could possibly have seen it in the 1630s. Its appeal was not only to contemporaries but also to future generations, symbolized by the young heir to the throne, Baltasar Carlos, whose spirited portrait hung on its walls. It was an appeal, in fact, to posterity.

The Olivares regime, in commissioning these works, and in mobilizing poets and painters and artists, was engaged in a gigantic exercise in self-projection. It was making, in what it hoped would be a permanent form, a statement about the way in which it saw itself, and the way in which it wanted to be seen by future ages. In making its statement it was bidding for fame, and claiming for itself a glory that would outlast time.

This being so, it is natural to wonder whether the most receptive contemporary audience for these celebratory statements may not have been the men of the regime that commissioned them. In fact, may not the perpetrators have been the first to fall for their own propaganda? This at least is what the evidence of the 1630s seems to suggest. Olivares and his men dominated the court and the government; but they were a small, inward-looking coterie, increasingly isolated from the outside world. Like Charles I and his circle, they had developed through the world of the arts and of the theatre their own elaborate illusion of power.[35] But because of their growing isolation, their own image of themselves and their accomplishments diverged at more and more points from the reality. This in turn provided splendid opportunities for Olivares' critics, who seized on the Buen Retiro as a symbol of the government's failings, and mocked Malvezzi as a mendacious hack. Olivares, they claimed, had taken Philip captive, and had closed his eyes to what was occurring beyond the confines of his court.

As soon as this began to happen, it is clear that the attempt to mobilize artists, writers, and intellectuals in the service of the regime had backfired disastrously. When Olivares fell in 1643 he fell because his regime had lost the last shreds of credibility. It had proclaimed unity, and yet – with the revolts of Catalonia and Portugal – the Spanish peninsula had been hopelessly fragmented; it had endlessly trumpeted Spain's triumph over its enemies, and yet it had visibly been defeated; it had insisted on the greatness of *Felipe el Grande,* and

---

[35] See Stephen Orgel, *The Illusion of Power* (Berkeley and Los Angeles, 1975).

yet, as a satirical poem unkindly remarked, 'the king is great as a hole is great.'[36]

The fiasco of the Olivares regime was a warning that the next generation took to heart. As a result of the Count-Duke's failure, activism by the central government was discredited, and it would come back only in the eighteenth century with the Bourbons, whose programme for the revival and modernization of Spain bore striking similarities to that of Olivares. The transformation of society by the state – especially in Spain – was to prove a long and slow process, and the habit of obedience was not easily instilled. In the seventeenth century there were important forces working in this direction: the desire for order, which looked for satisfaction to the king; Lipsian doctrines of social discipline; the overwhelming need to concentrate power in an age when warfare made heavy demands on society. But the political careers both of Olivares and Richelieu illustrate the extreme difficulties that faced the early seventeenth-century statesman in his attempt to enhance the authority of the crown and maximize the power of the state. The two men were using similar techniques, and the greater success of Richelieu may indicate not so much a greater skill in exploiting the apparatus of power, as the fact that the shortest road to absolutism at home lay through victory abroad.

The seventeenth-century leviathan possessed greater capacity than its predecessors for projecting a favourable image of itself to the world; and Louis XIV – who may have appropriated more from the Spanish tradition than has so far been allowed – would in due course develop that capacity to the full. But if the repertoire of illusionistic devices had grown, so too had the dangers involved in its use. The fate of Olivares showed how easily a gulf could open between rhetoric and reality; and if his regime came close to developing modern forms of propaganda, it paid a no less modern price when it fell into a pit of its own digging, known today as the credibility gap.

[36] 'Memorial a S. M. el rey don Felipe Cuarto', in Teófanes Egido, *Sátiras políticas de la España Moderna* (Madrid, 1973), p. 115.

IX

QUEVEDO AND THE COUNT-DUKE OF OLIVARES

The events of that terrible night of December 7, 1639, when two *alcaldes de corte* entered the Duke of Medinaceli's house and, in the utmost secrecy, carried off a frightened and shivering Quevedo to his narrow confinement in San Marcos de León, have etched themselves indelibly into the literary and political history of seventeenth-century Spain. Olivares and Quevedo, the ruthless statesman and the wayward genius, seem condemned to each other's company through all eternity – an irony that Quevedo himself would no doubt have been the first to appreciate. But this posthumous association is by no means unjustified; for the Quevedo of the 1620s and 1630s cannot be fully understood without taking into account his relationship with Olivares, just as the career of Olivares himself cannot be fully understood without taking into account his relationship with Quevedo. Each man, in his own way, helped to make, and unmake the other.

The story of the relationship between Quevedo and the Count-Duke is not, of course, a new one. It was told by Marañón in a brief chapter of his biography of Olivares,[1] and is related in more or less detail in the various studies of Quevedo and his works. I cannot add any dramatic documentation to it, other than one important but ambiguous letter, which I published some years ago. But perhaps, as a historian of the Count-Duke and his government, I can elaborate a little on the facts that we already have, and in this way add one or two insights which may help to deepen our understanding of Quevedo and his works.

It was, I believe, a combination of mutual necessity and mutual admiration that brought these two fundamentally incompatible men together, and harnessed them in an uneasy relationship which eventually proved intolerable to both. The evidence suggests that this relationship was at its closest in the late 1620s and early 1630s;

[1] G. Marañón, *El Conde-Duque de Olivares*, 3rd ed. (Madrid, 1952), ch. 11.

but the foundations for it were laid in 1621, in the opening months of the reign of Philip IV.

Let us start, then, by looking for a moment at the world in 1621, as seen from Quevedo's *señorío* of La Torre de Juan Abad, to which he had been banished following the disgrace of his patron, the Duke of Osuna. The death of Philip III on 31 March and the immediate downfall of his principal minister, the Duke of Uceda, transformed the political scene in Madrid, and at the same time created new opportunities – and new dangers – for Quevedo in his exile. Although he was himself absent from the court, Quevedo, who must have had good informants, captures brilliantly in his *Grandes Anales de Quince Días* the excitement of those first weeks of the reign of Philip IV – the death of the king, the attempted return to court of the Duke of Lerma, the triumph of the Count of Olivares and his faction, the replacement of Uceda by Don Baltasar de Zúñiga, and the beginnings of a reform programme designed to extirpate the evils which had flourished unchecked under the nerveless government of Philip III, and to call to account some of the more prominent figures of the old regime, including, to Quevedo's alarm, the Duke of Osuna.

Quevedo's interest in the intentions of Spain's new rulers was immediate and personal. He chafed against his exile, and, as the protégé of Osuna, had a natural foreboding that still worse might befall him. Moreover, as a man of letters, and one with strongly developed political instincts, he needed the stimulus and the patronage that only the court could give him. It is not therefore surprising that, like Góngora and many another man of letters in 1621, he should have hastened to make his obeisance to the men of the new regime. On 5 April – five days after the death of Philip III – he wrote to Olivares sending him a manuscript of his *Política de Dios*.[2] Less than three weeks later he dedicated to the new first minister, Don Baltasar de Zúñiga, his *Carta del Rey Don Fernando el Católico,* which may be read both as an implied criticism of the late king as measured against the ideals of kingship exemplified by Ferdinand the Catholic, and as an expression of hope that the young Philip IV would take Ferdinand as his model.

These various overtures to the men of the new regime clearly had some effect. He was allowed to return at least temporarily to Madrid, and even if he remained under suspicion, he had begun to purge himself of his association with Osuna and the ministers of Philip III. It was in March 1623 that his banishment came to an end – a month after the publication by the government of its *Capítu-*

---

[2] Luis Astrana Marín, *Epistolario completo de D. Franciso de Quevedo-Villegas* (Madrid, 1946), letter 60.

los de Reformación, on which, in effect, Quevedo bestows his blessing in his *Epístola satírica y censoria contra las costumbres presentes de los castellanos,* appropriately dedicated to that great reformer, Olivares.

The sycophancy which characterizes these various productions is obvious, but it seems to me that Quevedo is incomprehensible if one fails to take into account the blend of idealism with self-interest in his complex personality. Everything about his personal situation in the early 1620s pushed him towards an accommodation with the men of the new regime; but at the same time, for Quevedo as for so many Castilians, those men seemed to offer a dramatic revival of hope. We have to set the Quevedo of 1621 into the context of that widespread movement during the later years of Philip III for restoration and reform – a movement that found expression in the treatises of the *arbitristas* and the debates of the Cortes, and enjoyed the support of significant sections of the court and the bureaucracy.

One of the spokesmen of this movement, Fray Juan de Santa María, wrote in his *República y policía Christiana* of 1615: 'The title of king is not purely honorific; it is also vocational.'[3] In the first part of his *Política de Dios,* written some two years later, Quevedo comes back again and again to this same theme: 'The king is a public person; ...kingship is not a diversion but a duty.'[4] For both men, the restoration of kingship was an indispensable precondition for the restoration of Castile. A bad king was ruled by favourites; a good king chose good ministers. Everything that happened in those first weeks of the reign of Philip IV suggested that Castile once more had a real king. His ministers, Zúñiga and Olivares, set out with the proclaimed intention of restoring the standards of integrity and good government that prevailed under Philip II. In August of 1621 Almansa y Mendoza wrote in one of his newsletters that 'the reign of the king, our lord, Philip IV, is a golden age [*siglo de oro*] for Spain, and such happy beginnings promise prosperous ends.'[5] This was a sentiment which Quevedo could share. If Philip was still too young and inexperienced to fulfill on his own all the duties of kingship, he had at least placed his confidence in men who were dedicating themselves to the heroic task of reforming the abuses that had been allowed to proliferate during the reign of his father, and to restoring the ancient Castilian virtues that had been eroded by the long reign of self-interest, luxury and sloth.

Olivares, therefore, as the puritanical reformer, as the man who refused gifts and favours as ostentatiously as his predecessor, the Duke of Lerma, had accepted them, seemed to be the answer to

---

[3] (Ed., Lisbon, 1621), fo. 16.
[4] *Política de Dios, Govierno de Christo,* ed. James O. Crosby (Madrid, 1966), p. 100.
[5] *Cartas de Andrés de Almansa y Mendoza* (Madrid, 1886), p. 53.

12   Follower of Diego de Velázquez, *Francisco de Quevedo*.

Quevedo's prayers; and it was in good conscience that he could
dedicate to him the *Política de Dios*. Olivares for his part could hardly
fail to welcome, although no doubt with a certain wariness, the
adherence of a writer with such a mordant pen. During his years in
Seville Olivares had acquired the reputation of being a generous
patron to men of letters and learning. When he moved to Madrid he
carried this tradition of patronage with him – in a letter of 1615
Quevedo describes a public procession into Madrid in which
Olivares appeared flanked by two poets in a flamboyant bid to
outshine the Duke of Sessa, who had as his companion the great

Lope de Vega.[6] During his years in power, Olivares made use of his exalted position to attract to himself the leading literary and intellectual lights of his day, partly because his own tastes ran in that direction, and partly because his long-term aim as the principal minister of the crown was to make the court the focus of literary and artistic patronage, so that Philip IV should be renowned as a monarch glorious in the arts of peace as well as those of war – in letters as well as arms.[7]

In welcoming Quevedo to this coterie of court intellectuals, Olivares was not, of course, animated solely by an altruistic desire to see the arts in a flourishing state. He was a man with an acute sense of the power of the pen, and was always alive to the opportunities for image making. He knew that poets, playwrights and artists could confer lustre on his regime; and he was anxious to prevent them, in so far as possible, from placing their services at the disposal of his critics. Quevedo, as Olivares was quick to appreciate, was the kind of intellectual whom one would rather have in one's own camp than the enemy's, and it is not therefore surprising to find him in the entourage of the king and Olivares on their visits to Andalusia in 1624 and to the Crown of Aragon in 1626.

1626 and 1627 are the years of the first printing of several of Quevedo's works – the *Política de Dios,* the *Buscón,* the *Sueños.* But the imprints are in Zaragoza and Barcelona, for the times were not propitious for publication in Castile. The ban imposed in 1625 on the printing in Castile of comedies, novels and other works of this kind was motivated by the concern of the Junta de Reformación to protect the morals of the young,[8] but a likely ulterior motivation was Olivares' increasing anxiety about the growth of what might be called a literature of opposition. In June 1627, amidst mounting agitation over the inability of the government to check the spiralling inflation, a new decree specifically forbade the printing of 'letters and relations, apologies and panegyrics, gazettes and news-sheets, sermons, discourses and papers on affairs of state and government ...*arbitrios,* verses, dialogues or anything else, even if short and of very few lines,' without prior approval by the authorities.[9]

The stringent new censorship regulations created a climate conducive to the denunciation of successful authors by their rivals. It is probable that this was the fate that overtook Quevedo, who found

---

[6] *Epistolario,* letter X.

[7] For this policy, see Jonathan Brown and J.H. Elliott, *A Palace for a King. The Buen Retiro and the Court of Philip IV* (New Haven and London, 1980).

[8] For the prohibition, see Jaime Moll, 'Diez años sin licencias para imprimir comedias y novelas en los reinos de Castilla: 1625–1634', *Boletín de la Real Academia Española,* 54 (1974), pp. 97–103.

[9] *Novísima Recopilación,* lib. VIII, tit. XVI, ley IX.

himself banished again in the spring of 1628. He complained to the Count-Duke of calumnies,[10] and his enemies were apparently spreading stories that his *Política de Dios* was intended as an attack on the Olivares regime.[11] One can never be sure of Quevedo's motivation, but my own view is that at this time he was a committed supporter of Olivares and his programme. On the other hand, his gift for acid comments made him the most awkward of allies, and his violent support of the cause of St. James in the co-patronage controversy could hardly have been better calculated to antagonize the Count-Duke. Olivares had a deep personal devotion to the figure of St. Teresa. As a child, his mother had made an apparently miraculous recovery from an illness after being visited by St. Teresa in the family palace of the Counts of Monterrey in Salamanca;[12] and the saint's heart, encrusted with diamonds, was the Count-Duke's most prized possession.[13] In the circumstances, it is not surprising that Olivares should have been happy at this moment to let Quevedo cool his heels in La Torre de Juan Abad.

But the exile was a short one: in January 1629 Quevedo was back in Madrid, and it is now that he seems to have entered into his period of closest association with Olivares and his circle. By this time Olivares had surrounded himself with a group of friends and dependents, who were spoken of as his *hechuras,* or 'creatures', and who looked upon him as their *patrón.* These constituted the men of the Olivares regime, a mixed bunch of relatives, ministers, secretaries and men of letters, who had thrown in their lot with the Count-Duke, and regarded themselves as committed to the support and defence of his policies. It would be an overstatement to say that Quevedo ever fitted easily into any group, but there were a number of these men with whom Quevedo had close personal or intellectual affiliations, and who no doubt helped to pull him back into the fold.

Among these we should probably give special prominence to the Count-Duke's Jesuit confessor, Hernando de Salazar, who seems to have served as an intermediary between Quevedo and Olivares,[14] and also to the governor of the archbishopric of Toledo, Don Alvaro de Villegas, presumably a relative, and one of the Count-Duke's closest confidants.[15] Quevedo had another relative in high places,

[10] *Epistolario,* letter XCIX (5 May 1628).

[11] *Epistolario,* letter CVII (to Juan Ruiz Calderón, 1 Aug. 1628).

[12] Efrén de la Madre de Dios and O. Steggink, *Tiempo y vida de Santa Teresa* (Madrid, 1968), p. 434. For St. Teresa and the co-patronage controversy, see below, p. 260.

[13] In his will, he bequeathed it to the queen (Real Academia de la Historia, M-189, *Testamento del Conde Duque de Olivares,* 16 May 1642, fo. 29v.).

[14] *Epistolario,* letter CII (Salazar to Quevedo, 30 May 1628).

[15] *Epistolario,* letters C and CI. For Villegas' importance at this time, see J.H. Elliott and J.F. La Peña, *Memoriales y cartas del Conde Duque de Olivares* (Madrid, 1978), 1, p. 212.

too, although the relationship has passed largely unnoticed.[16] This was Jerónimo de Villanueva, the Protonotario of the Crown of Aragon, who by 1629 was already on his way to becoming the right-hand man of Olivares and the second most powerful political figure in Spain. Villanueva, fourteen years younger than Quevedo, was the son of Agustín de Villanueva, secretary of the Council of Aragon under Philip III, and of Doña Ana Díaz de Villegas, Quevedo's cousin. On the death of his mother, Quevedo went to live in the home of Agustín de Villanueva, who had been appointed his guardian, so that he must have known Jerónimo from his earliest years. The Villanueva-Quevedo relationship was therefore extremely close. The political implications of this relationship for our understanding of Quevedo's association with the Olivares regime deserve further exploration; but there are other implications, too, which are not without interest. For the great-great-great grand-parents of Jerónimo on the paternal side are alleged to have been burnt by the Inquisition of Aragon as Judaizers.[17] It may therefore have been in a household of *converso* relatives that Quevedo spent some of his most impressionable years.

If, as seems likely, Quevedo's friends in the Olivares circle helped to ensure that his new exile was a short one, there is no doubt that Olivares needed his services in 1629 as never before. His reform programme had ground to a halt, stopped in its tracks by the obstructions thrown up by the Cortes, the municipal oligarchies, and the bureaucracy. The inflation of 1626 and 1627 had finally been checked by the government's belated deflationary measures of August 1628, but these had only served to add to the general economic distress. Spain's involvement in the War of the Mantuan Succession was proving to be a disastrous miscalculation on the part of Olivares, and the disaster was compounded by the reports which reached Madrid at the end of 1628 that the Dutch had seized the treasure fleet. The Count-Duke and his government were the targets of intense popular hostility and an increasingly vocal opposition. Satires and pasquinades circulated freely in Madrid; so, too, did a major indictment of the regime, clandestinely printed – the *Discursos* of Mateo Lisón y Biedma, the deputy for Granada in the Cortes of

---

[16] But see Mercedes Agulló y Cobo, 'El monasterio de San Plácido y su fundador, el madrileño don Jerónimo de Villanueva, Protonotario de Aragón', *Villa de Madrid*, 13 (1975), nos. 45–46, pp. 59–68 and no. 47, pp. 37–50. See also for Villanueva, Elliott and La Peña, *Memoriales y cartas*, 1, p. 80 n. 44, and for Quevedo and Villanueva, Luis Astrana Marin, *La vida turbulenta de Quevedo* (Madrid, 1945), p. 67.

[17] Archivo Histórico Nacional, Inquisición, legajo 3687[2], paper by Don Pascual de Aragón, 23 Feb. 1652. The family in question were called Cabra, a name which will be familiar to readers of the *Buscón*.

Castile, who had become a major spokesman of the constitutional opposition and a source of growing exasperation to Olivares.

During the spring of 1629 the Count-Duke's position was still further undermined, as a result of sharp disagreements within the Council of State, and then between Olivares and the king himself, over the direction of Spain's foreign policy. This was the moment for which Olivares' opponents among the nobility had been waiting, and he knew perfectly well that once he stumbled, they would be quick to strike. He needed all the help he could get; and in particular it was vital to vindicate the record of the regime, so as to bring home to the world the unceasing vigilance of the Count-Duke on behalf of his royal master. In this public relations exercise three men seem to have borne the burden of the day – Olivares' friend from Seville days, the Count of La Roca, who had just completed his biography in manuscript; Antonio Hurtado de Mendoza, the house poet of the regime; and Francisco de Quevedo.[18]

There are two complementary works by Quevedo in defence of Olivares which can be dated to this critical time in the spring or early summer of 1629. The first of these is his *romance*, the *Fiesta de Toros Literal y Alegórica*, which Blecua ascribes to this year because of its reference to the queen's pregnancy.[19] The other is his *comedia*, *Cómo ha de ser el privado*. When Artigas published this in 1927, he dated it to late 1627 or early 1628, and this seems to have been at least tentatively accepted.[20] But this dating is unacceptable, because of the reference at the end of the play to Piet Heyn's capture of the treasure fleet in the autumn of 1628, the news of which reached Madrid in December of that year, and not in 1627, as Artigas says. Beyond this, there is a further contemporary reference which appears to have escaped notice. The play ends with a celebration of the marriage of the Infanta to the Prince of Transylvania. The Infanta María was in fact married by proxy to the King of Hungary on 25 April 1629,[21] and Quevedo may well have written the play for a palace performance during the marriage festivities.

As Artigas was the first to point out, the *romance* and the *comedia* go hand in hand. In the *romance* Quevedo goes to the palace and finds the Count-Duke in his rooms besieged by petitioners. We get a brilliant little vignette of two hours in the life of the *privado*. In comes Jerónimo de Villanueva with a pile of letters:

---

[18] For the conjuncture of 1629, see the introduction to Docs. 1–X in Elliott and La Peña, *Memoriales y cartas* (Madrid, 1980), 2, and Brown and Elliott, *A Palace*, p. 162.

[19] Francisco de Quevedo, *Obra poética*, ed. José Manuel Blecua (Madrid, 1971), 3, p. 5.

[20] Miguel Artigas, *Teatro inédito de Don Francisco de Quevedo y Villegas* (Madrid, 1927), pp. xxi–xxii; Raimundo Lida, *Letras hispánicas* (Mexico, 1958), p. 150.

[21] *Relación diaria* (manuscript in author's possession).

El Protonotario entró,	*The Pronotario entered, and like*
como diestro, cara a cara,	*a skilled swordsman, face to face,*
y luego rompió en el Conde	*promptly broke over the Count's*
sesenta pliegos de cartas.	*head sixty sheafs of letters.*

The Protonotario is followed by the great Ambrosio Spínola, who was very much in and out of the palace these days, before leaving for Italy to take command of the army of Milan at the end of July – which enables us to date the poem to the first half of the year. There is a junta to be attended; supplicants thrust *memoriales* into his hands. Quevedo's Conde Duque is a bull at bay, worn down by his assailants.

Esta es la vida que tiene,	*This is the life he leads, this is the*
éste el séquito que alcanza;	*applause he earns; if anybody*
si alguno se lo codicia,	*envies him it, then much good*
que mal provecho le haga.	*may it do him.*

This same image of Olivares as the indefatigable minister, his every moment devoted to the cares of office, is presented at much greater length in *Cómo ha de ser el privado,* which from a historical standpoint is a fascinating play. As Artigas realized, it is in essence a dramatization of the Count of La Roca's *Fragmentos de la Vida de Don Gaspar de Guzmán,* which is also designed to represent a supremely conscientious and disinterested minister, tested and purified by the fires of public and private adversity. The English marriage negotiations and their breakdown, treated at length by La Roca, provide Quevedo with an appropriate plot, which enables him on the one hand to defend the Count-Duke's foreign policy record as being based on considerations of faith and not reason of state, and on the other to lead up to a triumphant dénouement in the repulse of the English invaders at Cadiz and the happy conclusion of a Catholic and Habsburg marriage for the Infanta. But beyond and above this is the theme of the triumphant combination of a *rey justiciero* and a *ministro desinteresado,* a theme which might indeed be described as the depiction in theatrical terms of the political theory developed in the *Política de Dios.*[22]

The element of propaganda in all this is obvious to the point of blatancy. The Duke of Lerma's career had reinforced the traditional Castilian image of the *privado* as unscrupulous, self-interested and corrupt, and Olivares, who preferred to describe himself as a *ministro,* had been determined from the beginning to prove that he was a very different kind of *privado* from his predecessor. Quevedo also

[22] See also Melvina Somers, 'Quevedo's ideology in *Cómo ha de ser el Privado', Hispania,* 39 (1956), pp. 261–8.

seized the opportunity to deliver a number of messages about his patron's policies, including at one point a direct appeal to the people which was immediately relevant to the economic situation in 1629. The favourite, the Marquis of Valisero (an anagram of Olivares), is informed that:

La murmuración ha sido   *The word has been that owing to*
que por su culpa han subido   *him the price of everything has*
los precios de todo.   *risen.*

This report of popular discontent at rising prices gives Valisero the opportunity to make an appeal for patience:

El pueblo tenga paciencia,   *Let the people have*
porque a daños que han traído   *patience because it is*
los tiempos no se ha podido   *not possible to cure by*
dar remedio con violencia.   *violent means the*
Tiempo al tiempo se ha de dar,   *injuries that the times*
y cuando de este accidente   *have brought with*
tuviera culpa el presente,   *them. Time needs*
yo, ¿qué puedo remediar?   *time to work, and*
...También yo estos males lloro...[23]   *even if the present is*
                                     responsible for this
                                     misfortune, what
                                     remedy have I?...I
                                     too bewail these ills.

It would, however, be a mistake to regard this play as merely a rather cynical propaganda exercise. The hands of the Count-Duke were unusually clean by seventeenth-century standards, especially after his hopes for his family had been dashed by the death of his daughter in 1626 (represented in the play as the death of Valisero's son and heir). From this moment he has nothing to live for but the service of the king. It is also true that he was the prisoner of his papers, and could say, like Valisero in the play: 'The king entrusted me with the *consultas*, and now he holds me captive.'[24] Indeed, what is most striking about Quevedo's depiction of the Count-Duke to anyone who has studied Olivares' own papers and those of his entourage, is its faithfulness to the image which Olivares had of himself.

There are times when, in reading Quevedo, one can almost hear Olivares himself speak. In the *romance*, we read: 'The Count for the sake of his country condemned himself to the post of favourite, like

[23] Artigas, pp, 42–3.
[24] *Ibid.*, p. 42: 'Las consultas me entregó el rey, ya me ha aprisionado.'

the galley-slave to his oar.'[25] In a letter of 1625 to Gondomar, Olivares uses this same image: 'I am committed to dying, clinging to the oar.'[26] Then again, compare Valisero's remark in the play: 'he has once again charged me with an unparalleled task'[27] with the following very characteristic remark in a letter written by Olivares two years before: 'It is all hard work.'[28] Or with an equally characteristic remark: 'I can do no more. There is only one of me.'[29] Valisero's interpretation of his functions as first minister, whose duties are to advise but not to decide –

el ministro singular	*The principal minister, although he can*
aunque pueda aconsejar	*advise, cannot make decisions.*
no le toca decidir[30] –	

is exactly the interpretation which Olivares himself is constantly expounding. 'Once the prince has reached his decision', Olivares writes to the Marquis of Aytona, 'the minister must totally forget his his former opinion, and accept that he was wrong.'[31]

The attitudes and the phraseology in Quevedo's play are close enough to those of Olivares to suggest, if not necessarily a close personal association between the two men, at least a close proximity. But if the Count-Duke's influence on Quevedo is very marked, it may also be that Quevedo for his part had some influence on Olivares. The idea of disinterested service was central to Olivares' image of himself, and this idea is developed and refined in Quevedo's play, as the favourite loses his son and heir:

Ya no soy hombre de casa,	*I am no longer a family man.*
Este afán me quitó el cielo.[32]	*Heaven deprived me of that*
	calling.

All that now remains for him is to serve the king. In a way, Quevedo has here created the part for Olivares to play; and Olivares not only plays it to perfection, but even adds lines that might have been written for him by Quevedo, like this one written four years later to the Marquis of Aytona: 'I have no father, sons nor friend, save him who serves the king...'[33]

But behind the common language we must also see a common

---

[25] Blecua, 3, p. 7: 'El Conde...se condenó por su patria a privado, como a remo...'

[26] Elliott and La Peña, *Memoriales y cartas*, 1, p. 112.

[27] Artigas, p. 41: 'ha vuelto a cargar en mí un trabajo sin igual'.

[28] Archivo del Duque de Medinaceli, legajo 79, Olivares to Aytona, 19 Sept. 1627.

[29] Archivo General de Simancas, Estado, legajo 2336, voto del Conde Duque, 2 Oct. 1635.

[30] Artigas, p. 11.

[31] Archivo del Duque de Medinaceli, legajo 79, Olivares to Aytona, 15 Oct. 1631.

[32] Artigas, p. 95.

[33] Archivo del Duque de Medinaceli, legajo 79, Olivares to Aytona, 30 Dec. 1633.

philosophy – the neo-Stoic philosophy of Justus Lipsius. The neo-Stoic Quevedo presents the favourite in his play as a Spanish Seneca',[34] as the wise and disinterested councillor unmoved by adversity. But if we recall the impact of Justus Lipsius on Quevedo, we should also recall the impact of Lipsius on the academies and literary circles of early seventeenth-century Seville, with which the young Olivares enjoyed such a close association. His intimate companion of those years, the Count of La Roca, was one of the most eager publicists of Justus Lipsius in Spain; and the works of Lipsius are well represented in the catalogue of the Count-Duke's library. Everything suggests that Olivares had steeped himself in Tacitus and Lipsius, and had found the guiding principles of his life in Christian stoicism.[35]

If, as I believe, the writer and the statesman lived in the same neo-Stoic world, there existed a certain affinity between them that went beyond immediate personal interest. Olivares in adversity was a man to command admiration, and Quevedo in the late 1620s was ready to admire, and indeed to support him. Towards the end of that same year, 1629, we find him once again busily defending the Count-Duke and his policies in that vicious polemical tract, El Chitón de las Tarabillas – undoubtedly the 'insolent little book' to which the dis-affected courtier, Matías de Novoa, refers in his memoirs, when he writes of the 'great friendship' that the Count-Duke was now dis-playing for Quevedo, perhaps (as he suggests) out of fear of Quevedo's 'satirical genius'.[36]

Luis Astrana Marín argued that the Chitón was a reply to the clandestine Discursos of that gadfly of the Olivares regime, Lisón y Biedma.[37] The suggestion is plausible, although it seems likely that Quevedo was given an even wider brief. In June 1629 an anony-mous paper was circulating in the court, fiercely criticizing the king and his minister.[38] Olivares was accused of destroying Spain with his mistaken policies – his attempts at reform, his devaluation of the currency, the wars in Italy – and even Piet Heyn's capture of the treasure fleet was laid at his door. The king for his part was no more than a ceremonial ruler, who had let his kingly duties be appropriated by the Count-Duke, and the time had come for him to throw off this subjection and prove himself a king. The argument of the Chitón suggests that, if Lisón's book was Quevedo's primary

[34] Artigas, p. 86.
[35] See Elliott and La Peña, Memoriales y cartas, 1, pp. xlvi–xlviii.
[36] Historia de Felipe IV, Rey de España, in Codoin 69, pp. 73–4.
[37] La vida turbulenta, p. 397; Jean Vilar, 'Formes et tendances de l'opposition sous Olivares: Lisón y Viedma, defensor de la patria', Mélanges de la Casa de Velázquez, 7 (1971), pp. 263–94.
[38] Reproduced by Matías de Novoa, Codoin 69, pp. 74–6.

target, he was under orders to reply at the same time to the anonymous manifesto, and possibly, also, to other attacks, now lost.

That he was writing under orders, and indeed to a brief, is suggested by the similarity between the *Chitón* and a paper written by his friend, Antonio de Mendoza.[39] The arguments and the allusions in these two polemical tracts are close enough to suggest that Quevedo and Mendoza were working in collaboration, and were being primed with the same materials, perhaps by the Count-Duke's confessor, Salazar.[40] For example, both men argue that, while there have undoubtedly been reverses and defeats in the reign of Philip IV, the same could be said of the reigns of Charles V and Philip II – Charles' defeat before Algiers, for instance, or the loss of the Invincible Armada. Disasters like these are inevitable accompaniments of the exercise of power, as Quevedo insists: 'These calamities are inseparable from dominion.'[41]

Between them, Quevedo and Mendoza developed what was to be the official party line of the Olivares regime. They portrayed a king who had wisely placed his confidence in a vigilant and disinterested minister, doing his best to save the Monarchy while subjected to intolerable attacks and calumnies. Although admitting inevitable setbacks, they come out strongly in defence of the Count-Duke's reform programme, and of his handling of the currency crisis, in which, as Quevedo argued, he had liberated Spain from the 'empire of a hundred per cent.'[42] They dwelt, too, on the foreign policy successes, and in particular on the great victories of that *annus mirabilis* of 1625, which now entered the official mythology as the year which first revealed to an admiring world the young Philip IV in all his greatness. It was this official mythology which was to provide the iconographic programme for the decoration of the great central hall of the Retiro, the Hall of Realms, between 1633 and 1635. Velázquez's *Surrender of Breda* and Maino's *Recapture of Bahía* are the expression in visual form of the polemical arguments developed by Quevedo and Mendoza in defence of the Count-Duke's policies.[43]

The Quevedo of the late 1620s and early 1630s therefore needs to be set into the context of this tight little coterie of the friends and dependents of Olivares, all placing their talents at their patron's disposal. They did not go unrewarded for their efforts. In 1630, the

---

[39] 'Papel en que Don Antonio de Mendoza...discurre sobre un libro que salió impreso sin autor', in *Discursos de Don Antonio de Mendoza*, ed. Marqués de Alcedo (Madrid, 1911), pp. 73–100. For the reasons given here, I am unable to accept the tentative dating of this *discurso* to the middle or late thirties in Gareth A. Davies, *A Poet at Court: Antonio Hurtado de Mendoza* (Oxford, 1971), p. 52.

[40] Astrana Marin, *Epistolario*, p. 196n.

[41] Quevedo, *Obras completas*, ed. Felicidad Buendía, (6th., Madrid, 1966), 1, p. 812.

[42] *Ibid.*, p. 808.   [43] See Brown and Elliott, *A Palace*, ch. 6.

Count of La Roca was appointed ambassador to Venice; and
Quevedo was apparently offered, but refused, the post of ambassador to Genoa. But in 1632 he accepted the title of secretary to
the king.[44] Even if this secretaryship was purely honorific, he does
seem to have been exercising some administrative duties at the time,
for in May 1633 the formal transactions for the Count-Duke's purchase of the town of Loeches are conducted before 'Francisco de
Quevedo, secretary of His Majesty and *oficial mayor de la escribanía de
cámara* of the Council of Orders for the Order of Santiago.'[45] This
occurred at Aranjuez, where the court was then in residence, and it is
clear that in the early 1630s he remained very much a member of the
Olivares circle, exercising certain official functions in the palace,
and producing pieces to order for court occasions, like the play
written in collaboration with Mendoza, *Quien más miente, medra más,*
written at the request of Olivares in celebration of the queen's
birthday in 1631.[46] Then, in September 1634, the secretary of the
Tuscan embassy reports that he had been commissioned to write a
comedia to celebrate the birthday of Prince Baltasar Carlos, the production to be supervised by the ubiquitous Protonotario, Jerónimo
de Villanueva.[47]

All this suggests that Quevedo was still very much *persona grata* in
the palace until at least the end of 1634; and on the outbreak of war
with France in 1635 we again find him using his talents on behalf of
the crown, in his *Letter to Louis XIII*, one of the numerous responses
from the Spanish side to the French manifesto justifying the war.
But if we can still place him among the group of professional propa-
gandists to which the government could turn in emergencies, I think
we can detect in 1634–35 the first signs of an alienation from the Olivares regime which will soon convert Quevedo into an implacable
opponent of the Count-Duke and his works.[48]

---

[44] *Obras completas*, 2, Doc. CLXIX.

[45] Transcript in library of the late Dr. Gregorio Marañón of document from the Real
Academia de la Historia, Salazar M.63, Escrituras CLXIV, 9/869, *Venta de Loeches al Conde-
Duque*. I am grateful to Don Gregorio Marañón for allowing me access to this library.

[46] Davies, *A Poet*, p. 48.

[47] Archivio di Stato, Florence, Mediceo, filza 4960, letter from Bernardo Monanni, 30 Sept.
1634.

[48] This lecture was delivered before I had an opportunity to see the important new edition of
La Hora de Todos by Jean Bourg, Pierre Dupont and Pierre Geneste (Paris, 1980). In their long
introduction to this work the editors adduce reasons for regarding several episodes, in addition
to the *Isla de los Monopantos*, as specifically 'anti-Olivarist', and date some of these episodes to the
autumn of 1633 and others to the winter of 1634–35 on the basis of contemporary events to
which they see allusions in the text. If their 1633 attributions are correct, and their interpretations
are upheld, the alienation of Quevedo from Olivares comes about a year or so earlier than I have
suggested here.

As far as the dating is concerned, there is no doubt that the editors have picked up many
contemporary references which had hitherto escaped notice (although the reference on p. 131
to the dismissal of Cardinal Trejo from the presidency of the Council of Castile in '1632' is
misleading, since he was in fact relieved of his post in November 1629). As the editors suggest (p.

I have no simple explanation to offer of this dramatic change of attitude – dramatic, that is, if I am right in assuming that Quevedo's partisanship of Olivares during the first part of the reign was more than a matter of mere convenience. There may at this moment have been important changes in Quevedo himself, if we recall that searing letter on old age and death which he wrote to Don Manuel Serrano del Castillo in August 1635.[49] I think that we should also take into account the growing intimacy of his relationship with the Duke of Medinaceli, whose estates made him a neighbor of Quevedo at La Torre de Juan Abad.[50] We know far too little about this cultivated aristocrat, but he belonged to that group of great nobles who, for good reasons and bad, were deeply opposed to the Count-Duke and his methods of government.[51]

149), the reference to Gaston d'Orléans as the 'próximo heredero' to Louis XIII would certainly seem to date the *Isla de los Monopantos* to before the birth of Louis XIV in September 1638. But other allusions may still permit a certain latitude in dating. If the Doge of Venice (Episode XIII) refers to the Dutch as having occupied one of the Barlovento islands (here identified, no doubt correctly, as St. Martin), Quevedo, for the purposes of this piece, could still have described the island as being under Dutch occupation, even after the news of its recapture by a Spanish expeditionary force. Illustrative vignettes of this type do not depend for their general veracity on absolute contemporaneity.

As regards the incorporation of so many episodes into the 'anti-Olivarist' canon, it should be noted that this is primarily done on the basis of a systematic survey of assumed disagreements between Quevedo and Olivares in different areas of Spain's policy. Here I must admit to a certain scepticism. The discussion of foreign policy is much better documented than the discussion of domestic policy for the Olivares period, and it is not difficult to find discrepancies between the known or presumed views of Quevedo on Genoa, Savoy, etc., and the fluctuating attitudes and policies of the regime toward these states during the years 1631–35, as revealed in the deliberations of the Council of State, to which Quevedo was, of course, not privy. It would not, however, be impossible to prove that Olivares himself was an 'anti-Olivarist' on the basis of this technique, since short-term tactical considerations in the conduct of foreign policy sometimes appear to run counter to long-term policy objectives. On the present evidence, I do not see Quevedo as using these episodes to launch a sustained attack on the Count-Duke's conduct of Spain's relations with individual states.

But in spite of what seem to me to be examples of excessive editorial ingenuity, I would certainly not dispute the underlying 'anti-Olivarist' tone of parts of the *Hora de Todos*, which would certainly be compatible with my views on Quevedo's relationship with the regime from 1634–35 onwards, although less so for the years before 1634. In particular, the editors seem to me to make a particularly strong case in their analysis of the discussion in episode XXXVIII as to whether the King of England should lead his armies on campaign. Here there is no doubt about the allusion to similar debates in Madrid. While the editors may be right to relate this discussion specifically to the debate at court in 1634–35 as to whether Philip IV should lead his army into France, it should be pointed out that this was one of the most permanent themes of the opposition to Olivares. It had already provoked a rift between Olivares and the king in 1629 (see Elliott and La Peña, *Memoriales y cartas*, 2, introduction to Docs. I–X), and would continue to be agitated into the early 1640's.

[49] Astrana Marín, *Epistolario*, letter CLII.

[50] See *Le Dialogue 'Hospital das Letras' de D. Francisco Manuel de Melo*, ed. Jean Colomès (Paris, 1970), p. 52.

[51] For a brief biographical note on Don Antonio Juan Luis de la Cerda, seventh Duke of Medinaceli, see Astrana Marín, *Epistolario*, p. 235 n. 1. To this it is worth adding that, according to the *Relación diaria* (see above, note 21), Medinaceli had already fallen foul of the authorities on two occasions for disorderly behaviour and had been placed under arrest (September 1626 and April 1631).

In Medinaceli's household Quevedo could not fail to have been made aware of the indignities and humiliations to which the Count-Duke was subjecting the old houses of Castile. The classic case of this occurred in the second half of 1634, when that great but arrogant commander, Don Fadrique de Toledo, was not only stripped of his offices and honours for defying the orders of the king, but was persecuted into, and even beyond, the grave. Following his death on 10 December, his catafalque was dismantled on royal orders as soon as it was built – that same catafalque which provided the theme for Quevedo's famous sonnet.[52] James Crosby's discussion of the different drafts written by Quevedo for the concluding lines of this sonnet conveys a vivid sense of the indignation and outrage felt by Quevedo at this treatment of a hero – and perhaps also, depending on the interpretation of those ambiguous last words, 'it frightens speech' ('da...al discurso miedo'), a sense of the danger of speaking out in the Spain of Olivares.[53]

Ironically, this same Don Fadrique de Toledo, in a letter written to a nephew two years earlier, had made a similar comment on the perils of free speech: 'Everything here is going in such a way that I dare not be the one to tell you about it...In Spain we cannot even write...'[54] The attempt by the Olivares regime to safeguard itself by exercising a tight control over public opinion could hardly fail in the long run to antagonize a man like Quevedo, who had neither the inclination nor the ability to curb his tongue.

Quevedo's resentment at the acts of injustice perpetrated by an authoritarian regime does not, however, mean that he was automatically beginning to support all forms of opposition to its measures. On the contrary, he objected to the resistance of the Cortes of Castile in 1636 to the crown's tax demands, and wanted the king to take a high hand with the Cortes.[55] Indeed, what he seems to have wanted was not less kingship, but more; and increasingly he appears to have felt that the Count-Duke was impeding the proper exercise of kingship. It was during these years 1634–36 that he was writing the second part of the *Política de Dios,* and if the first part can be seen as a criticism of the regimes of Lerma and Uceda, the second part contains passages which suggest a criticism of that of Olivares. It is above all the *style* of the Olivares government to which he takes exception – the exploitation of the king by his ministers, and his

---

[52] Blecua, 1, no. 264 (*Venerable túmulo de Don Fadrique de Toledo*).

[53] See James O. Crosby, *En torno a la poesía de Quevedo* (Madrid, 1967), pp. 31–37. Also Brown and Elliott, *A Palace*, pp. 172–74 for his representation in the Hall of Realms.

[54] Archives des Affaires Étrangères, Corresp. Politique, Espagne, 17, fo. 20, Don Fadrique de Toledo to Don Luis Ponce de León, 8 Jan. 1633. He was writing from Lisbon.

[55] Astrana Marín, *Epistolario*, letter CLXI (to Don Sancho de Sandoval, Jan. 1636).

isolation from what was going on in his kingdom. In particular, I
believe that the Buen Retiro, with which Quevedo had been closely
associated in its opening years, had become for him the symbol of
what was wrong with the regime, for it served to divert the king
from the duties of his office. In Chapter XIII of Book II of the *Política
de Dios*, Quevedo discusses the problem of royal recreation. 'Palaces
for the idle prince', he writes, 'are sepulchres of a living death...';
and if the king wishes to relax, he should turn to other forms of
work. Listen, he urges, to the complaints of the aggrieved. Kings
are day labourers, who should be paid according to their hours of
work.[56]

The king could not see what was happening in Spain because he
was held captive by Olivares and his men. The Count-Duke, therefore, who was once the hero of Quevedo's scenario, is now
becoming its villain; and perhaps it is precisely because of the extent
of Quevedo's disillusionment with Olivares that he now turns upon
him with such vicious hostility. In the late 1630s the Spanish Seneca
is banished from Quevedo's works as if he had never existed. Now
spending much of his time away from the court, Quevedo can brood
in isolation on the hero who has failed him.

The antipathy which Quevedo was beginning to feel towards
Olivares was as extreme as the adulation which he had previously
lavished upon him. The change of attitude reflected less a change in
the behaviour of Olivares himself, than in Quevedo's perceptions of
him. The strains of fifteen years of government, and the unremitting
pressures of war, had certainly taken their toll of the Count-Duke: he
was more brusque, more authoritarian, than he had been in the first
years of power, and had surrounded himself with yes-men. But he
was still deeply committed to the reform of Spain and the restoration
of its greatness. What had become apparent since the mid-1620s,
however, was the terrible price that Castile was paying for his
policies. The insatiable fiscal demands of the crown in order to pay
for the war had intensified the social and economic ills from which
Castile was already suffering. While the poor were oppressed, the
nobility were harried. At the same time, a new plutocracy had arisen,
which was making its money out of the sufferings of others – a
plutocracy of tax-gatherers, of government officials drawn from that
letrado class which had always been for Quevedo an object of
contempt and disgust, and of the crypto-Jewish Portuguese financiers who had become so closely identified with the Olivares regime.

It was these men and their world who were mercilessly satirized in

[56] Ed. Crosby, pp. 211ff. For the Buen Retiro as a symbol of the failings of the Olivares
regime, see Brown and Elliott, *A Palace*, ch. 8.

La Hora de Todos. As Conrad Kent has argued,[57] Quevedo uses this
work to launch a broad-based attack on the Olivares reform programme, which was seeking to transform the character of Spain.
The reformers and the *arbitristas,* with their new-fangled foreign
notions, are depicted as the subverters of traditional Spanish values.
The tax-collectors are sponging up the wealth of the people; the
Machiavellians have perverted true politics with their doctrine of
razón de estado – a sharp dig at Olivares who was accused by his
enemies of being a Machiavellian; the ministers and the bureaucrats
have stripped the king of his authority and transformed themselves
into a self-perpetuating caste, excluding all others from access to the
monarch.

These attacks on the Olivares regime were at least partially veiled,
but in the episode of the Isla de los Monopantos the assault was
direct. Pragas Chincollos, the governor of the island, is, of course, an
anagram of Gaspar Conchillos, and so directly links Olivares, as Don
Gaspar de Guzmán, with his great-grandfather, Lope Conchillos, the
Aragonese *converso* secretary of Ferdinand the Catholic. The six
learned advisers summoned to the Sanhedrin are, in so far as they can
be firmly identified, members of Olivares' intimate circle, including
José González as Pacas Mazo; Hernando de Salazar, the inventor of
ingenious fiscal expedients, as Alkemiastos; and Villanueva, the
Protonotario, as Arpiotrotono.[58] All these men were once the close
associates of Quevedo. Now he rejects them and all their works,
castigating them as Machiavellian intriguers, immoral money-
grubbers, and unprincipled agents of an international Jewish conspiracy intended to subvert the proper ordering of the world.

Whether Olivares was aware of the Isla de los Monopantos we
have no means of knowing, but he certainly kept dossiers on the
opponents of the regime. Quevedo's recall to Madrid in January
1639, and the simultaneous offer to the Duke of Medinaceli of the
viceroyalty of Aragon,[59] may indicate that the Count-Duke was
concerned to keep close watch over two men whom he saw as actual
or potential dissidents. Then, ten months later, comes Quevedo's
arrest in Medinaceli's house.

Some years ago I found and published a short letter of 1642 from
Olivares to the king.[60] This letter throws a new and rather lurid light

[57] In 'Politics in *La Hora de Todos*', *Journal of Hispanic Philology*, 1 (1977), pp. 99–119. Jean
Bourg and his fellow-editors of the 1980 Paris edition of *La Hora de Todos* were apparently unaware of this article.
[58] For a discussion of these identifications, first made by Fernández-Guerra, see note 573 of
the Jean Bourg edition of *La Hora de Todos.*
[59] Astrana Marín, *La vida turbulenta*, p. 498.
[60] 'Nueva luz sobre la prisión de Quevedo y Adam de la Parra', *Boletín de la Real Academia de
la Historia*, 169 (1972), pp. 171–82. Reprinted, with a short commentary, in Elliott and La
Peña, *Memoriales y cartas*, 2, Doc. XV.

on the causes, or possible causes, of Quevedo's arrest, but, like so many documents, it raises at least as many questions as it answers. The letter as a whole is concerned with the arrest of a friend of Quevedo, and a former protégé of Olivares and publicist for the regime, Adam de la Parra. In discussing the justification for this arrest, which turns out to have been prompted by some scurrilous verses written by Adam de la Parra about the influence of *conversos* in high places, Olivares makes a specific reference to the arrest of Quevedo in 1639.

The Count-Duke's words, which – one has to remember – were written in a private note for the king, and were not for public consumption, deserve close examination. He is discussing, in relation to Adam de la Parra, the ethical and practical problems involved in shutting a man away for life, and he takes as his example the case of Quevedo. 'In the affairs of Don Francisco de Quevedo', he writes, 'it was necessary for the Duke of Infantado, as a self-confessed intimate of... Quevedo, to accuse him of being "treacherous (*infiel*), an enemy and critic of the government and, finally, an intimate friend of France, and in correspondence with the French"'; and, he goes on, even this was insufficient to get him put under lock and key, and it took the president of the Council of Castile and José González (Quevedo's Pacas Mazo!) to come up with a solution.

What are we to make of these words of Olivares? That Quevedo was 'an enemy and critic of the government' is obvious enough, and the charge would cover any written or spoken attacks on the regime, including the Isla de los Monopantos, and the notorious verses addressed to the *Católica, sacra y real majestad,* which have traditionally been regarded as the immediate cause of Quevedo's arrest. But it is the other charge that comes like a bolt from the blue: that Quevedo was 'infiel' – a word reserved by Olivares for those he regarded as traitors[61] – and, more specifically, that he was in secret correspondence with the French.

When Quevedo was released in 1643 the king observed that he had been arrested 'for grave cause.' Is it conceivable that Quevedo, who has always been regarded as the epitome of patriotism, should have been in collusion with the enemy? Here we can only enter the realm of speculation, and everyone will have to reach his own decision on the basis of his judgment of Quevedo and his complex character. My own guess, which is no more than a guess, is that Olivares did have some incriminating evidence against Quevedo, although the extent to which that evidence had any substance, or was simply planted by one or other of his many enemies, remains open to question. Here I

---

[61] See *Memoriales y cartas*, 2, pp. 187 for Olivares' use of the word *infiel*, which does not, I think, bear in this context the religious connotations ascribed to it on p. 179 of my article.

would add one further piece of archival information. Between 1639 and 1642 a French agent called Guillermo Francisco sent back regular reports from Madrid to his contacts in France. On 10 January 1640 he reported the arrest of Quevedo, and retailed the usual charges – that he was accused of being the author of various tracts against the regime, and perhaps, too, of the set of verses which the king had found beneath his napkin. But in passing, he makes an interesting reference to the Duke of Medinaceli. At Medinaceli's house, he says, 'all the wits of the court used to assemble and converse, and would lavish praise on the King of France and Monsieur the Cardinal; and in particular they would comment on how the king was to be found with his armies, encouraging the soldiers with his presence, whereas the King of Spain never left Madrid, in spite of there being so many places where his presence was needed.'[62]

Medinaceli's house, then, was a meeting-place for the dissidents, as we already know from Francisco Manuel de Melo's description of the conversations which took place there;[63] and these dissidents were making unfavourable comparisons between Philip IV and Olivares on the one hand, and Louis XIII and Richelieu on the other. Even if Quevedo had savaged Richelieu in his *Visita y Anatomía de la Cabeza del Cardenal Armando de Richelieu* four years earlier, this would not preclude him from judging that matters were being managed more efficiently in France than in Spain. Indeed, the recent course of the war would point to this very conclusion. But whether Quevedo went any further than this is difficult to say. It would not be surprising if French agents had an entry to Medinaceli's house, and had made some contact with the opponents of the regime. Spain itself was, after all, at this very moment, in close contact with the domestic opponents of Richelieu, and each side was doing its best to engineer the downfall of the principal minister of the other. It does not seem to me impossible that the Quevedo of 1639 was so consumed and corroded by his hatred of Olivares that he was willing at least to listen to the overtures of the enemy.

In the misery of his confinement in San Marcos de León, Quevedo did his best to work his passage back. He replied to the *Proclamación Católica* of the rebellious Catalans with his *Rebelión de Barcelona ni es por el güevo ni es por el fuero,* incidentally making use of a popular refrain which it so happens that Olivares himself had used three years earlier in a letter about the Portuguese troubles of 1637 – 'no es por el güevo sino por el fuero.'[64] He also wrote, and dedicated to the

[62] Bibliothèque Nationale, Paris, Fonds français, 10,760, f. 24.
[63] *Le Dialogue 'Hospital das Letras'*, p. 53.
[64] British Library, Additional Ms. 28, 429, Olivares to Conde de Basto, 18 Dec. 1637. *No es por el güevo sino por el fuero* – 'not for the egg (i.e. because of hunger) but for the *fuero* (ie. laws and liberties).'

Count-Duke, his reply to the manifesto of the Portuguese rebels of 1640. His abasement before Olivares in the petitions which he wrote to him from prison is the abasement of a broken man; and it failed to restore to him his liberty. When this came, it came only after the fall of Olivares in 1643, and indeed only after the king had been persuaded, apparently with some difficulty, to give his approval. His imprisonment was, after all, 'for grave cause.'

We have, then, if my reading of Quevedo's career is correct, a sad and twisted story of a twisted man. If Quevedo is unique, perhaps the story itself is not, for it illustrates all too vividly the dilemma of the intellectual in the world of politics. The combination of opportunism and idealism induces him to throw in his lot with a new government which promises to bring about major reforms on which he has set his heart – in Quevedo's case, the purification of a country that had almost sunk beneath the weight of corruption, along with the restoration of its ancient greatness and virtues. The regime runs into trouble, and he devotes his energies to defending it from the assaults of its enemies, incurring at the same time the charge that he is prostituting his talents for the sake of self-advancement. Then comes the moment when the doubts begin to grow. The failures of the regime outweigh its successes; some of its actions run counter to his own deeply felt beliefs. At this point, as the contradictions become acute, the strains prove to be simply too great. Bitterness and disillusionment take the place of hope. He then defects, and throws in his lot with the opposition, in the belief that any change can now only be a change for the better. We do not know if Quevedo was the author of those terrible lines penned on the news of the Count-Duke's death in his exile at Toro in 1645:

Al fin murió el Conde-Duque,	*At last the Count-Duke is dead;*
plegue al cielo que así sea;	*God willing, this is true. If it be*
si es verdad, España, albricias,	*so, congratulations are in order,*
y si no, lealtad, paciencia.[65]	*Spain, and if not, loyalty and*
	patience.

But he did write that *Panegírico* to Philip IV on the Count-Duke's fall, in which he expressed his belief that a new day had dawned for Spain, a day which had given the king back to himself.[66] Once again, as he thought in 1621, Spain had found its saviour. And once again, as in 1621, Quevedo was mistaken.

[65] A la muerte del Conde-Duque. Romance', in Teófanes Egido, *Sátiras politicas de la España moderna* (Madrid, 1973), p. 174.
[66] *Obras completas*, 1, p. 947.

PART IV

THE QUESTION OF DECLINE

INTRODUCTION

Spain's seventeenth-century experience has traditionally been discussed and interpreted in the context of 'decline'. From the seventeenth century onwards, Spain's decline has been a fertile topic for *ex cathedra* pronouncements, especially by foreigners. These pronouncements, although they range across the centuries, possess a distinct family resemblance. There is not much, either in content or in tone, to separate these two observations made from the vantage-point of England, one dating from the 1680s and the other from the 1830s. 'Spain...is a clear demonstration that misgovernment, in suffering all manner of Frauds, and neglecting the interest of a nation, will soon bring the mightiest Kingdoms low, and lay their honour in the dust.'[1] 'All the causes of the decay of Spain resolve themselves into one cause, bad government.'[2] Their clear, confident tones reflect the inner certainties of those who have no doubt that their own country has managed matters better.

The old stereotypes tended to dominate discussion of the decline of Spain, at least until the 1930s, when the subject was both reviewed and renewed for a modern readership by the American economic historian Earl J. Hamilton.[3] As the author of a famous pioneering study on the inflationary consequences of American bullion for Early Modern Spain,[4] Hamilton was well equipped to survey the decline of Spain in its economic aspects but less so when he occasionally wandered into non-economic fields.[5] Even in his own field of expertise, however, Hamilton, for all the importance of his contribution, was beginning to look vulnerable by the 1950s, as his arguments about the impact of American silver came under critical scrutiny, and

---

[1] Slingsby Bethel, *The Interest of the Princes and States of Europe* (2nd ed., London, 1681), p. 77.
[2] Thomas Babington Macaulay, *Critical and Historical Essays*, 3 vols. (London, 1843), 2, p. 45 ('War of the Spanish Succession'. First published 1833).
[3] 'The Decline of Spain', *Economic History Review*, 1st series, 8 (1938), pp. 168–79.
[4] *American Treasure and the Price Revolution in Spain, 1501–1650* (Cambridge, Mass., 1934).
[5] Cf. the remark in his 1938 article that 'The golden age in literature and the fine arts and the silver age in money (during the sixteenth century) were succeeded by a bronze age in the seventeenth century.'

new areas of Spanish economic history began to be explored. It was my awareness of this, and of the need to take more recent work into account, that prompted me to attempt a fresh survey of my own, published in *Past and Present* in 1961. I wrote it, as its first footnote makes clear, with a recent and scintillating article on the Spain of Don Quijote by the distinguished French historian, Pierre Vilar, very much in mind, even if I could not follow Vilar in his Marxist interpretation of decline.

By chosing for my article the same title as that used by Hamilton, 'The Decline of Spain', I was in fact committing myself to a semi-Hamiltonian approach to the topic. This essay was to be Hamilton up-dated for a new generation of readers, and I therefore confined myself largely to the kinds of theme addressed by Hamilton. But at the same time I tried to make it clear that the economic aspects of decline were only part of a larger story, most of which still remained to be told. That remains as true today as in 1961. I also expressed some reservations about a debate structured in terms of the concept of 'decline', partly because of the imprecision of the concept itself when applied to distinct, if related, developments, and partly because I felt that the use of traditional categories would make it harder to see old problems in new ways. Here I had in mind particularly the tendency, both inside and outside Spain, to treat Spanish phenomena as in some ways unique and attributable to innately Spanish failings. I therefore attempted, although very summarily, to open up the subject by suggesting the existence of some striking similarities between economic conditions in Spain and in other seventeenth-century societies.

Since the publication of my discussion of 'The Decline of Spain', a vast amount of new research has been undertaken on many aspects of Spanish economic history in the sixteenth and seventeenth centuries, not least by a new generation of native Spanish historians, who have made great advances, in particular, in the study of regional and local communities.[6] It was precisely the absence of work at the local level which made earlier generalizations about Spanish economic conditions so precarious, and in due course these new studies should make possible a richer, and much more sophisticated, synthesis. At present, however, their very proliferation is making synthesis more, and not less, difficult, as the history of Spain becomes fragmented into the history of its regions. Yet at the same time, recent work, especially in Spanish demographic history,[7] has tended to vindicate

[6] For a recent survey with extensive references to these studies, many of them locally published in Spain, see Carla Rahn Phillips, 'Time and Duration: a Model for the Economy of Early Modern Spain', *American Historical Review*, 92 (1987), pp. 531–62.

[7] Notably Vicente Pérez Moreda, *Las crisis de mortalidad en la España interior, siglos XVI-XIX* (Madrid, 1980).

my remarks about the need to set the problem of the decline of Spain into the wider context of a seventeenth-century European recession.

But there is always a danger that the discovery of close parallels between Spanish and general European conditions in the seventeenth century will cause the problem of the 'decline of Spain' to disappear, as if by a sleight of hand, as Spain's recession is subsumed into a general European recession. In spite of the reservations that I expressed about the word 'decline', it has an obvious usefulness as long as the ways in which it is being used are made clear. Nobody, for instance, would dispute that the seventeenth century saw a *relative* decline of Spanish power, when compared with its principal European rivals. This is a historical phenomenon that requires explanation. As part of that explanation I emphasized the decline of Castile, the most populous and wealthy of the realms of sixteenth-century Spain. This decline of Castile was – as far as our knowledge allows – a *relative* decline, in the sense that other parts of the Iberian peninsula, especially along the periphery, either suffered less than Castile from the seventeenth-century recession, or even made modest gains, so that, over the course of the century, there was some shift in the internal balance of economic forces, to Castile's detriment. There also seems to me a considerable, and growing, weight of evidence that Castile in the middle decades of the seventeenth century experienced an *absolute* decline in national wealth and productivity as measured against the levels it had attained during the first two thirds of the sixteenth century, even if the boundaries and contours of this process cannot at present be determined with precision.

No doubt what appears from one angle of vision as a process of decline will be seen from another as a process of adjustment.[8] There is no objective criterion to determine what constitutes 'decline' as against 'adjustment'. As I have come to see more clearly since first writing on the decline of Spain, the indicators of national decline are themselves culturally determined. Societies set their goals, and gauge their failures and achievements, in accordance with yardsticks determined by their own values and preconceptions and those of their neighbours and rivals. Pierre Vilar emphasized in his article the extreme interest of the treatise written in 1600 by Martín González de Cellorigo analysing the ills of Castile, and I was struck when reading this treatise by the recurrence of the word 'decline'. More extensive reading of the works of Cellorigo's contemporaries persuaded me that seventeenth-century Spaniards themselves had a tendency to conceptualize the current problems of their society in terms of *declinación*. The fact that they should have been doing this seemed to

---

[8] 'Seventeenth-century Castile experienced a long, slow and painful adjustment to the crisis of the late sixteenth century,' Phillips, 'Time and Duration', p. 545.

me to add a new dimension to the whole question of decline. It was this dimension that I sought to explore in the essay on 'Self-perception and decline', published in *Past and Present* in 1977.

It proved easier to trace the manifestations of a tendency to cast the debate about national problems in terms of decline, than to assess the wider implications of this line of thinking. Some of these I attempted to pursue in my study of *The Count-Duke of Olivares* (1986), whose policy of national reformation and renewal seemed to me to constitute a response to the challenge of perceived decline. But the problem remains elusive. In particular, it is not clear how pervasive was the decline mentality among the governing elite of seventeenth-century Spain. Nor is it clear to what extent this way of thinking helped generate a creeping fatalism, that itself effectively paralysed the will to act. Such questions are necessarily complex because they go to the heart of the relationship between events themselves, the perception of those events, and the formulation of public policy. The three constituent parts of this relationship all have to be addressed if we are ever to solve the old conundrum of the 'decline of Spain'. Partial interpretations, however valuable in themselves, remain inadequate.

There remains one further question, separate but related, to which I turn in the final essay in this volume: the capacity of a society to generate great works of art and literature even in times of economic adversity. This essay was written for the catalogue to an exhibition held in Madrid and London in 1982–3, and devoted to Murillo, a painter whose once high reputation had itself gone into spectacular decline. Much of the thinking behind it, however, was inspired by my researches into the literary and artistic environment of the Spain of the 1630s and the building of the palace of the Buen Retiro. Economically the seventeenth century was for Spain an age of iron, but culturally it was an age of gold. Although I offer certain explanations for the paradox, it seems likely that the paradox itself is more apparent than real, and that there is no necessary correlation, one way or the other, between the state of the economy and creativity in the arts. But no writer or artist – not even a Murillo – is entirely an island to himself, and at some level the contemporary political, social and economic situation is bound to impinge on the kind of work he produces, and his ways of seeing and describing the world. One day, perhaps, these subtle relationships will be better understood for seventeenth-century Spain. In the meantime, this final essay will serve as a salutary reminder that there is something more to Spain's seventeenth century than the question of decline.

X

THE DECLINE OF SPAIN[1]

By the winter of 1640, the Empire which had dominated the world scene for the best part of a century seemed at last, after many a false alarm, to be on the verge of collapse. In October of that year, after the revolt of Catalonia but before the revolt of Portugal, the English ambassador in Madrid wrote home of 'the state of Christendom, which begins already to be unequally balanced.'[2] Six months later he was writing: 'Concerning the state of this kingdom, I could never have imagined to have seen it as it now is, for their people begin to fail, and those that remain, by a continuance of bad successes, and by their heavy burdens, are quite out of heart.'[3] Olivares' great bid between 1621 and 1640 to turn back the pages of history to the heroic days of Philip II had visibly failed; and, like everything about Olivares, his failure was on the grand scale. The man whom eulogists had portrayed in the days of his greatness as Atlas, supporting on his shoulders the colossal structure of the Monarchy, was now, Samson-like, bringing it crashing down with him in his fall.

The dissolution of Spanish power in the 1640s appears so irrevocable and absolute that it is hard to regard it as other than inevitable. The traditional textbook approach to European history of the sixteenth and seventeenth centuries has further helped to establish the idea of the inevitability of Spain's defeat in its war with France. Spanish power is first presented at its height under Philip II. Then comes, with the reign of Philip III, the *decline of Spain,* with the roots of decline traced back to Philip II, or Charles V, or even to Ferdinand and Isabella, depending upon the nationality, or the pertinacity, of the writer. After the lamentable scenes that have just been portrayed, the early years of Philip IV come as something of an embarrassment,

[1] Readers of this essay will appreciate how much I, in company with other historians of Spain, owe to the ideas of M. Pierre Vilar, 'Le Temps du Quichotte', *Europe,* 34 (1956), pp. 3–16. [Later published in English as 'The Age of Don Quixote', in *Essays in European Economic History, 1500–1800,* ed. Peter Earle (Oxford, 1974), pp. 100–13.]

[2] P(ublic) R(ecord) O(ffice, London) SP 94.42 f. 51, Hopton to Windebank, 22 Sept./2 Oct. 1940.

[3] PRO SP 94.42 f. 144, Hopton to Vane, 3/13 April 1641.

217

since the ailing patient not only refuses to die, but even shows vigorous and unexpected signs of life. But fortunately the inexplicable recovery is soon revealed as no more than a hallucination. When a resurgent France under Richelieu at last girds itself for action, Spain's bluff is called. Both diagnosis and prognostication are triumphantly vindicated, and the patient dutifully expires.

It is not easy to reconcile this attractively simple presentation of early seventeenth-century history with our increasing knowledge of the discontent and unrest in Richelieu's France.[4] If Spain may still be regarded as a giant with feet of clay, France itself is coming to seem none too steady on the ground. This naturally tends to cast doubt on the validity of any concept of a French triumph in the first half of the century as being a foregone conclusion. Yet the lingering survival of the traditional view is easily understood. France had a population of some sixteen million, as against Spain's seven or eight, and it is commonly argued that, in the end, weight of numbers is bound to tell. It is also argued that the fact of Spain's decline is notorious and irrefutable, and that a power in decline will not win the final battle.

The argument from the size of populations is notoriously dangerous when used of a period when governments lacked the resources and the techniques to mobilize their subjects for war. Victory in war ultimately depended on the capacity of a state to maintain a continuing supply of men (not necessarily nationals) and of credit, and this capacity was by no means the exclusive prerogative of the large state. But the decisive argument in favour of an inevitable French victory is obviously the second: that Spain was in a state of irrevocable decline.

The phrase *decline of Spain* automatically conjures up a series of well-known images. Most of these are to be found in Professor Earl J. Hamilton's famous article,[5] which remains the classic statement of the theme: 'the progressive decline in the character of the rulers'; mortmain and vagabondage, the contempt for manual labour, monetary chaos and excessive taxation, the power of the church and the folly of the government. These so-called 'factors' in the decline of Spain have a long and respectable ancestry, and both their existence and their importance are irrefutable. Most of them can indeed be traced back to the writings of seventeenth-century Spaniards themselves – to the treatises of the economic writers or *arbitristas*, of whom Hamilton says that 'history records few instances of either such able diagnosis of fatal social ills by any group of moral

[4] See B.P. Porshnev, *Die Volksaufstände in Frankreich vor der Fronde* (Leipzig, 1954) and R. Mousnier, 'Recherches sur les Soulèvements Populaires en France avant la Fronde', *Revue d'Histoire Moderne et Contemporaine*, 5 (1958), pp. 81–113.
[5] 'The Decline of Spain', *Economic History Review*, 1st series, 8 (1938), pp. 168–79.

philosophers or of such utter disregard by statesmen of sound advice.'
The word *decline* itself was used of Spain at least as early as 1600
when González de Cellorigo, perhaps the most acute of all the *arbit-ristas*, discussed 'how our Spain...is subject to the process of decline
(*declinación*) to which all other republics are prone.'[6] Vigorously as
González de Cellorigo himself rejected the determinist thesis, the
condition of Spain seemed to his contemporaries graphic evidence of
the validity of the cyclical idea of history, of which the concept of
decline formed an integral part.

The skilful dissection of the Spanish body politic by contemporary
Spaniards, each anxious to offer the patient his own private nostrum,
proved of inestimable value to writers of later generations: to Protes-tants of the later seventeenth century, and to rationalist historians of
the eighteenth and nineteenth, who saw in the decline of Spain the
classic instance of the fatal consequences of ignorance, sloth and
clericalism. Apart from its important additions on Spanish wages
and prices, and its rejection of the traditional thesis about the grave
results of the expulsion of the Moriscos, Hamilton's article would
seem to belong, in content as in approach, to the eighteenth- and
nineteenth-century historiographical tradition.

It would be pleasant to be able to record that, in the twenty years
since Hamilton's article was published, our knowledge and under-standing of seventeenth-century Spain have been significantly enlar-ged. But, in most of its aspects, our picture of the reigns of Philip III
and IV remains very much as it was drawn by Martin Hume in the
old *Cambridge Modern History* over fifty years ago. The one signifi-cant exception to this story of historiographic stagnation is to be
found in Hamilton's own field of monetary history. Whatever the
defects either of Hamilton's methods or of his generalizations, both
of them subject to growing criticism, historians now possess a vast
amount of information on Spanish monetary history which was not
available to Hume; and the work of a generation of historians, cul-minating in the monumental study of Seville and the Atlantic by M.
and Mme Chaunu,[7] has revealed much that is new and important
about the character of Spain's economic relations with its American
possessions.

It could, however, be argued that these advances in the fiscal and
commercial history of Habsburg Spain have been achieved only at
the expense of other equally important aspects of its economic life.
Hamilton's pioneering example has encouraged an excessive concen-tration on the *external* influences on the Spanish economy, such as

[6] Martín González de Cellorigo, *Memorial de la política necessaria y útil restauración a la república de España* (Valladolid, 1600), p. 1.
[7] H. and P. Chaunu, *Séville et l' Atlantique (1504–1650)*, 8 vols. (Paris, 1955–9).

American silver, to the neglect of *internal* economic conditions.[8]
Little more is known now than was known fifty years ago about
Spanish forms of land tenure and cultivation, or about population
changes, or about the varying fortunes of the different regions or
social groups in the peninsula. It could also be argued that
Hamilton's lead, together with the whole trend of contemporary
historical writing, has produced a disproportionate concentration
on *economic* conditions. Explanations of the decline in terms of
Spanish religious or intellectual history have become unfashionable.
This is understandable in view of the naïveté of many such explanations in the past, but it is hard to see how an adequate synthesis can
be achieved until detailed research is undertaken into such topics as
the working of the Spanish church, of the religious orders and the
educational system. At present, we possess an overwhelmingly
economic interpretation of Spain's decline, which itself is highly
arbitrary in that it focuses attention only on certain selected aspects of
the Spanish economy.

If this leads to distortions, as it inevitably must, these become all
the greater when, as so often happens, the decline of Spain is treated
in isolation. The very awareness of crisis among late sixteenth- and
early seventeenth-century Spaniards prompted a flood of pessimistic
commentaries which helped to make the subject exceptionally well
documented. The extent of the documentation and the critical acute-
ness of the commentators, naturally tended to encourage the assumption that Spain's plight was in some ways unique; and this itself has
led to a search for the origins of that plight in specifically Spanish
circumstances and in the dubious realm of allegedly unchanging
national characteristics. But considerably more is known now than
was known twenty or thirty years ago about the nature of social and
economic conditions in seventeenth-century western Europe as a
whole. Much of the seventeenth century has come to be regarded as a
period of European economic crisis – of commercial contraction and
demographic stagnation after the spectacular advances of the sixteenth century – and certain features which once seemed peculiarly
Spanish are now tending to assume a more universal character. The
impoverished *hidalgos* of Spain do not now seem so very different
from the discontented *hobereaux* of France or the gentry of England.
Nor does the contempt for manual labour, on which historians of
Spain are prone to dwell, seem any longer an attitude unique to the
peninsula. A study like that by Coleman on English labour in the

---

[8] This point is well made in the useful bibliographical survey of recent work on this period
of Spanish history: J. Vicens Vives, J. Reglá and J. Nadal, 'L'Espagne aux XVIe et XVIIe
Siècles', *Revue Historique*, 220 (1958), pp. 1–42.

seventeenth century[9] suggests how 'idleness', whether voluntary or involuntary, was a general problem of European societies of the time, and can be regarded as the consequence, as much as the cause, of a backward economy: as the outcome of the inability of a predominantly agrarian society to offer its population regular employment or adequate remuneration for its labour.

Seventeenth-century Spain needs, therefore, to be set firmly back into the context of contemporary conditions, and particularly conditions in the Mediterranean world, before recourse is had to alleged national characteristics as an explanation of economic backwardness. It may be that idleness *was* in fact more widespread, and contempt for manual labour more deep-rooted, in Spain than elsewhere, but the first task must be to *compare*: to compare Spanish conditions with those of other contemporary societies, and then, if it is possible to isolate any features which appear unique to Spain, to search for their origins not only in the realm of national character, but also in the conditions of the soil and the nature of land-holding, and in the country's social and geographical structure.

Some of the difficulties in breaking free from traditional assumptions about the decline of Spain must be ascribed to the powerful connotations of the word 'decline': a word which obscures more than it explains. Behind the phrase *decline of Spain* there lurk different, although interrelated, phenomena. The decline of Spain can, in the first place, be regarded as part of that general setback to economic advance which mid-seventeenth-century Europe is said to have experienced, although the Spanish regression may well prove to have been more intense or to have lasted longer. Secondly, it describes something more easily measured: the end of the period of Spanish hegemony in Europe and the relegation of Spain to the rank of the second-rate powers. This implies a deterioration in Spain's military and naval strength, at least in relation to that of other states, and a decrease in its ability to mobilize the manpower and credit required to maintain its traditional primacy in Europe.

Any attempt to analyse the reasons for the decline of Spanish *power* in the middle decades of the seventeenth century must obviously begin with an examination of the foundations of that power in an earlier age. Olivares, between 1621 and 1643, was pursuing a foreign policy which recalls that of Philip II in the 1580s and 1590s. The general aims of that policy were the same: the destruction of heresy

---

[9] D.C. Coleman, 'Labour in the English Economy of the Seventeenth Century', *Economic History Review*, 2nd series, 8 (1956), pp. 280–95.

and the establishment of some form of Spanish hegemony over Europe. The nominal cost of the policy was also the same, though the real cost was greater. Philip III's ministers maintained that Philip II was spending nearly 13 million ducats a year between 1593 and 1597; Philip IV's ministers in 1636 estimated an expenditure of just over 13 million for the coming year,[10] and estimates were always liable to prove too conservative, in view of the rising premium of silver in terms of Castilian *vellón* (copper coinage), and of the sudden emergency expenses that invariably arose in time of war.

While the policy, as well as its nominal cost, remained the same under Philip IV as under Philip II, the basis of Spanish power under the two kings was also unchanged. It was, as it had always been, the resources of the Crown of Castile. Philip IV's best troops, like Philip II's, were Castilians. Philip IV's principal revenues, like Philip II's, came from the purse of the Castilian taxpayer, and Philip IV relied, like his grandfather, on the additional income derived from the American possessions of Castile.

The primacy of the Crown of Castile within the Spanish Monarchy, stemming as it did from its unique value to its kings, was obvious and acknowledged. 'The King is Castilian and nothing else, and that is how he appears to the other kingdoms', wrote one of the most influential ministers at the court of Philip III.[11] Olivares found himself as dependent on Castile as Philip II had been. But the assistance that Castile could render Olivares proved to be less effective than the assistance it rendered Philip II, and was extracted at an even greater expense. From this, it would seem that we are faced with a diminution of Castile's capacity to bear the cost of empire, and consequently with the problem, in the first instance, not so much of the decline of Spain as of the *decline of Castile,* which is something rather different.

Three principal foundations of Castile's sixteenth-century primacy were its population, its productivity and its overseas wealth. If the process by which these foundations were slowly eroded could be traced in detail, we should have a clearer picture of the chronology of Castile's decline. But at present our knowledge is fragmentary and inadequate, and all that is possible is to suggest something of what has been done, and the areas still to be investigated.

Spain's great imperial successes of the sixteenth century had been achieved primarily by the courage and vitality of the surplus population of an overcrowded Castile. Figures for the population of

[10] A(rchivo) G(eneral de) S(imancas) Hacienda leg(ajo) 750 no. 231, consulta, 23 Aug. 1636.
[11] AGS Cámara de Castilla leg. 2796 Pieza 9 Inquisición f. 329, Don Pedro Franqueza to Dr. Fadrique Cornet, 22 Jan. 1605.

sixteenth-century Spain are scanty and unreliable, but it would probably now be generally agreed that Castile's population increased during much of the century, as it increased elsewhere in Europe, with the fastest rate of increase in the 1530s. The population of the peninsula, excluding Portugal, in the middle of the sixteenth century, is thought to have been about 7½ million, of which 6½ million were to be found in Castile.[12] But perhaps even more significant than the overwhelming numerical predominance of the Castilian population is its superior density. As late as 1594 there were 22 inhabitants to the square kilometre in Castile, as against only 13.6 in the Crown of Aragon. The great empty spaces of modern Castile seem so timeless and so inevitable, that it requires an effort of the imagination to realize that Castile in the sixteenth century was relatively more populous than the rich Levantine provinces; and here, indeed, is to be found one of the fundamental changes in the structure of Spanish history. In the early 1590s the central regions of Castile accounted for 30.9 per cent of the population of Spain, whereas they now account for only 16.2 per cent. The political preponderance of Castile within Spain therefore rested in the sixteenth century, as it now no longer rests, on a population that was not only larger but also more densely settled.

This relatively dense Castilian population, living in an arid land with a predominantly pastoral economy – a land which found increasing difficulty in feeding its rising numbers – provided the colonists for the New World and the recruits for the *tercios*. It is not known how many Castilians emigrated to America (a figure of 150,000 has been suggested for the period up to 1550), nor how many died on foreign battlefields; nor is it even known how many were required for the armies of Philip II. Although foreign troops already represented an important proportion of the Spanish army under Philip II, the contrast between military conditions under Philip II and Philip IV is none the less striking. Native Castilians, who formed the *corps d'élite* of the army, were increasingly difficult to recruit. By the 1630s, Olivares was desperate for manpower. Provincial governors were reporting the impossibility of raising new levies, and the majority of the recruits were miserable conscripts. 'I have observed these levies', wrote the English ambassador in 1635, 'and I find the horses so weak as the most of them will never be able to go to the rendezvous, and those very hardly gotten. The infantry so unwilling to serve as they are carried like galley-slaves in chains, which

---

[12] For this and the following information about population figures, see J. Vicens Vives, *Historia Económica de España* (Barcelona, 1959), pp. 301 ff; Ramón Carande, *Carlos V y sus Banqueros*, 1 (Madrid, 1943), p. 43; and J. Ruiz Almansa, 'La problación española en el siglo XVI', *Revista Internacional de Sociología*, 3 (1943), pp. 115–36.

serves not the turn, and so far short in number of what is purposed, as they come not to one of three.'[13]

The explanation of this increased difficulty in recruiting Castilian soldiers may be found to lie primarily in changed military conditions. Philip IV had more men under arms than Philip II, and the demand on Castile was correspondingly greater; better chances of earning good wages or of obtaining charity at home may have diminished the attractions of military service abroad; the change from the warrior Charles V to a sedentary, bureaucratic monarch in Philip II, no doubt had its influence on the Castilian nobles, whose retreat from arms would in turn add to the difficulty of recruiting their vassals for war. All these problems deserve investigation,[14] but, in the search for the origins of Olivares' troubles over manpower, it would be natural to look also to the exhaustion of Castile's demographic resources.

Here, contemporary accounts may be misleading. There are numerous complaints of depopulation in late sixteenth-century Castile, but some of these can be explained by movements of population within the peninsula rather than by any total fall in numbers. There was a marked drift of population from the countryside to the towns, most of which grew considerably between 1530 and 1594; and there was also, during the course of the century, a continuous migration from *north* Castile – the most dynamic part of the country under Ferdinand and Isabella – into central Castile and Andalusia. This southwards migration, which may be regarded as a continuation by the populace of the *reconquista*,[15] was not completed before 1600. For all those Castilians who could not themselves cross the Atlantic, Andalusia became the El Dorado. The population of Seville, the gateway to the Atlantic, rose from 45,000 in 1530 to 90,000 in 1594, and, between those dates, the populations of all but two of the larger towns of the southern half of Spain increased, while several of the northern towns, like Medina del Campo, recorded a marked decline.

A survey of conditions in north Castile alone might therefore provide a false picture of the state of the population in the Crown of Castile as a whole, and it does not seem on present evidence that an overall decline in population can be established before the end of the 1590s. All that *can* be said is that Castile's population became concentrated in the towns, particularly those of the centre and south,

---

[13] B(ritish) L(ibrary) Egerton Ms. 1820, f. 474, Hopton to Windebank, 31 May 1635.

[14] Some of them are in fact now being examined by Mr. I.A.A. Thompson of Christ's College, Cambridge, who is researching into the Spanish military system in the late sixteenth and early seventeenth centuries. [See now I.A.A. Thompson, *War and Government in Habsburg Spain, 1560–1620* (London, 1976).]

[15] Chaunu, *Séville et l'Atlantique*, 8 (1), pp. 257–8 and 265.

and that it lost some of its most vital elements through emigration and military service. Then, in 1599 and 1600, famine and plague swept up through Andalusia and Castile, causing fearful ravages in the countryside and in the densely packed cities. Unfortunately, there are no figures for the losses for these years. One village, near Valladolid, reported that no more than eighty inhabitants survived out of 300, but it is impossible to say how this figure compares with others elsewhere.[16]

Although the traditional view of its importance has been questioned,[17] it is hard to avoid the conclusion that the plague of 1599–1600 marks the turning-point in the demographic history of Castile. Hamilton's figures, while too unsatisfactory as a series for the immediate years of the plague to allow of any comprehensive statistical deductions, do at least point to a very sharp increase of wages over prices in the following decade, and suggest something of the gravity of the manpower crisis through which Castile was passing.

This crisis was exacerbated by the expulsion of the Moriscos ten years after the plague. The figures of the expelled Moriscos used to range to anything up to 1 million. Hamilton reduced them to 100,000. The recent meticulous study of the size and distribution of the Morisco population by M. Lapeyre,[18] shows that between 1609 and 1614 some 275,000 Moriscos were expelled from Spain. Of these 275,000 perhaps 90,000 came from Castile and Andalusia, and the rest from the Crown of Aragon – above all, Valencia, which lost a quarter of its population. If Hamilton underestimated the number of the Moriscos, he also underestimated the economic consequences of their expulsion. The consequences to the Valencian economy were very grave,[19] but it is important to remember that the Valencian and Castilian economies were distinct, and that Castile would be only marginally affected by the disruption of the economic life of Valencia. But Castile also lost 90,000 Moriscos of its own. These Moriscos, unlike those of Valencia and Aragon, were predominantly town-dwelling, and they undertook many of the more menial tasks in Castilian life. Their disappearance would naturally produce an immediate dislocation in the Castilian economy, which is reflected in the relationship between prices and wages for the crucial years of the expulsion, but it is not known how far this dislocation was remedied

[16] AGS Hacienda leg. 409 no. 222, consulta, 27 Aug. 1601. [Bartolomé Bennassar, *Recherches sur les grandes épidémies dans le Nord de l'Espagne à la fin du XVIe siècle* (Paris, 1969), p. 62, estimates the population losses between 1596 and 1602 as 500,000, approaching a tenth of the total population.]

[17] Chaunu, *op. cit.*, 8 (2), pt. 2, pp. 1267–8.

[18] Henri Lapeyre, *Géographie de l'Espagne Morisque* (Paris, 1959).

[19] See J. Reglá, 'La expulsión de los moriscos y sus consecuencias', *Hispania*, 13 (1953), pp. 215–67 and 402–79.

by Old Christians taking over the jobs previously occupied by Moriscos.

The present picture of the Castilian population, therefore, suggests a rapid increase slackening off towards the end of the sixteenth century, and then a catastrophic loss at the very end of the century, followed by the further loss of 90,000 inhabitants through the expulsion of the Moriscos. After that, almost nothing is known. Figures available for towns in 1646 show heavy losses, and there was another disastrous plague between 1647 and 1650. Where Hamilton suggests a 25 per cent decline during the course of the seventeenth century, there are others who believe that the population remained stationary rather than actually diminishing. All that can be said at present with any certainty is that Olivares was making heavy demands on the manpower of a country whose population had lost its buoyancy and resilience, and had ceased to grow.

In so far, then, as Castile's primacy rested on its reserves of manpower, there was a marked downward turn in its potentialities after the 1590s. Castile's national wealth, on which the Habsburgs relied for the bulk of their revenues, also shows signs of depletion. One of the principal difficulties involved in measuring the extent of this depletion is our ignorance of economic conditions in Castile in the first half of the sixteenth century. It is hard to chart the descent when one is still trying to locate the summit. But the researches of Carande and of Lapeyre[20] have gone far to confirm that the first half of the sixteenth century is a period of quickened economic activity in Castile and Andalusia, presumably in response to a growing demand. This was a time of population increase and of sharply rising prices. Indeed, Dr. Nadal had shown, on the basis of Hamilton's own figures, that there was a faster proportional rise of prices in the first half of the century than in the second, although American silver shipments were much greater in the second half than in the first.[21] The average annual rise in prices from 1501–62 was 2.8 per cent, as against 1.3 per cent from 1562–1600, and the highest maximum rise in any decade occurred between 1521 and 1530, long before the discovery of Potosí. This sharp upswing in prices during Charles V's reign may be attributable to a rising scale of aristocratic expenditure, to the dramatic growth of Charles V's debts, which he financed by the distribution of *juros*, or credit bonds, and to a vastly increased demand: an increased demand for food from Castile's growing population, an increased demand in north Europe for Castilian wool,

[20] Carande, *op. cit.*; Henri Lapeyre, *Une Famille de Marchands: les Ruiz* (Paris, 1955); and see Ladislas Reitzer, 'Some Observations on Castilian Commerce and Finance in the Sixteenth Century', *Journal of Modern History*, 32 (1960), pp. 213–23 for a detailed bibliography.

[21] Jorge Nadal Oller, 'La revolución de los precios españoles en el siglo XVI', *Hispania*, 19 (1959), pp. 503–29.

and an increased demand for wine and oil and textiles, and for almost all the necessities of life, from the new American market. This was the period which saw the development of large-scale wine and oil production in Andalusia, and of cloth production in the towns of Castile, to meet the needs of the New World; and it was also the great age of the Castilian fairs – international institutions which linked the Castilian economy to that of Italy and northern Europe in a complicated network of reciprocal obligation.

If it is accepted that the reign of Charles V represents a period of economic expansion for Castile, the first clear signs of a check to this expansion appear in 1548, when the country was experiencing one of the five-year periods of highest price increase for the entire sixteenth century. In that year the Cortes of Valladolid, moved by the general complaint of high prices, petitioned the crown to forbid the export of Castilian manufactures, even to the New World, and to permit the import of foreign goods, which would be less expensive for the Castilian consumer than Castile's own products.[22] The assumption that the export trade was pushing up Castilian prices above the general European level appeared sufficiently convincing for the crown to agree to the Cortes' request in 1552, except in so far as Castilian exports to the Indies were concerned. The consequences of the new anti-mercantilism were exactly as might have been expected, and six years later the prohibition on exports was lifted at the request of the Cortes themselves. The whole episode, brief as it was, augured badly for the future of Spanish industry.

During the reign of Philip II foreign merchants succeeded in forcing wider and wider open the door that they had suddenly found so obligingly ajar in the 1550s, and Castile's industries proved unable to resist the pressure. Professor Hamilton gave the classic explanation of this industrial failure in his famous argument that in Spain, unlike France or England, wages kept pace with prices, and that therefore Spain lacked the stimulus to industrial growth which comes from a lag between wages and prices in an age of price revolution.[23] This argument, if correct, would naturally furnish a vital clue to the *decline of Spain;* but the evidence behind it has recently been critically examined, and the whole argument has been increasingly questioned.[24] Professor Phelps Brown has shown how

[22] José Larraz López, *La época del mercantilismo en Castilla (1500–1700)* (Madrid, 1943), pp. 31 ff.

[23] Hamilton, 'The Decline of Spain', and 'American Treasure and the Rise of Capitalism (1500–1700)', *Economica*, 9 (1929), pp. 338–57.

[24] David Felix, 'Profit Inflation and Industrial Growth', *Quarterly Journal of Economics*, 70 (1956), pp. 441–63. See also for criticisms of Hamilton: Pierre Vilar, 'Problems of the Formation of Capitalism', *Past and Present*, no. 10 (1956), pp. 15–38; Ingrid Hammarström, 'The "Price Revolution" of the Sixteenth Century', *Scandinavian Economic History Review* 5 (1957), pp. 118–54; and Jorge Nadal, 'La revolución de los precios'.

Hamilton's own figures would indicate that a Valencian mason's wages by no means kept pace with the rising cost of living, and indeed lagged farther behind prices than those of his English equivalent[25] (although, if comparisons of this kind are to be really satisfactory, they require a knowledge of comparative diets and household budgets such as we do not yet possess). Hamilton does not provide sufficiently connected series to allow similar calculations for other parts of the peninsula, but his hypothesis that Spanish wages kept abreast of prices would seem so far to be quite unfounded. Indeed, further investigation may well show a marked deterioration in the living standards of the mass of the Castilian population during the first half of the century. Such a deterioration, combined with the high level of Castilian prices in relation to those of other European states, would go a long way towards explaining the peculiar structure of Castile's economy by the end of the century: an economy closer in many ways to that of an east European state like Poland, exporting basic raw materials and importing luxury products, than to the economies of west European states. In so far as industries survived in Castile they tended to be luxury industries, catering for the needs of the wealthy few and subject to growing foreign competition.

Castile's industrial development, then, would seem to have been hampered not only by the crown's fiscal policies and by unfavourable investment conditions, but also by the lack of a sufficiently large home market. This lack of a market for cheap manufactures points to an economy in which food prices are too high to leave the labourer and wage-earner with anything more than the bare minimum required for their housing, fuel and clothing. One of the most important reasons for the high price of food is to be found in the agrarian policies pursued by the kings of Castile even before the advent of the Habsburgs. Their traditional practice of favouring sheep-farming at the expense of tillage – a practice vigorously continued by Ferdinand and Isabella – meant that Castile entered the sixteenth century with a dangerously unbalanced economy. While the demand for corn increased as the population grew, the sheepowners of the *Mesta* continued to receive the benefits of royal favour. The corn-growers, on the other hand, were positively hampered, not only by the presence of the ubiquitous and highly privileged sheep, but also by the *tasa del trigo* – a fixed maximum for grain prices, which, after being sporadically applied in the first years of the century,

---

[25] E.H. Phelps Brown and Sheila V. Hopkins, 'Builders' Wage-rates, Prices and Population: Some Further Evidence', *Economica*, 26 (1959), pp. 18–38.

became a permanent feature of the crown's economic policy from 1539.[26]

The consequences of this short-sighted policy towards the agricultural interest, at a time of rapid population increase, require no comment. Professor Braudel has shown how, in the last decades of the century, Castile, in common with other south-European states, became heavily dependent on grain supplies from northern and eastern Europe.[27] Castilian agriculture was simply incapable of meeting the national demand for food. What is not clear is whether agriculture was expanding, but not expanding fast enough to keep pace with the population, or whether agricultural production for the home market was actually falling off in the later sixteenth century. There are indications that more land was being cultivated in south Spain after the middle years of the century, but this may have been more to meet the needs of the American market than to satisfy home demand. The debates of the Castilian Cortes under Philip II give an impression of mounting agrarian crisis, characterized by large-scale rural depopulation, but unfortunately, apart from the tentative pioneering survey by Viñas y Mey,[28] agrarian questions in this period remain unstudied. There are signs that the smaller landowners in Castile were being squeezed out in the later sixteenth century: it was harder for them than for the large landowners to survive the misfortunes of bad years, and they were liable to run into debt and find themselves compelled to sell out to their more powerful neighbours. This still further encouraged the concentration of land in the hands of a small number of powerful landowners, at a time when mortmain and the entail system were working powerfully in the same direction. It is customary to find historians frowning upon this process, as if the consolidation of estates in a few hands was in itself necessarily inimical to agrarian progress. But a large landlord is not automatically debarred from being an improving landlord. It would be very useful to know how far, if at all, improving landlords *were* to be found among the great lay and ecclesiastical landowners, and also to what extent they were diverted from corn-growing by the profits of sheep-farming, or by the production of wine and oil for the American market.

The discussion in the Castilian Cortes of 1598 on agrarian conditions suggests that by this time the crisis was acute,[29] and certainly

---

[26] See Eduardo Ibarra y Rodriguez, *El problema cerealista en España durante el reinado de los Reyes Católicos* (Madrid, 1944), and Carande, *op. cit.*, 1. pp. 78–9.

[27] F. Braudel, *La Méditerranée et le Monde Méditerranéen à l'époque de Philippe II* (Paris, 1949), pp. 447–70.

[28] C. Viñas y Mey, *El problema de la tierra en la España de los siglos XVI–XVII* (Madrid, 1941).

[29] *Actas de las Cortes de Castilla*, 15 (Madrid, 1889), pp. 748 ff.

the movement of the great Castilian nobles to take up residence at
court after the accession of Philip III did nothing to lessen it. Philip
III's government found itself vainly legislating against absentee
landlords, in the hope that an overcrowded court could be cleared
overnight, and the lackeys and servants who thronged the streets of
Madrid would be compelled to return to the land. But much more
than legislation against absentee landlordism was required to save
Castilian agriculture. If the real causes of rural depopulation are to be
found, they must be sought, in the first instance, at the level of village life. It is here that the dearth of good local histories in Spain
becomes particularly serious. Apart from what can be learnt from the
discussions of the Cortes, and from one useful but necessarily general
article by Professor Domínguez Ortiz,[30] little can so far be said about
the exact nature of the crisis that was overwhelming Castilian rural
communities in the late sixteenth and early seventeenth centuries.

It is, however, clear that the Castilian village was pitifully unpro-
tected. There was, for instance, the little village of Sanzoles, which
in 1607 addressed to the crown a petition that has survived at Simancas.[31] It raised a loan for municipal purposes, to place itself under
royal jurisdiction instead of that of Zamora cathedral, and then, as
the result of a series of bad harvests, found itself unable to pay the
annual interest. The creditors moved in on the village and so haras-
sed its inhabitants that eventually, out of ninety householders, no
more than forty remained. Communal indebtedness was frequent
among Castilian villages, and it obviously became particularly grave
when even a handful of villagers moved away, and the reduced
population found itself saddled with obligations that it was now
even less able to meet. But the money-lender and the powerful
neighbour were only two among the many natural enemies of Castilian villages. They were exposed also to the merciless attentions of
the tax-collector, the recruiting-sergeant and the quartermaster. Unfortunately we do not yet possess the information to tell us what
proportion of a seventeenth-century villager's income went in
taxes. A speaker in the Cortes of 1623 suggested that, in a poor man's
daily expenditure of 30 maravedis, 4 went in the *alcabala* and *millones*
alone;[32] and besides these and other taxes paid to the crown – taxes
which the peculiar fiscal structure of Castile made particularly heavy
for the peasant – there were also dues to be paid to landlords and
tithes to the church. Then, in addition to the purely fiscal exactions,
there were all the vexations and the financial burdens connected with

[30] 'La ruina de la aldea castellana', *Revista Internacional de Sociología*, no. 24 (1948), pp.
99–124.
[31] AGS Hacienda leg. 473, consulta, 25 Mar. 1607.
[32] *Actas de las Cortes*, 39, p. 142.

the quartering and recruiting of troops. Villages along the principal military routes, particularly the road from Madrid to Seville and Cadiz, were dangerously exposed, and billeting could be very expensive – 100 ducats a night for a company of 200 men, according to a report made in the 1630s.[33]

The persistence of these many afflictions over a long period of time left the villager of Castile and Andalusia very little inducement to remain on the land. He would therefore either move with his family and become swallowed up in the blessed anonymity of the great towns, or he would join the army of vagabonds that trudged the roads of Castile. We have, then, the spectacle of a nation which, at the end of the sixteenth century, is dependent on foreigners not only for its manfactures but also for its food supply, while its own population goes idle, or is absorbed into economically unproductive occupations. Accusing fingers are commonly pointed at church and bureaucracy as important agents of decline, in that they diverted the population from more useful employment. But is it not equally likely that the growth of church and bureaucracy was itself a consequence of contemporary conditions: of the lack of incentive to agricultural labour at the village level, and of the inability of the Castilian economy to provide its population with adequate employment? The nature of the economic system was such that one became a student or a monk, a beggar or a bureaucrat. There was nothing else to be.

What could be done to revitalize a flagging economy, and increase national productivity? There was no shortage of ideas. The *arbitristas* – the economic writers – of the early seventeenth century, men like González de Cellorigo, Sancho de Moncada, Fernández Navarrete, all put forward sensible programmes of reform. Royal expenditure must be regulated, the sale of offices halted, the growth of the church be checked. The tax system must be overhauled, special concessions be made to agricultural labourers, rivers be made navigable and dry lands irrigated. In this way alone could Castile's productivity be increased, its commerce be restored, and its humiliating dependence on foreigners, on the Dutch and the Genoese, be brought to an end.

The ideas were there; and so also, from the truce with the Dutch in 1609, was the opportunity. This opportunity was thrown away. The ineptitude of the Lerma régime, its readiness to dissipate the precious years of peace in a perpetual round of senseless gaiety, is one of the tragedies of Spanish history, and goes far to explain the fiasco that finally overwhelmed the country under the government of Olivares.

[33] BL Add. Ms. 9936, Papeles tocantes a las Cortes, f.2.

But behind this inert government, which possessed neither the courage nor the will to look its problems squarely in the face, lay a whole
social system and a psychological attitude which themselves blocked
the way to radical reform.

The injection of new life into the Castilian economy in the early
seventeenth century would have required a vigorous display of personal enterprise, a willingness and ability to invest in agrarian and
industrial projects, and to make use of the most recent technical
advances. None of these – neither enterprise, nor investment, nor
technical knowledge – proved to be forthcoming. 'Those who can,
will not; and those who will, cannot', wrote González de Cellorigo.[34] Why was this?

The conventional answer, useful so far as it goes, is that the social
climate in Castile was unfavourable to entrepreneurial activity. The
Castilians, it is said, lacked that elusive quality known as the
'capitalist spirit'. This was a militant society, imbued with the
crusading ideal, accustomed by the *reconquista* and the conquest of
America to the quest for glory and booty, and dominated by a church
and an aristocracy which perpetuated those very ideals least propitious for the development of capitalism. Where, in Castile, was that
'rising middle class', which, we are told, leavened the societies of
northern Europe until the whole lump was leavened? 'Our republic',
wrote González de Cellorigo, 'has come to be an extreme contrast of
rich and poor, and there is no means of adjusting them one to another. Our condition is one in which there are rich who loll at ease or
poor who beg, and we lack people of the middle sort, whom neither
wealth nor poverty prevents from pursuing the rightful kind of
business enjoined by Natural Law.'[35]

These words were published in 1600, and accurately describe
Castilian society at that time, but they cannot be said to describe it in
1500. For, however uncapitalistic the dominant strain in sixteenth-
century Castilian life, there *were* vigorous 'people of the middle sort'
in the Castile of Ferdinand and Isabella and of Charles V. The towns
of north Castile at that time could boast a lively bourgeoisie – men
like Simón Ruiz, willing to engage their persons and their fortunes in
commercial enterprise. But the decay of commercial and financial
activity in north Castile, which is patent by 1575, suggests the
disappearance of such people during the course of the century. What
happened to them? Doubtless they acquired privileges of nobility.
The passion for *hidalguía* was strong in Castile, and a title secured not
only enhanced social standing, but also exemption from taxation.

[34] *Memorial de la política*, p. 24 v.
[35] *Ibid.*, p. 54.

Yet it is hard to believe that this is an adequate explanation for the disappearance from the Castilian scene of men like Simón Ruiz. All over Europe it was the practice of merchants to buy their way into the nobility, and yet it was not everywhere so economically stultifying as it proved to be in Castile.

It would seem desirable to press farther than this, and to turn away for a time from repeating the conventional arguments about contempt for commerce and the strength of the aristocratic ideal, to the technical and neglected subject of investment opportunities.[36] What was happening to wealth in sixteenth-century Castile? Much of it was obviously going, as it was going elsewhere, into building and jewelry, and all the expensive accoutrements connected with the enjoyment of a superior social status. But it was also being invested, and unproductively invested, in *censos*, or personal loans, and in *juros*, or government bonds. Sixteenth-century Castile saw the development of a highly elaborate credit system – a system which no doubt received much of its impetus from the exigencies of the crown's finances. Anyone with money to spare – a noble, a merchant, a wealthy peasant – or institutions, like convents, could lend it to private persons, or municipal corporations, or else to the crown, at a guaranteed 5, 7 or 10 per cent. A proper study of *censos* and *juros* in Spain could tell us much about the reasons for its economic stagnation, especially if related to similar studies for other parts of Europe. *Censos* and *juros* might almost have been deliberately devised to lure money away from risky enterprises into safer channels, of no benefit to Castile's economic development. Indeed, in 1617 the Council of Finance complained that there was no chance of a Castilian economic revival as long as *censos* and *juros* offered better rates of interest than those to be gained from investment in agriculture, industry or trade.[37]

To this unwillingness to engage one's person and one's money in risky entrepreneurial undertakings, there must also be added Castile's increasing technological backwardness, as an explanation of its failure to stage an economic recovery. This backwardness is suggested by the failure of Spanish shipbuilders between the 1590s and the 1620s to keep pace with the new techniques of the north-European dockyards.[38] It was commented upon by foreign travellers, like the Frenchman Joly, who remarked in 1603 on the backwardness of the

---

[36] An indication that this question may at last be arousing attention is provided by the pioneering article of Bartolomé Bennassar, 'En Vieille-Castille: Les Ventes de Rentes Perpétuelles', *Annales, Economies, Sociétés, Civilisations*, xve année (1960), pp. 1115–26.

[37] AGS Hacienda leg. 547 no. 58, consulta, 3 Sept. 1617.

[38] See A.P. Usher, 'Spanish Ships and Shipping in the Sixteenth and Seventeenth Centuries', *Facts and Factors in Economic History for E.F. Gay* (Cambridge, Mass., 1932), pp. 189–213.

Spaniards in the sciences and the mechanical arts,[39] and Olivares himself in the 1630s was complaining of the Spanish ignorance of modern engineering techniques: 'I am certain that no man who comes from abroad to see Spain can fail to blame us roundly for our barbarism, when he sees us having to provision all the cities of Castile by pack-animal – and rightly so, for all Europe is trying out internal navigation with great profit.'[40]

While these technical deficiencies can presumably be attributed in part to the general lack of business enterprise in Castile, they should also be related to the whole climate of Castilian intellectual life. Here we are seriously hampered by the lack of a good study of the Castilian educational system. Why was it that science and technology failed to take root in Spain, at a time when they were beginning to arouse considerable interest elsewhere in Europe? It may be that further investigations will show a greater degree of scientific interest in Spain than has hitherto been assumed, but at present there is no evidence of this.[41] Indeed, such evidence as does exist points in an opposite direction – to the gradual separation of Habsburg Spain from the mainstream of European intellectual development. Early sixteenth-century Spain was Erasmian Spain, enjoying close cultural contacts with the most active intellectual centres of Europe. From the 1550s there was a chilling change in the cultural climate. The *alumbrados* were persecuted, Spanish students were forbidden to attend foreign universities, and Spain was gradually sealed off by a frightened monarch from contact with the contagious atmosphere of a heretical Europe. The conscious transformation of Spain into the redoubt of the true faith may have given an added intensity to Spanish religious experience under Philip II, but it also served to cut Spain off from that powerful intellectual current which was leading elsewhere to scientific inquiry and technical experiment.[42]

The period between 1590 and 1620, then, sees a rapid erosion of two of the principal foundations of Castile's sixteenth-century primacy, and consequently of Spain's imperial power: a decline both in Castile's demographic vitality and in its productivity and wealth. Recent investigations have also confirmed that it sees the erosion of the third foundation of Castile's primacy, in the form of a drastic

[39] 'Voyage de Barthélemy Joly en Espagne (1603–1604)', ed. L. Barrau-Dihigo, *Revue Hispanique*, 20 (1909), p. 611.

[40] BL Add. Ms. 25,689 f. 237, consulta del Conde Duque a SM.

[41] A collection of essays on Spanish science, of very varying quality, was published in Madrid in 1935 under the title of *Estudios sobre la ciencia española del siglo XVII*.

[42] For the intellectual isolation of Spain as a factor in the decline, see especially Santiago Ramón y Cajal, *Los tónicos de la voluntad*, 5th edn. (Buenos Aires, 1946), pp. 203 ff; and Claudio Sánchez-Albornoz, *España, un enigma histórico* (Buenos Aires, 1956), 2, p. 553.

reduction in the value, both to the crown and to Castile, of Castile's possessions overseas. The great convoy of volumes launched by M. and Mme Chaunu has brought home to us the enormous significance of trade between the port of Seville and Spanish America. It is, they suggest, in the 1590s that the *Carrera de las Indias* shows its first signs of serious strain. In 1597 it became clear for the first time that the American market for European goods was overstocked, but already from about 1590 the upward trend of Seville's trade with the Indies was losing speed. Although the trade fluctuated round a high level between the 1590s and 1620, its whole character was changing to the detriment of the Castilian economy. As Mexico developed its industries and Peru its agriculture, the colonies' dependence on the traditional products of the mother country grew less. There was a decreased demand in America for the Spanish cloth, and for the wine, oil and flour which bulked so large in the transatlantic shipments of the sixteenth century. The consequences of this were very serious. The galleons at Seville were increasingly laden with foreign goods, although unfortunately we do not know the relative proportions of Spanish and non-Spanish cargoes. With less demand in America for Castilian and Andalusian products, less of the American silver carried to Seville is destined for Spanish recipients, and it is significant that Spanish silver prices, which had moved upwards for a century, begin their downward movement after 1601. Moreover, the changes and the stresses in the transatlantic system began to undermine the whole structure of credit and commerce in Seville.

The principal beneficiaries of this crisis were the foreigners – the hated Genoese ('white Moors' as an irate Catalan called them[43]), the Portuguese Jews and the heretical Dutch. Foreign bankers ran the crown's finances; foreign merchants had secured a strangle-hold over the Castilian economy, and their tentacles were wrapping themselves round Seville's lucrative American trade. Castile's sense of national humiliation was increased by the truce with the Dutch in 1609, and bitterness grew as the Dutch exploited the years of peace to prise their way into the overseas empires of Spain and Portugal. The humiliating awareness of the sharp contrast between the dying splendour of Castile and the rising power of the foreigner is one of the most important clues to the psychological climate of Philip III's Castile. It helps to accentuate that sense of impending disaster, the growing despair about the condition of Castile which prompts the bitter outbursts of the *arbitristas;* and it turns them into fierce patriots, of whom some, like Sancho de Moncada, betray a hysterical xenophobia.

[43] Acadèmia de Bones Lletres, Barcelona. Dietari de Pujades 1, f. 135, 1 Dec. 1602.

The resulting mental climate goes far to explain some of the more baffling characteristics of the age of Olivares. Insufficient attention has been paid to the many signs of a revival of aggressive Castilian nationalism between 1609 and 1621 – a nationalism that would seem to have been inspired by Castile's growing sense of inferiority. Consciously or subconsciously Castilians were arguing that peace with heretics, itself deeply humiliating, was politically and economically fruitless, since it had done nothing to check the advance of the English and the Dutch. Yet, if the foreigner triumphed in the contemptible arts of commerce, Castile could at least evoke the spirit of its former greatness – its military prowess. The answer to its problems was therefore a return to war.

This appears to have been the attitude of the great Castilian viceroys of Philip III's reign, the Osunas and the Alcalás, and it was in this climate of aggressive Castilian nationalism, with its strong messianic overtones, that Olivares came to power in 1621. In the person of Olivares one finds curiously blended the two dominant strains of thought of the reign of Philip III: the reforming idealism of the *arbitristas* and the aggressive nationalism of the great Castilian proconsuls. With his boundless confidence in his own powers, Olivares determined to combine the programmes of both. He would restore Castile to economic vigour, and simultaneously he would lead it back to the great days of Philip II when it was master of the world.

But the ambitious imperial programme of the Conde Duque depended, as the imperial programme of Philip II had depended, on the population, the productivity and the overseas wealth of Castile, and each of these had undergone a serious crisis between 1590 and 1620. It would conventionally be argued also that Philip II's imperialism was dependent, and indeed primarily dependent, on the flow of American silver coming directly to the crown; and in so far as that flow had diminished by the second and third decades of the seventeenth century, the attempt to revive Spain's imperial greatness was in any event doomed. Here, however, the popular conception of the role played by the king's American silver supplies can be misleading. The silver remittances to the crown at the end of Philip II's reign averaged about 2 million ducats a year. This was little more than the annual sum raised by ecclesiastical taxation in the king's dominions, and under a third of the sum which Castile alone paid the crown each year in its three principal taxes.[44]

The American remittances were important, in the long run, less

---

[44] This can be deduced from papers and *consultas* of the Council of Finance in AGS Hacienda for the years 1598–1607, and particularly leg. 380.

for their proportionate contribution to the crown's total income than for the fact that they were one of the few sources of revenue not pledged for many years in advance. Their existence assured a regular supply of silver which was necessary if the bankers were to continue to provide the king with credit. During the decade 1610–20 the remittances began to fall off. Instead of the 2 millions of the early 1600s, the President of the Council of Finance reported in December 1616 that 'in the last two years hardly a million ducats have come each year',[45] and by 1620 the figure was as low as 800,000. It recovered in the 1620s, but between 1621 and 1640 1½ million ducats represented an exceptional year, and not more than a million ducats could be expected with any degree of confidence; in fact, about half the sum that Philip II could expect.

This was serious, but it was not crippling in relation to the overall revenues of the crown. Under Philip IV, as under Philip II, it was not America but Castile that bore the main burden of Habsburg imperialism, and Castile was still paying its 6, 7, or 8 million ducats a year in taxation. But during the 1620s it became increasingly expensive for Castile to raise these sums. Since 1617 large new quantities of *vellón* coinage had been manufactured, and by 1626 the premium on silver in terms of *vellón* had risen from 4 per cent in 1620 to some 50 per cent.[46] This meant in practice that a tax collected in *vellón* would now buy abroad only half the goods and services for which it was nominally supposed to pay.

Olivares tried to compensate for the disastrous drop in the purchasing power of Castilian money by raising the level of taxation in Castile and inventing a host of ingenious fiscal devices to extract money from the privileged and the exempt. In many ways he was extremely successful. The Castilian aristocracy was so intensively mulcted that a title, so far from being a badge of exemption, became a positive liability, and the Venetian ambassador who arrived in 1638 reported Olivares as saying that, if the war continued, no one need think of possessing his own money any more since everything would belong to the king.[47] While this fiscal policy, when applied to the Castilian nobles, caused no more than impotent rumblings of discontent, it proved to be self-defeating when adopted towards what remained of the Castilian merchant community. The long series of arbitrary confiscations of American silver remittances to individual merchants in Seville, who were 'compensated' by the grant of rela-

[45] AGS Hacienda leg. 542 no. 1, Don Fernando Carrillo to King, 23 Dec. 1616.
[46] Earl J. Hamilton, *American Treasure and the Price Revolution in Spain, 1501–1650* (Cambridge, Mass., 1934), Table 7, p. 96.
[47] *Relazioni degli Stati Europei*, ed. Barozzi and Berchet. Serie 1. Spagna, 2 (Venice, 1860), p. 86.

tively worthless *juros*, proved fatal to the town's commercial life.[48] Olivares' tenure of power saw the final alienation of Spain's native business community from its king, and the final defeat of native commercial enterprise in the name of royal necessity. The crumbling of the elaborate credit structure of Seville and the collapse of Seville's trading system with the New World between 1639 and 1641,[49] was the price that Olivares had to pay for his cavalier treatment of Spanish merchants.

In spite of Olivares's ruthless exploitation of Castile's remaining resources, there was never enough to meet all his needs. Castile's growing inability to meet his demands for manpower and money naturally forced him to look beyond Castile for help. To save his beloved Castile, it became imperative for him to exploit the resources of the peripheral provinces of the Iberian peninsula, which had been under-taxed in relation to Castile, and which were under no obligation to provide troops for foreign service. It was this determination to draw on the resources of the Crown of Aragon and Portugal which inspired Olivares' famous scheme for the Union of Arms: a device which would compel all the provinces of the Spanish Monarchy to contribute a specified number of paid men to the royal armies.[50]

Olivares' scheme of 1626 for the Union of Arms was in effect an implicit admission of a change in the balance of economic power within the Spanish peninsula. Behind it lay the contemporary Castilian assumption that Castile's economic plight was graver than that of the other regions of Spain. How far this assumption was correct, it is not yet possible to say. The various regions of the peninsula lived their own lives and went their own ways. A decline of Castile does not necessarily imply the simultaneous decline of the Crown of Aragon and Portugal, both of them living in different economic systems, and shielded by separate monetary systems from the violent oscillations of the Castilian coinage.

Yet, if we look at these peripheral kingdoms, we may well think that the prospects were a good deal less hopeful than Olivares believed them to be. Aragon: a dry, impoverished land. Valencia: its economy dislocated by the expulsion of the Moriscos. Catalonia: its population growth halted about 1625,[51] its traditional trade with the

[48] See Antonio Domínguez Ortiz, 'Los caudales de Indias y la política exterior de Felipe IV', *Anuario de Estudios Americanos*, 13 (1956), pp. 311–83. The same author's *Política y hacienda de Felipe IV* (Madrid, 1960), is an important contribution to the study of the crown's financial policy in the reign of Philip IV, based as it is on previously unused documents from Simancas.

[49] Chaunu, *op. cit.*, 8 (2), pt. 2, pp. 1793–1851.

[50] For the Union of Arms, see my *The Revolt of the Catalans. A Study in the Decline of Spain (1598–1640)* (Cambridge, 1963).

[51] Catalan population problems are admirably treated in J. Nadal and E. Giralt, *La Population Catalane de 1553 à 1717* (Paris, 1960).

Mediterranean world contracting after the plague of 1630. Portugal: its Far Eastern empire lost to the Dutch under Philip III, its Brazilian empire in process of being lost to the Dutch under Philip IV.

Even if Olivares overestimated the capacity of the other territories of the peninsula to bring him the help he needed, he none the less knew as well as anyone else that he was engaged in a desperate race against time. If France could be beaten swiftly, the future would still be his. Then at last he could undertake the great reforms which only awaited the return of peace, and which would enable Castile to devote itself as effectively to the task of economic reform as it had already devoted itself to the successful prosecution of the war. In 1636, at Corbie, he very nearly achieved his aim. A little more money, a few more men, and French resistance might have crumbled. But the gamble – and Olivares knew it *was* a gamble – failed, and, with its failure, Olivares was lost. The Franco-Spanish war inevitably turned after Corbie into the kind of war which Spain was least able to stand: a war of attrition, tedious and prolonged. Such a war was bound to place heavy strains on the constitutional structure of the Spanish Monarchy, just as it placed heavy strains on the constitutional structure of the French Monarchy, since Olivares and Richelieu were compelled to demand assistance from, and billet troops in, provinces which had never been assimilated and which still possessed their own semi-autonomous institutions and their own representative bodies. The Spanish Monarchy was particularly vulnerable in this respect, since both Catalonia in the east, and Portugal in the west, were uneasily and unsatisfactorily yoked to the central government in Madrid. When the pressure became too great, as it did in 1640, they rose up in arms against that government, and Castile – for so long the predominant partner in the Monarchy that it took its superiority for granted – suddenly discovered that it no longer possessed the strength to impose its will by force.

The great crisis in the structure of the Monarchy in 1640, which led directly to the dissolution of Spanish power, must therefore be regarded as the final development of that specifically Castilian crisis of 1590–1620 which this essay has attempted to describe; as the logical dénouement of the economic crisis which destroyed the foundations of Castile's power, and of the psychological crisis which impelled it into its final bid for world supremacy.

It seems improbable that any account of the *decline of Spain* can substantially alter the commonly accepted version of seventeenth-century Spanish history, for there are always the same cards, however we shuffle them: mortmain and vagabondage, governmental ineptitude, and an all-pervading contempt for the harsh facts of economic life. Instead of continuing to be indiscriminately scattered they can, however, be given some pattern and coherence. Yet even when the reshuffling is finally done and all the cards are fairly distributed, it remains doubtful whether dissent will be possible from the verdict on Spain of Robert Watson's *History of the Reign of Philip III,* published in 1783: 'her power corresponded not with her inclination';[52] nor from the even sterner verdict of a contemporary, González de Cellorigo: 'it seems as if one had wished to reduce these kingdoms to a republic of bewitched beings, living outside the natural order of things'[53] – a republic whose most famous citizen was Don Quijote de la Mancha.

[52] p. 309.
[53] *Memorial de la política,* p. 25 v.

XI

SELF-PERCEPTION AND
DECLINE IN EARLY
SEVENTEENTH-CENTURY SPAIN

In the early summer of 1625 the Count of Gondomar, now old and sick, was reluctantly setting out on what was to be his last diplomatic mission to northern Europe. When he reached Irún he sat down to write a long letter to the Count-Duke of Olivares, the effective ruler of Spain for the past four years. The letter, described by Olivares as being in the nature of a general confession, contained four principal charges against his conduct of Spain's affairs, of which the first and most wide-ranging was that *se va todo a fondo* – 'the ship is going down'.

The Count-Duke replied at length on 2 June with a forceful point by point rebuttal, couched in that theatrical style so characteristic of the man. How many old and disgruntled men, he asked, had not said exactly the same thing, ever since the world was first created? Gondomar, as a man who read books, must know that kingdoms whose imminent demise was announced had gone on to flourish for many centuries afterwards. Indeed, within Spain itself, was there a single century in which historians had not lamented 'what we lament today'? 'By this', he continued, 'I do not mean to say that these are happy times', nor even that things were better than in 1621 when Philip IV came to the throne. But at least there had been no mutinies in the armies, and no rebellions at home, and one could even point to some modest achievements:

> And I conclude by saying that I do not consider a constant and despairing recitation of the state of affairs to be a useful exercise, because it cannot be concealed from those who know it at first hand. To make them despair of the remedy can only weaken their resolution, while it cannot fail to have adverse effects on everyone else...As far as I am concerned, your words can do no harm. I know the situation, I lament it, and it grieves me, but I will allow no impossibility to weaken my zeal or diminish my concern. For, as the minister with paramount obligations, it is for me to die

unprotesting, chained to my oar, until not a single fragment is left in my hands. But when such things are said where many can hear them, wanton damage is caused.[1]

The Count-Duke's words – realistic, perhaps, or stoical, but certainly prophetic – offer a poignant insight into the dilemmas of a statesman grappling with the monumental difficulties of a society 'in decline'. The country over which he was called to preside in the final years of its greatness has served as the classic textbook example of a society which fails to respond adequately to the challenges that confront it and pays the supreme penalty, relegation to the sidelines of history. The reasons for that failure have been the source of endless historical inquiry;[2] but if the results of that inquiry have not so far proved commensurate with the quantity of effort devoted to it, one possible explanation may be found in a certain unwillingness to probe beyond a supposedly 'objective' situation in search of more subjective evidence of the kind provided by the Count-Duke's letter to Gondomar. For later generations the general picture seems clear enough: they see, and attempt to measure, 'decline'. But how did men who, like Olivares, lived through those times seek to understand their predicament and explain it to themselves? And what contribution did their perception of the situation make to the actual process of 'decline', by influencing the way in which they reacted, or failed to react, to events?

The constant interplay between action and perception should form an integral component of the study of a society 'in decline'. The very fact, for instance, that Gondomar and Olivares in speaking of their country as a sinking ship had recourse to a classical image of the state which was a commonplace of their times, suggests a view of government and its problems which itself may consciously or subconsciously have influenced their behaviour and responses. Storms, after all, are acts of God, beyond the control of a captain, whose skills may serve for nothing when the crisis comes.[3]

[1] Olivares to Gondomar, 2 June 1625: Biblioteca del Palacio, Madrid, Ms. 1817. The text of this letter is published in full in John H. Elliott and José F. de la Peña, *Memoriales y cartas del Conde Duque de Olivares* (2 vols., Madrid, 1978–80), 1, Doc. 5. I have not so far been able to locate Gondomar's letter to the Count-Duke.

[2] For bibliographical references, see ch. 10.

[3] Martin González de Cellorigo in the dedication to his *Memorial de la política necessaria y útil restauración a la república de España* (Valladolid, 1600), also refers to the dangers of a general shipwreck. For the image of the ship of state in this period, see Michael D. Gordon, 'The Science of Politics in Seventeenth-Century Spanish Thought', *Pensiero politico*, 7 (1974), pp. 379–94, and his 'John Bodin and the English Ship of State', *Bibliothèque d'humanisme et renaissance*, 35 (1973), pp. 323–4.

Such a study should not be beyond the bounds of possibility for seventeenth-century Spain – a society almost obsessively dedicated to the written word.[4] It left behind it a wide variety of evidence from which to piece together its view of itself and its world. In part this can be done from its rich imaginative literature, even if this contains elements of distortion that can easily mislead.[5] Similar difficulties surround another source that has yet to be effectively exploited for Spain – the printed sermon for the special occasion. But there is also a massive quantity of material, in print and manuscript, which specifically addresses itself to what contemporaries identified as major problems of their times. This includes the discussions and documentation of the councils and juntas engaged in the government of the Spanish Monarchy, the debates of the Cortes of Castile, and the innumerable tracts and treatises, published and unpublished, which sought to analyse and prescribe remedies for Castile's many woes.

The expedients recommended in these treatises were known as *arbitrios*, and their authors as *arbitristas* – an appellation which makes its appearance before the end of the sixteenth century.[6] An almost exact contemporary English equivalent of the two words exists in 'projects' and 'projectors', even to the pejorative overtones which they both acquired. The *arbitrista* was the product of a society which took it for granted that the vassal had a duty to advise when he had something to communicate of benefit to king and commonwealth, the assumption being that he would also benefit himself. Sometimes a crook and more frequently a crank, he might recommend anything from a secret alchemical formula infallibly guaranteed to refill the king's depleted coffers, to the most grandiose political and military projects, like those put forward with characteristic obduracy by that

[4] Some faint idea of the scale of this obsession may be obtained from the alarming information that by 1603 a *visita* (the ordinary form of inquiry) begun in 1590 into the government of a recent viceroy of Peru had so far made use of 49,555 sheets of paper. See Lewis Hanke, 'El visitador licenciado Alonso Fernández de Bonilla y el virrey del Perú, el conde del Villar', in *Memoria del II congreso venezolano de historia* (Caracas, 1975), 2, p. 28 note 49.

[5] See Joseph Pérez, 'Littérature et sociéte dans l'Espagne du Siècle d'Or', *Bulletin hispanique*, 70 (1968), pp. 458–67, for a useful discussion of this problem.

[6] Baltasar Alamos de Barrientos, writing in 1598, warns the king to beware of 'the specious reasoning and false presuppositions of the *arbitristas*': Antonio Pérez, *L'art de gouverner*, ed. J.M. Guardia (Paris, 1867), p. 308. If the dating and text of Alamos' discourse are trustworthy, this would pre-date by fifteen years the first appearance of the word *arbitrista* in literary usage – by Cervantes – as cited in Jean Vilar's pioneering study of the figure of the *arbitrista* in Spanish Golden Age satire, *Literatura y economía* (Madrid, 1973), p. 48. In writing this essay I have made extensive use of this and other work by Jean Vilar, whose promised study of Spanish political and economic writers of the seventeenth century should transform our knowledge of the subject.

enthusiastic expatriate, Colonel Semple, for whom Spain's only hope lay in union with Scotland.[7]

Some *arbitrios* were so secret that their proud authors would only be prepared to disclose them in private audience with some great minister. Some, laboriously written and hopefully presented, disappeared without trace into the gaping caverns of the Spanish bureaucracy. Others, favourably received by men in high places, became the subject of formal discussion by groups of ministers. If the councils in Madrid not infrequently found themselves ordered to examine what might at first sight appear to be wildly implausible schemes, it was because some leading figure in the administration had allowed himself to be talked into it by the author, or simply felt that the most improbable project was perhaps worth a chance. The members of a special junta convened to consider another batch of projects from the ever ready pen of Sir Anthony Sherley were reminded by Olivares of the example of Columbus.[8] Unfortunately for seventeenth-century Spain, however, the analogy did not hold.

The *arbitristas* also circulated their manuscripts among acquaintances, or resorted to the printing-press in the hope of influencing a public opinion which was beginning to make its presence felt in the Spain of Philip III and Philip IV.[9] Colmeiro's nineteenth-century listing of Spanish economic tracts written during these two reigns, between 1598 and 1665, contains 165 titles.[10] These, however, are only the survivors – fragments of a vast literature, only in part economic, which proliferated especially in the opening and closing years of the reign of Philip III, and much of which has long since disappeared without trace. While many of these tracts and proposals for ingenious projects no doubt richly deserved the oblivion which overtook them, the unfortunate connotations of the word *arbitrista*, together with changing fashions in economic theory, have too often

---

[7] Vilar, *Literatura y economía*, pp. 198–9.

[8] Olivares, *consulta* of 8 Sept. 1626: A[rchivo] G[eneral de] S[imancas], Estado, legajo 2645, no. 23: 'In relation to these projects, it occurs to him how wild those of Columbus must have seemed, and yet what benefits they brought to this monarchy.' I owe this reference to the kindness of Dr. Conrad Kent. The king had already used identical words about Sherley in replying to a *consulta* of 4 August. Which of the two men was repeating his master's voice? For Sir Anthony Sherley's projects, see Xavier-A. Flores, *Le Peso político de todo el mundo d' Anthony Sherley* (Paris, 1963).

[9] For public opinion and opposition in Habsburg Spain, see especially J.A. Maravall, *La oposición política bajo los Austrias* (Madrid, 1972); Teófanes Egido, *Sátiras políticas de la España moderna* (Madrid, 1973); Jean Vilar, 'Formes et tendances de l'opposition sous Olivares: Lisón y Viedma, defensor de la patria', *Mélanges de la Casa de Velázquez*, 7 (1971), pp. 263–94. The government's use of propaganda to influence public opinion is examined in the pioneering study of José M. Jover, *1635. Historia de una polémica y semblanza de una generación* (Madrid, 1949).

[10] Manuel Colmeiro, *Biblioteca de los economistas españoles de los siglos XVI, XVII y XVIII* (Madrid, 1861). See Vilar, *Literatura y economía*, pp. 172–5, for this and the following points.

tended to preclude the dispassionate examination of a literature of economic and social debate which contains a number of works of high quality and interest. While a few select names, like Sancho de Moncada and Fernández Navarrete, have found their way into discussions of European economic thought,[11] the *arbitristas* as a group remain too little known.

Belatedly, however, a reassessment, based on a closer acquaintance with the men and their writings, is now well under way. There are various ways, not necessarily mutually exclusive, in which their work can be approached. The *arbitristas* were drawn from among certain groups in Spanish society – academics and clergymen, government officials, military men, members of the urban patriciate and the mercantile community – and there is ample scope for the study of their origins and affiliations. In so far as they tended to speak for different constituencies, their corporate ties and regional links – like those of the 'Toledo School' – become a subject of importance. Their suggested remedies, too, can be classified in terms of differing economic doctrines – bullionist or anti-bullionist, proto-physiocratic or protectionist.[12]

The proposals and prescriptions of the *arbitristas*, however, are not the only aspects of their thought which deserve attention. While they display an interesting and often important diversity, they are united by their shared belief that something had gone seriously wrong with the society to which they owed allegiance. It is this collective awareness of disaster or impending disaster, as expressed by a group of deeply concerned and articulate men busily engaged in searching for some way of escape, which makes seventeenth-century Castile an almost perfect laboratory in which to examine a 'declining' society's attitude to itself. What did these men see, or fail to see, as they looked at society, the economy and the state? Why did they see it in the way they did? What were the images and points of reference which they used, and how did these images affect their own responses

[11] For example, Joseph A. Schumpeter, *History of Economic Analysis* (London, 1954; repr. 1967), p. 168.

[12] For the role of Jean Vilar in this reassessment, see note 6 above. He identifies and discusses the 'Toledo School' in his contribution to the Fifth International Congress of Economic History held in Leningrad in 1970 ('Docteurs et marchands: l' 'Ecole' de Tolède'), and in his important introduction to his edition of Sancho de Monacada, *Restauración política de España* (Madrid, 1974). For Spanish anti-bullionist thinking, see Pierre Vilar, *Crecimiento y desarrollo* (Barcelona, 1964), pp. 175–207. The Instituto de Estudios Fiscales of the Ministerio de Hacienda in Madrid is publishing a collection of reprints of 'Clásicos del Pensamiento Económico Español', including Jean Vilar's above-mentioned edition of Moncada's *Restauración política de España* of 1619, Jean Paul Le Flem's edition of Miguel Caxa de Leruela, *Restauración de la abundancia de España* (Madrid, 1975), and Pedro Fernández Navarrete, *Conservación de monarquías y discursos políticos*, ed. Michael D. Gordon (Madrid, 1982).

and those of the men they sought to influence? Until the *arbitristas* are better studied and known, and their relationship to the organs of government and opposition charted with precision, the answers to these questions are bound to remain both generalized and tentative. But even now they can hint at something of the richness of interplay between a society and its image of itself, which can help bring us closer to an understanding of 'decline'.[13]

During the sixteenth century Castile, as the acknowledged head of a global empire, had enjoyed a series of spectacular successes. During the last years of Philip II, however, it began visibly to falter. The late 1580s and the 1590s seem in retrospect the critical years: the years of major reverses in Spain's north European policies, of another official 'bankruptcy' in 1597, of the death of the old king himself in 1598, and of the famine and plague which swept through Castile and Andalusia at the end of the century, and claimed perhaps half a million victims out of a population of the order of six million.[14]

These setbacks and disasters struck a society which had been conditioned to success, and it is clear that seventeenth-century Spaniards felt an urgent need to explain to themselves what was happening to them. This need was all the more urgent because recent events contrasted so strikingly with the expectations which their society had created for itself. During the sixteenth century Castile had developed a powerful strain of messianic nationalism.[15] The achievement of world-wide empire and an extraordinary run of victories had helped convince Castilians that they were the chosen people of the Lord, especially selected to further His grand design – a design naturally cast in cosmic terms as the conversion of the infidel, the extirpation of heresy, and the eventual establishment of the kingdom of Christ on earth. But if Castile was indeed the right arm of the Lord, how was the sudden series of disasters to be explained? Why did God now seem to have abandoned His own?

In a cosmology which postulates a natural, if not always clear-cut,

[13] The idea of decline has not so far received the attention that has been lavished on the idea of progress. For a discussion of this question and a useful bibliography, see Randolph Starn, 'Meaning-Levels in the Theme of Historical Decline', *History and Theory*, 14 (1975), pp. 1–31. See also Peter Burke, 'Tradition and Experience: The Idea of Decline from Bruni to Gibbon', *Daedalus* (Summer 1976), pp. 137–52.

[14] See my *Imperial Spain, 1469–1716* (London, 1963), pp. 279–95, for a discussion of the setbacks of the late sixteenth century. See also Bartolomé Bennassar, *Recherches sur les grandes épidémies dans le nord de l'Espagne à la fin du XVIe siècle* (Paris, 1969), and Antonio Domínguez Ortiz, *La sociedad española en el siglo XVII*, 2 vols. (Monografías histórico-sociales, 7–8, Madrid, 1963–70), 1, pp. 68–70.

[15] See the introduction by Miguel Herrero García to a belated example of this kind of thinking, Fray Juan de Salazar's *Política española* of 1619 (Madrid, 1945). M. Herrero García's *Ideas de los españoles de siglo XVII*, 2nd edn. (Madrid, 1966) is a useful compendium of the ideas of Spaniards about themselves and others.

relationship between divine dispositions and human morality, there was one obvious answer. Castile had provoked the divine wrath, and was paying the price of its sins. This did not necessarily mean, however, that God had cast it aside for ever. On the contrary, disaster might even be represented as cause for hope, as it was by the Jesuit Pedro de Ribadeneyra, when he attempted to explain the defeat of the Spanish Armada. The disaster was, he argued, yet another sign of God's special favour, since it would oblige Castilians to strengthen their faith, purify their intentions, and reform their manners and morals.[16]

There was, therefore, a supernatural explanation of Castile's troubles, of which the natural corollary was a moralizing puritanism. There would be no more victories, warned Mariana, moralist, *arbitrista* and historian, until morals were reformed.[17] The age revealed its corruption in sexual immorality and religious hypocrisy; in the idleness and insubordination of youth; in luxurious living, rich clothing and excessive indulgence in food and drink; and in the addiction to the theatre and to games of chance. To this catalogue of evils a new one was added in the later years of Philip III – the effeminate fashion among men for wearing their hair long. A diarist writing in 1627 came to the conclusion that this was a 'contagion from England', introduced during the course of the negotiations for an Anglo-Spanish match.[18]

Spain could only be cleansed of these vices by a programme of national regeneration beginning with the court. It was assumed that such a process of purification would 'oblige' God to look favourably again on Castile and continue His former mercies to it. This direct equation between national morality and national fortune was one that weighed heavily on the rulers of Spain, who had been taught to consider themselves personally responsible for the defeats and the sufferings of the peoples committed to their charge. 'I consider that God is angry with me and my kingdoms for our sins, and in particular for mine', was the best explanation that Philip IV could find for the Dutch capture of Wesel and 's Hertogenbosch in 1629.[19]

[16] 'Carta de Ribadeneyra...sobre las causas de la pérdida de la Armada': Pedro de Ribadeneyra, *Historias de la Contrarreforma*, ed. Eusebio Rey (Madrid, 1945), pp. 1, 351–2.
[17] Juan de Mariana, *De spectaculis*, in his *Obras* (Biblioteca de Autores Españoles, 31, Madrid, 1854), p. 460. Guenter Lewy, *Constitutionalism and Statecraft during the Golden Age of Spain* (Geneva, 1960), p. 29, dates this essay to 'well before 1599'.
[18] *Dietari de Jeroni Pujades*, 4 vols. (Barcelona, 1975–6), 4, pp. 87–8. According to Pujades, who is writing of Catalonia, the second Count of Santa Coloma has the distinction of being the first to persecute the long-haired young.
[19] *Papel que escribió S.M....*: A[rchivo] H[istórico] N[acional, Madrid], libro 857, fo. 182. For the idea of 'obliging' God, see the *consulta* of the Junta de Reformación of 11 January 1626 quoted in Angel González Palencia, 'Quevedo, Tirso y las comedias ante la Junta de Reformación', *Boletín de la Real Academia Española*, 25 (1946), p. 81.

It might appear at first sight that in an intensely religious society this supernatural interpretation of unexpected misfortune left little more to be said. But if seventeenth-century Spaniards, like their contemporaries in other parts of Europe, operated within a narrow theological framework bounded by sin and grace, punishment and reward, they also operated within a more secular framework which implied an alternative, although not mutually exclusive, interpretation of the terrible drama that was unfolding before them. This was a naturalistic, rather than supernatural, interpretation and it owed more to the Graeco-Roman than to the Judeo-Christian tradition in European thought.

In this alternative scenario Spain was no longer seen *sub specie aeternitatis*, its fortunes determined by the dictates of an inscrutable deity. Instead it was squarely placed within the temporal process, governed by those same forces which dictated celestial and terrestrial movements in the natural world. The idea of an infinite cyclical process, by which all living organisms were subject to growth, maturity and decay, was deeply embedded in European thinking, as was Polybius' application of it to the rise and fall of states. The organic conception of the state in sixteenth-century Europe reinforced the analogy, and history confirmed it. Renaissance historiography had dwelt on the *inclinatio* or the *declinatio* of Rome.[20] If all great empires, including the greatest of them all, had risen only to fall, could Spain alone escape? This hardly seemed likely, and one of the most acute of the *arbitristas*, González de Cellorigo, devoted the first chapter of his book, published in 1600, to the theme of 'how our Spain, however fertile and abundant it may be, is subject to the *declinación* to which all republics are prone.'

The fateful word had been uttered – *declinación*. It was a word which was here associated with a purely natural process, and as such it raised theological issues of which González de Cellorigo was well aware. There were, he explained, differing opinions on the causes of the decline of states. Some attributed it to the movement of the planets, some to the natural instability of all things human, and others to the cyclical processes of nature itself. But astrological and natural determinism were unacceptable to the Christian, who was bound to see in every event, great or small, the hand of an omnipotent God whose judgements were inscrutable.[21]

There was, then, an escape clause: the miraculous could occur. But

---

[20] For theories of historical decline in Renaissance and post-Renaissance Europe, see Starn, 'Meaning-Levels in the Theme of Historical Decline', and Santo Mazzarino, *La fine del mondo antico* (Milan, 1959), English trans. by George Holmes, *The End of the Ancient World* (London, 1966).

[21] Cellorigo, *Memorial*, fs. 1–4.

barring this, there was an inevitability about the process, which might by human agency be slowed down, but could never be reversed. The analysis of what had gone wrong would vary from *arbitrista* to *arbitrista*, but all began, whether openly or tacitly, with the mental image of a *degenerative* process to which their country was inexorably subject. As might have been expected of an age when the analogy between the state and the human body was a commonplace, the process of decline tended to be described in terms of a wasting disease. Jerónimo de Ceballos, for instance, writes of the:

> similarity between the government of a polity and the human body, which also suffers from excess or natural causes; and the same thing happens to the republic, which goes into *declinación* either by bad government...or by natural causes which proceed from time itself...for everything which has a beginning must decline towards its end, just like the rising and the setting sun.[22]

The result of the analogy from the human body was that the medical metaphor was ubiquitous.[23] For Fernández Navarrete 'the illness is extremely serious.' For Sancho de Moncada, whose *Restauración política de España* was published in 1619, Spain had changed more in the last four or five years than over the last forty or fifty, like an old but healthy man, who suddenly in the space of a few days is laid low by the illnesses which will carry him to the grave. For Lisón y Biedma 'this sick man is Your Majesty's monarchy, which is suffering in the head, namely the royal treasury....' A state paper presented to the Cortes in 1623 declares that monarchies are 'mortal and perishable', and compares the condition of Castile to that of one of those bodies described by Galen as being slowly corrupted by evil humours which yet keep it lingering on, so that the doctors dare not expel them for fear of inducing sudden death.[24]

Diseases could, of course, be diagnosed, and indeed the *arbitristas* behaved as if they were so many doctors, anxiously examining the patient for symptoms and each prescribing his own exclusive nostrum. Since, however, remedies are supposed to yield beneficial results, *arbitrista* thinking is distinguished by the paradox that, while the illness must be regarded as terminal, all the same there is hope. But the hope is essentially for a stay of execution: the doctor may

---

[22] Jerónimo de Ceballos, *Arte real para el buen govierno de los Reyes, y Príncipes, y de sus vassallos* (Toledo, 1623), f. 4.

[23] See José Antonio Maravall, *La cultura del barroco* (2nd, ed., Barcelona, 1980), pp. 148–9. (Eng. trans., *Culture of the Baroque* (Minneapolis, 1986), p. 65).

[24] Pedro Fernández Navarrete, *Conservación de monarquías* (Madrid, 1626), discurso 49; Moncada, *Restauración*, discurso 1, cap. 2 (ed. Vilar, p. 97); Mateo de Lisón y Biedma, *Discursos y apuntamientos*, pt. 2, 21 Nov. 1622, f. 15ᵛ; *Actas de las Cortes de Castilla*, 38, pp. 141, 146.

not be able to prolong the patient's life indefinitely, but at least by applying the right remedies he may be able to check the fever's course.

Medicine aims to conserve where it cannot restore. If, as Ceballos asserted, 'Your Majesty is the doctor of this republic, and your vassals are sick',[25] good government was a prerequisite for the survival of the patient. *Arbitrismo* therefore properly concerned itself with government as well as with economic and social affairs, on the reasonable assumption that the first necessity was 'physician, heal thyself.' There was an art or 'science' of government which, like that of medicine, had to be studied and learnt.[26] But of what did it consist? Essentially it was an art of conservation, whether in relation to foreign or domestic affairs. 'Good government is more a matter of knowing how to conserve than acquire', the Duke of Lerma was told,[27] and this became a commonplace of seventeenth-century Spanish political thought. The instinctive response to *declinación* was *conservación* – a word which winds its way through political literature and the records of conciliar debate in the reigns of Philip III and Philip IV.[28]

Still better than conservation was actual restoration – that *Restauración política de España* which provided the title for Sancho de Moncada's book. But those seeking to restore a body afflicted by a wasting disease cherish the image of a healthy state sometime in the past. There was, however, no clear agreement as to when the organism had attained its highest point of perfection. The men who came to power in 1621 consciously looked back to what they believed to be the high standards of government and probity which prevailed under Philip II.[29] More often the ideal was seen as the reign of Ferdinand and Isabella, itself frequently viewed as the age in which the Castilian virtues of an idealized middle ages, after being

[25] Ceballos, *Arte real*, f. 30.

[26] Cf. Alamos de Barrientos: 'this science (*ciencia*) which they call of state': *Advertencias políticas*, Hispanic Society, New York, MS. HC 380/80 f. 10; 'To know how to govern is a science': Moncada, *Restauración*, discurso 9, cap. 1 (ed. Vilar, pp. 229–30).

[27] 'Carta que Duarte Gomez escribió al duque de Lerma', 20 Nov. 1612, f. 7, in Duarte Gómez Solis, *Discursos sobre los comercios de las dos Indias* (Madrid, 1622).

[28] Cf. the royal confessor in a debate on the Netherlands in the Council of State, 1 Aug. 1628: AGS, Estado, legajo 2042; 'perhaps the greatest deed which Your Majesty could perform is to sustain and conserve entire and in peace the great monarchy that God has given you.' For the theme of *conservación*, see Maravall, *La cultura del barroco*, pp. 273–6 (*Culture of the Baroque*, pp. 129–30) and for Spanish political theory of this period, his *La philosophie politique espagnole au XVIIᵉ siècle* (Paris, 1955).

[29] In April 1621 Baltasar de Zúñiga told the Genoese ambassador that it was the new king's intention to 'restore everything to the state it was in during the time of King Philip II.' Register of correspondence of G.B. Saluzzo, 6 Apr. 1621: Archivio di Stato, Genoa, Lettere Ministri, Spagna 2429.

temporarily corrupted by the civil disorders of the fourteenth and fifteenth centuries, shone forth in all their glory. According to González de Cellorigo, 'our Spain in all things reached its highest degree of perfection. . . in those times', and then there set in a decline 'to which no certain beginning can be given.'[30]

Whether the point of perfection was placed in an idealized middle ages or an idealized reign of the Catholic kings, the scenario tended to unfold in a similar way. In former times Spaniards had lived sober, hard-working lives, practising frugal virtues, and dedicated to religion and the martial arts. But then the Indies had been discovered, and Castile had gained a world-wide empire. Gradually wealth and luxury had 'corrupted the good customs of men',[31] and idleness had prevailed. From this point the analogy with the fate of Rome was irresistible. The Jesuit Pedro de Guzmán, writing in 1614, recalled the words of Bishop Osorio that 'idleness has destroyed the greatest empires in the world, those of the Persians, the Greeks. . . and the Romans.' Fray Juan de Santa María, a leading figure in the opposition to the government of the Duke of Lerma, quotes Sallust to the effect that 'when a kingdom reaches such a point of moral corruption that men dress like women, . . . that the most exquisite delicacies are imported for its tables, and men go to sleep before they are tired, . . . then it can be regarded as lost, and its empire at an end.'[32]

The historical law behind all this was spelt out by a minor literary figure, Juan Pablo Mártir Rizo, in a life of Maecenas which he published with a dedication to Olivares in 1626:

> Empires are easily preserved with the customs they acquired at the start, but when idleness replaces hard work, luxury replaces sobriety, and arrogance steps in where justice should prevail, then fortune and manners are changed, and empires are undone unless a remedy is found.[33]

[30] Cellorigo, *Memorial*, f. 31. For the idea of corruption, see Pedro Sainz Rodríguez, *Evolución de las ideas sobre la decadencia española* (Madrid, 1962), esp. pp. 63–5. For the middle ages as seen through the eyes of Lope de Vega, see Renato I. Rosaldo Jr., 'Lope as a Poet of History', in *Perspectivas de la comedia*, ed. Alva V. Ebersole (Chapel Hill, 1978), pp. 9–32.

[31] Ceballos, *Arte real*, f. 32ᵛ. See also Mariana, *De spectaculis*, p. 460, and Caxa de Leruela, *Restauración de la abundancia de España*, cap. 21 (ed. Le Flem, p. 60).

[32] Pedro de Guzmán, *Bienes del honesto trabajo y daños de la ociosidad* (Madrid, 1614), p. 81. Fray Juan de Santa María, *República y policía christiana* (Lisbon, 1621 edn.), p. 200. For the importance of Santa María's book, see Jean Vilar's introduction to Moncada, *Restauración*, pp. 17–18. Santa María's *República y policía christiana* appeared in English translation in 1632 under two different titles: *Christian Policie: or, the Christian Commonwealth* (London, 1632, STC 14803.7 and 14831), and *Policie Unveiled* (London, 1632, STC 14831a).

[33] Juan Pablo Mártir Rizo, *Historia de la vida de Mecenas* (Madrid, 1626), fs. 88ᵛ–89. For details of the author, see José Antonio Maravall's introduction to the volume containing Mártir Rizo's *Norte de príncipes* and his *Vida de Rómulo* (Madrid, 1945).

It was, therefore, the deviation from the guiding principles of the heroic age of greatness which was the true source of disaster. Like other societies Castile had created an image of itself and of its past, which had helped to shape its expectations and its goals. The disappointments and reverses of the late sixteenth and early seventeenth centuries created a crisis of confidence, because they implied that Castile was falling short of the goals – essentially military and religious – which it had set itself. This failure was then set into the context of *declinación*.

The implications of the supernatural and the naturalistic explanations of Castile's troubles were the same. The answer, in both instances, was to go back: to reform and to restore. Over and over again the message of the reformers of the first three decades of the seventeenth century was a message of return. Return to the primeval purity of manners and morals; return to just and uncorrupt government; return to the simple virtues of a rural and martial society. The future essentially lay in the past. How was return to be achieved? By a programme of national regeneration and re-dedication, of which the purifying process represented by the expulsion of the Moriscos from 1609–14 – the uprooting from Castile of a 'cursed and pernicious seed'[34] – was an early manifestation. Sumptuary legislation should be enforced in order to curb the excesses of modern dress; the theatres should be shut down and the publication of frivolous books be banned; nobles should be sent back to their estates, and their sons be trained to become good horsemen and good soldiers; and the farmer and the rural labourer should be rescued before it was too late.[35] The rustic virtues were idealized in the increasingly urbanized Madrid of the early seventeenth century by a theatre which glorifid the independence and integrity of the peasant and the rural community – the only uncontaminated part of the commonwealth.[36]

If this were the sum total of the Castilian reform movement of the seventeenth century, it would seem very similar to the response of earlier societies to a time of troubles. The sense of decline, the idea of a lost virtue, the idealization of traditional rural values are characteristic of ancient Rome, and of the late medieval Islamic world, as seen through the eyes of Ibn Khaldun.[37] But in the seventeenth-century Castilian response to the national predicament, there is an

---

[34] Céspedes y Meneses, quoted in Herrero Garcia, *Ideas de los españoles*, p. 573.

[35] See the documents collected in *La Junta de Reformación. Documentos procedentes del Archivo Histórico Nacional y del General de Simancas..., 1618–1625*, ed. Angel González Palencia (Archivo Histórico Español, 5, Valladolid, 1932), and especially Doc. 4, the famous reform *consulta* of 1 February 1619, at pp. 12–30.

[36] See Noël Salomon, *Recherches sur le thème paysan dans la 'comedia' au temps de Lope de Vega* (Bibliothèque des hautes études hispaniques, 31, Bordeaux, 1965).

[37] Mazzarino, *End of the Ancient World*, chs. 1–4; Ibn Khaldun, *The Muqaddimah*, trans. Franz Rosenthal, 2nd edn. (Princeton, 1967).

additional and disturbing element, which helps to differentiate it from these earlier responses, and makes the Castilian experience an interesting forerunner of that of other societies in the modern and contemporary world. It is an element which certainly had its echoes in other parts of early seventeenth-century Europe, and not least in the 'depressed' England of the 1620s,[38] but which seems to have been felt on a scale and with an intensity that transform quantitative into qualitative difference.

The indicators of decline so far mentioned have been largely moral indicators, even if they also have some bearing on government and the capacity for war. 'Decline' does not seem to have been used of the arts and letters, as it was in the Rome of Pliny and Quintilian, presumably because of their obviously flourishing state.[39] At least from the 1620s, however, it was being used by Spaniards in relation to their country's international position and military power. The Count-Duke of Olivares, when discussing the setback to Spanish arms in Italy in 1629, wrote of the terrible discredit it brought upon king and nation, 'which still continues on its decline'. Philip IV himself, writing in 1634, described the recommendation by the Council of State in 1629 that a new truce should be made with the Dutch at any price, as marking the moment when 'my monarchy began by general consent, and visibly, to decline.'[40]

But as long as victories alternated with defeats, 'decline' was more obviously applicable to the domestic situation than to Spain's great power status. But decline of what, and in relation to what? The decay of manners and morals provided one set of indicators, but there was also another set, pointing to a different kind of decline. These indicators were essentially economic and fiscal. They included the state of the crown's finances, which a minister described in 1629 as having been in 'continuous *declinación*' during his thirty-nine years in the royal service;[41] the fiscal burden, especially on the peasantry; the excess of imports over exports and the consequent ruin of domestic industry; the disorders of the debased *vellón* coinage; and perhaps the most alarming of all the indicators in the eyes of contemporaries, the decline of population.

'Never', wrote Luis Valle de la Cerda in 1600, 'in seven hundred years of continuous war, nor in one hundred of continuous peace,

---

[38] See esp. B.E. Supple, *Commercial Crisis and Change in England, 1600–1642* (Cambridge, 1959), ch. 9, 'Economic Thought'.

[39] Mazzarino, *End of the Ancient World*, p. 34. For a view of the state of the arts in Spain, see the quotation of 1628 from Sebastián de Alvarado in Henry Kamen, 'Golden Age, Iron Age: A Conflict of Concepts in the Renaissance'. *Journal of Medieval and Renaissance Studies*, 4 (1974), p. 136.

[40] Olivares to Gonzalo Fernández de Córdoba, 4 May 1629: AGS, Estado, legajo 2712; *consulta*, 16 Mar. 1634 (Philip IV's reply): AGS, Estado, legajo 2048.

[41] AHN, Estado, libro 856, f. 141ᵛ.

has Spain as a whole been as ruined and as poor as it is now.'[42] But what was the evidence for this? Much of it, inevitably, was impressionistic. The decline of agriculture was confirmed by the sight of deserted villages, and by the scarcity of rural labourers, the causes of which were analysed at length by Lope de Deza in 1618.[43] The decline of trade was confirmed by the presence of the ubiquitous foreign merchant. The decline of industry was confirmed by the flood of foreign imports. Such evidence naturally suffered from the defect of its origins, and the problems of evaluation were difficult. What, for instance, was the truth about the Toledo of Philip III, which complained so loudly of its troubles that when González de Cellorigo went there in 1619 he expected to find it a desert? Yet on his arrival it seemed to him much less affected than other towns by the 'common *declinación* of these kingdoms, to which everything in the world is subject.' The streets were full of people, the houses occupied, the buildings in good shape....[44]

Local memory and the impressions of visitors were both very imperfect guides to the reality and the extent of 'decline'. But serious attempts were made to find other and more reliable forms of evidence. The very uncertainty over recent population trends itself served as an incentive to search for some kind of statistical precision. Sancho de Moncada was one of those who wanted decisions to be based on facts, not theories, and referred to the parish registers as showing that in 1617 and 1618 there were only half as many marriages as there had been in earlier years.[45] Global population figures were not easy to come by, but the paper presented to the Cortes of Castile in 1623 on the state of the realm made use of the tax assessments of 1584–5 and 1591 as the basis for its conclusion that population had declined by a third since the last of these assessments. But the administration was sufficiently uncertain of its figures to expatiate on the need to introduce into Castile 'what is called a *census* in Latin and a *censura* in romance.'[46]

The fact that reformers should fasten on economic and demographic phenomena – more or less accurately observed and described – no doubt stems in part from the tradition of government

---

[42] Luis Valle de la Cerda, *Desempeño del patrimonio de su Magestad*...(Madrid, 1600), f. 156ᵛ.

[43] Lope de Deza, *Govierno polytico de agricultura* (Madrid, 1618).

[44] Cellorigo to president of Council of Castile, 5 Feb. 1619: B(ritish) L(ibrary) Add. Ms. 14,015, f. 216. For a modern view of Toledo's problems at this moment, see Michael Weisser, 'The Decline of Castile Revisited: The Case of Toledo', *Journal of European Economic History*, 2 (1973), pp. 614–40.

[45] Moncada, *Restauración*, discurso 2, cap. 4 (ed. Vilar, p. 137). Vilar makes this point admirably in his introduction, esp. p. 64. For the same approach in the work of Pedro de Valencia, see J.A. Maravall, 'Reformismo social-agrario en la crisis del siglo XVII: tierra, trabajo y salario según Pedro de Valencia', *Bulletin hispanique*, 72 (1970), p. 50.

[46] *Actas de las Cortes*, pp. 135–6, 180.

based on local inquiry which had led to the compilation of that domesday survey, the famous *Relaciones topográficas*, under Philip II.[47] It reflects too the great tradition of economic debate in sixteenth-century Spanish universities. But it also reflects an awareness of, and participation in, the wider, west European debate of the later sixteenth and seventeenth centuries about the relationship of power, population and productivity. The better informed *arbitristas* knew their Bodin and their Botero – 'the book is common', wrote the professor of moral philosophy at Salamanca in 1624 of Botero's *Reason of State*.[48] It was in his famous book VII that Botero argued the case for a large population as a source of national wealth, and then went on to say that 'if Spain is accounted a barren land this is not due to any deficiency of the soil but to the sparseness of the inhabitants.'[49]

In a world where population was seen as the basis of wealth and power, demographic trends came to provide the touchstone of decline. If indeed it was true that 'the more people there are who eat and clothe themselves, the more is spent and bought and sold, and this in turn increases the royal revenues',[50] then Spain's plight was grave. Gondomar noted as much in a superb letter written in March 1619, six months after returning from England. Who that had travelled outside the peninsula could not fail to be aware on his weary homeward journey of the 'depopulation, poverty and misery of Spain today'?[51] The relationship between population and productivity was endlessly discussed – often, as by Sancho de Moncada, with considerable sophistication.[52] But the discussion always started from the standpoint that Castile had too few people, although from the strictly economic point of view this was not perhaps the most critical problem for a society unable to feed or employ such people as it had.[53]

[47] See Noël Salomon, *La campagne de Nouvelle Castille à la fin du XVIe siècle d'après les relaciones topográficas* (Paris, 1964).

[48] Angel Manrique, *Socorro del clero al estado* (Salamanca, 1624; repr. Madrid, 1814), p. 55. Antonio de Herrera had produced a Spanish translation of Botero in 1592.

[49] Giovanni Botero, *The Reason of State*, trans. by P.J. and D.P. Waley (London, 1956), p. 145.

[50] Manrique, *Socorro del clero al estado*, p. 58.

[51] *Correspondencia oficial de Don Diego Sarmiento de Acuña, conde de Gondomar*, 4 vols. (Documentos inéditos para la historia de España, 1–4, Madrid, 1936–45), 2, p. 135.

[52] Cf. Vilar's introduction to Moncada, *Restauración*, p. 66. Moncada was one of those who realized that Spanish 'idleness' might be the involuntary result of unemployment: *ibid.*, discurso 1, cap. 2 (ed. Vilar, p. 108).

[53] Interestingly, however, Martínez de Mata, the *arbitrista* of a later generation, notes when writing in the 1650s that the heavy population losses of the last twenty years had been useful in purging the body politic of evil humours, since it would have been impossible to find sustenance for so many people: Francisco Martínez de Mata, *Memoriales y discursos*, ed. Gonzalo Anes (Madrid, 1971), p. 337.

Alongside the supernatural and the naturalistic interpretations of Castile's predicament, then, there existed a more scientific vein of interpretation which – while not necessarily rejecting the other approaches – sought to identify and analyse specific economic and social problems, like depopulation, as amenable to correction by the appropriate policies, properly applied. It was an interpretation which assumed, in line with contemporary thought in other parts of western Europe, that it lay within the capacity of men and governments to increase productivity and maximize power. Whereas the bias of the first two interpretations was towards a moral response, and towards the restoration of health to a disordered body politic, this more scientific explanation saw the problem in terms of mistaken policies which could be changed for better ones.

The changes demanded, however, were changes in the management of the economy rather than the ordering of society. Modern society, thinking in terms of structure, sees the solution to its problems in terms of structural change. Seventeenth-century society, thinking in terms of organisms, was concerned with restoring health, not with transforming structures. It would purge, and bleed, and if necessary amputate, to get the constitution back to a harmonious balance. Strong arguments would be put forward in seventeenth-century Castile for reducing the wealth and power of those elements in the body politic, like the church, whose excesses disturbed the equilibrium of the whole.[54] But the hierarchical order of society was regarded as fixed and immutable. *Arbitristas*, satirists and playwrights might mock or criticize the abuses and the extravagances of contemporary social behaviour, but they accepted the foundations on which it rested as a matter of course.[55]

One of the great themes of González de Cellorigo's treatise was that things had gone wrong because the social balance had been upset – all moderation and just proportion had gone, as men aspired to a higher social status than that of their fathers. This was a commonplace of the times, repeated by *arbitristas* and royal ministers and echoed by playwrights.[56] Once again, inevitably, it pointed to return – return to an age when society was in balance. The same held true of many of the economic recipes that were proposed, like Caxa de Leruela's suggestions for the revival of the sheep industry. They looked to the past as a model, and therefore change took the form of

[54] See Domínguez Ortiz, *La sociedad española en el siglo XVII*, 2, ch. 8.

[55] For the containment of social tension in Spanish baroque thought, see Maravall, *La cultura del barroco*, esp. ch. 1.

[56] Cellorigo, *Memorial*, fos. 54ᵛ–56. For a playwright on this theme, see especially the words of the tailor, Homo Bono, in Tirso de Molina's *Santo y sastre*, act 1, scene 2 (*Obras dramáticas completas*, 3, Madrid, 1968 edn., p. 56).

restoration. But where the supernatural and the naturalistic interpretations of decline inevitably looked back to the past, this was not
necessarily true of the more scientific approach. The past might
provide one model, but it was not the only one. For those who saw
economic problems in the context of an international discussion
about the presumed relationship of population, productivity and
national power, another possible model existed. This model was
provided not by an idealized version of the national past, but by the
present practice of contemporary states.

If, as Sancho de Moncada wrote, 'experience has shown that
republics which used to be poor, like France, Flanders, Genoa and
Venice, have prospered by producing their own manufactures; while
Spain, rich in fruits and silver fleets, has grown poor by its failure to
do so',[57] then the answer was to go and do likewise. There was
nothing new in this kind of recommendation,[58] but as the contrast
between the economic situation of Spain and that of its rivals
appeared to sharpen, so the sense of urgency increased. 'It would be
wise to make use of imitation in so far as is compatible with our
nature and disposition', recommended a special junta which was
considering a proposal for the establishment of overseas trading
companies on the model of the Dutch. 'We must bend our efforts to
turning Spaniards into merchants', declared Olivares in his im-
perious way.[59]

Some Spaniards, therefore, were beginning to see decline in terms
of economic backwardness relative to other contemporary societies.
Once things began to appear in this light, the correct response was
not to restore but to innovate. Early seventeenth-century Spain, in
becoming aware of its 'barbarism' – to use the word employed by
Olivares of its technical deficiencies in internal transportation as seen
through foreign eyes[60] – therefore provides an early scenario for
what was in due course to become the world-wide drama of
modernization and traditionalism. Already the principal themes had
been suggested and the actors were taking their allotted places on the
stage. Here was a society which felt itself increasingly threatened and
disoriented as two currents of reform competed for attention – one
pressing for a return to the ancient ways, the other for innovating
change.

Innovation was not easy to justify in a world which instinctively
tended to assume that all change was for the worse. The received

[57] Moncada, *Restauración*, discurso 1, cap. 12 (ed. Vilar, p. 110).
[58] Cf. the *Memorial del Contador Luis Ortiz a Felipe II* (Madrid, 1970), p. 75.
[59] *Consulta* of Junta del Comercio, 13 Mar. 1624: AGS, Estado, legajo 2847; Olivares'
memorandum on government, 25 Dec. 1624: BL Egerton Ms. 2053, f. 217.
[60] 'barbaridad', in *consulta del conde-duque*: BL, Add. Ms. 25,689, f. 237ᵛ.

opinion was voiced by a leading minister of the crown: 'novelties (*novedades*) are absolutely bad when they run counter to the established forms of state and government.' 'Novelties have always brought great difficulties and inconveniences in their train', argued opponents of a proposed fiscal reform in the Cortes of 1623. On the other hand, as one of the *arbitristas* wrote, 'new needs and new situations demand a search for new remedies.' In the circumstances it is not surprising that *novedad* and *novedades*, as somewhat ambiguous words, acquired a certain fashionability in the Madrid of those years.[61]

It would, however, be misleading to postulate a clear-cut division between traditionalists and innovators in early seventeenth-century Spain. The currents, in fact, were hopelessly mixed. Proponents of innovating economic remedies also tended to think in terms of collective guilt and moral regeneration. Jerónimo de Ceballos, who proposed the introduction of a national banking system, also wished Castile to devote its energies to the reconquest of Jerusalem.[62] What does become increasingly apparent, however, is the incompatibility of the two reforming traditions when they meet on specific issues. The extravagances of dress, for example, were highly offensive to those who saw in them a conspicuous misuse of wealth and an indication of dangerous social confusion as men and women aped the fashions of their superiors. But against the rising pressure for new sumptuary decrees, Gregorio López Madera could write in 1621 that 'although frugality and moderation are very good for private individuals, and greatly desired by the zealous, they are not good for the republic as a whole, for they take away employment.'[63] In this anticipation of the doctrine of private vices, public benefits, new economics and ancient morality met in open conflict.

The perception of decline gave powerful urgency to the movement for reform. During the last four years of the reign of Philip III this movement developed an irresistible momentum, as *arbitristas*, sections of the bureaucracy, and the urban patriciate, through its spokesmen in the Cortes, clamoured for something to be done. Even the indolent government of the Duke of Lerma was forced to take note. 'We do not deny, gentlemen, within these four walls', said the president of the Council of Castile to the Cortes in 1617, 'that there is

[61] Fernando Carrillo to king, 10 June 1621: AHN, Estado, libro 613; *Actas de las Cortes*, 39, p. 221; Manrique, *Socorro del clero al estado*, pp. 45–6. See also Maravall, *La cultura del barroco*, ch. 9, on 'novedad'.

[62] Ceballos, *Arte real*, f. 149.

[63] *La Junta de Reformación* , p. 106. For a comparable view by a British contemporary, see Thomas Mun, *England's Treasure by Forraign Trade* (London, 1664; repr. Oxford, 1928, 1949). p. 60.

a general weakness in this body of king and kingdom, and that the remedy is for us to recognize and feel it reciprocally, for this will promote a concern to put things right.'[64] But it was not until 1621, with the advent of a new king and a new government, that Spain acquired a régime which, in its sense of urgency, seemed to match the mood of the times.

Under the government of Zúñiga and Olivares, the results of twenty years of national introspection began to acquire legislative embodiment in a programme of reform and regeneration devised and directed by the principal ministers of the crown. The perception of a society in decline therefore became the starting-point for governmental action. Instinctively resorting to the rhetoric of the *arbitristas* the administration told the 1623 Cortes that 'it is essential to press ahead with the cure, and this may have to consist of cauterization if nothing else works, because sometimes one can restore life to a patient *in extremis* by treating him as such.'[65]

Inevitably as the Olivares régime pushed ahead with its programme, the incompatibilities in the attitudes that had created a climate for reform became increasingly apparent. There are many reasons for the failure of the Olivares reform programme of the 1620s,[66] but among them must be included this conflict of attitudes – conflict to be found not only within the ranks of the administration, but also within the Count-Duke himself, as a man who mirrored with almost uncanny accuracy the fears and aspirations of the Castile of his times.

In the desire to return to the pure values of a heroic past, the régime embarked on a programme of *reformación*, designed to purify manners and morals and so make Castile once again worthy of its providential calling. Sumptuary excesses were curbed; brothels were ordered to be closed; and from 1625 to 1634 no licences were granted for the printing of novels and plays because of their tendency to corrupt the manners of the young.[67] This same spirit, however, helped to reinforce the arguments for the return to war after a period of relative peace – a war which would first distort, and then destroy, the programme of reform. Advocating the resumption of active hostilities in the Netherlands in 1621 the Count of Benavente argued in the Council of State that idleness made the naturally brave Spaniards effeminate, and that it was necessary to have 'a good war,

---

[64] *Actas de las Cortes*, 29, pp. 424–5.

[65] *Ibid.*, 38, pp. 146–7.

[66] For the reform programme and its failure see J.H. Elliott, *The Count-Duke of Olivares* (New Haven and London, 1986).

[67] For the *capítulos de reformación* of 10 February 1623, see *La Junta de Reformación*, Doc. 66, at pp. 415–55. For the ban on plays and novels, see Jaime Moll, 'Diez años sin licencias para imprimir comedias y novelas en los reinos de Castilla, 1625–1634', *Boletín de la Real Academia Española*, 54 (1974), pp. 97–103.

or else we lose everything.'[68] The overwhelming concern with 'reputation' in the conduct of Spanish foreign policy was at least in part the compensating response of ministers uneasily conscious of their country's *declinación*. Ironically it was Olivares' son-in-law, the statesman of a new generation, who despairingly observed after fifty years of obstinate effort culminating in the great disasters of the middle years of the century that 'the true reputation of states does not consist of mere appearances.'[69]

Yet in order to recover its strength and fight its wars more effectively, Castile found itself driven into the present while clinging to the past. The Olivares programme required innovating change, whether for tax reform or commercial recovery or technical advance. This change tended to draw on foreign ideas and expertise, and involved the introduction of new and disturbing elements into the centre of national life. The sudden prominence at the court of crypto-Jewish Portuguese bankers and businessmen symbolized the inner contradictions of a programme of reform which had depicted purification as essential to survival, and now had recourse to those very elements which the popular mind most associated with the contamination of Castile.[70]

The social effects of the administration's attempts to introduce change in the context of what was conceived of as 'decline' still have to be systematically explored. Was it, for instance, pure coincidence that the 1620s proved to be a decade of violent controversy over Castile's patron saint? The canonization of Teresa of Avila in 1622 gave a new impetus to the movement to make her the patron of Castile in place of, or alongside, St. James. Against the partisans of the warrior saint who had delivered Spain from the Moors were ranged those of a modern saint, who was both Spanish and a woman. In the great co-patronage controversy that divided Castile into two opposing camps, the nation's disasters, from floods to plagues of locusts, were attributed either to the anger of St. James at his possible displacement, or alternatively to the lack of effective advocacy in heaven, such as St. Teresa might supply.[71]

[68] *Consulta*, 17 July 1621: Archivo de los Condes de Oñate, legajo 104. I owe this reference to the kindness of the Marqueses de Torre Blanca.

[69] Quoted in R.A. Stradling, 'A Spanish Statesman of Appeasement: Medina de las Torres and Spanish Policy, 1639–1670', *Historical Journal* (1976), p. 19.

[70] There is a rapidly growing literature on the Portuguese Jews in seventeenth-century Spain. See especially Julio Caro Baroja, 'La sociedad criptojudía en la corte de Felipe IV', in his *Inquisición, brujería y criptojudaismo*, 2nd edn. (Barcelona, 1972), and Yosef Hayim Yerushalmi, *From Spanish Court to Italian Ghetto* (New York, 1971).

[71] For a brief but entertaining account of the co-patronage controversy, see T.D. Kendrick, *Saint James in Spain* (London, 1960), ch. 4; see also Américo Castro, *La realidad histórica de España*, 3rd edn. (Mexico, 1966), pp. 394–9.

A violent polemic over the identity of a nation's symbolic representative hints at a deep underlying disagreement over national identity itself. The awareness of 'decline' was itself the precipitant of change, but deep divisions arose over the direction of that change. As the reform programme faltered, so the satirical attacks on the *arbitristas* sharpened, and the disillusion with reform itself became more acute. The combination of an unsuccessful reform programme with crippling defeat in war – the yardstick by which Castile instinctively judged national failure or success – was the worst thing that could have happened, aggravating the bitterness, the fatalism, and the sense of collective guilt.

Still more ominous was the reinforcement of the stockade mentality in Castilian society. This mentality, which looked on Spain as surrounded by foreign enemies and in imminent danger of subversion by the enemy within, found coherent expression in a writer of genius who had for a time given active support to the reforming régime of Olivares, and then broke violently with it. In his brilliant and savage *La hora de todos* of the 1630s Francisco de Quevedo excoriated the *arbitristas* as pernicious meddlers and as the harbingers of foreign ideas which would corrupt and destroy the values that had made Castile what it was. 'To survive', says one of his characters, 'let us cling fast to the aphorism that "what always was done, always should be done", for this, if observed, will preserve us from *novedades*.'[72]

By an alchemy worthy of the most ingenious *arbitrista*, 'decline', then, was transmuted into a kind of success, as what later generations would call the 'eternal truths of Spain'[73] soared transcendent above the corrupting temporal process. Drawing on their own image of Spain, the opponents of reform rallied, and rallied again, over the course of the centuries. But so too did the reformers, who in the course of the eighteenth century began to look back to the *arbitristas* with interest and respect.[74] This respect was not unjustified. All self-perception contains an element of self-deception, but it varies in degree. Those who perceived that the ship was indeed sinking in the 1620s were not in fact far wrong. But a sinking ship needs to be relieved of some of its ballast, not steered on to the rocks.

[72] Francisco de Quevedo y Villegas, *Obras completas*, 6th edn., 2 vols. (Madrid, 1966), 1, p. 260, and see Conrad Kent, 'Politics in *La hora de todos*', *Journal of Hispanic Philology*, 1 (1977), pp. 99–119. I have also found helpful the essay by Juan Marichal, 'Quevedo: el escritor como "espejo" de su tiempo', in his *La voluntad de estilo* (Madrid, 1971).
[73] José M. Pemán, *Breve historia de España* (Madrid, 1950), p. 381.
[74] See the introduction by Gonzalo Anes to Martínez de Mata, *Memoriales y discursos*, pp. 82–90.

13   Diego de Velázquez, *The Count-Duke of Olivares on Horseback.*

XII

ART AND DECLINE IN
SEVENTEENTH-CENTURY SPAIN

In the winter of 1683–84 Samuel Pepys seized the opportunity afforded by a visit on government business to Tangier to cross over into Spain and do some sight-seeing in Andalusia. This at least was the intention, but during his six weeks in Seville it poured with rain. Neither prayers in the city's churches, not solemn processions through its streets, succeeded in halting the torrential downpour, which put a sad damper on Pepys' sight-seeing, and – to his intense disappointment – prevented him from making a trip to Málaga. But nothing – not even the rain in Spain – could dampen Pepys' habitual curiosity. Although he did not keep a diary during those weeks in Spain, he did jot down notes on points that attracted his attention, or 'contraries' and 'extraordinaries' as he called them: 'no chimneys in Spain'; 'rare to see a Spaniard drunk'; 'fleas are a mighty plague in houses'; 'no chamber-pots in all the country.'[1]

For all the sharpness of observation, it is sad that we do not have the more considered reflections of this most qualified of English tourists on the country which was still, at the time of his birth in 1633, the greatest power in Europe. How much one would have given to have heard the views of this robust representative of a rising Britain on a declining Spain! But his one summary judgement is predictably harsh:

> Men of the Toga who have never been in the World do govern all in Spain, and men of the Spada [the sword] are put into most employments at sea without knowing anything of their business, and so their state is governed and will be lost. In a word, never were a people so overrun with fools in all states as they are.[2]

If this should seem the characteristically arrogant remark of a supercilious foreigner, it is worth noting the comment of a Spaniard

---

[1] *The Tangier Papers of Samuel Pepys*, ed. Edwin Chappell (London, 1935), pp. 254–63.
[2] *Ibid.*, p. 168.

who complained to Pepys about 'how their country is under a fata-
lity in all their businesses of state.' This despairing observation
reflects a mood of fatalism which had become fashionable in seventeenth-century Spain. As early as 1600, twelve years after the defeat
of the Invincible Armada, Martín González de Cellorigo, an acute
observer of the economic and social problems of his native Castile,
used the word *declinación* – 'decline' – in relation to its condition.[3]
The notion of decline – a decline of power, a decline of prosperity, a
decline of national greatness – was often evoked in the following
decades by ministers and government officials, and by the numerous
commentators and analysts who anxiously diagnosed the state of the
Spanish body politic and prescribed a wide variety of differing and
often contradictory remedies to effect a cure.[4] The image seemed
especially appropriate because of its associations with the fate of
another great empire, that of ancient Rome.

The analogies between the Roman and Spanish experience had
always been regarded as close, and now, in the seventeenth century,
became painfully closer. Sixteenth-century Spain, under the government successively of Ferdinand and Isabella, of the Emperor Charles
V, and then of Philip II, had conquered and colonized a world-wide
empire, even greater than that of Rome. The language of Castile, its
laws, its arms, were supreme over wide portions of the globe. Here
was an empire on which, as Ariosto had said, the sun never set.

Or so at least it was thought. But then, after a series of shocks and
setbacks, the mood began to change. The crisis of confidence can be
traced back to the last few years of the sixteenth century. The defeat
of the Armada came as a severe psychological shock to a Castile
which had come to think of itself as the chosen nation of the Lord.
The death of the old king, Philip II, in 1598, meant change after
decades of firm and well-tried government – change to a young and
manifestly ineffectual new king, Philip III, who abandoned his
father's practice of poring far into the night over state papers, and
entrusted the business of government to the hands of favourites.
Then, in 1599–1600, Castile and Andalusia were hit by famine and
plague, which claimed perhaps half a million victims in a population
of some six million. On top of this, acute financial troubles,
culminating in state bankruptcies, forced Spain into peace – with the
French in 1598, the English in 1604, and into a humiliating twelve-
year truce with the rebellious Dutch in 1609. The Spain of these years
was the Spain of Don Quijote, of which the first part appeared in

---

[3] Martín González de Cellorigo, *Memorial de la política necesaria y útil restauración a la
república de España* (Valladolid, 1600), f. 1.
[4] Above, ch. 11.

1605 and the second in 1615 – a Spain which, like a bemused knight errant, showed signs of having lost its bearings in a changing world. 'It seems', wrote González de Cellorigo, as he surveyed the parasitic rentier society with its extravagant dreams and conspicuous consumption and neglect of economic realities, 'it seems as if one had wished to reduce these kingdoms to a republic of enchanted beings, living outside the natural order of things.'[5]

There were many moralists in the Spain of Philip III who felt that something had happened to Castile's moral fibre, and again they recalled the Roman analogy. One of them quoted Sallust to the effect that 'when a kingdom reaches such a point of moral corruption that men dress like women,...that the most exquisite delicacies are imported for its tables, and men go to sleep before they are tired..., then it can be regarded as lost, and its empire at an end.'[6] It is not surprising, then, to find that in 1621, on the death of Philip III, a new regime comes to power on a wave of popular acclaim – a regime committed to an austere programme of economic and moral reform. The new king, the sixteen-year old Philip IV, chose as his principal minister a man of very different stamp from his predecessors: Don Gaspar de Guzmán, known to history as the Count-Duke of Olivares (Pl. 13). He was a ruthlessly energetic and authoritarian figure, who was determined to save his country from disaster and bring about a great national revival. For two decades, the 1620s and 1630s, Spain felt the smack of stern and purposeful government.

Olivares sought on the one hand to restore Spain's former imperial grandeur, reviving its military virtues and leading it back to war. On the other, he embarked on a programme for national recovery, grappling with the problem of inflation and planning a whole series of measures to increase productivity. But the two decades of the Count-Duke's government ended in disaster. Reform had to be sacrificed to war, and the crippling burden of war taxation imposed intolerable strains on Spain's political and social fabric. In 1640 both Catalonia and Portugal revolted against the government of Philip IV, and although Catalonia later returned to allegiance, Portugal was lost for ever.

Sir Arthur Hopton, the British ambassador in Madrid during these years of disaster, wrote to London in 1641: 'I am induced to think that the greatness of this monarchy is near to an end.'[7] Two years later, in 1643, Olivares fell from power.

Hopton's judgment was right. Under Olivares, the Spain of the

[5] González de Cellorigo, Memorial, f. 25v.
[6] Fray Juan de Santa María, República y policía christiana (Lisbon, 1621), p. 200.
[7] Public Record Office, SP. 94.42, f. 192, Hopton to Vane, 26 July/4 August 1641.

House of Austria had shot its final bolt. The second half of the reign of Philip IV was at best a holding operation, as a disillusioned and world-weary monarch struggled to maintain what he could of Spain's former power and primacy. On Philip's death in 1665, only the fragile life of his pathetic son, Carlos II, stood in the way of the extinction of the male line of the dynasty.

The history of Spain during the last thirty-five years of the seventeenth century is often equated with the moribund existence of the last of the Spanish Habsburgs. This is not entirely fair. From around 1680 there are in fact some flickering signs of renewal, even in Castile, the depressed central region of the Iberian peninsula, which had borne the heaviest fiscal burdens. But the long-expected and long-delayed death of Carlos II in 1700 effectively marks the end of an era.

Looking back over those hundred years between the death of Philip II in 1598 and of his great-grandson in 1700, there seems no good reason to contest the established view that this was the century of Spain's decline – a decline partially concealed from the world during the first decades of the century by the lingering survival of fading imperial glories and the short-lived burst of energy during the regime of Olivares. But the disasters of the 1640s stripped off the mask to reveal the hollowness within. The Spain of Murillo – the Spain visited by Samuel Pepys in 1683, the year following the artist's death – was a once-great imperial power reduced to second-class status, an object of European derision.

Yet when we speak of a country in decline, what do we really mean? To some extent the indicators of decline change with the perspective of different ages, but some of the characteristics of the Spanish condition appear instantly recognizable: a marked reduction in military and diplomatic effectiveness; an inability to generate new sources of wealth and to cope with the causes and consequences of inflation; a failure of leadership and a paralysis of the political will; the fossilizing of traditional institutions; a narrow, inward-looking frame of mind, given to excessive self-examination, and always prone to relapse into fatalism. These characteristics are all to be found in seventeenth-century Castile – a society with a vast, top-heavy bureaucracy, and an entrenched and privileged elite in church and state, a society of rentiers and parasites, clinging to its ancient ways and setting an exaggerated store by outward appearances.[8]

But there is another possible angle of vision. Spain's century of

---

[8] For the history of Spain in the seventeenth century, see the following: Antonio Domínguez Ortiz, *The Golden Age of Spain, 1516–1659* (London, 1971); J.H. Elliott, *Imperial Spain, 1469–1716* (London, 1963); Henry Kamen, *Spain in the later Seventeenth Century, 1665–1700* (London, 1980); John Lynch, *Spain under the Habsburgs*, 2 (2nd. ed., Oxford, 1981).

decline, the seventeenth century, is also known as the Golden Age of its arts. In literature, it is the century of Cervantes, of Góngora and Quevedo; in the theatre, of Lope de Vega and Calderón and Tirso de Molina; and in painting, of El Greco, Ribera, Zurbarán, Velázquez and Murillo. The great creative impetus admittedly seems to belong to the first, rather than the second, half of the century. Calderón and Murillo, who died in 1681 and 1682 respectively, are generally represented as the last surviving giants in a land increasingly peopled by pygmies. But at least where painting is concerned, the verdict may have been prematurely returned. Inside Spain, and, still more, outside it, far too little is known of the artists at work in the second half of the century; the Golden Age of Spanish painting may well have been too abruptly terminated by historians and art-historians anxious to ring down the curtain.

But whether or not Spain's Golden Age is prolonged beyond the death of Velázquez in 1660, the fact remains that a remarkable age of literary and artistic creativity coincided with an age of political and economic decline. This apparent paradox raises some difficult questions. Is there, or need there be, any correlation between a nation's cultural vitality and its economic performance? Is it possible that national misfortune actually serves as a stimulus to cultural achievement, whether by promoting an escapist search for alternative fields of endeavour, still unmarked by failure, or by giving artists and men of letters that extra dimension of awareness which enables them to see the realities beneath the glittering surface?

It is easier to find support for this last hypothesis in the realm of literature than of painting. *Don Quijote* is, after all, a brilliant disquisition on the complex relationship of illusion and reality. But how far can even Don Quijote be convincingly related to a crisis of confidence in a society which has begun to see itself as afflicted by the symptoms of decline?

When it comes to painting, the problem is still more difficult, for reasons suggested by a consideration of Velázquez's remarkable portrait of the aging Philip IV (Pl. 14). At first glance it would seem that Velázquez had stripped away all the majesty of kingship to reveal the pathetic figure behind the mask – a weak, defeated and disillusioned man. But this is to ignore the Spanish tradition of royal portraiture to which Velázquez faithfully adhered. The Kings of Spain are normally depicted with great simplicity, and with none of the traditional appurtenances of royalty (Pl. 15). This iconographical tradition, which persists to the end of the seventeenth century, reflects certain assumptions about Spanish kingship that tend to be overlooked. The Kings of Spain were the greatest monarchs in the world, and their greatness was taken for granted. Therefore there

14 Diego de Velázquez, *Philip IV*.   15 Alonso Sánchez Coello, *Philip II*.

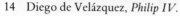

was no need to insist on the trappings of power, as the painters of lesser European monarchs tended to insist on them. The very austerity and simplicity of the king's image in Spanish painting was itself an indication of his overwhelming majesty. It may well be that Velázquez, as a supremely great artist, could not but reveal the human frailties of the king he served. But there seems no reason to doubt that the intention, at least, was to produce an official royal image, and it would be surprising if any contemporary read this portrait as a symbol either of the weakness of Spain's king or of the waning of its power.

The attempt to find hidden correspondences between the psychological or economic health of a society and its cultural creations is a hazardous enterprise, as the example of Velázquez's portrait of Philip IV suggests. In some instances at least, such correspondences may indeed exist, although perhaps at such a deep and subtle level that the writer or artist is himself unaware of them. In other instances, there seems to be no sign of correlation. It would be hard to deduce from the paintings of Murillo that he spent his working life in a country experiencing the traumas of economic crisis and military defeat, and in a city that suffered a catastrophic loss of population as the result of a devastating plague, and saw its prosperity ebbing away.

The example of Murillo suggests a need to move away from the more speculative aspects of the relationship between creativity and decline, and to examine the kind of circumstances that may have favoured artistic endeavour in seventeenth-century Spain, in spite of Castile's acute economic troubles. Some clues to the character of this society and the ways in which its organization, interests and aspirations helped to shape the work of the creative artist, can be gleaned from a survey of its three leading cities: Toledo, the spiritual capital of Habsburg Spain; Seville, its effective economic capital; and Madrid, its political capital. Certain recurring themes in the social and cultural history of Spanish urban society suggest a common underlying pattern, which makes more understandable the achievement of Murillo and his fellow artists.

It was in Toledo that El Greco settled in 1577, and here that he lived and worked until his death in 1614.[9] Toledo liked to think of itself as a second Rome. Its archbishop was primate of Spain, and the archbishopric possessed vast revenues and enjoyed enormous influence. Periodically Toledo also served as the seat of the court until the decision of Philip II in 1561 to make Madrid his capital.

The fortunes of Toledo might almost be taken as symptomatic of the fortunes of Spain as a whole. In the mid-sixteenth century it was a flourishing city of some 60,000 inhabitants. It had a fine cathedral, an impressive clerical establishment, a resident local nobility and a small but respectable university. It also had an important merchant community, which derived its wealth from the sale and export of local manufactures – textiles, especially fine silks, and the famous Toledan steel blades.

But during the nearly 40 years of El Greco's residence in Toledo, its fortunes took a turn for the worse. Harvest failure made his first two years in the city, 1577 and 1578, two of the hungriest years in Toledo's history. While harvest failures were a normal hazard of the times, the late sixteenth century and the first two decades of the seventeenth saw a progressive weakening of the Toledan economy, for reasons not yet fully clear. The removal of the court to Madrid led to the departure of some of the local nobility, along with their spending power. But above all, there were growing difficulties in the textile industry, on which Toledo's prosperity depended, partly because of competition from cheaper foreign textiles, and partly because of the high level of taxation and the lack of incentives to invest. The resulting lack of work and opportunities precipitated a

---

[9] The discussion of Toledo and El Greco which follows draws on the introductory essays to the catalogue of the 1982 exhibition of El Greco, *El Greco of Toledo* (Boston, 1982), and especially those of Richard Kagan and Jonathan Brown. I am especially indebted to the latter for his help and advice on many points on the history of art in seventeenth-century Spain discussed in the pages that follow.

migration to Madrid, and by 1646 the city's population was down to 25,000 – less than half its size at the time of El Greco's arrival.

El Greco's Toledo, then, was a city beginning its slide into decline, although the situation seems only to have become acute in the years after his death in 1614. By that time the city authorities were expressing grave concern; but when Martín González de Cellorigo went there in 1619 in his capacity as an official of the Inquisition expecting to find a desert, he was agreeably surprised: 'Although', he wrote, 'it enjoyed greater prosperity in the past, Toledo is less affected than anywhere else by the common decline from which these kingdoms are suffering.' The streets, he explained, were crowded, the houses occupied, the buildings well maintained.[10]

Consequently, at least into the reign of Philip IV, Toledo represents a case of very relative decline in comparison with many of the other cities of Castile. In El Greco's time it still boasted an extremely wealthy church and a civic elite of substantial families that had made their money in trade. It was among the members of this elite that El Greco found his patrons. Members of the great Toledan families – many of them educated at Toledo University – dominated municipal life and the cathedral chapter. They possessed an intense civic pride; a genuine interest in scholarship and learning; and a strong concern with religion.

It is not surprising that El Greco, who liked to think of himself as an intellectual artist, should have felt at home in this late Renaissance city. He may have been attracted to it in the first instance by Luis de Castilla, a Toledan cleric and classical scholar, who first made El Greco's acquaintance in Cardinal Farnese's household in Rome. Luis de Castilla was the illegitimate son of Diego de Castilla, dean of the Toledo cathedral chapter, and it was probably he who arranged for El Greco to be commissioned to paint *The Disrobing of Christ,* for the vestuary of the cathedral sanctuary (Pl. 16).

El Greco was not the easiest or most obliging of artists as far as patrons were concerned. He came from Italy with an elevated image of the standing of the artist, to find that the artist in Spain was regarded as no more than an artisan, and paid an artisan's wages. But his contacts and friendships with leading members of Toledo's lay and clerical establishment proved to be his salvation. In times of trouble his friends would rally round, either because they enjoyed his company or recognized his genius, which stood out all the more strongly against the prevailing mediocrity of painting in Toledo at the time of his arrival. The workshop of El Greco was able to survive because the canons of Toledo, the scholars, the merchants, continued

---

[10] Above, p. 254.

16　El Greco, *The Disrobing of Christ.*

to come forward with requests for their portraits, and to commission altarpieces for their family chapels, or persuade convents and parish priests to follow suit.

Toledo, therefore, was still a relatively prosperous city with an affluent and enlightened civic elite; a city proud of its great traditions, but, at least in El Greco's day, in touch with the outside world. The enclosed and mystical character of religion in the Toledo of El Greco has been exaggerated in an attempt to explain the idiosyncracy of his paintings. The city was very much in the mainstream of orthodox Counter-Reformation spirituality, with its emphasis on the sacraments and the saints, and on pious and charitable works. But those decades saw a particularly strong movement for spiritual and ecclesiastical reform, under the direction of successive archbishops; and the intellectual life of the Toledan elite combined with the highly-charged religious atmosphere to create an ideal environment for El Greco – one in which he could develop to the full his virtuoso Mannerist style, so well adapted to capturing the kind of Counter-Reformation spirituality practised in the city he had made his home.

In the second great city, Seville, where Velázquez was born in 1599, a similar pattern emerges.[11] Sixteenth-century Seville was the great metropolis of the western world, a city whose streets, at least in the popular imagination, were paved with the gold and silver of the Indies. By 1600, it was one of the largest cities in Europe, with a population of around 150,000. The life of this teeming port town was geared, like that of Spain, and indeed of all Europe, to the regular annual arrival of the New World treasure fleets. Trade with the New World was nearing its peak at the time of Velázquez's birth; but for the first two decades of the seventeenth century vast quantities of silver were still being shipped to Seville from the mines of Mexico and Peru. Although some of this silver belonged to the king, much of it was sent back on account to private individuals. The settler community in the Spanish Indies provided an expanding market for European goods, and especially for luxury items, which were purchased with American silver. Works of art were also in demand, and during the seventeenth century Seville studios turned out standard works for the American export trade: run-of-the-mill religious paintings for remote convents in Mexico or the Andes, or still-lifes for the houses of gentry and merchants in Cartagena, Lima and Mexico City.

But by 1640, under the impact of war and financial difficulties,

[11] For the history of Seville in the seventeenth century, the best studies are those of Antonio Domínguez Ortiz, *Orto y Ocaso de Sevilla* (2nd. ed., Madrid, 1974) and *Historia de Sevilla*, 4 (Seville, 1976).

the fleets were arriving with increasing irregularity, and Seville's American trade was clearly in deep trouble. Then, at the end of Spain's fateful decade of the 1640s, the city suffered a devastating plague, which wiped out half its population. Recovery was painfully slow, and the Seville visited by Pepys in 1683 was a much diminished city, living in the last sunset rays of the wealth of the Indies, as its primacy passed to Cadiz.

But the Seville of Velázquez and Zurbarán, and even the later seventeenth-century Seville of Murillo, remained immensely wealthy in spite of its vicissitudes. Its wealth was inevitably distributed with extreme inequality – nowhere in Spain were the social contrasts starker. An affluent elite, reinforced by returning *indianos* (men who had made their fortunes in the Indies) indulged spectacularly in conspicuous consumption. But there was also a vast, poverty-stricken sub-world of unemployed and underemployed – vagabonds, rogues, street-urchins, casual labourers, dock-workers, hawkers, pedlars, water-sellers, all of them anxiously wondering where and how to get a square meal. According to Sancho Panza's grandmother, 'there are only two races in the world, the haves and the have-nots',[12] and the distinguishing criterion was food. Seventeenth-century Spanish society was obsessed with food. The contrasts are nowhere more neatly pointed than in two of Murillo's paintings: *The Prodigal Son Feasting* (Pl. 17), which can be regarded as a seventeenth-century version of conspicuous consumption; and his *Peasant Woman and Boy* (Pl. 18) with its depiction of life on the poverty line.

Seville, like Toledo, was dominated by a network of families, many of which had originally made their money in trade, and then invested it in houses and land, in government bonds, in silver and precious objects. Like Toledo, it contained aristocratic families, like the Dukes of Alcalá and the Counts of Olivares, who played their part in municipal life and lived on fairly easy terms with the civic elite. It was a city, too, with strong civic pride, but because of its character as an emporium of trade, it was much more open than inland Toledo to external influences. It maintained close commercial ties not only with the New World, but also with Italy and the Netherlands. It is not therefore surprising that the young Velázquez, as apprentice, and then son-in-law, to the Sevillian artist Francisco Pacheco, should have had access to northern engravings, like Peter Aertsen's engraving of a *Woman Cleaning Fish, with the Supper at Emmaus,* which may have served as an inspiration for his kitchen scene in the National Gallery in London, with Christ in the house of Mary and Martha (Pl. 19).

---

[12] *Don Quijote*, part 2, ch. 20.

17   Bartolomé Esteban Murillo,
The Prodigal Son Feasting.

18   Bartolomé Esteban Murillo,
Peasant Woman and Boy.

19   Diego de Velázquez, *Kitchen Scene with Christ in the House of Mary and Martha.*

20   Bartolomé Esteban Murillo, *The Return of the Prodigal Son.*

ARTE

DE LA PINTVRA.

SV ANTIGVEDAD,

Y GRANDEZAS.

DESCRIVENSE LOS HOMBRES EMINENTES
que ha auido en ella, afsi antiguos como modernos, del dibu-
jo, y colorido; del pintar al temple, al olio, de la iluminacion,
y eftofado, del pintar al frefco, de las encarnaciones, de poli-
mento, y de mate; del dorado, bruñido, y mate. Y enfeña
el modo de pintar todas las pinturas
fagradas.

POR FRANCISCO PACHECO
vezino de Seuilla.

Año   1649.

CON PRIVILEGIO.

En Seuilla, por Simon Faxardo, impreffor de libros,
a la Cerrajeria.

21 Title page of Francisco de
Pacheco's *Tratado del Arte de la
Pintura*, 1649.

The Sevillian elite, like that of Toledo, was a cultivated elite,
combining strong humanist interests with the doctrinal and practical
concerns of Counter-Reformation Catholicism. Again, as in Toledo,
the cathedral canons, drawn from the great city families, played an
important part in the city's cultural life. They were prominent in the
informal literary academies which sprang into existence in the
sixteenth century, like that of Canon Pacheco, which on his death
was taken over by his nephew, Francisco Pacheco.[13] Here the young
Velázquez, who entered Pacheco's household as an apprentice in
1611, would have heard discussions on literary themes, artistic
theory (Pl. 21), and the great doctrinal issues of the day. One of the
most intensely debated of these issues was the Immaculate Conception, which became a favourite subject for seventeenth-century
Spanish artists, and especially those of Seville.

Seville was the most theatrical of Spanish cities. It conducted its
civic and religious life in a splendid blaze of drama, with the whole
city participating in the processions for the great religious occasions,

---

[13] Seville's academies are discussed in Jonathan Brown, *Images and Ideas in Seventeenth-
Century Spanish Painting* (Princeton, 1978).

organized by the church and the confraternities. In a city dedicated to display, those who had money were expected to spend it lavishly for the enjoyment of the community. The result was a high degree of private and corporate patronage, which naturally spilt over into commissions to local artists. A good proportion of this patronage, especially in the second half of the century after the plague of 1649, was directed towards religious and charitable foundations. It is therefore natural that much of the work of Murillo and his Sevillian contemporaries should have been commissioned by churches, confraternities and convents, like his *Return of the Prodigal Son* (Pl. 20), commissioned by the confraternity of the Caridad – a brotherhood devoted to charitable works for the poor – for the church of their hospital.

Murillo himself was a member of this confraternity, and was in touch with many of the leading figures in the religious life of the city. One of these, and one of his closest friends, was a canon of Seville cathedral, Don Justino de Neve, of whom he produced a brilliant portrait (Pl. 22). Neve was a characteristic Sevillian patron. He came of a family of rich Flemish merchants established in Seville; he became a canon in 1658, and devoted his wealth and energies to founding a hospital for elderly priests, the Hospital de los Venerables, to which he bequeathed his portrait on his death in 1685. The inventory of his possessions shows that he owned four large and four small clocks, one of which sits on the table beside him.[14]

It is significant that the Count-Duke of Olivares, the favourite and first minister of Philip IV, was a native of Seville – though of an earlier generation than Neve – and spent his formative years in the city, between 1607 and 1615. He was in touch with the city's leading scholars and writers. He was a well-known figure at meetings of the academies, including that of Pacheco, and he spent lavishly on cultural patronage. His own tastes ran more to books than paintings – he built up one of the great libraries of the seventeenth century – but his Seville years seem to have imbued him with a strong sense of the profound importance of patronizing and cultivating the arts and letters.

This attitude was to be of enormous importance when he acquired power at court in Madrid in 1621. Madrid – the late-comer in this trio of cities – was a boom town. In 1561, when Philip II chose it as his capital, it was little more than an overgrown village. By 1621 it had a population approaching 150,000, almost as large as that of Seville. It was a parasitic city, an artificial capital which lived for and off the court, and sucked in the wealth, not only of the surrounding

[14] Diego Angulo Iñiguez, *Murillo* (Madrid, 1981), 1, pp. 463–65; 2, pp. 325–56.

22   Bartolomé Esteban Murillo, *Don Justino de Neve*.

region, including Toledo, but also of Spain's European and American possessions. For Madrid was the capital of a world-wide empire.

Madrid, therefore, like Toledo and Seville, boasted a wealthy, leisured elite – an elite, in this instance, of the high aristocracy who rented or built houses in Madrid to be near the king, and of government officials, who waxed fat on the legal and illegal perquisites of office. Already under Philip III writers and artists were gravitating to Madrid in the search for patrons, and little coteries were forming around nobles with cultural interests; but the court of Philip III, whose interests did not extend beyond hunting, card-playing and church-going, set no very distinctive stamp on Madrid's cultural life. All this changed with the accession of Philip IV in 1621 and the advent of Olivares.

Olivares came to power with a clear sense of his mission – not only to revive the fortunes of a declining Spain, but also to make his royal master supreme in the arts both of war and peace. He wanted to make the court a brilliant centre of patronage, and he brought with him from Seville the traditions of his native city – splendour, stage-management, and generosity. And he also brought Sevillians. It was natural that he should give a welcome to writers and artists from his native city, not least among them the young Velázquez, who moved to Madrid in 1623 and became painter to the king. Under the inspired direction of Olivares the court of Philip IV blended the rather showy tastes and styles of Andalusia with the more sober traditions of the Spanish Habsburgs, whose official architecture continued to follow the austere lines of the Escorial.

Olivares set out to groom the sixteen-year old Philip for his destined role as the 'Planet King', the first luminary in the hierarchy of power and patronage. Philip embarked on an intensive reading course to supplement his very inadequate education; he was an enthusiastic theatre-goer; and he soon showed that he had a very discriminating eye for painting, like so many of his family. There seem to have been two critical events in the 1620s for his development as a patron and connoisseur. One was the extraordinary visit to Madrid in 1623 of Charles, Prince of Wales (Pl. 24). For the first time, Philip found himself face to face with a prince of his own generation, who was far more refined than himself and had an insatiable thirst for pictures. He was quick to learn the lesson. The other great event of the 1620s was the visit in 1628–29 of Rubens. Philip spent long hours in his company, as also did Velázquez, discussing paintings in the royal collection with him, and watching him at work. Rubens' visit was decisive both for the king and Velázquez, opening up new vistas and giving them a genuinely European vision of contemporary trends in art. In 1629 Philip gave Velázquez permission to visit Italy, in order to extend his knowledge of the great masters and get abreast of the most recent artistic developments. The opportunity had come at last for Spanish painting to break free from the rather archaic provincialism which until now had been one of its most distinctive features.

By the early 1630s, then, Philip IV had become exactly what Olivares had planned: the model of princely refinement, a discriminating connoisseur, a patron of arts and letters. All he lacked was a suitable setting in which to pursue his interests in the theatre and the arts. But Olivares provided him with this, too, by constructing for him the pleasure palace of the Buen Retiro, on the eastern outskirts of Madrid (Pl. 23). The Buen Retiro was run up at enormous speed – most of it in the three years 1630–33, under the frenetic personal direction of Olivares – and it showed. The palace was criticized by contemporaries as being unworthy of so magnificent a king; but at the same time Olivares came under attack for spending money on a pleasure palace in times of war, high taxation, and economic recession. Over ten years the costs probably came to about three million ducats – equivalent to one year's expenditure on Spain's army in the Netherlands.[15]

While it was true that the exterior of the Buen Retiro was undistinguished, the interior made up for this. 'The house', reported Hopton, 'is very richly furnished and almost all by presents, for the Count of Olivares hath made the work his own, by which means it hath not wanted friends.'[16] In practice he dragooned his unfortunate relatives, along with the entire Spanish establishment, into providing furniture, tapestries and paintings, and had Spain's viceroys scouring the earth for pictures to cover its walls.

Some paintings were specially commissioned for the Retiro, notably those which were to decorate its great ceremonial hall, the Hall of Realms, inaugurated in 1635. The Retiro, then, provided a splendid opportunity for the patronage of native artists like Velázquez and Zurbarán, but they could not be expected to cover all the walls in the short time available, and so it also became a great repository of paintings collected from all over Europe.

All told, about 800 paintings were acquired for the Buen Retiro, the great majority of them in that spectacular decade, the 1630s. This meant a vast increase in the size and range of the Spanish royal collection. When Philip IV came to the throne in 1621, there were around 1,200 paintings in the various royal palaces. In the 44 years of

[15] For the Buen Retiro and the court of Philip IV, see Jonathan Brown and J.H. Elliott, *A Palace for a King* (New Haven and London, 1980).
[16] *Ibid.*, p. 88.

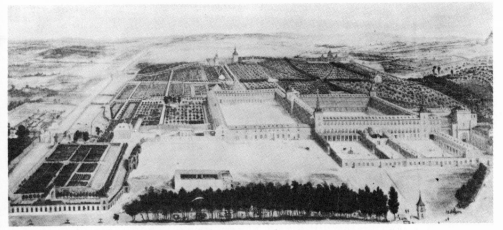

23   Jusepe Leonardo, *View of the Buen Retiro Palace.*

24   Juan de la Corte, *A Fiesta in the Plaza Mayor, Madrid, in honour of the Prince of Wales.*

his reign, he added at least 2,000 paintings to the collection, which is approximately the number of paintings in the Prado Museum today. Nor was it simply a question of quantity. Philip had a very good eye, and his tastes ran especially towards Rubens and the great Venetian masters. He would go to any length to add a masterpiece to his collection; his ambassadors were primed to be on the lookout for any important works coming on to the market; and when Charles I's collection was dispersed, the Spanish ambassador in London, acting under strict instructions from the king, picked up everything he could.

This royal obsession with picture-collecting was of momentous importance for the development of art and taste in seventeenth-century Spain. It had a major impact both on the tastes and interests of the Spanish ruling class, and on the artists themselves.

The social impact of the king's activities is pithily summed up in a letter of 1638 from Sir Arthur Hopton to Lord Cottington:

> They are now become more judicious in and more affectioned unto the art of painting, than they have been, or than the world imagines. And the king within this 12 month hath gotten an incredible number of ancient and of the best modern hands, and over with the Count of Monterrey came the best of Italy, particularly the Baccanalian of Titian, and in this town is not a piece worth anything but the king takes and pays very well for them, and in his imitation the Admiral of Castile, Don Luis de Haro and many others are making collections.[17]

Picture-collecting, in fact, became the fashion in the Madrid of the 1630s, especially in the circle of Olivares' relatives, friends and dependents, all of them anxious to imitate their royal master. Olivares' brother-in-law, the Count of Monterrey, who was immensely wealthy, returned in 1638 from Naples, where he had been serving as viceroy, with a very choice collection, including seven paintings attributed to Titian and thirteen to Ribera, and built a picture gallery to house them in the garden of his Madrid palace.[18] His cousin, the Marquis of Leganés, a general who served in the Netherlands and Italy, had a collection of some 1,300 paintings by the time of his death in 1655 – one that was particularly strong in Flemish paintings.[19] His nephew and successor as Philip's principal

[17] Ibid., p. 115.

[18] Alfonso E. Pérez Sánchez, 'Las colecciones de pintura del conde de Monterrey (1653)', Boletín de la Real Academia de la Historia, 174 (1977), pp. 417–59.

[19] José López Navío, 'La gran colección de pinturas del Marqués de Leganés', Analecta Calasanctiana, no. 8 (1962), pp. 259–330; Mary Crawford Volk, 'New Light on a Seventeenth-Century Collector: The Marquis of Leganés', Art Bulletin, 72 (1980), pp. 256–68.

minister, Don Luis de Haro, also had a splendid collection, part of which came through his wife; and Haro's son, the Marquis of Carpio, who died in 1687, while viceroy of Naples, was one of the greatest collectors of the age.[20]

The Olivares clan among the high nobility, which dominated Spain's political life between the 1620s and the 1680s, dominated its cultural life, too, as patrons and collectors. The habit of collecting extended, moreover, to government ministers and officials. Olivares' lawyer, José González, who ended his career as one of the principal ministers of the Spanish crown, had a collection of around 750 paintings at the time of his death in 1668. His widow's inventory shows that the principal room of his Madrid house was decorated with ten panels of a Brussels tapestry of the life of Jacob, along with fifty paintings, including several portraits. There were twenty more paintings in the dining-room, including portraits of himself and his wife; another thirty in the main first-floor room – two of them portraits of Olivares – and 100 paintings, including two originals by Teniers, in his summer quarters.[21] But the general effect may have been slightly marred by the framing. Pepys remarks in his notes on Spain: 'Tawdry frames in their best pictures of great masters and solemn things.'

By the time of Philip IV's death in 1665, then, the taste for picture-collecting was well established in court circles in Madrid; and the very fact that it was so fashionable must have had its impact on taste and patronage in the country at large, and not least in Seville. Here Cardinal Ambrosio Spínola, archbishop from 1669, set a magnificent example, commissioning works by Valdés Leal and Murillo for his palace, including the latter's famous *Virgin and Child in Glory* (Pl. 25). As the son of the Marquis of Leganés, that great collector of the reign of Philip IV, Spínola had presumably spent his early years in houses full of paintings.

For all the economic troubles of the later seventeenth century, the demand for paintings seems to have kept up – for religious paintings, in particular, to decorate family chapels and convents, and pious foundations; but also for still-lifes or *bodegones*; for the new genre developed by Murillo of cheerful scenes of street urchins,

[20] Gregorio de Andrés, *El Marqués de Liche, bibliófilo y coleccionista de arte* (Madrid, 1975). See also José M. Pita Andrade, 'Los cuadros de Velázquez y Mazo que poseyó el séptimo Marqués del Carpio', *Archivo Español de Arte*, 25 (1952), pp. 223–36, and Enriqueta Harris, 'El Marqués del Carpio y sus cuadros de Velázquez', *Archivo Español de Arte*, 30 (1957), pp. 136–9.

[21] See Janine Fayard, 'José González (1583?–1668), "créature" du comte-duc d'Olivares et conseiller de Philippe IV', in *Hommage à Roland Mousnier*, ed. Yves Durand (Paris, 1980), pp. 351–68. For another official engaged in collecting, see José Luis Barrio Moya, 'La colección de pinturas de don Francisco de Oviedo, secretario del rey Felipe IV', *Revista de Archivos, Bibliotecas y Museos*, 87 (1979), pp. 163–71.

25 Bartolomé Esteban Murillo, *The Virgin and Child in Glory*.

26 Bartolomé Esteban Murillo, *Boys Playing Dice*.

which were presumably produced in the first instance for a Seville clientele (Pl. 26); and for portraits, although many of these have disappeared with the dispersal or extinction of so many of Spain's great families.

Although some of this activity took place in provincial capitals, especially Seville, the court retained its preeminence as the centre and focus of artistic activity, in spite of the death in 1665 of Philip IV, one of the greatest royal collectors and patrons in seventeenth-century Europe. His son, Carlos II, seems to have added only a few works to the royal collection, but the habit of patronage had taken hold. And Philip, in addition to helping form the artistic taste of a whole generation of nobility, left another major legacy in the royal collection itself.

When Murillo, following in the steps of his fellow artist from Seville, Francisco de Herrera the Younger, paid his visit to Madrid in 1658, the royal and private collections in the capital contained a splendid sample of the works not only of Titian and his fellow Italians but also of the great northern masters of the seventeenth century, and especially Rubens and Van Dyck. The high baroque style that was now introduced into Seville by Murillo and his colleagues, and was adopted by the leading painters of the post-Velázquez generation in Madrid, among them Carreño de Miranda and Claudio Coello, directly reflects the influence of these Italian and northern masters. By making their work accessible to Spanish artists, the great collectors of the seventeenth century, beginning with the king himself, had helped to shape the vision of a whole generation of painters.

Artistic activity, drawing fresh inspiration from these foreign masterpieces, was sustained, both in Seville and Madrid, until the last years of the century. It is only then that the barren age of Spanish painting begins, to end nearly a hundred years later with the emergence of Goya. But the seventeenth century – this century of falling economic productivity, and of a dramatic decline in Spain's political influence and military power – had by any measure been a scintillating century for painting in Spain.

It may now be possible to get a little closer to the heart of this apparent paradox of a golden age of the arts coinciding with an iron age of political and economic disaster. No social or economic interpretation can explain genius – the genius of a Velázquez or a Murillo. But even genius needs a conducive climate in order to reach fulfilment, and it is clear that seventeenth-century Spain, for all its troubles, did manage to create a reasonably favourable climate, at least for writers and painters, although not, it seems, for architects.

The relative poverty of seventeenth-century Spanish architecture may provide a clue to the patronage of painters. Architecture requires a considerable – and, above all, a continuing – outlay of cash; and at every level of society in seventeenth-century Spain, from the king downwards, potential patrons were inhibited by acute problems of cash flow. It is therefore not surprising that great building enterprises are few, and rather undistinguished; and that even well-endowed religious orders take decades over the completion of their churches and convents.[22]

The patronage of writers and artists, on the other hand, can be managed more cheaply and on a more sporadic basis, without doing irreparable damage to artistic and literary enterprise, although there may be sad instances of individual casualties – men whose artistic careers are blighted by the ruin or death of their patrons, as happened

---

[22] See Virginia Tovar Martín, *Arquitectos madrileños de la segunda mitad del siglo XVII* (Madrid, 1975).

with Antonio de Pereda.[23] And it is here, in the exercise of patronage, that a key is to be found to the problem of artistic activity in an age of decline.

For effective patronage there must exist a group in society with both the means, and the desire, to support artistic enterprise. As this tale of three cities has suggested, the structure of Spanish society in the seventeenth century was such that there did indeed exist, in church and state, an affluent elite with sufficient reserves of wealth to escape the worst vicissitudes of the times. Indeed, those very vicissitudes may actually have encouraged the tendency to conspicuous consumption, precisely because, in an age of sudden inflation and no less sudden deflation, there was no inducement to save, and there were few economically productive outlets for the use of capital.

But, along with the means, there must also be the desire. In a hierarchical society like that of Spain, royal and aristocratic example was paramount; and here the natural taste of Philip IV and the impetus given to royal patronage of the arts by Olivares at the start of the reign, were of crucial importance. In a fragment of autobiography, Philip wrote that it was important not only to honour the profession of arms, but also 'those who have learned to improve themselves in letters, scholarship and the arts. For these two', he continued – arms and letters – 'are the two poles which govern the movement of monarchies, and are the foundations on which they rest, because together they form a perfect harmony, each supporting the other.'[24] This is as good an exposition as any of the underlying philosophy of his policy of patronage.

In 1621, at the beginning of Philip's reign, a commentator wrote enthusiastically that a *siglo de oro* – a Golden Century – was dawning in Spain.[25] As far as Spanish power, and the Spanish economy, were concerned, his prophecy proved wildly inaccurate. Spain's ruling class, and, with it, Spain itself, failed drastically to adapt to the requirements of a changing world, and paid the resulting price. But in the arts it was a different matter. Here a governing class which was fast losing the political and military touch that had given Spain its empire, turned, almost as if in compensation, to enlightened patronage. And so it became possible – not perhaps for the last time in the history of European civilization – for economic decline and cultural achievement to walk hand in hand.

---

[23] Pereda's career is discussed by Alfonso E. Pérez Sánchez in the exhibition catalogue, *D. Antonio de Pereda (1611–1678) y la pintura madrileña de su tiempo* (Madrid, 1978).

[24] Quoted by Brown and Elliott, *A Palace for a King*, p. 42.

[25] *Cartas de Andrés de Almansa y Mendoza* (Madrid, 1886), p. 53.

ACKNOWLEDGEMENTS

'Spain and its Empire in the Sixteenth and Seventeenth Centuries', in *Early Maryland in a Wider World*, ed. David B. Quinn (Wayne State University Press, Detroit, 1982), pp. 58–83.

'The Mental World of Hernán Cortés', *Transactions of the Royal Historical Society*, 17 (1967), pp. 41–58.

'The Discovery of America and the Discovery of Man' (Raleigh Lecture, 1972), *Proceedings of the British Academy*, 48 (1972), pp. 101–25.

'A provincial aristocracy: the Catalan Ruling Class in the Sixteenth and Seventeenth Centuries', in *Homenaje a Jaime Vicens Vives*, 2 vols. (Universidad de Barcelona, Barcelona, 1967), II, pp. 125–41.

'Revolution and Continuity in Early Modern Europe', *Past and Present: A Journal of Historical Studies*,★ 42 (1969), pp. 35–56.

'Foreign Policy and Domestic Crisis: Spain, 1598–1659', in *Krieg und Politik, 1618–1648*, ed. Konrad Repgen (Schriften des Historischen Kollegs, Kolloquien 8, Munich, 1988), pp. 185–202.

'The Court of the Spanish Habsburgs: a Peculiar Institution?', in *Politics and Culture in Early Modern Europe: Essays in Honour of H.G. Koenigsberger*, eds. Phyllis Mack and Margaret C. Jacob (Cambridge University Press, Cambridge, 1987), pp. 5–24.

'Power and Propaganda in the Spain of Philip IV', in *Rites of Power. Symbolism, Ritual and Politics Since the Middle Ages*, ed. Sean Wilentz (University of Pennsylvania Press, Philadelphia, 1985), pp. 145–73.

'Quevedo and the Count-Duke of Olivares', in *Quevedo in Perspective: Eleven Essays for the Quadricentennial*, ed. James Iffland (Juan de la Cuesta, Newark, Delaware, 1982), pp. 227–50.

'The Decline of Spain', *Past and Present: A Journal of Historical Studies*,★ 20 (1961), pp. 52–75.

'Self-perception and Decline in Early Seventeenth-Century Spain', *Past and Present: A Journal of Historical Studies*,★ 74 (1977), pp. 41–61.

'Art and Decline in Seventeenth-Century Spain', *Bartolomé Esteban Murillo* (Catalogue of the exhibition at the Royal Academy of Arts, London, 1983), pp. 40–51.

★ World copyright: The Past and Present Society, 175 Banbury Road, Oxford, England.

INDEX